When Oceans Merge

When Oceans Merge

the CONTEMPORARY SUFI AND HASIDIC
TEACHINGS OF PIR VILAYAT INAYAT KHAN
and RABBI ZALMAN SCHACHTER-SHALOMI

GREGORY BLANN

Foreword by NETANEL MILES-YÉPEZ

Adam Kadmon Books
Monkfish Book Publishing Company
Rhinebeck, New York

Paperback ISBN 978-1-939681-99-7
eBook ISBN 978-1-948626-00-2

Library of Congress Cataloging-in-Publication Data

Names: Blann, Gregory, author. | Miles-Yepez, Netanel, writer of foreword.
Title: When oceans merge : the contemporary Sufi and Hasidic teachings of Pir
    Vilayat Khan and Rabbi Zalman Schachter-Shalomi / Gregory Blann ; foreword
    by Netanel Miles-Yepez.
Description: Rhinebeck, New York : Adam Kadmon Books ; Monkfish Book
    Publishing Company, [2019] | Includes bibliographical references.
Identifiers: LCCN 2018056274 (print) | LCCN 2018057367 (ebook) | ISBN
    9781948626002 (ebook) | ISBN 9781939681997 (pbk. : alk. paper)
Subjects: LCSH: Sufism. | Hasidism. | Inayat Khan, Pir Vilayat--Teachings. |
    Schachter-Shalomi, Zalman, 1924-2014--Teachings.
Classification: LCC BP189 (ebook) | LCC BP189 .B62 2019 (print) | DDC
    296.7/12--dc23
LC record available at https://lccn.loc.gov/2018056274

Adam Kadmon Books, *a joint imprint of Monkfish Book Publishing Company and Albion-Andalus Books*
22 East Market Street, Suite 304
Rhinebeck, New York 12572
(845) 876-4861
monkfishpublishing.com
albionandalus.com

TABLE *of* CONTENTS

PART 2: REB ZALMAN SCHACHTER-SHALOMI

ACKNOWLEDGMENTS

I would like to express my deep appreciation to all those that helped in the formation of this book, whether through providing information or by reading through either parts or the entire the manuscript and suggesting edits and corrections. These include my wife Sylvia, Pir Zia Inayat-Khan, Pir Shabda Kahn, Puran Bair, Karima Bushnell, David Burrows, Paul Cohen, Susan Piperato, Colin Rolfe, and particularly Pir Netanel Miles-Yépez, who provided the foreword, several photographs, and many helpful editorial and content suggestions.

I would also like to thank the University of Colorado at Boulder for making available hundreds of archival lectures and interviews by Reb Zalman online, numerous excerpts of which are quoted in the book, with permission.

Special heartfelt love and appreciation goes to the two beautiful spiritual teachers whose inspiring lives and teachings form the foundation of this book, Pir Vilayat Inayat Khan and Rabbi Zalman Schachter-Shalomi. May their souls be blessed and ennobled.

LIST *of* ILLUSTRATIONS

1. Painting of Hazrat Inayat Khan (Painting by the author)
2. Joe Miller during a Thursday walk in Golden Gate Park in San Francisco in 1985 (Photo by the author)
3. Pir Vilayat Khan leading a retreat in the Sierras in 1985 (Photo by the author)
4. Pir Vilayat Khan with the author and his daughter Claire at the Abode in 1989 (Photo by Sylvia Blann)
5. Pir Vilayat Khan playing Beethoven's "Moonlight Sonata" at the author's home in November 1984 (Photo by the author)
6. Esoteric Week at Omega Institute in 1981 with Swami Satchitananda (Hinduism), Khempo Karthar Rinpoche (Buddhism), Reb Zalman Schachter-Shalomi (Judaism), Brother David Steindl-Rast (Christianity), and Pir Vilayat Khan (Sufism) (Photo courtesy of the University of Colorado Boulder's Zalman M. Schachter-Shalomi Collection)
7. Reb Zalman Schachter-Shalomi at the Dargah of Hazrat Inayat Khan, 1990, in Delhi, India (Photo courtesy of the University of Colorado Boulder's Zalman M. Schachter-Shalomi Collection)
8. Pir Vilayat Khan conducting a Universal Worship Service at the Abode in 1989 (Photo by the author)
9. Reb Zalman's photo of Thomas Merton at the Abbey of Our Lady of Gethsemani around 1963 (Photo courtesy of the University of Colorado Boulder's Zalman M. Schachter-Shalomi collection)
10. Reb Zalman officiating a wedding in Atlanta, Georgia, in 1985 (Photos by the author)

FOREWORD

The Merging of Two Oceans

The Making of a Sufi-Hasidic Lineage
and a Universal Priesthood

NETANEL MILES-YÉPEZ

Toward the One
The Perfection of Love, Harmony, and Beauty
The Only Being
United with all the Illuminated Souls
Who form the Embodiment of the Master
The Spirit of Guidance

Likhrat ha-eḥad
Ha-yaḥid ha-eḥad v'ha-m'yuḥad
Shleimut ha-ahavah, ha-tzedek v'ha-tif'eret
Ha-nimtza ha-yaḥid
Ha-kolel kol ha-n'shamot ha-ne'orot
Yotzrei hag'shammat ha-rabbi
Ha-ruaḥ ha-kodesh

Sometime in the mid-to-late '70s, my teacher, Rabbi Zalman Schachter-Shalomi—better known as "Reb Zalman"—took it upon himself to translate the universalist Sufi prayer "Toward the One" into the traditional Hebrew of Hasidic Jews in Eastern Europe. The prayer itself was composed in English by the first

Sufi master to bring Sufism to the West, Hazrat Inayat Khan, and is arguably one of the most popular nonsectarian prayers in the world today.[1]

Many years after he first encountered it, Reb Zalman wrote that he initially had trouble getting through a single recitation of the prayer:

> For even as I was speaking, I would be lifted "Toward the One" to regions of "Love, Harmony, and Beauty" where my feet no longer touched the ground of materiality, but instead were grounded in "The Only Being." I was overwhelmed by the energetic *qurb*—"proximity" to the One—in the words themselves. There was such holy precision in them and manifest spiritual energy that my heart could not fail to respond to them. And, as with other things that touched me powerfully from outside of the Jewish tradition, I immediately wanted to translate it into Hebrew, the language of my spiritual upbringing.[2]

As many people have often asked me how such an important Hasidic rabbi, trained in the traditional world of Judaism, could become a Sufi—indeed, a Sufi *sheikh* who was also interested in translating the "Toward the One" into Hebrew—I want to tell the story of how this happened, and indeed, of how this same Hasidic rabbi also contributed significantly to universalist Sufism through his relationship with Sufi master Pir Vilayat Inayat Khan.[3]

FROM HASIDISM *to* UNIVERSALIST SUFISM

Meshullam Zalman Schachter was born in Zholkiew, Poland, in 1924, and raised in Vienna, Austria, where his parents ran a small store selling textiles. In 1938, after the Nazi annexation of Austria, the family fled with their teenage son to Belgium where, in Antwerp, he first encountered Hasidim, in this case, of the famous Habad lineage.

Hasidism is the name given to a series of communal mystical movements in Judaism, the latest initiated by Yisra'el ben

Eliezer (1698-1760), called the Ba'al Shem Tov, from whom all latter-day Hasidic lineages stem. The Ba'al Shem Tov taught that God could be served joyfully through the body in ecstatic prayer, song, and dance, instead of through the harsh ascetic disciplines commonly practiced among mystics of his own time. He taught that "worlds, souls, and divinity" were all overlapping, interpenetrating realities, ultimately reducible to one divine reality, as it says in Isaiah 6:3, "the whole earth is filled with God's glory." Thus, the step between us and divinity is only a matter of perspective, overcome through a powerful intentionality *(kavvanah)* and cleaving to the Divine *(devekut)*.

Among the Hasidic lineages that sprang from the inspiration of the Ba'al Shem Tov was the Habad lineage, founded by Shneur Zalman of Liadi (1745-1812), a genius known for the tremendous sophistication of his mystical thought and his emphasis on deep contemplative practice.

In Antwerp, although from a family of Belzer Hasidim himself, the fourteen-year-old Zalman joined a radical group of young Habad* Hasidism with whom he began to experiment in authentic spiritual living. But when Antwerp was bombed by the Nazis a few months later, he and his family were forced to flee quickly in a coal train heading into France. After a period of internment in a refugee camp, the family made their way to Marseille, where Zalman met the son-in-law and future *rebbe* (master) of the Habad-Lubavitch lineage, Menachem Mendel Schneerson (1902-1994), who provided him with an introduction to Yosef Yitzhak Schneersohn (1880-1950), the sixth Lubavitcher Rebbe, to whom he attached himself shortly after his arrival in the United States in 1941.[4]

---

*   On the spelling of *Habad: Habad* is an acrostic for *Ḥokhmah, Binah, Da'at* (Wisdom, Understanding, and Knowledge), a triad of concepts at the heart of the Habad school or lineage of Hasidism. The guttural letter Ḥet in Hebrew may be transliterated by an Ḥ or Ch. Today, the organizational offshoot of the Lubavitch branch of that lineage has generally chosen to use the spelling, Chabad. However, since the particular school or lineage of Hasidism known as Habad is larger and more diverse than this organizational offshoot called Chabad, Reb Zalman, and many scholars, have believed it helpful to distinguish the larger lineage and teachings from the more limited organizational identity so well known today. —N.M-Y

The sixth Lubavitcher Rebbe, himself a refugee from the Holocaust, had recently established his headquarters at 770 Eastern Parkway in Crown Heights, Brooklyn, where young Zalman entered his *yeshiva* (seminary), training to become a Hasidic rabbi. In 1947, he was ordained and soon sent out by his *rebbe* to college campuses to bring Jews back to the traditional fold. A naturally talented and charismatic teacher with broad interests, he studied pastoral psychology at Boston University, and eventually (after a short period as a pulpit rabbi) became a college professor at the University of Manitoba in Winnipeg, Canada, teaching psychology of religion and Jewish mysticism.

By the late '50s and early '60s, Reb Zalman had noticed a generational shift among his Jewish students. Passionate in his desire to serve them, he sought to understand where they were coming from, exploring their questions as his own. It was clear that there was a deep spiritual impulse in them that was not being fed in the synagogues of the time. Though thoroughly grounded in the mystically-oriented tradition of Hasidism, he could see how the Jewish tradition in general was failing to meet Jewish needs in the wake of the Holocaust. Judaism in North America was a wasteland. Thus, many young Jews were finding their paths outside of Judaism in so-called "Eastern religions."

Already curious about other religious traditions, in the mid 1950s—in a move that separated him from other traditional Hasidim—Reb Zalman had begun to read deeply in mystical traditions at Boston University under the famous African-American Christian mystic, Rev. Dr. Howard Thurman (1899-1981), and soon began to seek out encounters with their practitioners. Before long, his knowledge of other traditions was considerable and became an integral part of the courses he taught in the psychology of religion.[5]

By the late 1960s, Reb Zalman was familiar with traditional Sufism through the writings of Idries Shah and had also read the universalist Sufi writings of Hazrat Inayat Khan. But it was not until the early 1970s that he made his first real connections with Sufis.[6] These were the disciples of Murshid Samuel or S.A.M. (Sufi Ahmed Murad) Lewis (1896-1971), also known simply as Murshid

Sam. A direct disciple of Hazrat Inayat Khan, Murshid Sam had become the leader of a new generation of universalist or Inayati Sufis, mostly "flower children" who had found their way to San Francisco. Contrary to common belief, Reb Zalman never met Murshid Sam, but first became acquainted with his successor, Pir Moineddin Jablonski (1942-2002), after being invited to teach in the Bay Area and connecting with the Sufi Choir. Remembering those first encounters, Reb Zalman told me: "I just fell in love with Moineddin, the kind of human being he was, and . . . still to this day, I thrill to the music of that Sufi Choir."[7]

As most of Murshid Sam's students were still in their twenties when he passed, they naturally looked to Reb Zalman, who was then approaching fifty, as an elder mentor. Many also wanted "a Jewish connection" through him and reciprocated by introducing the Hasidic master to Murshid Sam's Sufi dances and walking practices, as well as *wazifa* practices using the ninety-nine "beautiful names" of Allah. Thus, Reb Zalman began to study Inayati Sufism and practice *zikr* (the mantric repetition of the divine names) on his own. "I liked doing zikr," he said. "My sense in zikr was that it doesn't quite 'take' until you're passed boredom . . . you really needed to do it for a while."[8]

During one visit to the Bay Area, Reb Zalman was invited to a "holy man jam" (as these early interfaith gatherings were sometimes called) organized by Pir Vilayat Inayat Khan in Santa Rosa, at which the Sufi Choir would be performing. This was his first meeting with the charismatic son and successor of Hazrat Inayat Khan. The two men hugged, then Pir Vilayat looked Reb Zalman in the eyes and exclaimed, *"Majdhub!"*—"drunk"—recognizing Reb Zalman's God-intoxicated state. It was a Sufi compliment, and Reb Zalman said that he felt a clear heart attraction to Pir Vilayat at that time.[9]

In 1975, Reb Zalman was invited to teach for a semester at the University of California at Santa Cruz, allowing him to deepen his connections to the Bay Area Sufis. By now, he loved the teachings of Hazrat Inayat Khan and the practices of the Sufis. Of all the traditions to which he was exposed through the years, he said, "I was most at home among Sufis."[10] Thus, he decided to take initiation in the Inayati lineage of Sufism. As the lineage was universalist (and not confessionally bound to Islam), he felt this was not in conflict with his own commitments as a Jew and a rabbi. So he approached Pir Moineddin and asked him for initiation. Perhaps not surprisingly, Pir Moineddin demurred, feeling it was not his place to initiate an older and more accomplished master from another tradition. Instead, he suggested that Reb Zalman take initiation with Pir Vilayat.[11] Reb Zalman agreed to the suggestion, but only if Pir Moineddin would confirm the initiation afterward.

As it turned out, Pir Vilayat and Reb Zalman were both to participate in another holy man jam soon after, and thus the initiation was arranged to take place during the break. In preparation, Reb Zalman wished to go to a *mikveh* in order to do a ritual immersion. But, unable to find a kosher *mikveh* anywhere nearby, he immersed in a local pool. He then dressed to honor the occasion in a black silk caftan, a black silk belt, and a large fur hat, the traditional clothing of a Hasid. He would go to his Sufi initiation as a Jew. It was a statement.

After the first half of the program led by Pir Vilayat was finished, followed by a beautiful performance by Pandit Pran Nath, the Sufi *pir* and the Hasidic *rebbe*, each dressed in the robes of their respective traditions, went aside to do a thing rarely seen in the history of religions: to unite two esoteric traditions born from different religions.

Pir Vilayat closed his eyes for a long time and then proceeded with the initiation. When it came to the moment of "taking hand"—the initiation is often referred to as "taking hand" in Sufism, as one takes the right hand of the master—at the moment when one would expect to be called a *murid* or disciple, Pir Vilayat called Reb Zalman "a *sheikh*," a master.

Afterward, surprised by the turn the initiation had taken, Reb Zalman asked Pir Vilayat why he had called him a sheikh and not a murid.

Pir Vilayat answered, "As I was attuning to your presence, I found that I could not utter the word, 'murid'. . . . You are already a master."

Of course, it is well known that one of the great gifts of Pir Vilayat was his ability to attune and respond to the consciousness of the person before him. Thus, it seems that, somehow sensing Reb Zalman's state and station within his own tradition—being already a Hasidic *rebbe*—he found that he could only acknowledge him as a sheikh in the Sufi tradition.

Reb Zalman asked, "What are my duties then?"

Pir Vilayat responded, "Treat it as a degree *honoris causa* until you know."[12]

And that is just what Reb Zalman did for many years. Though he remained close to the Sufi communities of both Murshid Sam and Pir Vilayat, often teaching in them and offering guidance to many of their senior disciples, he always claimed, "In Sufism, I'm 'uncle' and not a 'papa,'" explaining that an uncle can give you advice, but doesn't have the responsibilities of a parent. As the spiritual leader of a burgeoning movement within Judaism at the time (later known as "Jewish Renewal"), it might be supposed that he did not want to take on the added responsibilities of being a Sufi sheikh to another community of disciples. And yet, this is not the end of the story; for the friendship between Reb Zalman and Pir Vilayat had only just begun and would continue to unfold in unexpected ways.

UNIVERSALIST SUFISM *and the* PRIESTHOOD *of* MELCHIZEDEK

The eldest son of Hazrat Inayat Khan, Vilayat Inayat Khan was born in 1916 in London, England, and grew up in the suburbs of Paris. When Vilayat was just ten years old, his father, in an act of great foresight, publically declared him his successor before departing on a trip to India, during which he died after a short illness in 1927.

When Vilayat was eighteen, reminded of his father's desire that he succeed him, he began to study philosophy, psychology, and Sufism with academic scholar, Louis Massignon, commuting between Paris and Oxford. Four years later, with all of Europe threatened by the Nazis, Vilayat returned to England, the country of his birth, and joined the Royal Air Force, and later the Royal Navy. As a mine-sweeping officer, Vilayat (then going by the name Victor) served on a flotilla of motor launches that swept the channels for mines. Often under heavy fire, his boat was once capsized, and he only narrowly escaped with his life.[13]

After the war, he worked for a time at the India High Commissioner's office in London, and at the Pakistani Embassy, where he served as Private Secretary to Ghulam Mohammed, the Finance Minister of Pakistan, and finally as a reporter for the Karachi-based newspaper *Dawn,* exposing atrocities by the French colonial regime in Algeria. But by then, having reached his early thirties, Vilayat felt that the time had come at last to dedicate himself entirely to Sufism.

The mystical movement of Sufism had first arisen in the early centuries of Islam, its principle teaching and practice being *zikr-ullah,* continual "remembrance of God." Although beginning as a highly ascetic tradition, it soon evolved into a tradition of divine love (utilizing the transformative power of love to yield the self for the sake of the divine Beloved) under the influence of a former slave, Rabi'a al-Adawiyya (ca. 717-801). In time, Sufism developed sacralized approaches to music, dance, and the recitation of love poetry, cultivating a state of ecstasy *(wajd)* in which the self is annihilated in the experience of union with God.

In search of his own Sufi roots, Vilayat sought out masters of his father's Chishti lineage in India and Pakistan; for, in the thirteenth century, the great Sufi master, Khwaja Mu'in ad-Din Chishti (1141-1236), carried the originally Central Asian lineage of Chishti Sufism into India, where it gave birth to a unique fusion of Indian and Middle Eastern spirituality, as well as new Sufi musical traditions *(qawwali)* and new breath practices influenced by the Yoga tradition.

In Hyderabad, Sayyid Fakhruddin Jili-Kalimi guided Vilayat in a traditional forty-day retreat, teaching him the methods of the Chishti-Nizami-Kalimi lineage, and ordaining him a Sufi *pir* or master upon its completion. However, on returning to Europe, he found that the organizational body of the Sufi

Movement founded by his father had gone in its own direction. Thus, he founded a new organization to spread the teachings of universalist Sufism.

Universalist Sufism can be traced back to 1910, when Pir Vilayat's father, Hazrat Inayat Khan (1880-1927)—then a brilliant young practitioner of Indian Classical music and a Chishti Sufi master—was charged by his own master, Sayyid Abu Hashim Madani (d. 1907) with bringing Sufism into the West: "Fare forth into the world, my child, and harmonize the East and the West with the harmony of your music. Spread the wisdom of Sufism abroad, for to this end art thou gifted by Allah, the most merciful and compassionate."[14] Coming to America, ostensibly as a musician, he gave concerts, after which, he would lecture on Sufism. In San Francisco in 1911, he met his first Western student, a Jewish woman named Ada (Rabia) Martin (1871-1947), who became the first American Sufi murid, and also the first American *murshida*, or acknowledged female spiritual teacher of Sufism.[15]

But in taking a Western murid, it soon became clear to Inayat Khan that it was not necessary, nor his mission, to spread Islamic Sufism in the West. The people he was teaching were already Jews and Christians, and there seemed no reason to interfere with their religion. Thus, he introduced them to Sufism without Islam, as an esoteric path and set of teachings that would catalyze or "turn on" what was dormant in their existing religious practice. Later, he would say, "If anybody asks you, 'What is Sufism?' . . . you may answer: 'Sufism is the religion of the heart, the religion in which the most important thing is to seek God in the heart of humanity.'"[16] Thus, universalist Sufism was born, and at the same time, the Inayati lineage.[17]

One aspect of Inayati Sufism's universalism was expressed in Hazrat Inayat Khan's teachings on "Universal Worship," a service honoring the major religious traditions, with its own prayers, rituals, and in some sense, a universal priesthood ordained to carry out the service and these rites.[18] Thus, Pir Vilayat began to deepen in his studies of all the major religions and their mystical traditions, learning their teachings and practices.

In 1969, he met Murshid Samuel Lewis, who introduced him to the Bay Area Sufi community, and for a time, the students of both teachers were closely affiliated, as we have seen. In 1975, Pir Vilayat's organization purchased a set of buildings (built in the eighteenth century by the Shakers) in New Lebanon, New York, which they now called the Abode of the Message. Pir Vilayat then took up part-time residence there, along with some seventy-five students and their children.[19] At about the same time, Reb Zalman accepted a permanent position as professor of Jewish mysticism and psychology of religion at Temple University in Philadelphia. From that time on, the two were more closely associated, and Reb Zalman was a frequent visitor at the Abode, as well as at Sufi circles in Philadelphia and Boston.

Thus, it was in this period that another important and possibly unprecedented initiation took place. Pir Vilayat now sought initiation from his friend Reb Zalman into nothing less than the Priesthood of Melchizedek.

In the Book of Genesis, chapter 14:1-12, we find that Chedorlaomer, the king of Elam, had held numerous other kingdoms under his control for over a decade. When these kingdoms eventually rebelled, he and his allies went out to defeat the rebel armies, taking still more lands and kingdoms. The kings of Sodom and Gomorrah then went to face Chedorlaomer in battle, but were quickly scattered, leaving him to plunder those cities, taking their stores and treasures as spoils of war and their people as slaves. Among the captives was Lot, the nephew of the biblical patriarch, Abraham (then called Abram).

Now Abraham was not a king of a land or a city, but something like a great tribal chieftain, leading a caravan of people and livestock, a traveling nation for whom he was prophet and provider. Thus, when he received the news about Lot's captivity, Abraham gathered over 300 of his strongest young men to get him back. They pursued Chedorlaomer and his armies as far as Dan and attacked them at night, putting them to flight and taking back all the treasures and captives of Sodom and Gomorrah. With just 300 men, Abraham defeated and scattered Chedorlaomer's four armies in a single raid![20] (Genesis 14:13-16)

Returning from his victory, he was soon met by two kings—the king of Sodom, and the king of Salem (Genesis 14:17). The king of Sodom, whose army had just been defeated, and whose lands were sacked by Chedorlaomer, was grateful and astounded by Abraham's victory over the mighty king. Thus, he offered Abraham a reward, saying, "Return my people to me; the property you may keep." But Abraham refused the gift and returned all. He was not going to have people saying that the king of Sodom made him rich. He was rich enough—*God provides* (Genesis 14:21-24). But when the king of Salem approached Abraham, he received quite a different response. Genesis 14:19-20 says:

> Now Melchizedek, the king of Salem, brought out bread and wine, for he was a priest of God, Most High, and he blessed him, saying, "Blessed is Abram by God, Most High, Creator of Heaven and Earth."

Abraham then gave him a tenth of the spoils and Melchizedek disappeared, never to be seen or heard from again. But both his identity and the meaning of this episode are biblical mysteries about which many have wondered and speculated through the centuries.

Nevertheless, there is much that can be understood from the Hebrew and the cultural context.

The first clues are given in his name and titles. Melchizedek in Hebrew is *malkhi-tzedek*, "king of righteousness." The Bible often names qualities rather than persons; thus, Adam is "earthling" and Eve is "life-giver." Likewise, in the Jewish mystical tradition, we are taught that when Adam named all the creatures of the earth, he named them according to their essence. So the Bible is telling us that Melchizedek was indeed a "king of righteousness," or a "righteous king."

Then we are given his titles. We are told that he is the king of Salem, or *shalem* in Hebrew. This is generally understood to be a reference to Jerusalem—*Yeru-shalayim*—the "city of peace." But in this form, king of Salem, or *shalem,* can mean that he was king of "wholeness," "completion" or "peace." This is supported by the fact that he is also "a priest of God, Most High"—*kohen l'El Elyon*—"God, above all."

But what does this mean that he was a "priest of God, Most High"? Aren't we usually told that Abraham is the "father of monotheism"? Here it sounds like there's someone else before him holding the monotheistic mantle, a priest of an unknown religion, bringing forth bread and wine in ritual and blessing Abraham from his place as the priest-king of Salem.

As we have already seen, there is an interesting dichotomy in the two kings that come out to meet Abraham. The king of Sodom is treated as a profane king (the later reputation of "Sodom and Gomorrah" perhaps indicating a culture of depravity already present and represented in him) who comes to Abraham offering money. The king of Salem, on the other hand, is righteous and comes offering bread and wine, offerings of peace and friendship. The first offer Abraham rejects, saying, "I don't need your money," indicating that he is sovereign or whole-in-himself; he is not indebted to anyone else for his power and position. He is essentially a king. Thus, the offer of the bread and wine from the king of Salem is accepted, as it is an offering between equals to establish friendship, and the tenth of the spoils is not a return gift from Abraham, but a tithe of ten percent to a priest of God, Most High.

In the ancient world, there are three primary archetypes of leadership, an ideal triad of powers that keep each other in check: the king, prophet, and priest. Abraham, of course, was a prophet from the time that he was called by God. *Lekh lekha*—"*Go out* from the land of your people . . . and be a blessing." (Genesis 12:1-2) Thus, he goes out into the world, a desert traveler with an open connection to God. In time though, he becomes the wealthy chieftain we have met, capable of defeating an army, and who, when offered money from the king of Sodom, refuses the reward and proves that he is sovereign, a king. And now, the priest-king, Melchizedek, seems to be initiating him into the priesthood of God, Most High, making him at once a king, prophet, and priest, the ideal leader of the ancient world.

Spiritually speaking, the prophet is perhaps most important, having an open connection to God. Being "tuned to the right frequency," the sacred message comes through the prophet. But the prophet is rarely tame in the Bible, and is frequently—if not by definition—at odds with conventional society. Thus, it is the priest who translates what comes through the prophetic connection to the people in a language that they can easily understand and assimilate, like bread and wine. So while it is the function of the prophet to channel the divine message, and the responsibility of the king to take care of the people's material needs, it is the priest who sees to their basic emotional and spiritual needs.

In the ancient world, there was an idea that bread and wine were divine gifts. They were not natural products—not grain from the earth or fruit from the trees—but substances transformed through an almost magical process (fermentation) into something else, bread and wine. Unlike today, the bread of that time was remarkably nutritious, a staple of the ancient diet, and wine a substance which, when taken moderately, was positively associated with pleasure and could be drunk safely when water was suspect. Thus, both were highly regarded, and the secret of their making was believed to be a gift bestowed by God (whether by an act of revelation, or by granting us the insight and intelligence to see beyond the obvious). Thus, the unusual Hebrew blessing, *Barukh attah Yah, Elohenu melekh ha-olam, ha-motzi leḥem min ha-aretz*, "Blessed are You, Yah or God, who brings forth bread from the earth."

Now, the priestly ritual is one that, even to this day in the Jewish and Christian traditions, is performed with bread and wine, symbols of sustenance and the joy of life. But both the grain and the grapes from which these are made, in a sense, have to "spoil" before they are transformed into something else. The priest is the person who knows how to work with what seems spoiled, as if patiently observing the fermentation process, waiting for the transformation to happen to the wine, or for the moment to bring the risen dough to the heat. In the same way, the priest, as the guide of souls, is able to say to the broken and contrite hearts (Psalm 51:17) who come for guidance—"I know you think you've messed up, that you've sinned, that you've gotten off track and your life is in ruin. But I'm here to tell you, this ruin can be salvaged, it can be transformed, it can become the catalyst for a new and different life!" This is the priestly function, to show us that out of destruction, out of something apparently spoiled, something wonderful and holy is possible, and thus the symbolic presence of the bread and the wine in the priestly ritual.

Having offered Abraham the bread and wine, and having blessed him as a "priest of God, Most High," Melchizedek promptly disappears. He is mentioned again in Psalm 110:4, where King David (also a prophet), speaks of a victorious ruler who is "a priest forever, after the order of Melchizedek." Then in the New Testament, Paul echoes this Psalm in the Book of Hebrews 5:6, saying that Christ is "a priest forever, after the order of Melchizedek." This, according to Paul, is a priestly line which stands outside of the inherited priestly line of the Levites (the descendants of Aaron, the brother of Moses). Thus, today, all Episcopal and Catholic Christian priests are ordained "after the order of Melchizedek."

Now, why would Pir Vilayat ask this initiation of Reb Zalman? About this we can only speculate. According to Reb Zalman, Pir Vilayat believed that Melchizedek was likely the *qutb* in his time—the spiritual "axis" around which the fate of humanity revolved—who was then passing the mantle of *qutb* to Abraham.[21] For him, as for many others, Melchizedek was the "father of all priests," and a figure who did not die, but who was taken up into heaven, like Elijah, or transformed like Khidr, and who can thus come and go between the worlds.[22] This, of course, is close to the Pauline view, which says of Melchizedek, "Without father, without mother, without genealogy, having neither beginning of days, nor end of life, but resembling the son of God, he remains a priest forever" (Hebrews 7:3).

Given these possible beliefs, I suspect that Pir Vilayat, as the head of the Universal Worship established by his father—ordaining religious (cherags) empowered to do ritual and lead the Universal Worship service—wished to anchor himself in the most ancient and authentic transmission of the "father of all priests," Melchizedek, for the benefit of those whom he ordained. And from whom could he best receive this transmission? Reb Zalman himself believed that his friend had sought this initiation from him with the understanding that the esoteric transmission of the universal priesthood had been passed to Abraham, and thus also through his descendants to our day.[23] And, as Abraham was the father of the Jews, who established and maintained a lineal priesthood (the *kohanim*, the priestly caste descended from Aaron the Priest, the brother of Moses), and as Reb Zalman was not only a descendant of Abraham, but also a *kohen*, belonging to the priestly caste of Jews, as well a Hasidic rebbe or master of the Jewish esoteric tradition, Pir Vilayat may have believed Reb Zalman could best offer him this transmission.[24]

It is not clear exactly when the initiation took place. According to Reb Zalman, it was in New York, and possibly connected with Pir Vilayat leading the Cosmic Mass at St. John the Divine in New York City. If that is so, then it may have been as early as the end of October 1975. It may also have followed a seminar in New York City by Pir Vilayat (possibly held in conjunction with the Cosmic Mass) which Reb Zalman attended, coming up from his home in Philadelphia.[25]

After the conclusion of the seminar, Reb Zalman said that he performed the initiation for Pir Vilayat, opening the ritual with the question—"Vilayat, son of Inayat Khan, do you know that this is merely an initiation from the outside in recognition of something you already possess?"

Pir Vilayat responded, "Yes."

"Good," said Reb Zalman. "Then we'll do it."

We do not know the form of the initiation, but at its conclusion, Reb Zalman wrapped Pir Vilayat in a special *tallit* or prayer shawl on which he'd written in Hebrew, *Kohen l'El Elyon*, "Priest of God, Most High," and proceeded to teach him a kabbalistic text so that he would have some context from within the kabbalistic tradition of what he had just received.

After this, Reb Zalman brought out three loaves of *ḥallah*, which his wife had baked in the form of a heart with two wings, and a bottle of old Tokay, which, according to him, "poured dark like blood." He then said to Pir Vilayat, "Priest after the Order of Malki-tzedek, consecrate the bread and wine for the consumption of all present," later commenting to me that the latter did so "beautifully."[26]

TWO PILLARS *of* INTERSPIRITUALITY

In the coming years, Pir Vilayat would speak of these mutual initiations as being of great importance to him, and for the development of the future of religion. In one letter, dated August 9, 1988, he wrote:

> Some years ago, Reb Zalman and myself initiated each other into our respective traditions. Our reciprocal blessings represent the thrust of our life's work, and an example of possible networking among religious leaders in the future. Our sharing of this bonding in the Spirit represents my high regard for Reb Zalman and the authenticity of his teachings. On the many occasions in which we have participated in interfaith conferences, I have been deeply appreciative of his keen insight, in-depth knowledge of the esoteric traditions, and his capacity to open hearts with the fullness of his love and laughter.[27]

In a later letter, dated June 4, 2002, speaking of Reb Zalman's work and significance in the context of the political crisis in the Middle East, Pir Vilayat also wrote:

> I consider that his contribution in the present world situation in the Middle East is particularly pertinent

because he is the one rabbi in the world today who is not only familiar with Sufism, but practices it. He is not only a sheikh . . . but has initiated me in the Order of Melchizedek. This is not only a political statement, but a religious one. I emphasize the importance of the role he is playing by trying to overarch the political structures with unity by making a religious statement.[28]

In his book *Awakening*, Pir Vilayat talks about the qualities of Abraham and Melchizedek with regard to the temporal and spiritual, as the naturally paired archetypes of sovereignty and holiness. Abraham represents the ideal of *noblesse oblige*, the obligation of the noble, or true nobility. This is the chivalrous ideal of obligation based on advantage and blessing, that those who "have" are obliged to assist and serve those who "have not." Thus, their status exists solely for the purpose of taking care of others. But this in itself is not whole without the quality of holiness, embodied in Melchizedek, the high priest. Of course he is not talking about the religious functionary, but the ideal priest who is connected to the Source, the prophet-priest who counsels the sovereign.[29]

For Reb Zalman, the initiation into Inayati Sufism was also connected with the idea of a "universal priesthood." It allowed him a freedom that was not possible for him as a Jew and a rabbi. It allowed him to perform non-Jewish weddings and other rituals for which he could not find a basis under Jewish law *(halakhah)*, i.e., to function as a priest or cherag of a universal spirituality. Thus, he also encouraged some among his Jewish students to become Inayati Sufis and to train as cherags in order to fulfill this function as well.[30]

In the years to come, Reb Zalman continued to study Sufism, eventually taking initiation into the Qadiri-Rufai *tariqa* under Sheikh Siddi-Hassan al-Moumani of Balata (who empowered him to lead zikr*)*, and the Halveti-Jerrahi tariqa under his friend, Sheikh Muzaffer Ozak (1916-1985). He also formed important connections and friendships with Bektashi and Melami Sufis. Nevertheless, his closest relationships continued to be with Inayati Sufis. Pir Moineddin would remain a valued friend and colleague until his passing in 2002, and Reb Zalman maintained close ties with his successors, Pir Shabda Kahn and Murshid Wali Ali Meyer. But it was with two of Pir Vilayat's senior-most disciples that Reb Zalman would develop very special "avuncular" relationships. Puran Bair would become a colleague, sometimes leading Sufi retreats for Reb Zalman, who in turn served as his rabbi and counselor (even conducting his son's *bar mitzvah* in green Sufi robes and a turban). And still closer was Thomas Atum O'Kane, former Secretary General of the Sufi Order, and Pir Vilayat's "second" for many years. Atum would form a close spiritual bond with Reb Zalman, seeking his guidance on spiritual matters and working directly with Reb Zalman as his academic advisor on both his master's thesis and doctoral dissertation.

It was not until the year 2000 that Reb Zalman finally broke his "avuncular vow" and initiated his first and only Sufi murid. This story—my own—is perhaps best told elsewhere. Nevertheless, it is worth noting that out of this relationship was formed a new Sufi-Jewish or Sufi-Hasidic branch of the Inayati lineage, the Inayati-Maimuni tariqa, recognized in 2004 by Pir Vilayat's son and successor, Pir Zia Inayat-Khan. It is also possible that, in my own ordination and initiation as his successor in 2002, we have an example of the form Pir Vilayat's initiation into the Priesthood of Melchizedek may have taken, as Reb Zalman also performed some version of it for me at that time.

To the best of my knowledge, the last meeting between Reb Zalman and Pir Vilayat took place in New York City in 2000. On that occasion, both were participants in a plenary session on "Future Visions" during the State of the World Forum.[31] Afterward, they shared a hotel room at the Hilton, staying up late into the night, singing and teaching one another songs from their respective traditions—"Qalbi" ("my heart") and "Hashiveinu" ("turn us back"). There were no more teachings to exchange, no more initiations to offer one another; they were simply free to play as children before God.[32]

May the Holy One bless you and keep you;
May the Holy One shine favor upon you;
May the Holy One countenance you,
And grant you peace.
Amen. (Numbers 6:24-26)

— *Pir Netanel Miles-Yépez of the Inayati-Maimuni Order*
Boulder, Colorado

ENDNOTES

[1] The "Serenity Prayer," attributed to the famed Christian theologian Reinhold Niebuhr, recited by members of Alcoholics Anonymous, is certainly more widely known and used.

[2] Schachter-Shalomi, Zalman, and Netanel Miles-Yépez. "Translating the Invocation of the Toward the One into the Hebrew of the Jewish Tradition." *Seven Pillars House of Wisdom*. June 10, 2009. (http://www.sevenpillarshouse.org)

[3] Over the sixteen years of our relationship, I heard Reb Zalman speak of his connections to Sufism (both traditional and universalist), as well as his relationship to Pir Vilayat Inayat Khan, on various occasions and in numerous contexts. The account I give here is synthetic and based upon my own memory of those various occasions. However, most of it can be verified from a recording of an early conversation between us in 2002, recorded in Reb Zalman's home library for a book we were then writing whose working title was, "A Deep Encounter: A Primer for a Jewish Deep Ecumenism." The project was later shelved after we realized that a major reorganization of the material was necessary. This recording, titled "Deep Encounter, Part 5 of 12. Islam" and dated March 3, 2002, is now available in the Zalman M. Schachter-Shalomi Collection of the University of Colorado at Boulder Archives. I cite it and other sources here mostly in support of my personal account.

[4] Schachter-Shalomi, Zalman, with Edward Hoffman. *My Life in Jewish Renewal: A Memoir*. Boulder, Colorado: Rowman & Littlefield Publishers, 2012: 25-34, 43-48, 53-56.

[5] Ibid., 87-92.

[6] See Schachter-Shalomi, Zalman M., and Netanel Miles-Yépez. "Deep Encounter, Part 5 of 12. Islam." March 3, 2002. (Recording:

JRRZ0001S0101N008). Zalman M. Schachter-Shalomi Collection of the University of Colorado at Boulder Archives. He may have made the acquaintance of various Perennialist Sufis by this point, having heard Seyyed Hossein Nasr (b.1933) speak, and having been introduced to Jewish zikr by Leo Schaya (1916-1985), though the dates of these meetings are uncertain.

[7] Schachter-Shalomi. "Deep Encounter, Part 5 of 12. Islam."

[8] Ibid.

[9] See Schachter-Shalomi. "Deep Encounter, Part 5 of 12. Islam."

[10] Schachter-Shalomi. "Deep Encounter, Part 5 of 12. Islam."

[11] At that time, the two organizations springing from Murshid S.A.M. and Pir Vilayat were closely associated, and it was not uncommon for Pir Moineddin to advise others to first seek initiation with his elder, Pir Vilayat.

[12] See Schachter-Shalomi. "Deep Encounter, Part 5 of 12. Islam."

[13] Inayat-Khan, Zia (ed.). *Caravan of Souls: An Introduction to the Sufi Path of Hazrat Inayat Khan.* New Lebanon, NY: Suluk Press, 2013: 73-74.

[14] Khan, Inayat. *The Sufi Message of Hazrat Inayat Khan: Volume 12: The Vision of God and Man.* Geneva: International Headquarters of the Sufi Movement, 1982: 150.

[15] Khan, Inayat. *Biography of Pir-o-Murshid Inayat Khan.* London: East-West Publications, 1979: 125.

[16] Khan, Inayat. *Religious Gathekas,* #1.

[17] A new emphasis in a Sufi lineage is often marked by the addition of a name to it, often the name of the innovator.

[18] A term coined in San Francisco in 1923. Van Voorst van Beest, Munira (ed.). *The Complete Works of Pir-o-Murshid Inayat Khan" Original Texts: Lectures on Sufism 1923 I: January–June.* London: East-West Publications, 1989:: xii.

[19] Inayat-Khan. *Caravan of Souls,* 75.

[20] Though the passage does mention allies.

[21] Meaning that the fate of a community, a nation, or maybe the world, turn on what this one person might do. A person might be the *qutb* for years or a single moment. At one point, Pir Vilayat believed the qutb was in Lebanon. All of this was heard directly from Reb Zalman.

In Pir Vilayat Inayat Khan, *Awakening: A Sufi Experience* (ed. Pythia Peay. Jeremy P. Tarcher: New York, 1999: 80-81), Pir Vilayat writes: "Melchizedek is recognized by Judaism, Christianity, and Islam, and thus represents a religious authority whom they each have in common. No doubt he sacrificed at the altar in Jerusalem, which is probably the stone now housed in the Dome of the Rock. I believe he must have lived in the cave that is at the top of the Mount of Olives—a place where I once took retreat—whereas most of his people at the time were living in tents. When I imagine the being of Melchizedek, I think of him as very, very holy, with a personality that is totally dedicated to attuning to the sacred. . . . Can you, for instance, put yourself back in time to that moment when Melchizedek, during a ceremony in which bread and wine were offered as a sacrament, anointed Abraham as king? In a moment of divine transmission, in which Melchizedek conferred upon Abraham God's blessings as His ambassador on earth."

[22] A student of Pir Vilayat (I believe it was Daena Ross) told me: "Pir Vilayat used to talk about him [Melchizedek] as the father of all priests. . . . He also talked about him as never really passing, that he was a real being on Earth, and you know, just like the tales of the Green Man, and Elijah."

[23] In the rabbinic tradition of Judaism, it is understood that Melchizedek bestows the priesthood on Abraham at this moment, who then becomes a "priest forever" (b. Ned. 32b; Lev. Rab. 25.6), an eternal or universal priest.

[24] At the end of the last talk he gave to the Boulder-Denver Inayati Sufi community, Reb Zalman gave the priestly blessing with the priestly gesture.

[25] Schachter-Shalomi. "Deep Encounter, Part 5 of 12. Islam." "The one [Cosmic Mass] that he did at St. John the Divine, he looked like a *kohein gadol*." Pir Vilayat led the Cosmic Masses at St. John the Divine in New York City on October 22 and 24, described in a *Time* magazine article, "Mish-Mass" (November 3, 1975), and perhaps again a year later. Thanks to Nancy Lakshmi Barta-Norton of the Inayati Order Archives for helping me to identify the dates.

[26] Schachter-Shalomi. "Deep Encounter, Part 5 of 12. Islam." In Reb Zalman's recorded words:

"At one point he had asked me to initiate him into the order of Melchizedek. So I had brought him a *tallis*, and I did a thing in which I had written, *kodesh l'Yah*, you know, so just like the high priest had, and we did that initiation after he did a seminar in New York.

"Then we had the initiation, and I know what he wanted. He wanted a connection with Malkhitzedek, on that level. So I asked him this question—'Vilayat son of Inayat Khan'—you know, like to do that—'do you know that this is an initiation that you don't need from the outside, that you have it already from the inside?'

"He said, 'Yes.'

"I said, 'Then in that case I might do the rest.'

"And Elana had baked a ḥallah, three ḥallahs, that looked like a heart, and two ḥallahs that looked like wings. And I'd gotten some special old wine that flowed like blood from Lipshitz's winery in Philadelphia. . . . So he had one cask of old Tokay, and it poured like, you know, it was dark like blood. And I figured that if he's gonna be doing the initiation according to the wine and bread. So after I'd brought him that, I said, 'Now that you're'—after the initiation, *yivarekha* and some other things were over—I asked him to consecrate the bread and the wine, and to share it with us. And it was wonderful."

[27] "Letter from Vilayat Inayat Khan to Greg Burton and Rochelle N. Grossman." August 9, 1988. The Pir Vilayat Inayat Khan Collection. The Inayati Order Archives–North America. Richmond, Virginia. Letter written endorsing Schachter-Shalomi's Wisdom School.

[28] "Letter from Vilayat Inayat Khan to Dana Lobell." June 4, 2002. The Pir Vilayat Inayat Khan Collection. The Inayati Order Archives–North America. Richmond, Virginia. Letter written recommending Schachter-Shalomi for the Templeton Prize.

[29] Here is also a suggestion of Reb Zalman in the archetype of Abraham and Pir Vilayat in archetype of Melchizedek. Pir Vilayat likewise connects two *waza'if* (names of divine qualities) to Abraham and Melchizedek. *Ya Qahr*, the sovereign, he connects with Abraham. *Ya Quddus*, holiness, he connects to Melchizedek.Vilayat Inayat Khan. *Awakening: A Sufi Experience*. Ed. Pythia Peay. Jeremy P. Tarcher: New York, 1999: 80-83.

[30] See Schachter-Shalomi. "Deep Encounter, Part 5 of 12. Islam."

[31] This information was given to me on July 22, 2017 by Richard (Nur) Gale, a student of Pir Vilayat who helped to organize the session set up by Joe Firmage, who financed it. Deepak Chopa and various scientists also participated.

[32] See Schachter-Shalomi. "Deep Encounter, Part 5 of 12. Islam

INTRODUCTION

This book brings together the perspectives of two contemporary, universalist spiritual teachers and friends, Pir Vilayat Inayat Khan and Rabbi Zalman Schachter-Shalomi, and explores the deep commonalities between the mystical paths of Sufism and Hasidic Judaism, which are their respective traditions. They were both progressive thinkers and creative trailbrazers within their own traditions, fearlessly exploring the cutting edge of spirituality, redefining and renewing our concepts of the Divine, stressing direct experience and realization, and always striving to uplift the hearts and souls of those around them.

These two beloved spiritual leaders met in 1975 and initiated one another, rekindling a cross-fertilization of traditions which echos the thirteenth-century blending of Jewish-Sufism in the spirituality of Rabbi Abraham Maimuni, the son of Maimonides. This has, in the twenty-first century, given rise to a new Sufi-Hasidic lineage known as the Inayati-Maimuni Order.

I am deeply grateful for having had the opportunity to study with these two teachers and hope to convey some of the richness of their unique contributions to the field of contemporary spirituality. Their teachings reveal the profound mystical depths and universal foundations that connect these two vast expressions of the Abrahamic tradition at a time when many of their respective followers in mainstream Judaism and Islam have become entrenched in open conflict. These two traditions are like vast bodies of water formed out of one great ocean—certainly Christianity, which is my own birth tradition, is the third great expanse of this ocean, and its perspective will also be considered in this book. Sufism and Hasidism represent the inner teachings of Islam and Judaism, and emphasize the religion of the heart—the love, compassion, and joy that is their true *raison d'etre*.

From the modern convergence of these two great traditions—which are historically distinctive, but inseparably rooted in the realization of divine oneness—comes the metaphor that inspires the title of this book, *When Oceans Merge*. The phrase harks back to the title of a Persian treatise called *Majma ul-Bahrain* (variously translated as "the merging of the two oceans," "the mingling of two seas," and "where the two oceans meet;" ca.1654-55) by Muhammad Dara Shikoh, son of the Mughal Emperor Shah Jahan, the grandson of Akbar and builder of the Taj Mahal. Dara Shikoh was a champion of coexisting heterodox mystical traditions, and the title of his famous work refers to the affinities between the traditions of Sufism and Vedanta, which freely commingle in India. The title is equally applicable to the underlying wellsprings of Sufism and Hasidism, which have both come forth from the fountainhead of prophetic inspiration transmitted through Abraham, the one who, four millennia ago, in an age of polytheism, received the revelation of the Divine Oneness, the indivisible singularity of the Source.

In sixth-century Arabia, in the time of the Prophet Muhammad, the righteous ones who upheld the Divine Oneness in the universal tradition of Abraham were called the *hanifiyyah*. These hanifs were distinguished from Jews, who followed the Jewish law which was revealed to Moses hundreds of years after the time of Abraham, and from Christians, who saw Jesus as the fulfillment of the law and the second person of the Trinity. The earliest Christian community in Jerusalem, headed by James the Just, the brother of Jesus, recommended, as a minimum commitment for Gentile converts to Christianity, the observance of the seven laws of Noah,[1] which comprised less restrictive guidelines (for instance, omitting the Jewish requirement of circumcision) which were revealed for all righteous humanity prior to the more specific Mosaic covenant with the Jewish people. With the subsequent rise of Judaism, the waters of the great spiritual ocean separated, and Christianity and Islam (which was the original primordial religion of Abraham) trifurcated into three great related sacred traditions. The Qur'anic revelations that came through the Prophet Muhammad confirmed some of the Jewish dietary laws, prophetic revelations, and biblical and midrashic stories of Judaism, along with the exalted station of Jesus (*Isa*) and the Virgin Mary (*Maryam*)—with the understanding that Islam represented not a new separate faith or "ism," but a continuation and renewal of the original Abrahamic tradition prior to its Jewish and Christian customizations. Reb Zalman once summed up this historical progression in conversation with a Sufi sheikh in Hevron (Hebron, Israel), who was amazed that a Jew could accept Muhammad as an authentic prophet and would want to join in the mystical practice of *zikr* with his Sufi dervishes:

> There was Ismail, the son of Ibrahim Habibullah, Abraham the friend of G-d. . . . Ismail still had the *Tawhid,* the knowledge of the oneness of G-d, but his children fell into the dark ages, into the *jahiliya*, into the unknowing. And so, they had lost their way to the oneness of G-d. So, *Ya Rahim, Ya Rahman,* the Merciful, the Compassionate, sent out a messenger to the children of Ismail to bring them back to Tawhid, to the oneness. I believe that he was a true messenger.[2]

Centuries after the Prophet's time, in thirteenth-century Egypt, Abraham Maimuni (Rabbi Abraham ben Moses Maimonides), along with his son, 'Obadyah, and other Jewish pietists of his time, saw the mystical path of Sufism—although practiced primarily by Islamic descendents of Ishmael—as having preserved the original spirit and praxis of the Jewish faith more faithfully than could be found in the Europeanized Judaism of the time, and thus looked to Sufism as an aid to Jewish renewal and restoration. As Pir Vilayat Khan recounts this history:

> The longstanding interface between Islam and Judaism deserves our attention. During the flowering of Kabbalah

in the eleventh and twelfth centuries, Kabbalists and Hassidim frequented the khanaqas of the Sufi mystics of Baghdad. Bahya ibn Paquda's *Duties of the Heart* bears the unmistakable imprint of the Sufi exhortations of the time, although he has reservations about the self-annihilation found amongst some Sufi ascetics. While the Crusaders were besieging Jerusalem, a large number of Jews fled to Cairo, fostering a Jewish-Sufi movement; they were, no doubt, encouraged by the progressive philosophy of Moses Maimonides, and even more so by the influence of his son, Abraham Maimonides, whose attachment to Sufis is known. The Jewish Sufis found in Sufism a restoration of practices that had been prevalent in Israel in former times. Abraham Maimonides was quoted as having said, in reference to the Sufis: The latter imitate the prophets (*of Israel*) and walk in their footsteps. But it was in the *Al-Maqalat al-Hawdiya* ("The Treatise of the Pool"), authored by 'Obadyah b. Abraham b. Moses Maimonides, the grandson of the renowned philosopher, that deep familiarity with precepts reserved for the Sufi initiates evidences an initiatic affiliation with a Sufi order.[3]

Abraham Maimonides was one of the most respected Jewish authorities of his time, during one of the most creative and formative eras of Jewish mysticism. Author Tom Block ventures that

It would not be too far of a stretch to say that the Sufi leanings of Abraham influenced virtually all mystical writings in Judeo-Arabic over the next two hundred years, the formative years of the Kabbalistic system! In fact, his works were still being studied by Kabbalists in sixteenth-century Safed, where the Lurianic Kabbalah was setting the scene for the entrance of Hasidism onto the Jewish mystical stage. . . . Jewish practitioners today of the Kabbalistic sciences and Hasidism certainly have no idea just how much of the *Sufi Way* is wrapped into their traditions.[4]

The mystical dimensions of Judaism which paralleled Sufism developed esoteric traditions based in part on the ancient oral transmission of the Torah, which was so important to the formulation of the Kabbalistic tradition, building on the visionary insights of Jewish mystics such as Moses de Leon, Isaac the Blind, and Isaac Luria. Then, in the time of Rabbi Israel ben Eliezer, the Ba'al Shem Tov (ca.1700-1760), a great wave of Jewish renewal appeared in the form of the Hasidic tradition in Eastern Europe, paralleling the mystic way of the Islamic Sufi orders, yet developing along distinctively Jewish lines. In Mughal India and the Ottoman lands, Sufism continued to expand its own traditions. Practitioners of both Sufism and Hasidism extolled love, engaged in regular prayers, sought the divine intimacy, studied and chanted the divine names, sang mystic hymns, spoke of the four worlds, emphasized allegorical, rather than literal, understandings of scripture, and both, to some degree, incorporated aspects of emanationism (in common with Neoplatonism), seeing all life as emanating from the One and Only Being and creation as an ever-ongoing emergence of the Source.

This reciprocal cross-fertilization, renewal, and development over the centuries has enriched the mystical traditions of both Sufism and Hasidism, as they have been handed down to the present generations. Likewise, in the Christian world, the Hesychasts and later monastic orders developed the inner teachings of Jesus and produced great teachers who shared commonalities with Sufism, such as St. Francis of Assisi, Meister Eckhart, and Thomas Merton. These three parallel mystical paths are currently undergoing fresh interpretations by forward-thinking teachers within these traditions whose love of the world's sacred legacies often extends to other paths beyond the traditional boundaries of their faith, as today's spiritual practitioners discover new dimensions of the sacred in a modern interspiritual Axial Age.

Pir Vilayat and Reb Zalman epitomize the new approach to spirituality. Both addressed the issues of exclusivism, fundamentalism, pluralism, and the modern contributions of science and psychology, reaching beyond the surface of the traditions to see the one essential religion, the one Divine Reality behind all the doctrines, creeds, and opposing claims on truth. They were futurists, steeped in the traditions of the past, yet dedicated to a vision of what spirituality could become in the coming centuries. They enjoyed deep friendships with spiritual teachers and progressive thinkers from other faith traditions, both Eastern and Western; and they studied and incorporated insights and practices from these traditions into their own teaching, bringing further enrichment, universality and fresh perspectives to their own path. Both authored multiple books, innovated within the traditions they represented, sought to update stale, literalistic understandings of the Divine, and were, to some extent, musicians—with music being an important ingredient in their method of sacred transmission and celebratory worship.

In writing about these two teachers, I detail various facets of their life journeys, their struggles, and their distinctive spiritual contributions, occasionally including in the narrative my own interactions, experiences, and dialogues with them, in an attempt to impart an experiential understanding of the progressive and changing spirituality in our times, as it flows forth from the mystical wellsprings of the Abrahamic tradition.

As for my own background, I was raised in a Protestant Evangelical Christian family, with a paternal grandfather who was a Wesleyan minister in Upstate New York and a maternal grandmother who started the first rescue mission in Nashville, Tennessee, in the 1940s. Raised in France and the United States, I studied liberal arts at Vanderbilt University and Peabody College in the early 1970s. I received initiation from Pir Vilayat in 1980 and met Reb Zalman the following year. Throughout the 1980s, I undertook an extensive study of the world's religions, attending various retreats and spending as much time as possible with Pir Vilayat, Reb Zalman, and a host of other spiritual teachers. During this same period, I began to lead a Sufi group in the Nashville area. In the 1990s, I received initiation from Sheikh Nur (Lex Hixon) in the Halveti-Jerrahi Order, an

Ottoman Sufi *tariqat* (order) based in Istanbul, and was invested as a sheikh in that order in 1994.

In the following years, I began to bring together the rich spiritual resources to which I had been granted access, and to write about the spiritual path, not as an academic scholar, but as a spiritual practitioner inside these living traditions, who is drawn to document the evolving teachings and new perspectives that are currently renewing and infusing these time-honored sacred traditions with new life. Sufism, as I understand it, is a religion of the heart; as such, its approach is open and life-affirming, placing a high value on peace, love, and harmony between people, while rejecting any political or ideological interpretation of religion that encourages violence against other faiths in the spirit of intolerance.

Today, with the resources provided by the internet and mass communication, we have more and more access to the wisdom offered by these great traditions (as well as new unaffiliated spiritual systems); yet the institutions associated with these traditions have too often tethered the spirit to outdated precepts and culturally limiting parochialism instead of freeing the spirit and allowing it to rise in love.

My first two books (*The Garden of Mystic Love* and *Lifting the Boundaries*) conveyed the history and teachings of the Sufi path, presenting the essential transmission as I had received it and interpreting it in ways that might speak to a contemporary Western audience while accentuating the authentic underlying universality of the tradition. In this book, I endeavor to take the process further by going to the heart of interspirituality and chronicling two highly innovative teachers who represent a progressive window on the universal, timeless, yet evolving aspects of contemporary spirituality with its roots in the authentic mystical traditions of the Abrahamic faiths. This resonates with my own spiritual orientation which is aptly summarized by the words of the Sufi 'Abdul Allah:

> *Qur'an, the Bible, or a martyr's cry, all these my heart can tolerate, since my religion is love alone.*[5]

Pir Vilayat Khan was a Sufi *murshid* (guide or teacher) who possessed a great gift for lifting people beyond their limited assessments of things into the higher realms of meaning and glorification. Born in London and raised in France, he was endowed with a predilection toward the meditative attunement of the *sannyasin* (a spiritual renunciate, retired from the life of a householder) and an intense desire for spiritual liberation, both for himself and for others around him. Pir Vilayat's genetic heritage made him a natural cultural bridge between East and West—with an American mother and an Indian father, he had sympathies for both worlds. A pioneer in the field of interspirituality, in the 1960s he launched an annual interfaith congress near Paris, founding a convocation of representatives of all the world's major religions that would continue for two decades, and he was the inspiration behind the founding of Omega Institute in upstate New York.

Pir Vilayat's father, Hazrat Inayat Khan, brought Sufism to the West in 1910 and bequeathed to the modern world a treasury of profound contemporary spiritual teachings that emphasized the universality of the spirit and the awakening of humanity to its own divine inheritance. This legacy became the touchstone for Pir Vilayat's teachings as he traveled the world, leading retreats and seminars which drew upon the practices and inner teachings of the great mystics of all traditions, with an emphasis on Sufis such as Ibn al-'Arabi and Mevlana Jalaluddin Rumi.

With his Oxford English accent and Indian robes, Pir Vilayat at times radiated an almost aristocratic air, which he balanced with a mirthful sense of humor. A master of meditation, he endeavored to uplift the consciousness of his listeners, reviving the memory of the soul's glorifications in the heavens. This was facilitated through guided meditations, Sufi *zikr*, and the sacred music of inspired composers from J. S. Bach to Samuel Barber, all utilized in the service of attuning the individual to the transcendent, eternal dimensions of reality behind the everyday, pedestrian world, with all its problems. In his talks, Pir Vilayat occasionally highlighted cutting-edge insights from contemporary physics, but when he spoke of the great Sufi masters and led zikr practices in a retreat setting, one felt strongly the intimate attunement of the dervish lover lost in rapturous contemplation of the Beloved.

Both Pir Vilayat and Rabbi Zalman Schachter-Shalomi lived long lives, just short of ninety years. Born of Jewish parents in pre-Holocaust Poland, Reb Zalman escaped with his family to America, where he continued his Hasidic training with the sixth Lubavitcher Rebbe, received ordination as a rabbi, earned degrees in psychology and religion, and, after a decade as a congregational rabbi, went on to become a university professor and progenitor of the Jewish Renewal Movement.

Both Reb Zalman and Pir Vilayat passed through the alchemical fire of suffering and struggle at an early age, Reb Zalman and his family narrowly escaping Hilter's regime, and Pir Vilayat losing his father at age ten, then his beloved sister, Noor, at the hands of the Nazis during his twenties, followed by the sudden death of his fiancé a few years later. In Reb Zalman's case, he not only lost close relatives, but saw the annihilation of many of the great Jewish rebbes of Europe in the smokestacks of World War II. The resultant Jewish anger at God over the Holocaust and the subsequent migration of so many contemporary Jews to Eastern religions and secularism fueled the spiritual fallout and impoverishment within modern Judaism that Reb Zalman longed to redress and heal throughout his adult life.

While Reb Zalman has been called the father of the Jewish Renewal Movement, he was also known by the affectionate monikers, "the hippie rabbi" and "the cyber rebbe." Possessing a penetrating mind and a big heart, Zalman's spiritual ecumenicism and modernizing tendencies, all in the service of revitalizing and updating Jewish spiritual practice, inevitably outgrew the insular restrictions of traditional Hasidism. He counted as friends practitioners and leaders from many other spiritual paths, including, along with Pir Vilayat: Thomas Merton, the Dalai Lama, Chögyam Trungpa Rinpoche, Father Thomas Keating, and Jean Houston, among many others. Though he founded a Jewish-Sufi order late in life, he never wavered in his goal of revivifying his root tradition of Judaism and reacquainting his followers with the neglected mystical depths of Kabbalah.

Reb Zalman endeavored to inspire fellow Jews to reach beyond the post-Holocaust wounding and rationalistic flattening of worship so prevalent in modern Judaism, striving to unveil the tradition's true universal, generic core, and mystical dimensions, without abandoning the distinctive Jewish practices, insights, humor, and love of knowledge which characterizes it. He opened up Kabbalistic teaching to non-Jews as well, reaching out to find common ground with other faiths. In later life, he championed spiritual eldering and women's ordinations, pointing to the duty of authentic religion to advocate a proactive "eco-kosher" approach to the environment in order to help heal Mother Earth. Like Teilhard de Chardin, he saw religion, the universe, and even our God concepts as always changing, growing and evolving toward an ever-greater expression of divinity.

Reb Zalman reflected on his own journey, saying,

> It was not my achievement that I have a foot in the past and a foot in the future; it was my given. I was uniquely placed to comprehend and bridge many worlds both by historical events and personal disposition. My real achievement was that I held fast to both.[6]

His friend and longtime colleague, Rabbi Arthur Green, described Reb Zalman's prolific intellectual pursuits as including "the language of psychedelics and New Age consciousness in the sixties, humanistic psychology in the seventies, Marshall McLuhan in the eighties, Ken Wilber and Integral Studies in the '90s, environmentalism and Gaian language in the new century, [and] more recently the latest studies in brain physiology and the relationship between brain, mind, and consciousness,"[7] all of which he was anxious to translate and infuse back into the language of the religious traditions which he loved. As Reb Zalman once remarked in reference to the currently available harvest of spiritual possibilities and our opportunity to consciously participate in the emergence of planetary consciousness, "In the history of our earth there are only a few times like ours. What a blessing to be incarnated now!"[8]

May you, dear reader, whatever your tradition, experience in this account of two modern spiritual innovators and their teachings, new and helpful seed-thoughts to ponder and assimilate on your journey to union with truth.

ENDNOTES

[1] Acts 15:1-31

[2] Schatcher-Shalomi, Reb Zalman, *Reb Zalman Among the Sufis*; excerpt of a 3/19/94 audio recording at the Hillel Foundation in Berkeley, CA; co-sponsored by the Aquarian Minyon, transcribed by Reuven Goldfarb with the assistance of Eliyahu (Khaled) McLean. Available at: http://sufi-tariqah.de/tarchiv/rebzalman.html.

[3] Khan, Pir Vilayat, *The Ecstasy Beyond Knowing*, Kindle edition, chapter 6 on Kabbala.

[4] From an article entitled, *Abraham Maimonides: A Jewish Sufi*, in the winter 2001 issue of *Sufi* magazine, London.

[5] Khan, Hazrat Inayat, *The Unity of Religious Ideals*, p.17; Sufi Order Publications, New Lebanon, NY, 1979.

[6] Phone interview by Ken Wilber entitled "Exile, Imprisonment, and the Journey Towards a Self-Conscious Spirituality," 2005.

[7] Quoted from "The One Who Walked Before the Camp; a Eulogy by Rabbi Arthur Green." Available at: https://aleph.org/resources/the-one-who-walked-before-the-camp-a-eulogy-by-rabbi-arthur-green+&cd=1&hl=en&ct=clnk&gl=us.

[8] From a talk by Atum O'Kane given during a training course on Spiritual Guidance in 2015.

PART I

Pir Vilayat Inayat Khan

the FORMATIVE YEARS

Pir Vilayat was born June 19, 1916, in London, England, the eldest son of Pir-o-Murshid Hazrat Inayat Khan and Ora Ray Baker Khan. Vilayat's father was a Sufi master and renowned musician from India (1885-1927) who is distinguished as the first teacher to bring Sufism to the Western world, coming in 1910. He eventually settled his family in Suresnes, a suburb of Paris, France, where he taught Sufism until his return to India and untimely death in 1927. Vilayat's mother was an American who, before meeting Inayat, learned yoga from her prominent half-brother, the graphic designer Pierre Bernard. This union produced four children who were biologically and psychologically a blend of East and West. Vilayat's younger siblings were Hidayat, who became a musician, conductor, composer, and a murshid in the Sufi Movement; and Khair-un-Nisa (or Claire) Harper, co-author of the book, *We Rubies Four*.

Vilayat's older sister, Noor-un-Nisa (meaning "light of womanhood"), was born in Russia in 1914, grew up in London and France, and is today considered a French war hero, having been posthumously awarded the Croix de Guerre. She is also the subject of several films documenting her clandestine work as a radio operator for the French Resistance during the Nazi occupation of France. Sadly, just days before she was to be smuggled out of France to the safety of England, she was betrayed by an associate and arrested by the Nazis, who shipped her to the concentration camp at Dachau, where she was beaten and killed in September 1944.

Vilayat had also volunteered for military duty as a defensive mine-sweeping officer in the British Navy, was involved in the Normandy invasion, and, on another occasion, had his own close encounter with death when his minesweeping boat was torpedoed and sunk in freezing waters. Vilayat survived the war, but was devastated by the tragic death of his sister, as was his whole family. His mother had already become severely depressed by her husband's death over a decade earlier. She moved with the family to England during the war and did some hospital work there, but the family kept the news of Noor's death from her due to her already weakened state. After the war ended, she returned to France with her daughter Claire and died there in 1949.

It is noteworthy that Hazrat Inayat Khan did not teach his children a spiritual doctrine of total nonviolence but advised them in keeping with Islamic principles of "pursuing good and forbidding evil." He told his children in 1926 that if another war came and external enemies threatened their home country of France, it was their duty to help defend the land, and not just passively enjoy its benefits and freedoms during times of peace.

In 1926, Hazrat Inayat Khan designated his ten-year-old son, Vilayat, as his successor in the Sufi Movement. However, when Inayat passed away the following year during his retirement to India, Vilayat was far too young to take on the role of spiritual leader, so the interim position fell to Inayat's brother, Maheboob Khan, who promised Vilayat that he would turn the leadership over to him when Vilayat felt ready.

Maheboob had been part of the Indian musical ensemble of family members who accompanied Inayat to the West in 1910. Together with his brothers Maheboob and Musharaff and his cousin 'Ali Khan, Inayat formed a quartet for a time, performing Indian classical music for American and European audiences, and briefly backed the exotic dancer Mata Hari (who was executed as a German spy in 1917), as well as the great modern dance teacher and performer, Ruth St. Denis. After a few years in the West, Inayat turned to teaching Sufism full-time instead of performing music.

Maheboob set a number of Hazrat Inayat Khan's English language poems and sayings from his *Gayan, Vadan, Nirtan*, to Western music using hauntingly beautiful, singable, oriental melodies, occasionally utilizing famous Indian melodies such as the Hindu "Hymn to the Sun." Maheboob died in 1948 before Vilayat was ready to assume the Sufi mantle and his uncle, 'Ali Khan, took over as head of the movement. 'Ali Khan had trained in the Western operatic style of singing and had a beautiful voice and a reputation as a healer, but he did not display the same sympathy toward Vilayat as Maheboob had, and blocked Vilayat when he finally asked to take over the leadership of the Sufi Movement in the mid-1950s.

Given the situation, Vilayat started his own movement, which he called the Sufi Order in the West. This organization, now known as the Inayati Order, is currently one of three major branches of universalist Sufism based on the teachings of Hazrat Inayat Khan. The other two major branches are the original Sufi Movement (with most of its activity in Europe) and the Sufi Ruhaniat International, founded in the late 1960s in San Francisco by another disciple of Hazrat Inayat Khan, Murshid Samuel Lewis, who innovatively brought through the Dances of Universal Peace prior to his death in 1971.

After the death of his father, Vilayat attended the Ecole Normale de Musique in Paris, where he studied composition with Nadia Boulanger, and attended the Sorbonne, which included classes with Igor Stravinsky. He graduated in 1940 with a degree in philosophy and psychology and went on to do graduate work at Oxford University, also studying Sufism with the Catholic Islamist and mystic Louis Massignon. Afterwards, Vilayat studied comparative religion at King Alfred Lancing College, near Brighton, and worked for a time as assistant to the Pakistani finance minister, Ghulam Mohammed. After the war ended, Vilayat fell in love with an attractive young woman named Myrtle Mitchell and asked for her hand in marriage. But his happiness was once again shattered when, in 1947, they went for a ride on his BMW motorcycle and the bike stand collapsed as they sped along, causing her to fall off the back and sustain injuries that resulted in her death. Two years later, his mother passed away.

In later years, Pir Vilayat occasionally mentioned this period as a time when he felt inconsolable grief. He eventually healed himself by listening to the high mass of Bach (in B minor) every evening for months, soaking in the glorification that came through the mass, and being lifted beyond his personal sorrows. He often played these glorious strains of music at the conclusion of his camps, having everyone dance freestyle and whirl to the music of his favorite composer, Johann Sebastian Bach, whom he felt had tuned into the angelic cosmic celebrations in the heavens and who could be thought of as a Western spiritual master who communicated the Divine through his music.

For a time, Pir Vilayat worked as a reporter for a Karachi-based newspaper, reporting on the Algerian independence movement, and exposing atrocities associated with it. A few years later, Vilayat married Mary Walls, a Roman Catholic, and later had a daughter named Maria.

During the 1950s, Pir Vilayat intensified his religious studies. His father had told him of great *rishis*, Hindu saints, in the Himalayas near the source of the Ganges, so he decided to hitchhike across India in search of such teachers on what he called his "guru hunt." Finally, high up in the snowy mountains, beyond the various *faqirs* (ascetics), yogis, and tourist areas, he came across some tracks in the snow which led him to a rishi in a cave. He approached the rishi with great deference. As Pir Vilayat later recounted it, the rishi motioned to him not to enter, so he sat down in the snow and began to meditate. When he opened his eyes a little while later, the rishi was in front of him. He looked at Vilayat and said simply, "Why have you come so far to see what you should be?" Pir Vilayat recalled that, in his youthfulness, he answered something like, "It is so wonderful to see this," but later came to realize that a better response would have been: "To become what I might be, I have to see myself in another myself who shows me who I truly am." The rishi also asked him, "Are you looking for a guru?" When Vilayat answered no, the rishi told him, "In that case you may come in." He allowed him to stay for three days, then sent him back into the world.[1]

This experience echoed an encounter that had occurred a century earlier when his father, Hazrat Inayat Khan, as a young man, had come across a great *mahatma* in Katmandu who was rapt in ecstatic meditation. His spiritual glance, or *darshan*, was very powerful, and Inayat was greatly influenced by him, receiving his blessing. The mahatma, or holy sage, also very much enjoyed Inayat's singing and his playing of the Indian stringed instrument the *vina* over the course of many subsequent visits.

Together, Vilayat and Mary made five trips across India. In preparation for his duties as pir and as his father's successor, Vilayat made rigorous Sufi retreats at Ajmer, Hyderabad, and the Mount of Olives in Jerusalem. He meditated near the Bodhi-tree in Bodh Gaya, undertook a retreat in the monastery of Monserrat in Spain, and visited the Greek Orthodox Christian community at Mount Athos. In Hyderabad, Vilayat made a significant forty-day retreat with Pir Fakhruddin Jili-Kalimi of the Chishti-Nizami-Kalimi lineage, the grandson of Kalimi Delevi (Hazrat Inayat Khan's teacher's teacher), who recognized Vilayat as a Sufi *pir* in his own right. This title was further confirmed in Ajmer by Diwan Saulat Husayn Chishti.

Finally, in 1956, after many years of preparation, Pir Vilayat felt ready to assume his place as his father's successor in the Sufi Movement. Faced with the realization that his uncle, 'Ali Khan, was not willing to turn over the reins to him, Pir Vilayat founded a parallel organization that operated in Europe and in the United States with summer camps at Chamonix, in the French Alps. At the time, there was still very little other Sufi activity in Europe and America.

In 1964, Idries Shah, a Naqshibandi Sufi living in England, wrote his seminal book, *The Sufis*, which, at the time, was one of the few English publications available that dealt with Sufism. Though Shah was ostensibly writing a survey of the Sufi influences in the Western world, he pointedly omitted all mention of

Hazrat Inayat Khan, who had first brought Sufism to the West. This likely reflected the influence of Shah's father, who had been a friend of Inayat Khan but also a critic of his establishment of the Sufi Order as an interfaith, rather than exclusively Islamic, order. When Annemarie Schimmel later published her classic book, *Mystical Dimensions of Islam*, she followed suit and only mentioned Khan in a small footnote saying that his brand of Sufism was very "modern and subjective, yet impressive."[2]

In order to put this into context, as well as the whole thrust of Pir Vilayat's teaching, it is necessary to pause here and briefly review the legacy of Hazrat Inayat Khan—how he came to the West and approached Islam and the perennial mystical tradition. It is said that initially Inayat Khan was reticent to give these teachings a name, but later he began to call it Sufism, or "the Sufi Message in our time" (or just "the Message"), which he identified as the timeless wisdom brought by all of the prophets.

As Mark Segwick observes in his book *Western Sufism; From the Abbasids to the New Age*, Hazrat Inayat Khan's perspective on Sufism was universalist, anti-exoteric, and emanationist, echoing Neoplatonic conceptions of the One perhaps as much as the influence of more theistic Islamic Sufism in the creationist tradition. In Pir Vilayat's presentation, Ibn 'Arabi's understanding of the Unity of Being (*Wahdat-al Wujud*) served as a reference point bridging traditional Sufism with the more emanationist pre-Islamic conceptions of the One Source typical of Plotinus. As a kind of modern English corollary of the foundational Islamic teaching, *La ilaha illallah* (Nothing exists except the One Reality), Hazrat Inayat Khan was inspired to give the modern English invocation,

> Toward the One, the perfection of love, harmony, and beauty, the Only Being, united with all the illuminated souls who form the embodiment of the Master, the Spirit of Guidance.

HAZRAT INAYAT KHAN

Painting of Hazrat Inayat Khan by the author

Inayat Khan was born in Baroda, India on July 5, 1882. He was descended from a musical family; his grandfather, Maula Bakhsh (1882-1896), was one of the most famous musicians of India, known as "the Beethoven of India." A true exemplar of Indian religious tolerance, Maula Bakhsh was a devout Muslim who had two wives, one Muslim and one Hindu, and studied with a Hindu master of Hindustani music. He formed a school with the goal of uniting southern Karnatic music with the Hindustani music of the North to systematize and further the study of Indian music. Although Inayat was raised as a Muslim, he was sent to a Hindu elementary school because it was the best school available. An important anecdote from Inayat's childhood involved his experience of making the five-times-a-day Islamic prayers (*nimaz*). In *Confessions: Autobiographical Essays of Hazrat Inayat Khan*, Inayat recounts the following story:

> My kinsfolk were Muslim, and I grew up devoted to the Holy Prophet and loyal to Islam, and never missed one prayer of the five which are the daily portion of the faithful. One evening in the summer time I was kneeling, offering my nimaz to Allah the Great, when the thought smote me that although I had been praying so long with all trust, devotion, and humility, no revelation had been vouchsafed to me, and that it was therefore not wise to worship Him, that One whom I had neither seen nor fathomed. I went to my grandfather and told him I would not offer any more prayers to Allah until I had both beheld and gauged Him. "There is no sense in following a belief and doing as one's ancestors did before one, without knowing the true reason," I said.
>
> Instead of being vexed Maula Bakhsh was pleased with my inquisitiveness, and after a little silence he answered me by quoting a sura of the Qur'an, "We will show them our signs in the world and in themselves, that the truth may be manifested to them."[3] And then he soothed my impatience and explained, saying, "The signs of God are seen in the world, and the world is seen in thyself." These words entered so deeply into my spirit, that from this time every moment of my life has been occupied with the thought of the divine immanence; and my eyes were thus opened, as the eyes of

the young man by Elijah, to see the symbols of God in all the aspects of nature, and also in that nature which is reflected within myself. This sudden illumination made everything appear as clear to me as in a crystal bowl or a translucent jewel. Thenceforth I devoted myself to the absorption and attainment of truth, the immortal and perfected Grace.[4]

Inayat went on to become a musician of great ability, both in singing and vina playing. The apex of his musical career came when he had the honor of playing for the Nizam of Hyderabad and was given the title "Tansen" and a royal ring by the Nizam, the highest musical honor possible in India. Soon afterwards, Inayat turned from the pursuit of music toward the spiritual path. After a long search for a suitable teacher, he met his spiritual guide, a Sufi murshid named Sayyid Abu Hashim Madani. Madani, an aristocratic Arab from Medina, initiated Inayat into the Chishti Order, as well as the Naqshbandi, Qadiri, and Suhrawardi orders. A story about Moinuddin Chishti, the great thirteenth-century saint who brought the Chishtiyya to India, is instructive as regards the approach of that lineage.

Usman Haruni was the seventh successor in the Chishti tariqat, a murshid with thousands of disciples, many of whom were very learned individuals who seemed qualified to succeed him. Haruni taught them the traditional forms of worship along with the deepest truths of mysticism, urging them to worship the nameless and formless God. Then one day, to the horror of his disciples, he announced that he felt called to go and prostrate himself before the hideous dark image of the goddess Kali. His pupils were aghast and refused to follow him to the temple of Kali, all except one very devoted disciple. The teacher tried to send him away as well, saying that perhaps the others were right to think he had taken leave of his senses, but the disciple still followed. After the teacher prostrated himself before the idol and the pupil still watched with sympathy, the teacher turned and asked him why he had followed and not left. He replied, "You have taught me the first lesson of the spiritual path: that none exists save God. How then can I exclude this image of Kali, if you choose to bow and prostrate yourself before it?'"[5] This disciple was Khwaja Moinuddin Chishti, who, having understood and passed his teacher's test, was designated as Haruni's rightful successor.

In Inayat's case, his own murshid received complaints from his other disciples that, in addition to his Islamic affiliations and Qur'an studies, Inayat had friends from other religions, and was setting the Zoroastrian Gathas to music and studying the Hindu Upanishads and the Christian Bible. To one of the students who brought this up, Abu Hashim Madani replied: "While you see the outward person of Inayat, I see his inner being. I cannot very well tell you what Inayat is and what he is to me, except that he is my beloved *mureed* [disciple] and I am proud of him."[6]

Though little of his teaching has come down to us, we can get some idea of Mandani's teachings from one of his sayings that has been preserved: "The only sin is to spend a moment without being in the divine consciousness."[7] When his own end drew near, Madani confirmed Inayat Khan as a Sufi murshid, and informed him that he had received spiritual instructions from Khwaja Moinuddin Chishti advising him to send Inayat to carry the wisdom of Sufism to the West. Madani blessed Inayat, saying, "Fare forth into the world, my child, and harmonize the East and the West with the harmony of thy music; spread the wisdom of Sufism abroad, for to this end thou art gifted by God. May God strengthen your faith."[8]

In 1910, Pir-o-Murshid Inayat Khan, accompanied by his brother and cousin, arrived in New York; his youngest brother would come slightly later. They toured the country, spent time in San Francisco, and performed their music for several years, but they found that most Westerners had little knowledge or appreciation of Indian music, although some souls were spellbound by Inayat's singing. Gradually, Inayat began to lecture on spiritual matters and realized that he had a wonderful gift for attuning and harmonizing souls, not only through music, but as a spiritual teacher. It was in San Francisco that he initiated his first disciple, Ada Martin, who was given the Sufi name Rabia.

Inayat Khan found her a very promising pupil and placed her in charge of organizing the first American Sufi group to study and further his teachings. She seems to have been the only disciple to whom Inayat taught the traditional Islamic prayers and practices. Before long she became the first of four *murshidas*—female murshids—initiated by Pir-o-Murshid Inayat Khan.

Back on the East Coast of the United States, Inayat met his future wife, Ora Ray Baker, but his travels soon took him and his brothers to England. When Ora's brother learned of the romance and of his sister's desired to marry a dark-skinned Indian, he passionately forbade it and even threatened Inayat's life. Her response was to travel secretly to England where she and Inayat were reunited and married. Soon thereafter, the extended family moved to Russia, where their first child, Noor-un-Nisa was born in 1914. However, they were soon forced to flee back to Western Europe as the Russian Revolution began to unfold. After enduring the hardships of World War I in London, the family finally settled in Suresnes, a suburb of Paris, in a large stone house that was occupied by Inayat, his wife and four children, two of his brothers, and a cousin, as well as their landlady and benefactress, Sheikha Gladys Lloyd.

Hazrat Inayat Khan felt that because of the Western emphasis on individuality and ego achievement, it was especially difficult for Westerners to relate to Sufism. This is because its principles are subtle and difficult to put in plain words. Sufism teaches a humble, selfless approach to life and it sees beyond the false individual self to the underlying unity that unites us. This goes counter to much of Western individualistic thinking and tends to come more naturally to those raised with the social conditioning of the East.

Yet Hazrat Inayat Khan also saw much of value in the West and stated that, "The day is not far off when, if not through religion then by science, the people in the West will realize the oneness of the whole being and that individuals are nothing more than bubbles in the sea."[9] Interestingly, he said that the religion of the future would be music. He also foresaw the contribution of women to the new spirituality, saying, "I see as clear as daylight that the hour is coming when woman will lead humanity to a higher evolution."[10]

Hazrat Inayat Khan related that before he came to the West he thought most people there were devout Christians, but after coming to the West he soon realized that this was not the case; rather, scientific materialism was very widespread, and most people's religious affiliations were rather casual. He felt that Protestantism, in rebelling against the prophetic message of the original Christian Church, had lost some of the richness and sacred sense of mystery that characterized the Orthodox and Roman Catholic Churches. He believed that it was the spirit of Islam, as felt in the West (with its lack of priestly hierarchy, human images or monasticism), that had eventually led to the Protestant Reformation, but these reforms had been mainly on the outer planes and had not absorbed the rich inner spirit of Islam.

When a woman at a lecture asked Inayat Khan why he didn't take Christianity back to the East, he replied that it had already come from the East. Another person asked him if he believed in the second coming of Christ. He responded that for him, Christ had never left. On the question of whether Jesus was the exclusive "only-begotten son of God,"[11] he explained that this phrase, *monogenes* in the Greek text, actually indicates "begotten of the One and Only Being"—one who is profoundly conscious of his divine inheritance. When Inayat had an opportunity to attend a papal mass in Rome at St. Peter's Church, his secretary who accompanied him was amazed to see that his murshid went into a state of great exaltation during the mass and at one point exclaimed, "How wonderful is the power of the living Christ!"[12] During his years in Suresnes, Inayat enjoyed spending time in meditation and contemplation at the magnificent Basilica of Sacre-Coeur (the Church of the Sacred Heart) in Montmartre, overlooking all of Paris.

In *The Unity of Religious Ideals*, Inayat Khan states:

> Truth is the soul of religion. When Jesus came to earth he did not say, "I have brought you a new religion never heard of by you or your ancestors." He said he had not

come to give a new law but to fulfill the law; in other words, "I have come to continue giving you that which you have received before and have not understood." . . . He who is always there has said, "I am Alpha and Omega. I exist every moment. When you call me, I am there. Knock at the door, and I will answer you." And those whose eyes are open do not need to go to a church and look at a picture or statue of the Lord. In the eyes of every infant, in the smile of every innocent child, they receive the blessing of Christ.[13] . . . The belief in Christ is in the Church, the book of Christ is with the clergy, the spirit of Christ is in the illuminated soul.[14]

In regard to Islam, Hazrat Inayat Khan felt that as a result of centuries of Western anti-Islamic sentiment against the religion, which was perceived as the greatest religious rival to Christianity, there was little chance of widespread acceptance of Islam in the West in his time. He found that even among his most open-minded followers, including Masons, Christian Scientists, and Theosophists, the very use of Islamic terminology elicited an uncomfortable resistance.

While he felt that Islamic principles contained much that would be of value to the West, he noted that in some cases Muslim literalism had restricted Islam from reaching its fullest potential. For example, he said, "Moslems have closed the doors of the mosque by saying that Mohammad was the seal of *Risalat*, which they interpret as the last of the prophets. They do not seem to realize" that this does not mean there is no further ongoing divine inspiration, only that Muhammad was the last who would claim to be a prophet and after him no successor would come openly claiming to be a prophet.[15] This agrees with the words of Jalaluddin Rumi:

It is said that after Muhammad and the prophets, revelation does not descend upon anyone else. Why not? In fact, it does, but then it is not called "revelation." It is what the Prophet referred to when he said, "The believer sees with the Light of God.". . . Therefore the meaning of revelation exists, even if it is not called revelation.[16]

Inayat Khan summarized the noble Prophet's contribution to humanity as follows:

> Mohammed's saying, "None but God exists," explained the essence of all previous messages most clearly. The lesson of Mohammed, once learned, left no need for continuance of prophetic teaching, because it proved that each being bears the divine source thereof within himself, and that the evolution of man has now prepared him for the kingdom which is within.[17]

It was often observed by Hazrat Inayat Khan's students that when he spoke of one of the prophets, he seemed to radiate the presence of that master. When he meditated on Muhammad or one of the Hebrew prophets, he seemed to take on their holy countenance. When he meditated on Buddha, one seemed to behold the living Buddha; and he was perceived by many who met him, or even saw him walking down the street, to be Christ-like in appearance, presence and sanctity.

the MESSAGE BROUGHT *by* HAZRAT INAYAT KHAN

At this point, we may ask: What is the Message that Hazrat Inayat Khan gave to humanity? We can begin to answer this by looking at a few sentences which contain some of his basic premises.

> Sufism is the religion of the heart, the religion in which the thing of primary importance is to seek God in the heart of mankind.[18]
> The note that the Sufi message is striking at the present time is the note which sounds the divinity of the human soul.[19]

In the *Sangatha* papers, Inayat Khan states that "Sufism is the essence of all religions," Sufism means "divine wisdom," and "God alone was the founder of Sufism."

> The Sufi's God is the only Being that exists. His teacher is the spirit of inner guidance; his holy book is the manuscript of nature, his community is the whole of humanity. His religion is love. [20]

> The Sufi message is the echo of the same divine message, which has always come and will always come to enlighten humanity. It is not a new religion; it is the same message, which is being given to humanity. It is the continuation of the same ancient religion, which has always existed and will always exist, a religion, which belongs to all teachers and all the scriptures. It is the continuation of all the great religions, which have come at various times; and it is a unification of them all, which was the desire of all the prophets.[21]

> There has never in any period of the world's history been a founder of Sufism, yet Sufism has existed at all times.[22]

> What is meant by the word Sufi? The word Sufi is derived from the Arabic word *Safa*, or *Saf*, which means, literally, pure, i.e. pure from distinctions and differences. In Greek the word means wise. Sufism cannot be called deism, for the Sufi does not consider God as an entity separate from oneself. Neither can it be called pantheism, because the Sufi not only sees the immanence of God in nature, but also realizes God's Essence in the infinite, naming God Allah, the Formless, the Colorless. . . . The Sufi is not an atheist, for the Sufi denies neither God nor God's Messengers. To the question, "Are you a Christian?," "Are you a Muslim?," "Are you a Jew?," the Sufi's answer would be "yes" rather than "no,"

for the Sufi opposes no religion but sympathizes with all. In fact, Sufism cannot be called a religion, for it does not impose either belief or principle upon anyone, considering that each individual soul has its own principles best suited for it, and a belief which changes with each grade of evolution.[23]

Sufism itself is the essence of all the religions as well as the spirit of Islam.[24]

The Sufis of ancient times brought wisdom to the Muslim world and presented that wisdom in Muslim terminology.[25]

The Sufi is a true Christian in regard to charity, brotherhood, and the healing of his own soul as well as the soul of another. He is not bigoted in his adherence to a particular Church, or in forsaking the other masters and their followers who came before and after Christ, but his at-one-ment with the Christ and his appreciation and practice of his truth are as keen as those of a true Christian. . . . The Sufi is a Catholic in that he produces the picture of his ideal of devotion in his soul, and he is a Protestant in giving up the ceremonials of the cult. . . .

The Sufi is a Brahmin, for the word Brahmin means, "the knower of Brahma," of God, the only Being. His religion lies in believing in no other existence save that of God, which the Brahmin calls *Advaita*. The Sufi has as many grades of spiritual evolution to pass through as the Yogi does. There is very little difference to be found even in their practices, the difference lying chiefly in the names. No doubt the Sufi chooses a normal life in preference to that of an ascetic, yet he does not limit himself to either the former or the latter. The Sufi considers the teachings of the Avatars to be the true manifestations of the divine wisdom, and he has a perfect insight into the subtle knowledge of the Vedanta. . . .

The Sufi is a Buddhist, for he reasons at every step forward on his spiritual journey. The teachings of the Sufi are very similar to the Buddhist teachings; in fact it is the Sufi who unites the believers and the unbelievers in the God-ideal and in the knowledge of unity.

The Sufi is a Muslim, not because many Muslims happen to be Sufis, nor because of his use of Muslim phraseology, but because in his life he proves what a true Muslim ought to be. . . . The Sufis are the ones who read the Qur'an from every experience of life, and see and recognize Muhammad's face in each atom of the manifestation. . . . Islam prepares one to become a Sufi.

The Sufi, like a Zoroastrian or a Parsi, looks at the sun and bows before the air, fire, water, and earth, recognizing the immanence of God in his manifestation, taking the sun and moon as the signs of God. . . .

The Sufi is an Israelite, especially in this study and mastery of the different names of God. The miraculous powers of Moses can also be found in the lives of the Sufis both past and present. In fact the Sufi is the master of the Hebrew mysticism; the divine voice heard by Moses on Mount Sinai in the past is audible to many a Sufi today.[26]

In a 1926 radio address, Hazrat Inayat Khan gave the following brief summary of the Message:

Beloved Ones of God, [the] Sufi Message is a message today being given to humanity. It is not a message of the East, but it is the message of the soul, and the spirit. The Sufi word means wisdom, which comes from the root *sofia*. It is the work of that wisdom to give the message today to humanity, in order that people may come together in a better understanding arising beyond the different sections of casts and creeds which divide mankind. The Sufi Message is an answer to the cry of humanity today; at this moment, when materialism is all-pervading and commercialism is continually on the increase. The Sufi Message respects all religions, recognizes all scriptures, regards all the prophets held in esteem by large sections of humanity, and sees (the) source and goal of all this wisdom in the One.[27]

In his book *Confessions*, Inayat Khan gives this brief account of his own path to the unity behind the different religions:

I first studied comparative religions with an open mind; not in a critical spirit but as an admirer and a lover of truth in all its guises. I read the lives of the founders, prophets, and seers with as much reverence as their most devout adherents. This brought me the bliss of realization of one truth, which all religions contain, as different vessels may yet hold the same wine. It was the conception of truth in all its manifold forms and expressions, ever borne by different messengers, who most wondrously, by their very diversity of garb, civilization, nationality, and age, revealed the one Source of the inspiration. To me their sole difference was caused by the laws of space and time.[28]

Inayat Khan said that instead of accepting all of the divine messengers as one boundless embodiment of truth, the followers had divided themselves along nationalistic and religious lines, yet no authentic prophet has ever come with the idea of dividing humanity into sects or to teach such a split. He sees all the illuminated souls who have come to give humanity the message of unity as delivering one essential teaching, inspired by the "Spirit of Guidance" (by which he means something similar to the Holy Spirit).

In relation to the Divine, he taught that each person must cultivate their own God ideal, and the messengers who founded the various religions, as well as masters, saints and one's spiritual teacher can all serve as models and stepping stones towards one's highest ideal. But one must not get stuck with any one limited conception or cover over God. As one grows spiritually, one must "shatter one's ideal upon the rock of truth"[29] and continually remold it ever nearer to the heart's desire. In the *Githa* papers Inayat Khan speaks in holistic terms of God—Who is beyond the opposites of good and evil—and the ideal that helps make the Divine comprehensible to one's mind and heart:

> No one can concentrate on God, because God is beyond all limitations and any limitation, even goodness, limits God; and for ages people have made this mistake. They have idealized God as goodness. Then for all evil they have had to imagine a Satan. . . . The Sufi therefore looks upon God as the origin and end of all things, as within and without all things. He may consider it impertinence to say God is in evil, yet he does not exclude one single atom from the being of God. . . . Since all in the garb of matter are to be separated one day in life, good or wicked, friends or foes, what alone is reliable is the ideal which man creates within himself, call it Christ, Buddha, Krishna or Mohammed.[30]

The practices and concentrations which Hazrat Inayat Khan gave were varied. He designated five branches of the Sufi Movement: the Esoteric school, Universal Worship, the Sufi healing work, *ziraat* (with its emphasis on nature, agriculture and the restoration of the earth), and the brotherhood/sisterhood work, which has taken forms such as soup kitchens and medical clinics in India for the poor. He also wished to have a physical temple built called the *Universel*, an interreligious shrine for all believers, which he envisioned built in a shape subtly suggestive of four Buddhas meditating back to back. Several modest versions of the *Universel* were built years after Inayat Khan's passing, though his followers have tended to interpret the *Universel* as being as much a spiritual ideal as a brick and mortar temple.

For those who took initiation in the esoteric school, Inayat Khan gave breathing practices, meditations, practices with sound (*mantra*, *wazifa*, divine qualities), English prayers and affirmations. Also, in keeping with Sufi tradition, attunement with the being of one's teacher was emphasized (*fana-fi-sheikh*), which is a stepping stone to the further attunement to the *rasul* or prophet (*fana-fi-rasul*), and finally to divine union (*fana-fil'llah*)."

In cultivating the devotional aspect, Inayat Khan was inspired in 1921 to found the Universal Worship Service. This service brings together the scriptures of all the major religions on one altar (usually including at least six: Hinduism, Buddhism, Zoroastrianism, Judaism, Christianity, and Islam) to show the unity of the various religions, and to consult their wisdom on various themes. At the time, such an interreligious service was quite innovative in the West, but today similar services and interfaith panels have become much more common. Of the service itself, Inayat Khan said:

> The Universal Worship, therefore, is the religion of the future, which brings to humanity the ideal of the unification of religion; the ideal of getting above the sectarianism and limited outlook of communities and groups.[31] . . . This Universal Worship which has been organized in the Sufi Movement was the hope of all prophets. The prayer and the desire of all great souls was that the light given in all the different forms such as the Buddhist scriptures, the *Qur'an*, the Bible or the teachings of Krishna or Zarathushtra, should be known by everyone. The work of the Sufi message is to spread the unity of religion. It is not a mission to promote a particular creed or any Church or religion. It is a work to unite the followers of different religions and faiths in wisdom, so that without having to give up their own religion they may strengthen their own faith and focus the true light upon it. [32]

Hazrat Inayat Khan asks: how can the worship of many gods and One God be united? He answers that "those who have many gods also worship one God. It is simply that they worship the different attributes of God. The great ones, in order to make God intelligible to man, have given Him different names."[33]

Inayat Khan was inspired to give three main prayers in English to be recited during the service and by his murids (disciples) in daily life. The first prayer, *Saum*, features optional movements which include prostrations, and contains some phrases reminiscent of the *Fatiha* in the Islamic prayers. The second prayer, *Salat*, is addressed to the divine messenger or prophet—the one who models the God ideal for human beings—calling on various prophets, including, Rama, Buddha, Abraham, Christ, Muhammad, and other messengers. The third prayer, *Khatum*, focuses mostly on the disclosure of inner light, love, and peace, and serves as a kind of benediction.

Inayat Khan's emphasis on the divine unity extended to psychology as well. Rather than dividing behavior into good, divinely approved impulses, as opposed to other unacceptable impulses, coming from the devil or the primitive unconscious, he taught that there is a divine origin behind every impulse. However, a desire which is thwarted, repressed or condemned by society or one's family, can become distorted and alienated from its original purpose, so that the underlying divine impulse becomes no longer recognizable and the impulse appears negative, destructive, or evil. In Inayat Khan's own words:

> To repress desire is to suppress a divine impulse. Those who distinguish between divine and not divine certainly make the greatest error, as either all is divine or nothing is. The only difference is the same as that between the machine and the engineer. The mind of God is working and at the same time the instrument, the machine of God is working; therefore that which arises as a desire has God as its source and is thus a divine impulse.[34]

As an alternative to repression, he taught the way of skillfully mastering an impulse, utilizing its energy as a sailor uses the boat's sails to harness the wind. Rather than trying to annihilate the limited self, he advised cultivating a transformative friendship of the lower self with the Divine, filing the sharp thorns of egoism from the rose of one's being, and allowing the small ego to blossom and enlarge beyond narrow self-interest, until the heart is open and loving towards all beings—for each person is but a cover over the Divine. In his *Gayan*, Inayat Khan writes:

> Every form I see is Thine own form, my Lord,
> And every sound I hear is Thine own voice;
> In the perfume of flowers I perceive the fragrance of
> Thy spirit . . .
> Whomsoever I see, I see Thee in his soul;
> Whoever aught gives to me, I take it from Thee.
> To whomsoever I give, I humbly offer it to Thee, Lord;
> Whoever comes to me, it is Thou who comest;
> On whomsoever I call, I call on Thee.[35]

Inayat Khan also gave a valuable insight about personal accomplishment when he observed that "If a desire is not fulfilled, it means that the person did not know how to desire; failure is caused by indistinctness of motive."[36] Often people have a vague feeling of dissatisfaction about their life, but simply haven't been able to get in touch with what it is they really deeply desire at the soul level.

In a discourse entitled "Deity and Divinity" (*The Unity of Religious Ideals*, part 2), Hazrat Inayat Khan lays out his understanding of humanity's inherent divine core of inner light and how it relates to Christ's teaching. The passage is rounded out by a few other related sayings.

> The word "divine" comes from *Deva*, God (fem. *Devi*), and the word *Deva* is derived from *Div*, which means "light." Every soul is itself a light, but a light which is surrounded by clouds, clouds which have risen from the earthly impressions and surrounded the human heart. These clouds keep the soul covered; but the *Deva* or *Div* is always there. One reads in the Bible that no one should keep his light under a bushel. The hint to raise the light high shows us

that *Deva* or the divine spark is within man. That divinity, even when it is human, is infinite. Only the expansion of this light and the disclosing of it are necessary. The prophets and great avatars, the messengers who have come to the world from time to time, have been examples of the expansion of this divine spark, and what they gave to the world has been the outcome of this divinity.

Divinity is like the seed, which grows in the heart of the flower; it is the same seed, which was the origin of that plant, and it comes again in the heart of the flower. In a similar way the same God, who was unmanifested as the seed of the plant of this creation, rises again towards fulfillment; and in that fulfillment He produces the seed in the heart of that flower which is divinity.

Some religious authorities have tried to recognize the divinity of Christ while ignoring the divinity of humanity. They have tried to make Christ different from what may be called human. But by doing so they have not been able to keep the flame alight, for they have covered the main truth that religion had to give to the world, which was that divinity resides in humanity, that divinity is the outcome of humanity, and that humanity is the flower in the heart of which divinity was born as a seed. And by this they have not done any good to religion; on the contrary they have harmed religion, trying to make man something different, not knowing that all is in man—angel, *jinn*, and animal. . . .

No doubt, compared with God divinity is the imperfection of God, but it is still the perfection of man. It is just like a drop of water, which is entirely, and absolutely water, and yet it is a drop in comparison with the ocean. The ocean is God, but the drop is divine.[37]

The first self we realize is the false self. Unless the soul is born again it will not see the kingdom of heaven.

The soul is first born into the false self; it is blind. In the true self, the soul opens its eyes. Unless the false self is fought with, the true self cannot be realized. Therefore endurance is necessary. Patience is necessary."[38]

If man dived deep enough within himself he would reach a point of his ego where it lives an unlimited life.[39]

Make God a reality and God will make you the truth.[40]

Hazrat Inayat Khan's teachings are wide-ranging and have been collected into fifteen volumes, and little justice can be done to them in a few pages. Space does not permit more than a mention of his highly interesting volume on the *Mysticism of Sound*, a book which, according to Pir Vilayat, the German composer Karlheinz Stockhausen used to carry with him wherever he traveled, saying it was like a Bible for musicians. Another remarkable book by Inayat Khan is *The Soul, Whence and Whither*, which describes the soul's descent through the various planes of existence toward manifestation. The theme is captured in a very succinct form in a saying from the *Gayan* of Hazrat Inayat Khan: "The angels were made to sing the praises of the Lord; the jinns to imagine, to dream, to meditate; but man is created to show humanity in his character."[41] The interested reader is encouraged to further investigate the books of Hazrat Inayat Khan, which are primarily edited transcriptions of extemporaneous talks he gave over the years, which have an easily readable style and are now freely available on line.

After Hazrat Inayat Khan's death in 1927, it would be almost forty years before these teachings were given new life and popularity in the West, particularly in the United States. This came about through the efforts of two of his disciples, Murshid Samuel Lewis and Hazrat Inayat Khan's eldest son, Pir Vilayat Khan, whose story we now resume in the late 1950s.

the FLOWERING *of* UNIVERSAL SUFISM *in the* 1960s

In 1958, Pir Vilayat began his own organization, separate from the Sufi Movement, at first called the Sufi Order in the West. Actually, he was reviving the original London Charter of the

Sufi Order as incorporated by his father back in 1915. By the late 1960s, the organization had become active in the United States, growing to over one hundred centers around the country. Pir Vilayat was an early advocate of interspiritual convocations. Every spring from 1965 to 1986, he held an interfaith congress near Paris, inviting participation from representatives of all the world's major religions.

In the years following Hazrat Inayat Khan's passing, Murshida Rabia Martin, entrusted with carrying on the Sufi Work in the United States, had traveled to Europe in hopes of being designated Inayat Khan's successor but was not accepted in this capacity by the Sufi Movement there. After some time, she contacted the Indian spiritual master Meher Baba and became convinced that he was the *qutb,* or axis of the age. Meher Baba in turn convinced her to follow him. Before her passing in 1944, she appointed as her successor her khalifa, Ivy Duce, who subsequently turned over the American Sufi organization and its lands to Meher Baba, reorganizing the order under the name "Sufism Reoriented." Pir Vilayat also visited Meher Baba in India in the late 1950s to pay his respects but declined Meher Baba's invitation to follow him instead of his father.

One of the leading disciples working with Murshida Rabia from 1919 until her passing was Samuel Lewis, who was designated as one of her khalifas and had been expected by many to be her successor. Sam attempted to make the transition to the new organization under Meher Baba and Ivy Duce, but found he didn't fit in well and soon left to pursue other spiritual options. It wasn't until the late 1960s, when Sam was in his seventies, that his path crossed with Pir Vilayat and Sam's lifetime of spiritual training blossomed in a dramatic way as "spiritual leader of the hippies." As Samuel Lewis became an important American Sufi teacher and universalist in his own right, it is worth pausing to mention a few biographical details from his life.

MURSHID S.A.M.

Samuel L. Lewis (1896-1971), otherwise known as "Sufi Ahmed Murad" (S.A.M.), or simply "Murshid Sam," was born in San Francisco into an upper-middle-class Jewish family and appears to have been named after the Biblical prophet Samuel. From an early age he was attracted to the spiritual life and was prone to experience spiritual visions and directives from the unseen world, from personages such as Khidr.* He met Murshida Rabia Martin in 1919 and began to study Sufism with her. He was ini tiated in 1923 by Hazrat Inayat Khan and had six lengthy inter- views with him in 1926, during which his murshid asked him to produce commentaries on a number of his writings, which in time he did.

Besides his affiliations with the lineage of Hazrat Inayat Khan, Sam was attracted to study and receive initiation with a number of other spiritual teachers from various traditions, becoming an early American pioneer in the field of interreligious involve- ment. Starting in the 1920s, he studied with the Zen Buddhist Roshi Nyogen Senzaki, and helped him open the first official zendo in the United States. In 1930, he received the Dharma transmission from Zen Roshi Sokei-An Shigetsu Sasaki, and in the same decade began to study the yogic teachings of the non- dualist Indian sage Ramana Maharshi. In the 1950s, he met the Hindu master Swami Papa Ramdas and received his initiation in India. From Papa Ramdas, he received the powerful mantra, *Om Sri Ram Jai Ram Jai Jai Ram*, which Sam later utilized ex- tensively in the Sufi dances of the 1960s. The Sanskrit phrase means roughly: "May the Lord who dwells as light in my heart be victorious over every difficulty."

Murshid Sam also visited Egypt in the 1950s, where he was initiated into the Rifai and Shadhili Sufi Orders; and in West Pakistan in 1960 he was confirmed as a Sufi murshid in the Chishti-Kadri-Sabri Order by Pir Barkat 'Ali. Ruth St. Denis,

---

* Khidr is a mysterious figure endowed with mystical knowledge who is mentioned in Qur'an. He is sometimes seen in visions, guiding souls, and revealing divine wisdom.

the great dance artist whose oriental dances Hazrat Inayat Khan had accompanied half a century earlier, was a longtime friend of Murshid Sam, and planted in him the seeds of inspiration for developing spiritual dance as a practice in America. In 1966, he assisted in founding a Christian mystical school with Father Paul (Rev. Earl Blighton), called the Holy Order of Mans, where Murshid Sam gave talks on mystical Christianity and Kabbalah. In 1967, he was ordained "Zen-shi" by Master Kyung-Bo Seo of Korea.

Murshid Sam had a wide circle of friends and contacts, but probably none was more colorful and plainspoken than his good friend Joe Miller (1904-1992), whom Sam asked on his deathbed to take care of his disciples. Joe had a background in

Joe Miller during a Thursday walk in Golden Gate Park in 1985 (photo by the author)

Vaudeville and the Theosophical Society, as well as Buddhism, Vedanta, and Christian mysticism. Sought out by many for his down-to-earth wisdom and humor, he eschewed all high-falu-tin' spiritual titles and advised people to "fall awake," open their hearts to love and joy, to tune into the breath, and learn to BE— to really be themselves—not somebody else's idea of who they should be. His most famous and characteristic slogan was: "You can get more stinkin' from thinkin' than you can from drinkin'! But to FEEL is for real!"[42]

Every Thursday, for the last few decades of his life, Joe and his wife, Guin, would lead a walk through Golden Gate Park and invite the public to join them; the popular walks often attracted hundreds of casual participants. Sometimes Joe and Guin would wear T-shirts saying, "No religion higher than truth, no power greater than love!" At some point along the way, everyone would come together in an informal circle and Joe would give a short talk; there might be singing of a few spiritual songs and a simple dance or two. For those who wished to continue, the walk would proceed on to the beach, where Joe would treat everyone to ice cream bars purchased at the local Safeway store.

Joe was very close to Murshid Sam and described Sam as be-ing the kind of person of

> whom, if you had seen him on the street you would have said, "I don't know what to make of this guy. He's a crackpot or fanatic or he's nuts!" Actually, he was a combination of all three because in Sufism he'd be called a *[majdhub]*. A *[majdhub]* will not con-form to any particular pattern, and will continue to be eclectic in what they give to people and what they put out to help people live. And Sam was such a person.
>
> He struck a note that was not Sufism from some oth-er land, but Sufism became the flavor of the good earth here in the United States itself. It's an important thing! The important thing is that it's the flavor of what the people are here, what they'll put up with and what they won't put up with. And it's honest, straight-forward, and

if it was necessary to kick 'em and push 'em around, he'd kick 'em and push 'em around. But he was for real! . . . He was a down to earth person. He wouldn't give you any fancy trip on a nice pink cloud. No, rather than do that, he would kick you and say, Now what's the matter with you? Come off your high horse and look at things the way they really are! And realize your at-one-ment with the One! And radiate love to everybody! But no hooks on that love. Nothing taken back. Just let it flow out.[43]

While Murshid Sam had initiated and led Sufi *murids* since the 1940s, it was in the late 1960s that his work as a Sufi murshid really began to flower. Murshid Sam was a horticulturalist and often used the metaphor of planting seeds in a garden. He said he planted spiritual seeds year after year for decades but nothing came up. Then one year the entire harvest of all those planting seasons came forth in abundance. In 1967, Murshid Sam was hospitalized and, while lying flat on his back, received a spiritual revelation in which Allah appeared to him and told him, "I make you the spiritual leader of the hippies."[44]

Although this was unexpected, Murshid Sam was perfectly situated in San Francisco, the West Coast epicenter of the hippie revolution, where free love, drugs, and exotic spiritual centers of every kind abounded. Thereafter Murshid Sam began to solicit murids among the local hippies, seeking to take that vibrant energy and spiritual aspiration of the young people and give them a way to get spiritually high without drugs. It was at this point in 1968 that Pir Vilayat first began to visit and teach on the West Coast and made the acquaintance of Murshid Sam, who was twenty years his senior. The two teachers had corresponded by letter since 1954 when Murshid Sam had written to Pir Vilayat saying, "I am being guided to be Shams Tabriz to your Mevlana Rumi."

Murshid Sam received Pir Vilayat Khan, the son and successor of his Sufi teacher, with great respect, and urged his students to attend Pir Vilayat's talks. Murshid Sam quipped, "Pir Vilayat is not just a chip off the old block—he *IS* the old block!"[45] The two agreed to join forces to strengthen the Sufi message. Of Murshid Sam, Pir Vilayat later said:

> His joy was contagious, winning, devastating, and earmarked him as the Pied Piper of the new age, luring happy and not so happy people into new dimensions of being high. He could bring down the house by the punch of his opinion and build another one somewhere else. . . . "Why not do something rather than talk about it?" was his motto. If you wish to do something about joy and ecstasy, you will dance the dance of Shiva, and the world will dance with you. And so out of the traditional dervish whirl, emerged the dance of the happy people, and in no time it spread to the states and beyond the seas to Europe.[46]

During some of Pir Vilayat's talks, he spoke about the dance of the whirling dervishes and their Pythagorean roots. This, and Sam's own visionary inspirations, provided the catalyst for Sam to bring forth his own creative versions of spiritual dance, using simple folkdance steps, some whirling, and sacred phrases from the world's spiritual traditions, such as "*Allah, Allah, er-Rahman, er-Rahim*," "*Allaho Akbar*," "*Alhamdulillah*," and "*Sri Ram Jai Ram, Jai Jai Ram*." Murshid Sam had already been teaching his murids spiritual walks in the attunement of various prophets and astrological types, and the dances became a natural extension of these practices. In 1969, at Murshid Sam's urging, a Sufi choir was organized and led by Allaudin Mathieu, which sang and creatively harmonized some of these sacred phrases and songs. Murshid Sam originally called the dances that were coming through him "Sufi dances," but in his writings, he referred to them as "Dances of Universal Peace."

As foreseen by Murshid Sam, the dances became very popular (and are now done in fifty-four countries) and, after Murshid Sam's passing, his disciples continued the legacy by creating further dances and emphasizing spiritual walks and as part of the overall Sufi training. Not only are the dances a wonderful way to introduce people to Sufism, to whirling, and the chants of various other spiritual traditions, but they are a spiritual practice in themselves and a beautiful vehicle for creating community and generating joy, embodiment, and sympathy. The dances are usually simple enough to be done without any previous experience, yet they have depths that can appeal to the seasoned practitioner as well. For those with a Christian background, one of the most interesting dances that came through after Murshid Sam's passing was Neil (Saadi) Douglas-Klotz's dance to the words of the Aramaic Lord's Prayer, *Abwoon D'Bashmaya*, whose movements are reminiscent both of Jewish daavening and the standing zikr of the Sufis. The seed for this dance was planted by Murshid Sam, whose writings suggested it, and the dance was later brought to fruition through the inspiration of Dr. Neil Douglas-Klotz (Murshid Saadi).

Toward the end of Murshid Sam's life, his disciples created a full-length movie about him called *Sunseed*, which was directed by Amertat Fred Cohn. The film includes footage of various other spiritual teachers of the time, culminating with the inimitable Murshid Sam leading dances, loudly chanting the call to prayer on a hilltop while motorcycles race by, and shopping at the local market. *Sunseed* concludes with a scene from Sam's 1971 funeral service, which features a few spirited words of eulogy from Joe Miller and Pir Vilayat. Another shorter film featuring Murshid Sam was entitled *Dance to Glory*.

One of the more memorable exchanges in the film occurs as Murshid Sam, busily engaged in playing solitaire, converses with the off-camera director, Fred Cohn, about the fear some people have of the spiritual path. As Murshid Sam shuffles the deck, he remarks, "It's something very simple. A concept of spirituality has nothing to do with spirituality. It has to do with concepts. That's an entirely different subject!" As Murshid Sam continues to shuffle his cards, Cohn laments that some people just don't feel capable of being "spiritual." Murshid Sam shoots back, "That again is a concept ... Jesus said, 'Unless you become as little children yours is not the kingdom of heaven.' Nobody wants to be simple!" Cohn rejoins, "But the concepts are real to a lot of people and get in their way. . . ." Murshid Sam interrupts: "Sure! Concepts are real to a lot of people, and that's 'unsanity.'" Finally, after Sam flips over a few more cards, Cohn adds, "It's just so hard to break them of concepts." Murshid Sam replies, "Of course it is! That's why we don't solve problems. The solutions interfere with our concepts!"

This exchange captures the spirit of a teacher who valued real experience and realization over high-flown spiritual ideas which simply become abstractions in the mind. Murshid Sam famously said, "Sufism can't be taught; it has to be caught!"

In a subsequent scene, Murshid Sam is seen cooking breakfast in his kitchen while offering a running commentary. When asked by Cohn what he wants to do before he dies, Murshid Sam replies, "This is a very difficult question for someone who has experience of immortality direct!" Then he adds, "I want to see two or three of my disciples reach the stage of spiritual realization; then I could die in peace." Asked how he would be able to tell if they were enlightened, Murshid Sam replies, "I would see the light shining out through them!"

At his own request, Murshid Sam was buried at the Lama Foundation in northern New Mexico, an interspiritual commune and retreat center where he had often visited and taught toward the end of his life. At the foot of his tomb is Murshid Sam's devoted disciple Murshida Vera Corda (1913-2002), who encountered Hazrat Inayat Khan as a child, studied with Murshid Sam for decades, and after his passing, worked with Pir Vilayat. She became a pedagogue in the field of children's spiritual education—founding several New Age seed schools on the West Coast—and served for years as a mentor and guide for murids in the Inayati tradition.

Around 1969, Pir Vilayat and one of Sam's students, Jemila, later known as Taj Inayat, were drawn together. Taj was in the process of separation from her husband, Mansur Johnson, who was one of Murshid Sam's secretary/assistants and later the author of a biography of Sam, entitled *Murshid*, which, through Sam's personal diaries and letters, conveys the story of his life in the late 1960s. At the time, Pir Vilayat had grown apart from

Mary, his own wife in France, but owing to her Catholic background and her remaining affection for him, she never con-
sented to the possibility of a divorce. It is told that Pir Vilayat
had previously experienced dreams or visions of an unknown
woman who was his soul-mate, whom he immediately recognized in meeting Taj, and in this way felt a certain destiny in
their coming together as spiritual partners, after her divorce
from Johnson. Their union produced two sons, the eldest being
Saraphiel, born in 1971, who later became Pir Zia Inayat-Khan
(also known as Sarafil Bawa), Pir Vilayat's designated successor, who is currently the head of the Sufi Order, which in 2016
became designated as the Inayati Order. Pir Vilayat and Taj's
younger son is Kerubiel, also known as Mirza.

In 1970, Murshid Sam had established a nonprofit religious
corporation named the Sufi Islamia Ruhaniat Society (S.I.R.S.)
to preserve and further his legacy. After Sam's passing, most of
Murshid Sam's senior disciples were initiated and confirmed in
their ranks by Pir Vilayat, including Sam's successor, Murshid
Moineddin Jablonski (1942-2012). For several years, the order
functioned harmoniously under Pir Vilayat's leadership, but in
1977, the union unraveled, resulting in another branch of the
lineage, called the Sufi Islamia Ruhaniat Society (S.I.R.S.), now
renamed the Sufi Ruhaniat International.

The separation came about when Pir Vilayat issued a declaration designed to bring the Sufi Order more in line with his own
vision; it included a rule requiring abstinence from recreational
drugs. Pir Vilayat further indicated that he was restricting the
use of the Dances of Universal Peace in certain settings *(Gatha*
classes) and wanted leaders to remove any murids who didn't
follow these directives. The announcement was both unexpected and controversial because there had never been a restrictive
rule in the Sufi tradition of Hazrat Inayat Khan. While many
of Pir Vilayat's murids willingly accepted the terms of the declaration, others strongly opposed it, or opted out of the order.
Whether by intention or not, the effect of the declaration was to
push the heirs of Murshid Sam to go work on their own. After
collective deliberations and soul-searching, the declaration was

ultimately rejected by the majority of murids in the lineage of Murshid Sam.

Thereafter, Murshid Moineddin became acting head of an independent Ruhaniat Order which looks to Murshid Sam and Hazrat Inayat Khan as its primary lineage holders, and places special emphasis on sacred dance and music. Some twenty years later, good relations were restored between the two branches and teachers from both orders began to come together at various camps and forums. After Pir Moineddin's passing, Pir Shabda Kahn, another senior disciple of Murshid Sam, succeeded him as leader of the Sufi Ruhaniat International, a role he continues to fulfill to the present day. Shortly before Pir Vilayat's passing in 2004, Pir Shabda traveled to Suresnes to pay his last respects to his former friend and teacher and to thank him for his life's work. Pir Vilayat told Pir Shabda that in retrospect he felt that the Declaration had been a mistake and he wished to take it back, a sentiment he reiterated in a subsequent group meeting the next day. After this, the 1977 edict was formally rescinded in a letter issued by Pir Vilayat's son and successor, Pir Zia.[47]

PIR VILAYAT INAYAT KHAN *and* *the* BLOSSOMING *of the* SUFI ORDER

In 1975, an opportunity came for the Sufi Order to acquire a large wooded tract of land that had formerly been a Shaker religious community in the Berkshire-Taconic Mountains of Upstate New York. Because the Shakers believed in a celibate lifestyle their community gradually died off leaving a small village of nine-teenth-century wooden houses with herb gardens, surrounded by forest. In at least one respect, the Shakers shared a common tradition with the Sufis: the use of sacred dance. One of the Shakers' most enduring dance melodies was the popular tune, "Tis a gift to be simple," which they danced in a large circle (or concentric circles). Their land was purchased by the Sufi organization and there Pir Vilayat founded the Abode of the Message.

The Abode community became one of Pir Vilayat's homes until his death. He also lived part of the year at the family residence in Suresnes, near Paris, and traveled extensively. Pir Vilayat stayed at the Abode with his new family and, in keeping with his longing for the life of a recluse in a cave, he had a small pod built in the forest, with a splendid view, where he could meditate and work while still having immediate access to the latest electronic technology. The Abode served as Sufi headquarters and the central gathering place for retreats and spiritual camps in the United States and a home for a number of Sufi residents. Each year, Pir Vilayat would lead a summer camp and retreat at the Abode and another European camp in the Alps— in the early years located in Chamonix, France. Also, in 1975, Pir Vilayat founded the Children's Ashram Fund to finance the Hope Project in the Nizamuddin quarter of Delhi, India, as a way of addressing some of the dire poverty of the people who lived in the vicinity of the Sufi shrines there, including the *dargah* where Hazrat Inayat Khan is buried.

the ALCHEMICAL RETREAT

Pir Vilayat was a master of meditation and one of his greatest gifts was his ability to lead transformative retreats and lift people's consciousness very high. Early on, he developed what he called the Alchemical Retreat process, which he continued to modify and update for the rest of his life. The age-old process of spiritual retreat is one of the primary methods by which one can progress on the spiritual path, a period of time wholly dedicated to spiritual practice and meditation, away from one's busy schedule and the demands of everyday life. It is not a time to focus on or be introspective about one's personal problems. Rather, during the retreat, one redirects one's concentration away from middle-range ruminations in order to calm the trouble waters of the mind to a more tranquil and pure state of receptivity. Using various meditations and working with sound and light to lift one's consciousness, the conditions are prepared for deeper inspirations to emerge, effecting a transformation in one's being beyond the personality and one's usual limited assessments of one's problems.

In the past, it was customary to make lengthy retreats of forty days or longer, but in accommodation of the busy schedules of most modern working people, shorter periodic retreats are now recommended, having proven to be beneficial as well. These could be for as little as one day, three days, six days, or ten days; however, it should be noted that it usually takes a couple of days for the mind and heart to become sufficiently quiet to allow deeper inspirations and realizations to begin to flow. The retreat can be done either in an individual or group setting, but in either case should be taken under the guidance of a seasoned spiritual guide who can prescribe practices and periodically check on one's progress. This is because the retreat can trigger higher states of consciousness (Maslow's "peak experiences") and, in some cases, unresolved psychological issues from the unconscious which may require help in processing.

What Pir Vilayat developed was a six-stage retreat process based on the medieval alchemical texts, some of which had been used by the Sufis of the past (the root word for alchemy, *al-kimiya*, is Arabic). More recently, alchemy and transformation was a subject of deep interest and meaning for psychologist Carl Jung, who noticed an abundance of alchemical symbols spontaneously appearing in the dreams of his patients.

On the surface, the alchemical texts describe the transmutation of base metals, such as mercury, salt and sulphur, into silver and gold, but at another level, they can be seen as referring to the transformation of human beings from coarse consciousness into a more enlightened state, mercury, or quicksilver, representing the mind, salt the body, and sulphur the spirit. The basic alchemical principle is formulated in the Latin phrase, *"Solve et Coagula,"* which means "dissolve and congeal," an alchemical motto which expresses the process of transformation that occurs when elements are broken down so that they can reunite in a new form. In the process of dissolution, energy is released which catalyzes a reconstitution of the elements which reform in a more pure and refined state, like lead into gold. The transformative energy that is released has been called "the Philosopher's stone."

Pir Vilayat Khan leading a retreat in the Sierras in 1985 (photo by the author)

Before he developed the alchemical retreat, Pir Vilayat led early meditation retreats in which he helped people get very spiritually high, and they would leave the camp radiant with light. However, they were often unable to integrate their retreat experiences into their daily lives and either quickly lost their attunement or, in some cases, tended to become otherworldly and ungrounded in everyday life. It soon became clear that just getting spiritually high on retreat wasn't an adequate approach for householders. It is part of the syndrome which psychologists have criticized as the "spiritual bypass." Of relevance to this is a 1991 video interview with Atum O'Kane, in which Pir Vilayat referred to the rishi he met high up in the Himalayas whose being was filled with power, beauty, insight, and love. Pir Vilayat recounts that at the time,

> I thought to myself, maybe those are the conditions in which a human being develops these wonderful quali-ties, and maybe the kind of life that we lead in the West does not make for this kind of unfoldment. So I came back to the West with the hope of trying to communi-cate something of that. Of course, I lived in the caves and did those practices myself. I saw that the pursuit was, of course, *samadhi* [a high state of unitive consciousness] and I realized that the teaching that was brought into the West from the East, from India, was intended for ascet-ics; therefore, it makes people maladjusted to the world. Therefore, I realized that even my own impact was mak-ing people rather badly adjusted to life. That was in the sixties when people were seeking a way out of the es-tablishment. Now I'm beginning to realize that you can bring this in in a way that will supplement, or at least be complimentary to the way that people are in life—another dimension without pulling people out of their sense of responsibility in life. That's been my struggle.[48]

The alchemical retreat takes these factors into account, lead-ing one through a bell-shaped energy curve (as opposed to a curve that goes up until the end, then sharply down) where one lifts consciousness high and then from that more impersonal, distanced vantage point, is able to see how one is caught in var-ious patterns and limiting perspectives in everyday life. Then in the second half of the retreat, one begins to bring through qualities that can balance and strengthen one in life; these serve to ground one and facilitate a smooth return into everyday life invigorated with new perspectives, strength and resolve. This more balanced and effective approach is described below.

STAGES *of the* RETREAT

There are six stages in the alchemical retreat; the first three represent the minor mysteries and the last three the major mysteries. In the first half, one is awakening in God; in the second half, God is awakening in one's being. The six stages are symbolized by progressive combinations of: cross (representing the human being), crescent moon (receptivity to the divine guidance and light), and sun (divine illumination). The six symbols, including their corresponding planets, are:

1. Cross above Crescent Moon (divine light and inspiration is overshadowed, blocked by the ego-self); Saturn.
2. Crescent Moon above Cross (expanding consciousness and opening to the divine energies); Jupiter.
3. Crescent Moon alone (complete receptivity, transparency to the Divine); the Moon represents the feminine responsive quality and selflessness.
4. Sun (circle) above Cross (beginning of the divine descent into one's being, the alchemical betrothal); Venus.
5. Sun beneath Cross (divine illumination is further incorporated into the depths of one's being); Mars.
6. Sun alone (total illumination); Sun.

The first stage: In the alchemical retreat, the first stage involves discrimination of the parts of one's being (*separatio*). There are a great many practices that can be utilized at the beginning of the retreat. One of the classic Sufi practices at this stage is contemplating the pair of divine names, *Ya Hayy ul-Qayyum* (*Hayy* meaning the Ever-living, *Qayyum* meaning self-subsisting), and distinguishing between the transient and eternal aspects of one's being. Another type of separating action at this stage is *muhasabi*—the examination of conscience—in which one observes one's life, behavior, and shadow issues, seeing how shadow issues act to cloud the soul's light. Still another approach is the Buddhist practice of *Sattipatana* and the *Jhanas*. Here, one looks at how the physical body, the mind (with its conditioning), the personal emotions, and the psyche have all been built up over time and are subject to dispersal at death, yet none of them comprise one's true being, which is eternal. This is a stage of purification and disidentification from all that is foreign to one's essential being. (It is not that one rejects one's personality and the experiential wisdom that has been gained in life, but that one sees how this has all been built up and that it is not who one really is.)

Other attunements include the Christian practice of the Hesychasts, *Kyrie Eleison* ("Lord have mercy") and the bowing zikr, *Illa'llah Hu* ("only God exists"), both of which are done bowing and rising in the kneeling position and are given to aid in the negating of the limited sense of self. In Christian terminology, this act of self-emptying is called *kenosis* and the *via negativa*, the way of self-negating which opens the way to the divine self-disclosure. Hazrat Inayat Khan says: "No one has risen above the delusion of this life without giving up some of the habits, some of the inclinations, some of the tendencies of our everyday life in the pursuit of truth."[49]

In alchemical language, the first phase is called *nigredo* ("the blackening"), representing unconscious shadow energy, the dark night of the soul, a kind of breakdown or crucifixion of one's sense of self or ego. Pir Vilayat notes that sometimes one goes through such a stage naturally in one's life when everything breaks down; there may be some kind a catastrophe that occurs in one's life, a death, an identity crisis, or some event that devastates one, turning all of one's hopes and comforting beliefs to ashes, and making one feel "annihilated" in one's being. This is a natural part of the cycle of existence, as when the tree loses its leaves in the winter and turns its energy within. In the retreat process, one goes through this shattering under more controlled conditions while "accepting it as bearing within itself the promise of a rebirth." Such a breakdown can open the way to a breakthrough in understanding and compassion.[50] Hazrat Inayat Khan says: "The false ego is a false god; when the false god is destroyed the True God arrives."[51]

In the retreat process, one starts with separation (*separatio*), then applies heat to the process (*calcinatio*), leading to annihilation of the false self (*mortificatio)* and its limiting manifestations. Then one progresses to the next stage of *albedo* ("the whitening"), in which higher consciousness emerges out of one's personal consciousness. In the *calcinatio* (calcification) sub-stage, one is returning to the seed-stage, the primal condition of "all-possibility," letting go of everything one thinks one knows and entering the dark night of the mind and soul, out of which new possibilities may emerge. St. John of the Cross advises that, to arrive at Being, you must first pass through a stage in which you become nothing: "To come to what you are not, you must go by a way in which you are not."[52]

Pir Vilayat found various ways of helping people at the onset of a retreat to begin letting go of any tight sense of being a skin-encapsulated individual; this was done by attuning to what he called the "cosmic dimension" of consciousness. One of the ways this can be accessed is by meditating or walking in the woods, in the spirit of St. Francis or a Native American who is very in tune with nature, and getting into the consciousness of a tree, a bird in flight, a deer, or the stars at night, and experiencing oneself as at one with all things, rather than simply as an individual walking around, caught in the web of one's own thoughts and problems.

In *The Call of the Dervish*, Pir Vilayat speaks about the first retreat stage and its psychological ramifications:

> The alchemists of the Middle Ages were discovering the process of transformation. When you know the secret of the stages you go through in transformation, you understand what's happening to you. Something that happens to a lot of people in our time is the disintegration of personality. It's a very frightening thing, and people often go

to a psychiatrist and think there is something wrong with them. In fact, this disintegration is part of the process of transformation: you can't progress unless you disintegrate and are rebuilt again. An intelligent psychiatrist really provides for the continuity of a person's being in the middle of the disruption of the elements of his being. It's a question of earmarking the principle of your being and hanging on to the principle while all the contingency begins to scatter. If you let the principle of your being scatter, you're lost. . . . If you're distilling chemicals and they evaporate, you've lost your chemicals.[53]

Pir Vilayat goes on to say that "you can promote that dissolution, provided you know where you are going." But if the breakdown goes wrong, it can lead toward insanity. He continues,

Since life will break you down anyway, it's sometimes better to do it yourself. That's what the dervish does. . . . So you become conscious of the essence of your being, and that is the only safety. . . . If you look upon your personality as a continuity in change and then reach into the consciousness of what you have always been, beyond all change, that is the essence of your being. That is what we do in the practice of Samadhi, and it is the second stage.[54]

The second stage. In the second phase of the retreat there is a sense of rising, connected with the alchemical stage of distillation. The heat that is applied begins to separate the sulphur from the coarse salt so that it rises as a vapor, to be collected before it disperses. One identifies no longer with the body and personal consciousness but with pure spirit—in Sanskrit terms, one identifies with the eternal *Purusha* rather than the transient *prakriti*. The chanting of divine esmas (names) such *Ya Azim* (glorification), *Allah Hu* and the full zikr, *La ilaha illallah (Hu)*, can aid one at this stage in lifting consciousness higher still, as one transitions from the first to the third stage. Jalaluddin

Rumi shows the spirit in which the fiery heat is applied, saying: "Enough of phrases, conceits, and metaphors! I want burning, burning, burning!"[55]

Pir Vilayat points out that when the Greek initiates went through this same stage in the Eleusinian mysteries, they called it the "rise of Apollo." It is reminiscent of the phoenix rising from the ashes, or the sun rising in spring after the long, bleak winter. Hazrat Inayat Khan says, "Out of the shell of the broken heart emerges the newborn soul."[56]

The third stage represents the summit of the mountain where one has left behind one's personal self and enters into what is called the immaculate state, or stage of self-transcendence. This state is totally impersonal and beyond any qualities, beyond any forms in the physical universe, beyond the duality of subject and object—the realm of pure spirit, pure luminous intelligence, pure consciousness without content. The practices at this point involve working with light, with the subtle breath (Hindu breathing practices such as *qasab* and *shaghal*), and the more rarified Sufi esmas such as *Quddus* (the Holy Spirit), *Nur* (divine light) and *Hu* (the Divine Essence). At this stage, *samadhi* meditation practices can lift one's consciousness very high—"beyond the beyond," as Buddha says.

By meditating on formlessness and allowing the mind to become very still, beyond all thought and personal effort, and using the breath to lift one's consciousness very high, the retreatant can temporarily dissolve all sense of self, which can trigger a kind of ecstasy and a marvelous sense of freedom. By temporarily letting go of all thoughts and worldly cares, one can totally lose the sense of one's personal self and enter an indescribable condition of pure being, pure transcendence, in which one discovers oneself as "always having been" in the eternal realm—the timeless, formless and spaceless dimension of existence. In this state of upliftment, intoxicated by the vast, ever-expanding frontiers of consciousness, "the soul rides the wind," as Pir Vilayat says. The breath carries one aloft like Pegasus or Buraq into the boundless realms of transcendence. One's familiar sense of one's conscious awareness as restricted to a particular body recedes, and is replaced by a sense of time-lessly existing "always and everywhere," without boundaries.

In the Eastern traditions, such as Hindusim and Buddhism, the third stage may resemble the end of the path (*moksha*, lib-eration, *nirvana*), but in Sufism it represents a necessary step in a process of stripping away the false self, of disidentifying with it—a kind of ego death, where ones sees through the illusion of what one thought oneself to be (a temporary bundle of habits, thoughts and physical characteristics)—and identifies with the soul rather than the body and personality. One could put it in other terms and say that one is a being of light, who has become "thickened light" (to use Emerson's phrase) and accrued a body and psyche in order to incarnate in the physical world. This pure untainted soul (beyond the conditioning of the physical world) corresponds to the archetype of the "virgin soul" and its Christian idealization is the Virgin Mary in her immaculate condition, a state of inner purity necessary to give birth to the Divine.

This state of purification is followed by further stages in which one begins to "make God a reality," where the divine en-ergies are reborn and reconfigured in one's being. When the heart has been emptied of all that blocks the divine light, the heart metaphorically becomes the throne of God. In the words of Hazrat Inayat Khan, "This is not my body; it is the temple of God. This is not my heart; it is the altar of God."[57]

In distinguishing these two halves of the retreat, Pir Vilayat described the first half as leading to what could be called

> cosmic consciousness—one becomes aware of the boun-ty of one's being and one becomes aware that one is the divine consciousness looking at the universe. Actually, there are two awakenings: one is awakening out of the existential state (for example, you see yourself as a visitor from outer space who has donned a physical body). The other awakening is the opposite: the awakening in life. My father calls the first one the awakening of the human into God consciousness and the second the awakening of God into human consciousness. . . . [Or] we could say the

first is the awakening from the existential condition into a transcendental state, and the second one is the awakening of the total consciousness of the universe into each fragment or each focal point of itself.[58]

The fourth stage begins the incarnational descent of spirit into matter, the alchemical marriage of heaven and earth in one's being. One of the Sufi practices (*wazaif*) at this stage would be the concentration on the divine names, *Quddus-Hayy*. *Quddus* means (holy) spirit and *Hayy* means life, so *Quddus-Hayy* triggers the quickening of life-force, of aliveness with spirit, breaking through old forms that are no longer adequate containers for one's new realization. Also, *Ya Wahhab(o)* may be given to catalyze new creativity. *Wahhab* is the quality of granting and bestowing, which can release blocked energy and allow one's inspiration to come forth. During the retreat, such practices are both chanted and contemplated silently. At this stage, one may have the realization that all the threads, all the parts of the universe converge in the being of each one of us, like the ocean forming a whirlpool, a temporary form which is both an individual vortex and a state of existence with no boundaries separating it from the totality of the ocean.

Pir Vilayat explains that, in the fourth stage of the retreat, "The alchemical betrothal consists of rebirthing oneself consciously—that is, going through all the stages that are interwoven into one's present state—consciously instead of unconsciously. It's just like pulling apart all of the strands of the tapestry that make up oneself, and then reweaving them together in a new pattern. That would be rebirthing."[59]

He says one practice for doing this would be to review all the salient events in one's life, moving backwards in time, looking for an overview or panorama of one's life. Having done that, one can observe how the personality has evolved in the course of one's life, how one is now the result of what one learned and how one reacted to the challenge of events in one's life. For instance, a person who is driven to mistreat and harm others may be reacting to their own early life experiences of being beaten and mistreated by someone who, in turn, was also mistreated, and so on. It may help if one begins to see deeply the connection and discover the roots of the behavior.

Pir Vilayat speaks of finding "the cause behind the cause behind the cause." Discovering the root causes of the conditioning that we absorbed during our youth can help free us from some of the guilt, resentment, and self-hatred we bear as a result of the traumatic experiences of our youth, events over which we may have then had little control, but which continue to live on in us as negative patterns of behavior. Such psychological self-discovery, coupled with any glimpses of the soul's greater purpose which the retreat affords, can catalyze a personal breakthrough to greater mastery and maturity in life, born of the conviction that new choices and reappraised attitudes are now open to us.

Sometimes we discover unfulfilling life scripts, critical, or self-defeating internal attitudes, and recurring situations that are based on biases and negative feedback we received early on from loved ones and which we have, up until now, internalized as our own opinions and choices. But once we see this, we no longer have to continue with it as part of our belief system. Some events may have traumatized and damaged our personality and others may have made us stronger by facing them. Some events occurred when we were young and, if they happened today, our reaction might be totally different, especially when seen from the more detached clarity of the retreat perspective.

Through this life review, one may also begin to earmark various qualities in one's being; some may have been dominant in the past but new qualities may also be trying to emerge, qualities that need to be nurtured, reinforced, and given space to come through. It is at this point of earmarking the predominant qualities within oneself that concentration on the divine qualities is useful in seeing and working with the qualities that are coming through one, or where one needs balance: mastery (*Wali*), compassion (*Rahman*), beauty (*Jamil*), power (*Qadr*), sovereignty (*Qahr*), truth (*Haqq*), and so on.

Another possible concentration at this point would be what is called "the descent through the planes." The concentration involves tuning into the higher angelic and jinn planes and experiencing, as much as one is able, one's descent through the spheres of angelic light (accruing a body of light), then of the world of mind, of genius (the jinn plane, where one accrues mental and imaginative faculties), and seeing how all of that inheritance has joined with one's genetic biological inheritance to produce one's person on earth. As mentioned previously, a wealth of information on this subject is provided in Hazrat Inayat Khan's book *The Soul Whence and Whither,* which describes the various higher planes and how the soul, on its descent into physical incarnation, inherits strands of being from each plane.

In short, Hazrat Inayat Khan compares the soul to a ray of the sun (the Divine Source) which descends through the various heavenly spheres, accumulating qualities and propensities from each plane. This includes interfacing with souls who are on their return trip after incarnating on earth, souls who are now in the process of stripping away the accumulated "clothes" of each plane in order for the soul's pure ray to merge again with the Divine Source. (The soul, as a ray of the Divine, is never really separate from the Source, even on earth.) As Pir Vilayat adds, Hazrat Inayat Khan's teaching explains how, without invoking the explanation of reincarnation, a descending soul could, for instance, meet with the ascending soul of Beethoven, or some other musician in the higher planes, and then be born on earth with great musical gifts, even into a family previously devoid of musicians. Similarly, we could say we inherit from angelic and jinn parents as well as our biological parents. The idea is that we carry an inheritance from angelic and jinn parents, not just our biological parents.

Pir Vilayat suggests that, just as a plant grows by incorporating the rays of the sun and the nourishment of the earth into its being, at this stage of the retreat, one consciously incorporates both the heavens and the earth into one's being. He says: "That's what birth is: the moment when there's a contact between your having always been, with all the inheritance that you've brought, and the planet Earth. You are infusing the planet Earth with what you're bringing down from your soul, and when you leave after death, you have left a mark on the planet. One might say that for the Earth to unfold, it has to draw into itself all that has accrued to it from the higher planes."[60]

The fourth stage can also concentrate on the qualities of love and experiencing compassion for the suffering of the world. One of the many Sufi practice that goes with this concentration is *Ishq Allah Ma'bud lillah* (God is love and beloved, the subject and object of all love.) One may also begin to sense how it is out of an act of divine love and magnanimity that each of us has been brought into being and that, as bearers of the divine inheritance, we might express that loving kindness and compassion to all the other "ourselves" in the world, instead of being caught up in personal resentments and negative judgments.

Pir Vilayat often used the humorous line, "What you could be if you would be what you should be—but you don't be." Later, after receiving feedback from various people that they already felt weighed down with guilt by all the familial and societal expectations of what they "should be," Pir Vilayat realized they had a valid point and altered his saying to: "What you could be if you would be what you *might* be!"[61]

The fifth stage is the stage of affirmation, of fixing one's new realizations and resolutions, just as a photographic plate has to be immersed in a solution of fixative so that the image will be preserved and not quickly disappear. In the earlier stages of the retreat, the personality had to be left behind; in the fifth stage, it is rediscovered. Previously it was more conditioned and corrupted, but now, having undergone a purifying process during the first part of the retreat, it is closer to projecting one's real being. Now one needs the courage to affirm one's real being when returning to everyday life, amidst old acquaintances and family who will expect one to still be the same as before and may draw one back into old patterns of behavior that no longer adequately reflect one's deeper truth. Pir Vilayat says, "You can get very high, but if when you come down you get right back into your personality, everything is lost."[62] He advises that it is easy to say, "That's just the way I am," but that is not the spiritual way. After all, these old habits and imperfections do not adequately represent who you really are at a deeper level.

At this point, one begins to look at one's life's purpose, where one is going, and what might be the next step in life. What are the qualities one is manifesting, or the ones which are trying to come through, and can these be strengthened and balanced to help fulfill one's life purpose? Hazrat Inayat Khan teaches that every soul enters life with some purpose, but it is often well hidden and must be discovered. He says, "Blessed is he who sees the star of his soul, as the light is seen from the port in the sea."[63] If we do not clearly see it as a beacon, can we, like a person lost in a cave, intuit a little more light in one direction than in another or find clues along the way that point us in the right direction?

Here, practices with the divine qualities such as *Ya Alim* (divine insight) and *Ya Qadr* (the divine power) can be helpful. The divine power should not be confused with ego power; rather, it is like finding an immense impersonal power behind one's limited will power and allowing that to come through one's being. In this regard, Pir Vilayat attached special importance to his father's saying: "I discover within myself the self-same power that moves the universe."[64] Here, it is important to also consider the less heroic power of patience with difficult people or situations, which is so valuable in daily life.* Hazrat Inayat Khan points out that those who say, "I cannot stand this," or "I cannot tolerate that," simply show their weakness. Some retreatants may begin to see how they have given away their power and need to reclaim it through greater reliance on the Divine; others may realize that they are already too controlling and need to open up to the greater will. Thus the form of the practice will vary for each person, divine power being but one of qualities that can be contemplated at this point in the retreat.

In group retreats, Pir Vilayat sometimes utilized recorded music to help bring through the emotions of the different divine attributes, from a very meditative Indian raga, representing the quality of *Batin* (the inner, hidden, veiled one), to a Gloria by

---

*   The Arabic divine name for patience is *Sabr*.

Bach or Vivaldi that conveyed the sense of glorification represented by *Azim* (glory). He also emphasized practices with the
various chakras or latifas and practices with light. Some concentrations work toward discovering the inner light, and others
with radiating light toward others, with the insight that the light
you cast upon others is more important that the light they reflect to you. This means seeing and affirming another person
in their highest potential, their real being, and giving energy to
that (rather than seeing their defects and reacting to them), thus
uplifting the other person. This is one of the secrets of the Sufi
murshids: to always see others in their higher being—as they
could be—and to encourage them in manifesting their real being by treating them as if they already were doing so.

The sixth stage. The final stage of the alchemical process is
called "the spiritualization of matter and the materialization of
spirit." One becomes conscious of incarnating spirit and materializing matter. This is expressed in the prayer from the ancient Zoroastrian Gathas: "May I become an instrument of the
resurrection of the world!"[65] One begins to see oneself in all
forms of life and begins to discover the divine perfection in it
all, seeing the divine light in all beings; then one returns back
into the world with a new perspective. As Al-Hallaj stated: "The
light of the divine awareness has arisen in my heart, like the sun
over the horizon, and it will never set."[66] After the dissolution,
one is fully coagulated and fixed in the sixth stage. The archetype is the Christ being, the human who has awakened to the
divine inheritance—who has undergone the second birth of the
Divine—and is conscious of incorporating these energies in a
body made of the fabric of the planet yet is characterized by the
greatest humility.

There are many practices that could be given at this point.
Two of the divine names often used are *Wahhab(o)*, concentrating on the outpouring of divine qualities through one, and
Fattah (the opener of the way). The latter practice also entails
an inward pledge to uphold one's inner light and truth as a
channel of divine service, and reflects the covenant of *Alast*,
mentioned in the Qur'an,[67] in which, prior to their earthly

incarnation, all souls pledged to uphold the divine truth in this world of limitation.

Pir Vilayat quotes Ibn al-'Arabi as saying, "By discovering the divine consciousness in my consciousness, I confer upon God a mode of knowledge; by manifesting the divine qualities in my personality, I confer upon God a mode of being." He adds, "That's the purpose of the Sufis: it is, on one hand, to become aware of being the divine consciousness that is limited, that is funneled down, but is still divine—and of being the divine nature which is also limited but is still the divine nature."[68]

the COSMIC CELEBRATION

Between 1973 and 1983, Pir Vilayat conceived of a large-scale interreligious mythic pageant patterned on the Cosmic Mass in Teilhard de Chardin's *Mass on the World*. Working with other Sufis who were experienced in theatre and musical scoring (primarily Saphira Linden and Allaudin Mathieu), he brought together music, dance, myth, and drama in a powerful production that was not merely designed with an audience in mind, but spiritually involved the actors and participants. The pageant, called the Cosmic Celebration, grew out of the spiritual practices of murids at Sufi camps where individuals were given various roles that reflected qualities within themselves.

Gradually, this was developed into a spiritual spectacle which had a transformational effect on the hundreds of actors who played roles in the drama. The pageant was based on various motifs from the world's major religions as they relate to the stages of the Christian mass. These included Buddha's enlightenment, Abraham's sacrifice, Isaiah's baptism by fire, representations of the angelic planes, processions of white robed choirs, the triumphal entry of Muhammad into Mecca and Jesus into Jerusalem, Rama reuniting with Sita, and so on, all dramatically narrated by Pir Vilayat. The idea was to bring to life on earth the remembrance of the cosmic drama in the heavens, through acts of glorification, drawing upon the various transformative motifs of the different religions and mystery initiations rites.

The Cosmic Celebration was performed in New York City at the Cathedral of St. John the Divine and in various other cities. A 1978 long-playing record, a few film clips, and a slide show were made to record the drama for posterity.

Pir Vilayat Khan with the author and daughter, Claire, at the Abode in 1989 (Photo by Sylvia Blann)

CONNECTING *with* PIR VILAYAT KHAN

My first exposure to the Sufi Order was through the Dances of Universal Peace in 1978 when I was about twenty-six years old. A few years before, I had seen Pir Vilayat's first major book, *Toward the One*, with all its mystical sayings and illustrations, but it hadn't really spoken to me. At the time, I was more interested in the writings of Krishnamurti and Alan Watts. During the same year, I was invited to accompany the Gurdjieff movements on the piano, which drew me into the Gurdjieff Work as well. Soon, however, the joy conveyed in the Dances of Universal Peace and the open-heartedness of the American Sufis beckoned me in the direction of the Sufi path.

In the spring of 1979, my wife and I traveled to the Gurdjieff school in Charlestown, West Virginia, where we met Muzaffer Efendi and his dervishes, who were visiting America from Istanbul. There I also met the radio host and spiritual author Lex Hixon, with whom I would later study. Although I was, by this time, looking for a spiritual teacher and was very inspired by the experience of spending time with Muzaffer Efendi and joining in a traditional dervish zikr ceremony, I felt that the language and cultural differences, as well as the fact that the sheikh lived in Turkey, might not represent my best option. That door would reopen eleven years later (and I would eventually write about my experience in my book *Lifting the Boundaries: Muzaffer Efendi and the Transmission of Sufism to the West).*

In early January 1980, Pir Vilayat held a retreat in downtown Atlanta at the Omni Hotel, which I attended along with my wife and a few others friends. There were several hundred people in attendance. Pir Vilayat guided exquisite meditations and, toward the end, led us in whirling, a practice to which he had been introduced in Konya, Turkey, by the head sheikh of the Mevlevis, Suleyman Dede (who had, in turn, later visited America and paid his respects to Pir Vilayat at the Abode).

Pir Vilayat explained that the turn, or *sema*, arose out of Rumi's vision of the planets orbiting around the sun, each planet moved by its nostalgia for union with the Divine Source, but separated by the gravity pull—that is, the amount of density—of the ego. Each of Rumi's dervishes had impersonated a different planet in his whirling. While the knowledge of exactly how Rumi's dervishes attuned to each planet in their whirling has been lost, one can still imagine: Mercury whirling fast, Mars powerfully, Jupiter with great majesty, Saturn slow and perturbed, and Venus with beautiful grace. We were advised to think of a planet with which we had an affinity and whirl in that rhythm, and so we did. As for myself, I found that I was metaphorically gravitating toward Pir Vilayat. By the end of the weekend, I felt I had found my spiritual guide.

In June, we traveled to the Abode for a weeklong summer camp with Pir Vilayat, and there I received spiritual initiation from him, as well as his *darshan* (spiritual glance). Though he rarely did so in later years, at the time Pir Vilayat would, for about half an hour each day, sit in meditation at the front of the main tent and give darshan. One by one, a select number of persons would sit before him and receive a kind of spiritual reading from the Pir, in which he glanced at the person, closed his eyes and then spoke a few words about what he intuited as coming through their being.

Pir Vilayat's darshans were a modified version of what his father had done at the summer schools in Suresnes in the early 1920s. Hazrat Inayat Khan would meditate for hours in the morning and go into a transfigured state of samadhi in which he became lost to the outer world. Then several strong disciples would carry him into the meditation hall, where his murids sat in silence, and he would be placed behind a curtain at the front of the hall. One at a time, his disciples would be led behind the curtain to sit in front of their meditating master. Hazrat Inayat Khan would briefly open his eyes and exchange a glance with the murid, then close them and the disciple would be escorted out. Those who experienced Inayat Khan's darshan during those sessions reported that they were amazed at the light and divine power radiating from his glance, as though they were seeing into the windows of paradise.

In the case of Pir Vilayat, it was during the short ceremony of initiation, which was usually done in private, that one really experienced the power of his glance. The black pupils of his eyes sparkled and danced with light and vitality, and, as my wife observed, perceptible waves of energy radiated around his head subtly distorting the view of the trees behind him. During several such encounters with Pir Vilayat over the years, I also experienced invariably a kind of tingling, ecstatic energy in my own crown chakra when he raised his hands above me for the blessing.

During the summer camp, Pir Vilayat conducted a volunteer choir (in which I participated) performing a beautiful kyrie by the composer, Tomas Luis de Victoria. We also had the pleasure of hearing Pir Vilayat play a movement from Beethoven's "Archduke" Trio on cello, with Taj accompanying him on piano, and Shams Kairys on violin. It was the only time I heard him play cello, but a few years later, when Pir Vilayat came to our home town of Nashville to give a seminar and stayed with us, he sat down at our piano and played from memory a very soulful rendition of Beethoven's "Moonlight Sonata."

Pir Vilayat Khan playing Beethoven's "Moonlight Sonata" at the author's home in November 1984. (Photo by the author.)

As an occasional musician myself, I found that Pir Vilayat's love for a wide variety of spiritual music—from Indian ragas to Western classical music—and frequent use of music in his retreats and seminars, was one of the things I most appreciated about him. What I found interesting was that soon after receiving initiation with Pir Vilayat, I was inspired to compose a whole series of melodies, with which I set to music various sayings by Hazrat Inayat Khan. (I subsequently studio recorded them with the help of various musician friends and years later placed them on the internet under the title: "Thy Glorious Vision.") Although I did compose other music after this, I never again experienced such a concentrated burst of melodic creativity.

I found it noteworthy that, in addition to religious masters, saints and prophets, Pir Vilayat also considered many of the great composers to be spiritual masters in their own right. He sometimes used the beginning of the Fourth Piano Concerto of Beethoven as a teaching analog. At the beginning of the concerto, the piano enters with a soft, peaceful melody and the orchestra responds in a loud, overpowering way, yet the piano holds its own, and soon the orchestra softens, adjusting itself in order to better cooperate with the solo melody. Pir Vilayat took this musical lesson as a model that demonstrates how the individual can affirm their truth and influence the collective, rather than just being drowned out and absorbed by the collective will.

On occasion, Pir Vilayat also quoted the following statement of Johann Sebastian Bach to show the musician's profound understanding of the principles of cosmic and earthly harmony:

> In the architecture of my music I want to demonstrate to the world the architecture of a new and beautiful commonwealth. The secret of my harmony? I alone know it. Each instrument in counterpoint, and as many contrapuntal parts as there are instruments. It is the enlightened self-discipline of the various parts, each voluntarily imposing on itself the limits of its individual freedom for the well-being of the community. That is my message. Not the autocracy of a single stubborn melody on the one hand, nor the anarchy of unchecked noise on the other. No, a delicate balance between the two; an enlightened freedom. The science of my art. The art of my science. The harmony of the stars in the heavens, the yearning for brotherhood in the heart of man. This is the secret of my music.[69]

Within a year of joining the Sufi Order, I found a local Hindu music teacher and began a decade long study of Karnatic (South Indian) music, both vocal and on the Saraswati *vina*, which had been Hazrat Inayat Khan's instrument. We started a Sufi center in Nashville and began to invite senior teachers in the Sufi Order to visit and hold local seminars. I also began to attend retreats with Pir Vilayat and other spiritual teachers, such as the

Sufi healing conferences organized by Himayat Inayati at Light of the Mountains, near Asheville. There I met Rabbi Shlomo Carlebach, Matthew Fox, Reshad Feild, Wallace Black Elk, Grace Spotted Eagle, and various spiritual healers such as Rosalyn Bruyere, Dr. Olga Worral, and Marcel Vogel.

I encountered a number of other gifted teachers at Omega Institute, located in Rhinebeck, New York (formerly in Vermont), such as Rabbi Zalman Schachter-Shalomi, Brother David Stiendl-Rast, Swami Satchitananda, and the Indian bamboo flutist, Sachdev. Omega Institute was founded by Dr. Stephan Rechtschaffen and Elizabeth Lesser in 1977 under the inspiration of Pir Vilayat Khan, as an institute for spiritual studies both esoteric and practical, from Sufi studies to creative writing, yoga and African drumming courses, always featuring top teachers, musicians, and writers in their fields.

Esoteric Week at Omega Institute in 1981. On the interfaith panel were (left to right) Swami Satchitananda (Hinduism), Khempo Karthar Rinpoche (Buddhism), Reb Zalman Schachter-Shalomi (Judaism), Brother David Steindl-Rast (Christianity), and Pir Vilayat Khan (Sufism). (Photo courtesy of the University of Colorado Boulder's Zalman M. Schachter-Shalomi Collection.)

In 1982, my wife and I attended the Sufi Centennary (the 100th anniversary of Hazrat Inayat Khan's birth) in Suresnes, France and then traveled to Mount Dauphin in the French Alps to attend Pir Vilayat's annual summer camp. It was most interesting to hear Pir Vilayat lead trilingual talks and meditations in

French, German (or Dutch) and English, speaking a paragraph in each language in turn, always without prepared remarks.

REB ZALMAN *and the* JEWISH-SUFI CONNECTION

Although a fuller discussion of Reb Zalman follows in the second half of this book, we can begin to look at his association with Pir Vilayat at this point. Rabbi Zalman Schachter-Shalomi was a Hasidic rabbi, born in Europe eight years after Pir Vilayat, who immigrated to the United States in the 1940s as a refugee from Nazi persecution. He studied with two of the Lubavitcher rebbes and became a rabbi, then a university professor, and finally, the guiding light of the Jewish Renewal Movement. Over time, his spiritual horizons broadened to include an interest in other faiths in addition to his root tradition of Judaism. He befriended many of the leading contemporary spiritual lights of his time, such as Thomas Merton and the Dalai Lama, represented Judaism in numerous ecumenical gatherings, and developed a deep interest in the Sufism of Hazrat Inayat Khan.

He initially made a connection with Sufism on the West Coast in the mid-1970s through Murshid Sam's successor, Murshid Moineddin Jablonski, but was directed to Pir Vilayat when he expressed a desire to receive a Sufi initiation. Immediately recognizing Reb Zalman as an accomplished teacher of Judaism and Kabbalah, Pir Vilayat initiated him as a sheikh and senior advisor in the Sufi Order, and requested Reb Zalman's blessing in return.

Following this, Reb Zalman began an intensive study of Sufism and undertook a number of lengthy personal retreats with Puran Bair, a senior disciple of Pir Vilayat, who had worked with Pir Vilayat to develop the alchemical retreat process. Years later, Puran told me that Reb Zalman showed up for his first week-long retreat with a whole stack of spiritual books and several musical instruments, figuring the retreat was a good time to read, study and play music. (During those years, Reb Zalman's extremely busy schedule allowed him very little down time.)

Puran instructed him to leave the books and instruments outside the retreat space, because he was there to meditate and do Sufi practices, not to catch up on his reading. Reb Zalman understood and seemed to appreciate Puran's firm guidance in this regard, and continued to take periodic Sufi retreats for several years. Although Puran was not Jewish, his first wife, Saphira, was, and she wanted their children to learn about Judaism and have bar mitzvahs. Reb Zalman agreed to prepare Puran and his children for their bar Mitzvahs and also performed the ceremonies. Puran's son, Ethan, went on to become a rabbi.

Puran was Pir Vilayat's first khalif and had a background in science, technology, and business. Working closely with Pir Vilayat, he soon become an advanced practitioner of Sufi meditation and the spiritual technology of the heart. After nearly two decades in the Sufi Order, Pir Vilayat advised Puran and his second wife Susanna—also a student of Pir Vilayat—to start their own spiritual order, incorporating the latest scientific principles in conjunction with the teachings and insights of Pir Vilayat and Hazrat Inayat Khan, but without calling it Sufism. In this way, Pir Vilayat felt that a wider audience might be reached, including people in the business world—those who might be put off by the Sufi label and any Islamic associations it evoked, but who would otherwise receive great benefit from its teachings. The thriving organization that emerged from this directive is called *The Institute for Applied Meditation on the Heart*—"iamHeart."

Thomas Atum O'Kane, was another senior student of Pir Vilayat, one who functioned for twelve years as the Secretary General of the Sufi Order. Early on, he formed a deep connection with Reb Zalman when the rebbe relocated to the Philadelphia area where Atum lived, taking up a teaching post as professor of Jewish mysticism and psychology of religion at Temple University. Atum, a graduate student at the time, was thus able to study with Pir Vilayat as well as Reb Zalman. When Atum first made contact with Reb Zalman, he felt a deep affinity with him and realized that Reb Zalman manifested qualities ("juicy with life and a huge overflowing heart")[70] that were

not quite like the priests in his Catholic upbringing or his beloved teacher, Pir Vilayat, but were complimentary. Reb Zalman
quickly put Atum at ease by telling him, "You already have a
teacher; so just think of me as your Jewish spiritual uncle. There
are questions and issues that you can bring to your uncles that
you wouldn't bring to your father."[71]

Atum found Zalman's wise delineation of his relationship
as "spiritual uncle" perfect, and later found that, indeed, there
were personal issues on his journey which he could take to Reb
Zalman that were not necessarily the domain of Pir Vilayat. As a
university professor, Reb Zalman was also able to act as Atum's
advisor and mentor for his graduate and doctoral studies. Atum,
who functioned for a number of years as my spiritual guide, was
only one of many students of Pir Vilayat who received great benefit from their dual association with both of these marvelously
universal souls. After receiving his master's degree in psychological counseling and a doctorate in transpersonal psychology,
Atum graduated from the Guild for Spiritual Guidance, which
focuses on the depth psychology of Carl Jung, the vision of
Teilhard de Chardin, and the practice of Christian mysticism.
He went on to found the Spiritual Guidance Wisdom School,
which provides training and mentoring in spiritual guidance
throughout America, Canada, and Europe.

*Reb Zalman Schachter-Shalomi at the Dargah of Hazrat Inayat Khan, 1990, in
Delhi, India. (Photo courtesy of the University of Colorado Boulder's Zalman M.
Schachter-Shalomi collection.)*

Pir Vilayat also undertook an in-depth study of Kabbalah in his early years and occasionally led meditations on the Tree of Life and the ten *sephirot*, relating them to ideas in Sufism and giving their corresponding astrological archetypes. (Appendix 1 contains a short series of Kabbalistic meditations as led by Pir Vilayat. The chapter on Reb Zalman delves deeper into the Kabbalistic teachings from the Jewish perspective.)

a PILGRIMAGE *to* MOUNT SINAI

In 1984, an ecumenical meeting of religious leaders was organized, culminating on top of Mount Sinai. Among the Sufi pilgrims on this expedition were Pir Vilayat, his son Zia, Atum O'Kane, and Reb Zalman, who attended as a representative of the Jewish people and particularly of Moses, the prophet who received the divine revelation on Mount Sinai over 3,000 years ago. People of many other faith traditions participated in the expedition as well; yet, in order to get the Egyptian government's permission for the visit, the organizers had to agree not to publicize the event in the media for fear of repercussions from religious and political hardliners. Pir Vilayat described the purpose of the ecumenical gathering on Sinai as "a gesture of good will in a tough, violent world!" In a 1984 *Keeping in Touch* newsletter, he went on to say:

> Why, then, did we meet? Could you believe that there are still a few idealists in the world who will leave their jobs and homes, cancel their busy schedules at their own expense, out of pure dedication, in the belief that since there is a religious factor in any war, let alone the Middle East conflict, it is incumbent upon the more progressive spiritual leaders of various religious denominations to demonstrate their solidarity in their dedication to a spiritual ideal while respecting their differences of outlook and ritual?
>
> Obviously, numerically we represented a negligible fraction of the pleiades of rabbis, priests, ministers,

imams and Bikkhus on the planet. Therefore, one might well question what impact our symbolic action might have upon the conflicting religious masses, especially since we were deprived of the powerful tool of mass media. "Small is beautiful . . ." and we believed that our gesture may, however, loosen tensions a little bit in, let us say, the "software" of the programming of events materializing on the physical plane. For the least, it may be said that we had a marvelous time sharing in the spectacle of the most diverse types of people and cultures and attires, and discovered the joy of communicating together with an open heart. . . .

It was a striking expression of the spirit of the message of unity to which we are dedicated. We sang Hindu, Buddhist, Jewish, Christian, Muslim, and Sufi songs at the top of the Mount, where presumably Moses discovered the famous tablets. A Native American lit medicinal herbs at dawn. What a privilege to be ushered into the "holy of holies" at the St. Catherine's monastery, dating as early as the year 50 A.D.–a tribute to the fervor of the Hesychasts, the early monks of the desert whose caves are still to be seen where water flows generously betwixt the barren desert land.

Reb Zalman also penned an account in an article entitled "The Sinai Gathering: Prayers for Peace," which appeared in the June 1984 issue of the *B'nai Or Newsletter*. He described the many participants in the pilgrimage as

people who were attracted by the call of the voice of God today urging us peace. They were: Japanese Shinto priests and Buddhists of all varieties . . . a Native American shaman and healer . . . Moslem men and women . . . people from Egypt, the United States, and Israel. Sufis, some close to the Moslem tradition, others more universalist, doing zikr in the oasis and on the mountain and seeing some of their holy hopes on the verge of realization. Christians, Byzantine Orthodox, Copts, Melkites, Baptists, Anglicans, Quakers, Roman, and other Catholics, a rainbow of Protestants, praying and speaking in many tongues and doing this together. Some from Israel, others from Egypt, some from the USA and Europe. Jews from both Americas and Europe, from Israel and the Diaspora, secular and religious, New Age and traditional and feminist. The age range spanned from 11 to 80. . . .

Reb Zalman describes the culminating climb to the top of Sinai, that began long before daylight, at 2:00 a.m., and which involved hours of steep, arduous climbing up the eastern side of the mountain by starlight and flashlight in order to arrive at the top for sunrise. His account continues with a description of how a Native American Shaman named Philip

prepared a smoke offering of sage, sweet grass, and cedar and, holding the incense bowl, began his chant just as the sun's first pierce came to touch us. We felt presences of prophets and ancestors, chains of traditions from times more ancient than Jethro's forebears. . . . As soon as the sun was half risen over the horizon, the Japanese banzaied it three times, we davvened, zikkred, blew the shofar, and chanted, then Pir Vilayat Khan led us in a pledge to serve the spiritual government of the world with our body, mind, and soul; we each in our way accepted the Kingdom of God and pledged to bring it down into our lives and into our world. And all the bone-tired ague was forgotten for the moment. Soaring in songs celebrating the chains of transmissions that connected us with Sinai, we joined each other's refrains and hugged. . . . Oy was it ever a peak experience!

In commemoration of the burning bush, Reb Zalman removed his shoes, accompanied by the corresponding verse from Exodus, and then led the Jewish contingent in several prayers and blessings, culminating in the *Shema*, whose echo reverberated back from the mountain. Then Reb Zalman

> urged all present to join in a chant, each one in their way petitioning for peace in the name of those who otherwise would become the victims and visualizing the region united in peaceful interaction. Anna HaShem Hoshia was joined by Kyrie Eleison and Yah Rachman Ya Rachim and Hey Vah! Heh Vah! (peace in Japanese) while I recited the Malkhiyot prayer of the High Holy Days and we blew the shofar, Samuel Avital and I, and again that echo! Aleinu and BaYom HaHu with a Kaddish for the past victims of the Middle East wars was our contribution. Phillip Deer, the shaman, introduced his prayer with some heart words for the Traditional Peoples' vision, and by that time it was noon and the Moslems prepared for the Salaat in rows to prostrate themselves to ALLAHU AKBAR! . . . RAINBOW OF TRUTHS!

Reb Zalman relates that the pilgrimage concluded the next morning with a group visit to St. Catherine's monastery, with its library containing "the oldest extant manuscripts from the time of the Desert Fathers, who followed in the wake of the Jewish hermits and healers of the Qumran and Therapeutae-Essene tradition." The account of the pilgrimage is completed with Pir Zia's impressions:

> My most cherished memory of Reb Zalman is the memory of having climbed with him, and with many other peacemakers and pilgrims, the rocky path that leads to the peak of Mount Sinai in the Egyptian desert. We ascended the holy mountain in the predawn darkness, and as the sun slowly rose over the horizon, Reb Zalman sang joyous chants of divine praise. Standing on the summit, one could see the *wiratha* of Hazrat Musa (*'alayhi as-salam*)—the inheritance of Moses (peace be upon him)—radiating from his face.[72]

The Sinai pilgrimage by people of all faiths was emblematic of the collective need of humanity to renew its spiritual orientation, to inwardly ascend to the place where we all discover our connection with Spirit, with the eternal divine broadcast which not only revealed itself to Moses at Sinai in the distant past, but which continues to call us all to reaffirm our essential Source and oneness with the Universe.

a PIR VILAYAT INTERVIEW *with* ELLEN BURSTYN

In 1981 Pir Vilayat participated in a videotaped interview with actress Ellen Burstyn,[73] who had previously studied Sufism with him. The bond between them lent an air of intimacy to their discussion. As the topics they discussed touched on several key points in Pir Vilayat's teaching, the interview provides a good entry point to a further examination of his approach to spirituality.

At the time, the actress had recently starred in a film entitled *Resurrection*, which concerns a woman who is brought back from a near-death encounter and discovers that she now has healing powers, which prove to be a mixed blessing. The title of the film led to a discussion of the spiritual significance of resurrection. Pir Vilayat explained that he saw resurrection as a process that goes right to the core meaning of human existence. That is because if there is to be any preservation of the purpose of our earthly incarnation, then something of our experience, the know-how we gain on earth, must be eternalized, just as the essence of the flower is preserved in the form of perfume. Contrary to the Buddhist idea that life is transient and of no ultimate value and therefore one must liberate oneself from it, he says "there must be a process by which the experience of the human being is digested by the Total Consciousness." Otherwise there would be no point and nothing gained by the soul incarnating in the physical world. He continued:

> What I'm really saying here is that God is both dynamic *and* static. One mustn't think of the static archetypes—the

aidos of Plato—that remain there permanently, and everything is just simply reflecting these archetypes. The programming is totally spontaneous and inventive and creative just like in a toccata and fugue of Bach, for example. In that sense, one can say that evolution is a departure from the norm. It's always exploring new possibilities. Hazrat Inayat Khan used to say that one could think of God as an artist Who imagines a painting before He makes a painting, but once He starts it, He changes His programming because He finds new ways of doing it better than He had thought of before. So you mustn't think of things as preordained.

Pir Vilayat went on to point out that we are not just the paint and canvas but also part of the painter.

That's part of the beauty, that we're not just manipulated by an action beyond ourselves. You see, according to the Sufis, God wished that every fraction of Himself should be endowed with the qualities or the faculties that He enjoys in the totality, and therefore that includes His consciousness. Maybe today one should say "His and Her consciousness"—I don't know. You see, our language has been formed by our ancestors who were chauvinists, and so we're still using the same language which doesn't fit into our present way of thinking. So I have to excuse myself every time I say Him, but I think people know what I mean. . . . The universe is a hologram. These are the new views. That would mean everyone carries within themselves the totality of the divine inheritance.

Pir Vilayat described how our perception of the surface of things from a single localized vantage point gives us a very limited idea of the reality of things. For instance, if you see the outside of a house from the front, your knowledge of the house is still quite limited because you haven't seen the house from other angles or been inside. Similarly, if we just see the bark of the tree, we haven't really seen or experienced the tree except in its outer surface—not the tree's roots in the earth, nor its sap and interior aspects; and one hasn't entered into the very consciousness of the tree and experienced what it is like to be a tree. In the same way, in our dealings with other people and our assessment of our own problems, we are operating from a very narrow personal vantage point, so we see things in a partial way, filtered through our conditioned likes and dislikes and generally limited to a surface assessment of things.

Is there an alternative, more holistic mode of perception? This is where Pir Vilayat recommended entering the mode of consciousness which he called "turning within" or entering inverted space. Here, the physicist Dr. David Bohm's concept of the implicate and explicate order is helpful in understanding this mode of consciousness where we experience things beyond our usual subject-object duality, experiencing things from the inside. Dr. Bohm describes the implicate order or "enfolded" order as a deeper and more fundamental order of reality, where time and space relations are not the dominant factors in perceiving the material world.

Pir Vilayat sometimes alluded to the implicate state as a mode of diffuse awareness "where everything is all everywhere," and often used Ibn al-'Arabi's phrase to speak of the deeper apperception of "that which transpires behind that which appears." This contrasts with our usual outward, surface-bound perception of things, which, in Dr. Bohm's terminology, is called the "unfolded" order or explicate state. In short, experiencing the implicate state of things through meditation allows us access to a deeper, more inward perception of reality, beyond the outer world of appearances. Pir Vilayat often quoted Dr. Bohm's statement, "The physical world as we know it, is just a ripple on the ocean of reality."[74] As Pir Vilayat went on to say in the interview:

> One also has the ability sometimes to have an overview of oneself, to observe oneself as though one were another person, for example. Then one thinks, "What am I doing down here?" and "How is it possible that I let myself

be caught into this little vantage point?" and "How is it possible that I allowed myself to be so concerned about my little storms in my teacups, when in fact, I've missed the great show in the universe?" That's what I call the "Cosmic Celebration." I think that's what we are invited to, and if we fail to do it, we sink into terrible despair, and that's what's happening to a lot of people."[75]

the DIVINE PROGRAMMING

In *The Call of the Dervish*,[76] Pir Vilayat expands on the idea he touched on at the beginning of the interview, that is, his model of how the divine order behind the universe can manifest in a way that is both static and dynamic and can include perfection as well as imperfection. He first appeals to the theology of Meister Eckhart, who makes a contrast between *Gott* (God) and *Gottheit* (Godhead or Godhood), the former referring to the Creator God as a being, a thing, and the latter referring to Divinity, to Being itself, the transcendent "God(ding) beyond God," a process beyond change or becoming. Pir Vilayat speaks of the changing, evolving aspects of the Divine, saying, "When you get into the order of the universe, you realize that it is continually improving itself, so you can't limit God to the order, although it is a very important aspect of the Divine Being."[77] On the other hand, you can get to a place beyond the order where there is just intelligence, beyond multiplicity, beyond all attributes (*Gottheit).*

> We should say, then that God is both . . . changing and unchanging at some very high level. We could even say that it is an attribute of His perfection to change: it would be limiting if He could not change. So the order takes account of the feedback. Imagine a computer program that could program itself by building up information from the environment. You might set it off with a certain program, but in the end it would have a much larger program, because it would have to take into account the

feedback from the environment. That would be like the divine order that is continually reprogramming itself and perfecting itself; and yet behind all that is intelligence.

The original program is like the cause, and that is why many theologians have called God "the Cause," but the programming is not just limited to the cause, because it takes into account the feedback. Everything is not predetermined, because another factor is coming in, and that is purpose. In biology, for example, the species does not just adapt itself to the environment; it also adapts the environment to its own sense of purpose. So it's an inventive order that is always seeking out new horizons and new possibilities. There is a feedback, and the information gained is eventually incorporated into the order: what has been gained by God becoming man accrues to the divine consciousness, and that is what we mean by resurrection.[78]

UNIVERSALIST SUFISM *and* ISLAMIC SUFISM

In speaking of the Sufism of Hazrat Inayat Khan, Pir Vilayat says:

Every teacher, if he really has a contribution to make, is generally in advance of his time. He foresees perspectives that will be taken for granted in fifty years, but in his time they seem a little odd. When we started having the Universal Worship service [in 1921], in which we light candles for all religions and read texts of all religions, people were very shocked. . . . And yet for many people now it is just taken for granted, because the different religions are different aspects of the one religion, which is the religion of God, and the spearhead of civilization has grown into an understanding of the unity behind diversity."[79]

As Pir Vilayat saw it, even modern science is able to affirm the unity of existence: "The best credo of all times is that of modern physics—that everything is an unbroken, undivided wholeness.

That is the meaning of *'La illaha illa'llah hu'* ('Nothing exists save God'), of *'Shema Israel, Adonoi elohenu, Adonoi Eḥad'* ('Hear O Israel, the Lord thy God, the Lord is One')—the Buddhist principle of *'anata'*—that there is no such thing as multiplicity."[80] Yet, when one looks carefully at the great religions beyond their essential core agreements, one sees many differences in their approach and doctrines: Hinduism is polytheistic, Buddhism is nontheistic, Christianity affirms the divine incarnation, while Judaism and Islam affirm God's transcendence—they all disagree on the details.

For many years, Pir Vilayat both organized and participated in interreligious gatherings and panels. About these efforts, he said:

> I am sure that many people would have liked if the gurus teaching the different traditions would at last come together and explain their differences and their similarities and make us feel that we are all together on a great quest. And we have made some attempts at doing that. I in particular, but other people have done it too. Myself, I came to grief because one guru kept on answering all the questions and when I tried to restrain him, he said, "There is no stopping me." So these attempts are not always successful, or when they are, sometimes each one keeps telling his story and there is no real inter-relationship between them. But we are trying and have had seminars with gurus with whom at least I feel a very close connection. Sometimes we feel that we're getting a little bit closer together. We are very close in our feeling, but when it comes to the teachings, that's where it's important to show how it all dovetails. That does not mean that all the teachings are the same. Hazrat Inayat Khan said "unity is not uniformity" and so it's far from us to make the kind of syncretism which is one thing that happened in history. There was a syncretism of the School of Alexandria in the third century, and in Rome the Romans included the gods of all the religions."[81]

Pir Vilayat summarized the situation of the interreligious dialogue by saying: "If you try to find unity based on the juxtaposition of dogmas, you won't find it—they're contradictory. But if you go from the point of view of actual experience, of the mystics, then of course you find unity."[82]

In an address to his senior murids, Pir Vilayat went on to describe the perils of applying the name Sufism to the universalist teachings of his father:

> Now we are in a very vulnerable position because we say that we represent all traditions; on the other hand, I think that the teaching of Murshid is certainly not syncretism, is not just a synthesis of all the teachings that came before. There are some ideas that are very new. And then secondly we use the word Sufism which is really very debatable nowadays. We get attacked all the time. I get terribly rude letters by people purporting to speak in the name of Sufism. And it is generally just Islam, but they think it is Sufism. They condemn me for being a fake and using false pretensions that I am a Sufi. . . . The letters get quite aggressive.[83]

As an example, Pir Vilayat mentioned an episode that occurred during the early 1970s, when a group of conservative Sufis, apparently from Africa, attended one of his talks and got up and walked out as soon as he mentioned Buddha. They waited outside during the rest of his talk and then approached Pir Vilayat as he left, denouncing him and then repeating as they left, "We'll get you!" Pir Vilayat stood his ground and tried to explain to them that he was a recognized murshid in a Sufi Order from India where they adopt a more universal approach, but to no avail. "So I know that there's two totally opposite opinions about this," he concluded. "There are books which represent Sufism as being essentially the mysticism of Islam. And there are other books which show that it goes far beyond Islam."[84] Pir Vilayat went on to elaborate on the unique approach of the Sufis in the Indian subcontinent:

In Pakistan . . . which is a Muslim country, in the north, in Sind, there is a very large group of Hindus who are Sufis. And their name is the group of Abdul Latif.* Now it's true that he was a Muslim himself, but most of his pupils were Hindus. And they do not say "La illaha illa'llah, Muhammada Rasulillah," they just say "La illaha illa'llah hu," And they don't say the five prayers a day. And yet they are Sufis. So it isn't true to say that you can't be a Sufi if you are not a Muslim. I attended a lot of meetings of a very great murshid in Bareilly in India. His name was Aziz Mehrzam, a great murshid. I must say when I think of him he was like a king, he was a great being. And he had thousands of murids. And many of his murids were Hindus, Christians, all kinds. So this is not true. But it is true in the Arab countries through North Africa and in Syria and so on and so forth . . . [but] it doesn't apply in India.[85]

Pir Vilayat recounted that when Suleyman Loras Dede (1904-1985), the sheikh of Konya, Turkey, the Mevlevi leader who first brought the whirling dervishes to America, visited the Abode, the sheikh confided to him, "You know, I daren't come out with how we feel about the universality." Pir Vilayat added, "That's why he's so enchanted to find that we do." Both Ibn al-'Arabi and Jalaluddin Rumi have poems that say something very similar. In both they declare, "I am not a Hindu, not Muslim, etc. because I belong to the religion of the heart."[86]

a PIR VILAYAT RADIO INTERVIEW *with* LEX HIXON

In 1979, radio host Lex Hixon interviewed Pir Vilayat for his *In the Spirit* program on WBAI, broadcasting from New York City. Lex had interviewed Pir Vilayat previously and the two shared

---

* Followers of the Sindhi mystic poet, Shah Abdul Latif Bhittai (1689–1752), whom Seyyed Hossein Nasr described as a "direct emanation of Rūmī's spirituality in South Asia."

a common love for many different religious traditions but differed in the way they expressed and practiced their universality.
Prior to this interview, Lex had just returned from Istanbul after
spending a month with the Halveti-Jerrahi Sufi grand-sheikh,
Muzaffer Ozak, and his dervishes. There, Lex had been tremendously impressed with the way Islamic prayers and principles
were integrated in that order with Sufi mystical teachings and
practices, such as the standing zikr ceremony. Yet his joyful
Turkish encounter with Sufism, as lived in full integration with
mainstream Islam, had challenged some of his previously held
assumptions about universality, pluralism and the esoteric path,
presenting him with new questions. He told Pir Vilayat, "I, myself, in some way, have been drawn to try to accept the various
traditions and not just study them from the outside but somehow merge with them in a real way. But my faith in this process
was shaken this summer when I realized that perhaps one really
needed to be rooted in a single tradition in order to really do it
authentically." In light of this, he asked Pir Vilayat to speak to
this dilemma of deeply practicing only one religion in its mystical depth as opposed to involvement in several paths.

Pir Vilayat responded by noting that this represented a matter of conscience in which each person must decide for themselves how they feel most comfortable. He offered an analogy of
transplanting a plant from one country, in which it grows naturally, to another country with a different environment and noted that "scientists are now finding that when one does, they do
undergo some kind of mutation in order to adapt themselves."

Pir Vilayat pointed out that, while most Muslims observe the
external forms of the religion—the shariat—mystics such as Ibn
al-'Arabi, while basically conforming to the religious background
of their culture, generally "have their roots in the tradition but
they grow the branches of their tree into further dimensions."
He quoted the Islamic saying that "the real Islam is in exile,"*
which he understands as referring to the exile of the deeper aspect of Islam that is beyond the formalism of the shariat.

---

*   An apparent paraphrase of the hadith of the Prophet: "Islam was
born in exile and will return to exile. Blessed are the exiled."

Lex noted that, in what he experienced in Istanbul, the outer form and inner form were so harmoniously intertwined and
done by the sheikh "with such great joy and ecstasy that it doesn't
seem to make any sense to call it a mechanical outer form anymore." Pir Vilayat responded, "When it's the expression of an inner experience then of course it's very, very beautiful. Actually,
my father Hazrat Inayat Khan, when he was asked something
like this, said 'There is not one drop of blood in my veins that
is not Muslim.'" Pir Vilayat mentioned that "a lot of Muslims
think it's being untrue to the Prophet to speak of the unity of
all the prophets, but it's right there in the Qur'an."* Lex agreed,
adding that also in the Qur'an there is "the tremendous feeling
for the creation and its unity. It seems to me a wonderful basis
for science and for deep scientific investigation of the spirit."

Pir Vilayat added: "That's the thing that I've been underlin-
ing more and more—an accent which I find outlined in Hazrat
Inayat Khan's teaching—an accent on the importance of what
is achieved in the world, whereas of course the Hindu and
Buddhist teachings were very much oriented towards samadhi
or the nirvana state, which is beyond life, which is transcendental." Pir Vilayat said that the most important and personally
meaningful thing Hazrat Inayat Khan speaks about is

> experiencing the divine consciousness, or getting into
> the divine mind experiencing conditions in creation,
> which is diametrically the opposite to samadhi, where
> you reach the original state before creation. But it doesn't
> prevent me from still appreciating what Buddhism has
> to teach. I think one can show great interest in the mean-
> ing of life and what is achieved and at the same time
> experience detachment. . . . I've often found that peo-
> ple who are too eclectic lose their sense of loyalty. And
> I have sometimes found mystics who might be consid-
> ered to be narrow-minded. . . . I would say that some
> people can reach the top of the mountain better when

*   For example, verse 2:285 of Qur'an.

they are following a well-defined path, but I would rather sometimes leave the trodden paths and go through the brush and reach the top using perhaps paths that are not too well-defined.

Lex raised the point that each of us approach spirituality from certain background assumptions from our own culture, which we may not even realize is a bias; for instance, in the West, scientific and humanist values, as well as various forms of Jewish and Christian thinking. Lex said that he grew up as an agnostic with nonreligious parents, and then, in his early twenties, met Swami Nikhilananda of the Ramakrishna Order with whom he studied Vedanta for many years. He said he had recently realized that maybe Ramakrishna—who was a sort of all-embracing Sufi—was, in a way, the background tradition in which he himself was rooted, which may have subtly affected the way he was seeing the other traditions.

Lex mentioned that Swami Vivekananda had come to the West to the Parliament of the World's Religions in 1893, less than two decades before Hazrat Inayat Khan came to the West in 1910, and asked Pir Vilayat whether perhaps his father may have heard of this and, in turn, been inspired by Vivekananda to also come to the West. Pir Vilayat heartily agreed, adding that his father had even given him a picture of Ramakrishna to hang on his wall. They agreed that perhaps only in India could this harmony of religion have arisen during that time.

Lex asked Pir Vilayat whether he felt there should be people that uphold the major traditions or whether he thought the traditions would somehow fall away. When Pir Vilayat answered that he felt that the traditions were bound to fall away, Lex observed that this was a point where they definitely disagreed. Pir added, "I certainly wouldn't encourage people to leave their religion and believe in all religions together, and so on, or a new synthetic religion or anything like that. No, but I believe it is bound to happen."

The interview went on to examine the question of whether, as Lex contended, the exoteric religious forms and structures are an indispensable support structure for the deeper mystical aspects, with the religions containing "the highest possibility that human beings have," or whether the forms, rules, and religious dogmas are basically outer restrictions like those a parent gives a child, which are primarily "for the masses," as Pir Vilayat was suggesting.

Pir Vilayat opined that while there were some mystics who could experience ecstasy—for instance, without needing the sacrament of communion—for most people, the religious structure, with all its rules, was indeed necessary and that this is what he meant by saying that "religion was for the masses." However, he felt that too often these rules were enforced by fear, by a threat that if you didn't follow them you would go to hell. He summed up his position:

> What I'm saying is that, as time goes on, people are giving up forms, although they have value. . . . Why? Well, because we have given up whatever it takes to make a cathedral like Notre Dame. They are building other churches and so on which are technically wonderful in their way, but they are unable to do the same now as they were able to do then. And I think the same thing is probably happening with forms. Even in the Catholic Church they are changing their forms. That is because—well, the forms have their value and one shouldn't devalue the forms— but they do have to change, they do have to evolve.

Moving on, Lex asked Pir Vilayat about the nature of "the Message" of Hazrat Inayat Khan. Was it his own message, or the prophetic message or something else? Pir Vilayat clarified that he called it the "Message *in* our time" rather than the "Message *of* our time." Lex probed, "It's not referring to some message of the past—it's a totally contemporary message—coming down right now?" Pir Vilayat answered, "Yes, but it is the same message as ever; but it is always moving ahead." Lex clarified: "It's one message that always comes down?" When Pir affirmed that it was, Lex exclaimed: "I like that!"

Pir replied: "That's my credo!" Then he added that when his father was asked

"What is the message in our time?" he said, "It is the awakening of humanity to the consciousness of the divinity in man." In other words, that we've reached the point now when we can't go on any longer simply thinking of ourselves as being human, as a separate entity and a fragment of the totality, and limited by I-ness, but we have to be aware of the divine and universal dimensions of our being. That's the holistic message.

Lex concluded the show by reading a paragraph by the great Sufi metaphysician, Ibn al-'Arabi, and inviting Pir Vilayat to offer his own reflections on the passage, which he did beautifully, ending the interview on a most convivial note. Pir Vilayat then led a short zikr and Lex concluded the interview by telling Pir Vilayat: "There's not a drop of blood in you that is not Islam!"[87]

WORDS FROM *a* UNIVERSAL WORSHIP SERVICE

Pir Vilayat Khan conducting a Universal Worship Service at the Abode in 1989 (photo by the author)

When the Universal Worship service began in 1921, many of the murids who attended and participated as officiants in the services had roots in the Anglican Church, where quiet, dignified services and prayers were the model. As such, the form of the service—prayers, a reading from the world's scriptures by an officiant wearing a black robe, followed by a sermon and a closing benediction—in some respects, conformed to the model with which people were familiar. Like other forms which evolve with time and changing cultural expectations, the approach to the Universal Worship changed somewhat in Pir Vilayat's time so that it usually incorporated music from the various world's traditions, either recorded, performed, or sung as a congregation, and sometimes included spiritual dance. So while the form of the service was usually preserved, Pir Vilayat typically incorporated music and some dance when he led the service, often ending with free dancing or whirling to the joyful music of Bach, or perhaps Sufi music, which had the result of lifting everyone's consciousness through active participation in the glorious strains of the music.

Pir Vilayat also updated the prayers used in the service in order to avoid exclusively male gender phrases, so that, for instance, "Raise us above the distinctions and differences which divide men" was altered to end with "divide us." Pir Vilayat said that while his father's words should be preserved in tact as faithfully as possible, he felt that if Inayat Khan were alive today he would update the gender language in keeping with the times. (Two decades later, in 2016, the first in a series of carefully researched Centennial Editions of Inayat Khan's talks was released by Suluk Press, which sensitively updates the English usage and, as far as possible, avoids gender-specific language.)

In September of 1984, at the end of a powerful retreat for representatives (center leaders) at the Abode, Pir Vilayat led a Universal Worship service in which he minimized the use of forms, emphasized music and dance, and gave an inspiring talk, which included guided attunements to the spirit of the various religions and their founders in lieu of readings from scriptures. I have chosen to include here his opening impromptu remarks because they convey so clearly the spirit of Pir Vilayat, a Gemini who was always in search of new dimensions of consciousness and updated, innovative ways of expressing the inexpressible.

As he would sometimes say in jest: "The New Age is already old hat!" Here then, is the opening portion of his talk:

> We cannot just continue worshiping the way we worshiped before, because things move ahead. We don't think the same way as we thought a hundred years ago, two hundred years ago—and yet, organized religion is still doing the same old things. We can't compose as Schubert composed or Beethoven composed or Mozart or Bach composed—we can—there's somebody who does it, but it's an anachronism. It doesn't ring true. It doesn't correspond with the feeling of our time. And then, is "the Message" a "mishmash," as somebody said in *Time* magazine about the Cosmic Celebration? [Laughter] I've never forgotten it. [More laughter] Well, you know, one can learn from one's critics. Is it a collage? Well, you get a little bit of Hinduism and a little Buddhism and a little bit of Zoroastrians and then stuck together with some Judaism and Christianity and Islam, and then we say that's the Message?
>
> We are presented with a problem of how we are going to build a temple, the Universel. We say it's the temple of all religions. Is it a collage of all religions—is that what it is? You go to Jerusalem and see all these religions all fighting together, each one wanting their space. Is that the future of religion in our time? Get them to agree? Is that where religion is at? And here we have the whole problem—how is that temple going to be? Is at just going to be just the symbols of all religions? Is that the temple of the New Age? The New Wave?
>
> Here we have the whole problem of art—the artist. I went to an exhibition of modern art in Paris. This wonderful woman is organizing, finding genius wherever there is, and there's a tremendous amount of genius and talent all over the world—getting it all together, and exposing people to these new works of art. And of course, they have nothing in common with the art of the past. . . .

I asked her, "Is that your conception of art? Is it to make *tabula rasa?*" *Tabula rasa* means to eradicate everything that came before you and just start anew. And she said, "Yes." I remember Stravinsky telling me once, telling us at a class, that if you want to compose, don't listen to the music of Schubert or Chopin, or whatever. Never listen to any music past Bach. Bach is the last—Monteverdi, all you like, before but not after Bach. And he was saying, "Well, the reason is because one gets influenced by [them]. One is still thinking in the past and you have to think forward, and therefore, you have to, let's say, eradicate your predecessors so that you can move forward."

I've been thinking about this a lot, because it has to do with the meaning of the word, the Message. You know that in Coventry, for example, there was a cathedral that was in ruins because of the war. It was broken down, destroyed during the war, and the architects built a cathedral right next to it. But they built the new cathedral in such a way that the new cathedral looks upon the old one, but is not the old one—it's still something new. Somehow, the old one is kind of integrated in[to] the new, but it was done with so much sensitivity. And like, for example, Notre Dame is part of the new Paris, and if you had Notre Dame in New York, you wouldn't be destroying it to build a modern building.

So that what I'm saying is the past does continue to live in us. If we want to move forward, we have to carry the past with us, instead of abandoning it. We step on the shoulders of our predecessors, and that's why Buddha is still part of our being—not just Buddhism, if you like. Buddhism, well, is a system of teaching and is helpful to some people and some people can't go along with it, and so on—it's the same with all the different "isms." But Buddha is really part of our being. . . . We don't only inherit from our ancestors' bodies, but we inherit from our ancestors' souls. So that you could say that something of Buddha we've inherited in our being; and the same is true of Christ and the same is true of Krishna and Shiva, and Abraham and all.

Well, perhaps one of the symptoms of our being caught up in our sclerosis is that we still always think of those beings as past. We think of Buddha as walking in the solitude or sitting under the tree. We think of Abraham with a big beard and a tent and sheep and camels. And we think of Christ and all those things in history—historical Christ being crucified, and the Sermon on the Mount—all these things. We're still living in the past! The priests are still talking about Jesus doing this and that and the other thing. And Muhammad! Muslims saying, "Muhammad said to do this," or "You've got to do it because Muhammad did it." People are living right back in the past! If Muhammad were living today, he wouldn't say cut off the hand of one who is stealing. In fact, he might be the president of the commission on nonviolence. And Buddha may very well be married, and he might very well have been a psychotherapist. And Abraham may well not have a beard. And Christ—I think he might be in San Salvador in the concentration camps. He might not be accepted in the church because he wasn't a Christian. All these ideas that we have about the masters of the past—totally ideas! We're living in ideas instead of reality! And all that in the name of religion!

How can we carry the past into the future? Finding new ways and yet still honoring the quintessence of what is brought, but not limiting it with our little puny ideas. It's such a great task that I don't feel up to it. And when I stand here at this little altar and I think to myself, "Well, yes, it's rather sweet." [Laughter] It's very endearing—we try to represent here some candles that stand for the different religions and here we are, hoping for some miracle to happen. And we're caught right in the here and now and forgetting the cosmic celebration in the heavens! And we forget to relate between the heavens and the earth—I don't say the cosmic celebration is just in the heavens. It includes the whole earth, of course, but I don't see how repeating words in the prayer, if we're just repeating words, is going to make us participate in the cosmic celebration; or just doing all the things that one is supposed to do in the ceremony.

Now, it's true that when I wrote the "Cosmic Celebration," what I was saying is that what the prophets and masters and saints were trying to do was to remind us, produce human activities which are reminiscent of what we do remember of the cosmic celebrations in the heavens—that's true. And since we forgot that was the original reason why these ceremonies are made, we forget some of the aspects of those ceremonies. Like, for example, in the old churches in Spain there was—people go on a procession before coming into the church! Now that is reminiscent of the great processions in the heavens! We eliminate that because it's not rational, so then, the minister gives a talk, and that's what it gets reduced to in the end.

A brilliant mind gets a lot of people. Maybe it's the new wave—I don't know—it's possible. Rev. Schultz in the Crystal Cathedral in Los Angeles—I don't know how many people—10,000 or something—all in awe before this brilliant mind communicating something beyond the mind. Maybe that's the new form—I don't know. But I can only say that we are in search of something beyond the mind. If the mind does communicate ecstasy and glorification, yes, then we place the mind at the service of something greater. Otherwise, one gets entrapped in the mind. And sometimes, bypassing the mind is a better way! Not speaking—dancing! Yes. Dancing. Chanting, dancing—it's a way of bypassing the mind. Beauty—looking at crystals. Looking at the atoms and the planets—it's a way of bypassing the mind. Getting into our emotions—the depth, the sacredness of the emotions that are surging in the depths of the human heart—that's something sacred, it's something beautiful.

That's where we find God—not on an altar! So you see my quandary, standing here in front of this altar.[88]

On other occasions, in speaking of the symbolism of the altar, Pir Vilayat referred to Pierre Tielhard de Chardin's altar in nature when the Catholic priest found himself in the wilderness in China, on a paleontological expedition in the 1920s, without the accoutrements of the mass. Inspired by the magnificence of the surrounding natural landscape, he improvised, affirming, as Pir Vilayat paraphrased it, that the earth was the altar, the host the way that matter was transmuted into spirit, and the wine was the way suffering is transmuted into joy. Below is a partial quote from Teilhard de Chardin's *Mass of the World*:

Since once again, Lord—though this time not in the forests of the Aisne but in the steppes of Asia—I have neither bread, nor wine, nor altar, I will raise myself beyond these symbols, up to the pure majesty of the real itself; I, your priest, will make the whole earth my altar and on it will offer you all the labors and sufferings of the world. Over there, on the horizon, the sun has just touched with light the outermost fringe of the eastern sky. Once again, beneath this moving sheet of fire, the living surface of the earth wakes and trembles, and once again begins its fearful travail. I will place on my paten, O God, the harvest to be won by this renewal of labor. Into my chalice I shall pour all the sap which is to be pressed out this day from the earth's fruits. My paten and my chalice are the depths of a soul laid widely open to all the forces which in a moment will rise up from every corner of the earth and converge upon the Spirit. Grant me the remembrance and the mystic presence of all those whom the light is now awakening to the new day. This bread, our toil, is of itself, I know, but an immense fragmentation; this wine, our pain, is no more, I know, than a draught that dissolves. Yet in the very depths of this formless mass you have implanted—and this I am sure of, for I sense it—a desire, irresistible, hallowing, which makes us cry out, believer and unbeliever alike: "Lord, make us one."[89]

PIR VILAYAT'S VISIT *to* NASHVILLE

In early November 1984, a month after this Universal Worship service, Pir Vilayat came to Nashville, Tennessee, at our invitation, in order to hold a day-long seminar at a local Unity Church. He stayed at our house for a week and was later joined by his then personal secretary and nurse, Mariel Walters. This gave us an opportunity to spend significant alone time with Pir Vilayat and get to know him better, share meals and conversation. We were used to seeing him in a retreat setting, wearing Indian robes, so it was an adjustment to see him in more casual attire.

We soon found that Pir Vilayat not only had a sense of humor, but he was often full of mirthful jests. To give but a few examples, when he was going to borrow one of our cars to travel with his secretary on a day trip to Chattanooga, to hang-glide off the mountain peaks (at age 68!) and horseback ride, he turned toward me with an impish expression and said, "You know, I used to have somewhat of a reputation as a daredevil driver!" When we took Pir Vilayat to the Unity Church to give the seminar, we located a room where he could relax and meditate before starting. But for some reason, the room we were advised to use for this was lined with padding all around the walls, perhaps for soundproofing. When my wife, Sylvia ushered Pir Vilayat into the room, he looked around and drolly asked, "Is this how you treat your Pir? Putting him away in a padded cell?" We all had a laugh at this.

On a more serious note, Pir Vilayat also conveyed to us his own deep feeling of connection with the being of Christ. He said that just outside of Paris, in Passy, there is a church which has on its altar a very special statue which portrays Christ dancing for joy on top of the cross on which Jesus is being crucified. The image represents the eternal soul of Christ, who is beyond death and who could not in reality be killed on a cross. Pir Vilayat felt that this, far better than the usual sad image of the crucifixion, conveyed the real spirit of the resurrection that is at the heart of the Christian story.

During Pir Vilayat's visit, my wife recounted to him a recent dream in which he had appeared. He listened with interest as she told him how she had dreamed she was among a group of Sufis who were sitting on an idyllic grassy hillside during a springtime meditation retreat that he was leading. In the dream, Pir Vilayat had just instructed everyone to close their eyes and meditate in the silence. So she closed her eyes and meditated for a while, but then decided that she could better enter into the spirit of beauty and joy inherent in the meditation by blowing soap bubbles into the air. Opening a bottle of liquid soap she had brought along, she soon became absorbed in watching dozens of floating iridescent bubbles, shimmering with rainbow hues in the morning sun. Then she thought, "What if Pir Vilayat opens his eyes and disapproves of this?"

At this point in the retelling of the dream, I watched Pir Vilayat's expression change from bright anticipation to a look of mild concern over where the dream was going, as Sylvia emphasized the worry she had in the dream, that maybe Pir Vilayat might think she should have just followed the instructions to meditate with eyes closed and would therefore disapprove of her actions. Then she revealed that in the dream, Pir Vilayat did open his eyes, saw the bubbles, and with an expression of childish delight exclaimed, "O how beautiful!" after which she woke up. At this point, I looked back over at the real Pir Vilayat and saw an expression of relief on his face, which quickly lit up as he affirmed, "Yes! That's exactly what I would have done! In fact I might have enjoined everyone to get up and enjoy blowing bubbles and dancing for joy!"

a PEAK EXPERIENCE

Throughout the late 1980s, I continued to attend Pir Vilayat's retreats for representatives, and various trainings in order to lead retreats, dances and the Universal Worship service. I also began to lead occasional Sufi group retreats in Tennessee. One retreat I attended with Pir Vilayat was especially noteworthy because, during that retreat, I had a very powerful "peak experience" (to use Maslow's term) which, inasmuch as possible, I will attempt to share, although the experience was really beyond anything words could adequately convey. Perhaps it might best be characterized as an epiphany of the higher Self, or higher level of soul, for lack of a better term. In Sufi terms, it could be called a *tejelli* (a divine unveiling or epiphany) and a *hal*, a temporary mystic state of disclosure.

My sense is that the experience was triggered by the orientation of the Sufi teachings I was involved in, particularly the whole thrust of Hazrat Inayat Khan's teaching about awakening to the divinity of the human soul and finding God within the heart. Had I been, say, doing Buddhist *zazen*, the nature of the spiritual breakthrough might have been very different. Or, if I had experienced an epiphany of this kind within the Christian tradition, perhaps I might have interpreted it as an encounter with the Holy Spirit. In this regard, I am reminded of that marvelous *hadith* of the Prophet Muhammad, in which he recounted receiving the Divine disclosure: "I appear to My servants as they expect Me to appear."[90] Yet, this peak experience wasn't really like anything I could have anticipated. Through various samadhi practices, involving long, still meditations on formlessness, I had previously experienced what might be called a state of "no self," a blissful timeless and spaceless sensation, with no boundaries to consciousness, with no observing self and no real activity of thought for a time. However, this experience was very different. It was very dynamic and powerful, and yet there was some vestige of an observing witness which didn't seem to be the habitual ego-self.

The setting was Whidby Island, near Seattle, Washington, on June 15, 1989, toward the end of a weeklong group Sufi retreat with Pir Vilayat in which we had been doing quite a few powerful practices. In the morning, we met with Pir Vilayat and received some instructions. We were told to go off on our own and make 1,000 repetitions of zikr—significantly more repetitions than we were normally prescribed. Pir Vilayat mentioned that on his longer retreats, he had repeated the zikr thousands of times; it had been very powerful for him, and therefore he wished for his representatives to also go deeply into this practice, going beyond the mind through chanting.

The Chishti zikr which Pir Vilayat taught uses the words, "*La ilaha illallah Hu*," which means "Nothing exists except the One." To paraphrase Ibn al-'Arabi's explanation of its esoteric meaning: "No ego and no separate individual really exists, or ever has existed; there is only the One Source Who experiences the physical world through us and through the rest of creation." Therefore, in the repetition of zikr, one is first saying "no" to the idol, or the illusion of the separate ego self that one has built up; then one allows the divine energies, the One Reality, to be affirmed in its place. One is sweeping and cleansing the heart of the limited, small self, in order to empty, purify and make the heart a worthy throne for the Divine.

The traditional head movements of the zikr, as done in the Chishti lineage, involves a counterclockwise circle of the head as one says "*la ilaha*," after which the head comes forcefully down to the chest (third eye to solar plexus) on "*illa*" (shattering the ego, the limited illusion of the separate self); then the head rises heavenward without effort (as though one is being lifted or resurrected by the divine will) on "*'llah Hu*." Of course, Pir Vilayat had many variations on the practice of zikr—the zikr of love, the zikr of freedom, the zikr of the broken heart, the zikr of power, the zikr of majesty, and so on. In this case, Pir Vilayat had given instructions to imagine a crescent moon of receptivity to the divine action as the head circles from left to right and up, then experience the star of divine power in the heart and solar plexus region as the head descends to the chest, and finally one raises the head in glorification. The practice may be done slowly or quite rapidly, but in either case the head movements powerfully involve the body in the practice.

According to Puran Bair, the co-founder of the Institute for Applied Meditation on the Heart, it has been confirmed in laboratory studies that the head (and upper torso) movements of the

Chisti zikr churn the bioelectromagnetic currents around the heart. With the counterclockwise circular movements of zikr, these currents form a vortex of energy that corkscrews within, penetrating, then opening up the heart in a powerful way. I had done the practice of zikr for years, yet I wasn't prepared for the intensity I would experience as I went back to my tent and began the 1,000 repetitions that morning.

Gradually, toward the end of the repetitions of the zikr, I began to feel a very powerful being or presence emerge, which took over my voice and consciousness as I continued the intense chanting. Perhaps it could be said that the Higher Self began to come through as the chanter, as though aroused from a long, hibernating slumber and now trying to break through the thick veils of limited human understanding and heedlessness. This being felt very much like myself, but on a far more exalted and impersonal level than my usual sense of self. It was bursting with radiant power, overflowing surety, fearlessness and independence, seemingly eternal, deathless and immortal, and imbued with a shatteringly vast wisdom and cosmic self-realization that far surpassed any limited human knowledge. My chest region became intensely alive, expansive, and overflowing with presence, and my eyes felt radiant and wide as saucers. My familiar everyday identity was annihilated for a time, as though it were an inconsequential rag which had been cast aside in a heap, its meager knowledge absolutely dwarfed by this far greater, seemingly all-knowing entity. As Lex Hixon (Sheikh Nur) later observed when I described it to him, my description of the abandoning of the small self was reminiscent of the discarded garments of Christ left on the floor of the empty tomb after he resurrected.

Through all of this, there was still a small portion of my consciousness, impassively witnessing this. Through it, there was a sense that somehow the divine presence (or perhaps a great Cosmic Individual or powerful angelic being who is one localization of the One Being) was now awakening within, and this being had incarnated at my birth as myself, as this limited human being on Earth, yet up till now had not revealed itself. (My sense, after the fact, was that likely all humans have such a higher enlightened self but do not usually become so dramatically aware of it.)

I had the sense that, previous to my human birth, an arrangement had been set up by which a magnificently powerful and wise divine soul agreed to enter the limited and forgetful condition of a human person, with the goal of arousing self-awakening under adverse earthly conditions. But until its awakening, in its absence, the unreal lower self and personality had been built up as an effigy, as a necessary substitute for the Higher Self or "real I" (to use Gurdjieff's expression). On this day, it only showed itself very briefly—but in time, and with the lower level's maturity, it may come through in other forms or realizations, perhaps in a more subtly integrated manner.

I was particularly impressed with how, in relation to this awakening God-realized intelligence, all other mundane human knowledge and philosophical and religious speculations, seemed very banal, paltry, and tentative, based on best guesswork in the absence of direct understanding. Pir Vilayat had once told us that at Oxford they had a saying, "A philosopher is like a blind man in a dark room looking for a black cat that isn't there." This seemed to aptly describe the level of normal human cognition compared to the heightened cosmic awareness that was coming through. It wasn't discursive knowledge of facts and figures that this being possessed, but far beyond that, a profound understanding, presence and certitude about one's nature and place in the cosmos and an devastating appreciation of just how little the limited human brain can know of its own origin and the nature of consciousness, except through the awakening of the divine wisdom and presence within.

At the peak of the experience, there was a sense of being in touch with a higher sphere of intelligence and meaningfulness, of having access to vast knowledge which clarified all things—this in contrast to my usual sense of always seeking knowledge and answers to the great questions of life. Suddenly, the seeker identity was obsolete—for a brief time, the veils had been lifted and there were no more unanswered questions—one just felt intensely alive, amazed, powerful, and spiritually immortal. I felt a great certainty that this higher self existed far beyond the confines of the physical body—almost remote from human mundane concerns, and beyond gender differentiation. It didn't seem to have any judgments or moral agenda, but instead was far beyond that.

Soon it occurred to the fragment of witness consciousness left in me to consider what course of action could befit this state. If, at least temporarily, there are no more questions, nothing else to seek, then what? What needs to be done in this world in such an awakened state? The wordless realization came: to engage in service and help those who have not yet awakened, the bodhisattva ideal of Buddhism. The awakened Self does not mind putting the body to work, in contrast with the usual lower self's predisposition to comfort and ease. Seeing this, in light of a more awakened state of consciousness, I immediately resolved to go and work cleaning up in the kitchen, remembering that they had announced earlier that kitchen duty volunteers were welcome.

At first, when I started to leave my tent, the power of this presence was so intense that I felt almost as though waves of power were coming out of my eyes. I saw some others milling about in the distance, but I didn't want to approach or look at anyone while my gaze felt so intense. I remembered hearing how Hazrat Inayat Khan had said that at times, he had to veil the power of his gaze from other people. Gradually, that level of intensity subsided, and I realized the presence was beginning to fade, but it lingered to some degree as a kind of perfume or powerful memory for days, even months thereafter. I walked a short distance to the rustic camp kitchen area, offered my services and washed dishes in a state of great joy—having found and no longer seeking higher realization—glad to just do, to be, and to help, however small the task.

When I later recounted this to Sheikh Nur, he felt this joyous service aspect was very important, noting that I didn't decide to start a movement dedicated to service or something like that, but just went immediately to help out with a task near at hand. He felt this was how Mother Teresa began her ministry—not by first trying to build an organization of workers, but by just starting to help one ailing person on the sidewalk, then another, and people were spontaneously moved and inspired to join her work.

While the experience was fresh, I wrote down what I could. I remembered how Alan Watts had described such an experience as more common in the East, where the Divine is conceptualized less as a separate being outside oneself and where the response might be: "So you discovered that you're God. Congratulations! *Tat twam asi* (That thou art)." Upon reflection, I was initially troubled by the seeming polytheistic implications of my experience—as though what had appeared was one of many gods, or divine entities, as in the polytheistic Greek or Hindu tradition, rather than the pure sense of Oneness that perhaps I had expected in such an experience of awakening. Yet this presence really felt like it *was* myself, only at a much higher, more awakened level, rather than some deity who was separate from me.

Soon I concluded that it was best to think of it as something like God, or the divine energy, experienced as funneled down and focalized in the individual human mind and heart (part of the sensation had been of vast power localized in the chest area), a presence which had some vestige of individuality, but was still an inseparable part of the Oneness, the Totality. I also realized that spiritual inflation is a tremendous possible pitfall when the lord or god within awakens. (As Pir Vilayat says: "The danger of the ego is always lurking.") Yet further, it seems that each being is a potential god-self and may attain to realization of that state eventually—each body and mind being a veil over the great One who has manifested in that form. In association with this god-self experience, I am reminded of *Dhul Jalal wal Ikram*—the Arabic divine name which Pir Vilayat associates with the magnificent lord of one's being, and Krishna's appearance before Arjuna as the being of splendor, and that which is called *Atman* in the East—all names for something vast and ineffably mysterious which is unnamable yet powerfully real.

That afternoon I sent a message to Pir Vilayat briefly describing what I had experienced and asking some questions about it.

The next morning, I received word prior to a group session with Pir Vilayat that he would speak to my experience in the talk in the form of more general remarks. Here is the pertinent part of what he said:

> It is more accurate to call it "everlasting" rather than one's "eternal" being. Murshid [Hazrat Inayat Khan] distinguishes these two words carefully. Do not think of that model as static or sclerosed so it can't grow. It is continually recurrently remodeling itself—because its time pattern is different from that of the transient, perishable body. It's not transient. It's self-generating and motivating and regenerating. I suppose one could say that it's not subject to the arrow of time, which is called "becoming"—that's why we call it "eternal"—but it conforms to another time relationship which is moving from transcendence into transiency. One's real being is much more impersonal than one thought—it's cosmic. . . .
>
> What is in the trunk of the tree moves further and further out the branches and into the tips and leaves of the limbs. Ibn al-'Arabi speaks of a different sort of cause behind the cause than the usual mechanistic billiard ball model. Rather, one is moving causally from transcendence into transiency (the software working down into the hardware). The practice [of] *Majid-Mawjud* helps. * There is a further stage of bewilderment of that splendor which is trying to break through down into the nitty-gritty. And it is only the ecstasy of that splendor which will give us an insight into the purposefulness of everything. Ultimately, all experience is self-discovery.
>
> Just as the seed (and plant) takes in itself sun, water, earth, and air to grow, so are we transformers of energy, taking in impressions, food, emotions, etc., and using and converting them, transmuting as catalysts and fuel for the growth and unfoldment of our real being in the

---

*　　*Majid* means majesty; *mawjud* existentiation, groundedness.

midst of the transient realm—transforming the physical world into psyche, into the expression of our being. The energy we draw in from the universe, outer space—like light photosynthesized—is also being transmuted into matter. One can also, [through] the trees in the forest as they reach up, feel the One Being coming through with divine nostalgia, though they are limited by their tree-hood nature. A very small fraction of the richness of the whole can come through them, but more so in humanity—more of the soul or intention or thinking of God.

In Sufism, there are two poles of your being: [first], the hidden treasure [the unknown, unmanifest part]—the latent potentialities waiting to be discovered, unfurled. This is God in the beginning of time, or pre-eternity, *Azaliat*. Then [the other pole is] the Lord, or *Dhul Jelal wal Ikram*—God made a reality as the Lord (as You, or as any master). In Hinduism, *Brahma* or *Purusha* becomes *Ishvara*: God becomes the Lord—the progressive, dynamic aspect in time. In Islam, there is the feudal scheme [of sovereignty-suzerainty] in which the human is the divine vice-regent. What is preserved after death is the wisdom, the know-how, the aptitude that has been gained—the resurrection of the essence of one's being, enhanced through having made use of the physical body and its earthly experience.

It would be good to have a seventh stage in the alchemical process of resurrection. The sixth is already acknowledging it when it says: "the materialization of spirit and the spiritualization of matter." Since the physical plane is transient, it is not really the final purpose of life to incarnate God or the spiritual into this realm (and then to have it disperse). The final step would be the eternalization of the essence, resurrected beyond the transiency of the material world. "Die now"* and resurrect now, meaning: die to the old being you thought

---

*   "Die before death," a *hadith* attributed to the Prophet Muhammad.

you were, distill, and identify with that which is beyond physical death.[91]

I later found these quotes from Hazrat Inayat Khan relevant to the emergent quality of divinity in humanity:

> The more deeply we study matter, the more proofs shall we find of intelligence working through the whole process of continual unfoldment. There is a gradual awakening of matter to become conscious and through the awakening of consciousness, matter becomes fully intelligent in man. In matter, life unfolds, discovers and realizes the consciousness that has been, so to speak, buried in it for thousands of years.[92]
>
> The seed out of which the trunk, branches, leaves, flowers and fruit are made arises again at the end of the cycle. The same God, so little of whose perfection manifested in the plant, arises again and again in its pursuit of excellence trying to emerge as perfectly as possible in the midst of human imperfection.[93]

Years later, Pir Vilayat would record in his 1999 book, *Awakening*, a retreat experience of his own that bore some resemblance to the one I have described. In his description, Pir Vilayat begins by mentioning the words of the early Sufi master, Bayazid Bastami who wrote of seeing behind the veil of effigies to the Divine Reality hidden behind them. Pir Vilayat then goes on to say:

> Ultimately, we may reach a stage in our meditations where we discover a direct intuition of meaningfulness unmediated by physical phenomena. Hazrat Inayat Khan says that when intelligence is confronted with an object it becomes consciousness, and when it is voided of any content it returns to its ground, which is intelligence. Attainment of this "spiritual intelligence" is the ultimate realization of the mystics. Sufis

call this state of consciousness Jabarut, the ground out of which consciousness emerges. . . . So the mind, stripped of the distraction of transient thoughts is infused with an inborn sense of meaningfulness. This transcendent faculty appears only when one has given up trying to sort things out in a habitual fashion.

Once while on retreat in the Alps, I had just such a breakthrough experience—one that was dramatically reflected in the weather and surrounding landscape. After a stormy night in the mountains, precariously sheltered beneath the roof of a shepherd's shed, I observed the dark clouds and heard the thunderclaps gradually receding into the distance, swept away by a raging wind. As if in sympathetic resonance, my consciousness began to melt away, scattered into an infinite edgeless Universe. . . . Vanishing along with the storm were my concepts about the world, the Cosmos, my personal circumstances, unresolved problems, values, appropriate or inappropriate actions—even my teachings about the divine Qualities, the meaningfulness of life, egos, bodiness, the psyche. Suddenly, all these thoughts seemed so futile, worthless, and misleading!

Rather than flounder in a "dark night" of negativity brought on by the collapse of these mental structures, however, I clung to the very meaningfulness that had just shattered my commonplace thinking. It was the consummate quantum leap; it brought vividly alive the last words spoken by my father, Hazrat Inayat Khan, on his deathbed: "When the unreality of life strikes my heart, its reality is revealed to me." All my life, I thought to myself, I have prided myself on what I thought were valid theories about the Universe—unmasking the hoax of superstitions, dogmas, and conditioned responses to life. But instead of dismissing all these constructs, I realized that they had acted as stepping-stones that led me to this ultimate breakthrough. Even though I had no more use for them, they remained there for my use, like a ladder propped against a wall. While "I" became immersed in the sublime, wordless state of unity beyond life—existence unveiled into eternity. . . ."[94]

Pir Vilayat concludes this passage by pointing out that, like a pendulum, consciousness inevitably must swing back from such a sublime state into the individual personal perspective, yet one does not return empty-handed, but "emanating the exotic perfume of his or her spiritual realization."

After this retreat, I again attended the 1990 representative's retreat at the Abode, accompanied by my wife and daughter. I attended a Pir Vilayat seminar in Georgia in early 1991, but this was the last time I would see Pir Vilayat, because another chapter in my spiritual journey had by this time begun. Yet, for me, this did not mean any lessening of the initiatic link, and I still continue to draw strongly on the teachings I received in the Inayati Order and especially value its universal approach to spirituality.

DISCOVERING *in* OURSELVES *the* AWAKENING *of the* UNIVERSE

Until the end of his life, Pir Vilayat continued to advance in his thinking, moving further from conventional religious categories, labels (including Sufism), and God-talk. He began to use the word "Universe" interchangeably with the word God, in order to circumvent the inevitable theological associations that the word carried of a Deity Who existed outside, above and beyond the realm of earthly life, a concept which can stand in the way of a deeper mystical prehension of Reality. In his final book, *Awakening: A Sufi Experience*, he explains that "this transcendent force is what some call God and what I also call the 'Universe,'. . . Like a cosmic pull that exerts a force of its own over humanity, the Universe is constantly compelling us to break free of the conditioning of the past in order to transform and evolve." He says we are "participants in the evolution of the Universe," which for billions of years has been "fashioning its stardust into human beings. The planning of the Universe is affected by humankind's free, creative participation; thus the goal for humans is to become conscious of their profound impact upon the unfolding of creation." [95]

He quotes Sir Isaac Newton's daring statement, "I think as God thinks," and interprets it to mean that when "a physicist has a sense of the intention behind the workings of the Universe, it's because his mind thinks as the universe thinks, only less well...."[96] It is the same for those who intuit the divine intention behind their problems. Their thinking becomes cosmic, for it is isomorphic with (the "same as") the thinking of the Universe, like a small battery that is connected to a greater electrical power grid. "The consequence of linking one's thinking and awareness with the thinking of the Universe is that it brings about a dramatic change in how we see life—jumpstarting individuals out of their narrow thinking patterns that continue round and round in the usual deep ruts." As physicist David Bohm says, such a change in perspective can bring about a transformation "in the deep structures of the brain" and produce new and different ways of thinking. Pir Vilayat understands this as

> a breathtaking breakthrough that radically distinguishes the spirituality of the future from the past. The Universe is evolving toward an even greater destiny—and we are the means of this global transformation! . . . For while in the past individuals may have posited a "perfect God" who wreaks upon humankind a harshly preordained fate, a radically different image of the Divine is appearing on the horizon: the Universe as a Global Being of which the Cosmos is a body, whose intelligence flashes through our thoughts and emotions, sparking ecstasy and despair in the cosmic drama—and in which we participate by our individual free will.[97]

Our thinking reflects, on a microcosmic level, the macrocosmic intention and planning of the Universe, while our emotions mirror on a much smaller scale the greater Cosmic Drama. Our DNA is an expression of the ordering of the Universe and our conscious awareness—our "I am-ness"— like our breath (which is one with the air that surrounds us)—is a seamless part of the all-pervading consciousness and presence of the Whole, the Only Being that exists. "From this perspective," says Pir Vilayat, "the Universe is an impersonal virtuality—a limitless potentiality—that is not static but continually evolving through 'you' and 'me.' Revisioning God as the Universe has staggering implications for how we view reality.[98]

PIR VILAYAT'S LATER YEARS

Pir Vilayat lived on until 2004, always searching for new approaches to the Message brought by Hazrat Inayat Khan, always seeking to "reconcile the irreconcilables." A number of Pir Vilayat's senior murids became involved in Jungian and Transpersonal psychology, and others became spiritual teachers in their own right. In another Sufi order, they would have had the ranks of khalifs, sheikhs and murshids, and their equivalent feminine ranks, but in 1981 Pir Vilayat had elected to do away with the twelve levels of initiation and all the titles (except his own) in order to avoid hierarchical rivalries among his murids. For his part, Pir Vilayat sought to avoid the guru model and refrained from telling people what to do. Rather, he tried to lift people out of their limited assessments of situations to find their own creative solutions. He told Atum O'Kane, "I am a transitional figure. In the future there won't be gurus." He added that something like transpersonal psychology might fill its place.[99]

On June 30, 1996, at age 80, Pir Vilayat was able to fulfill a long-held wish on behalf of his sister Noor. On the grounds of Dachau concentration camp, where his sister had been murdered 52 years before, Pir Vilayat conducted a choir and orchestra in a moving performance Bach's B Minor Mass in honor of Noor and all victims of oppression. It was reported that the weather was gloomy and overcast, a condition which lasted through the mournful *crucifixus* section of the mass. But just as the strains of the joyous *resurrexit* section began, a great shaft of light appeared through the clouds, as though the heavens were

responding in affirmation of the prayers and glorification arising from the earth.

In 2000, Pir Vilayat held a turban-tying ceremony in Dehli
where he confirmed his son, Pir Zia, as his spiritual successor.
In his final years, Pir Vilayat completed several books (including
Awakening: A Sufi Experience and *In Search of the Hidden Treasure*)
and continued to give seminars up until the December before
his passing at age 87. Shortly before his death, he said: "I will not
be able to give seminars anymore, but I am working on seven
levels of light, and I will be with our mureeds that way."[100] Pir
Vilayat passed away at his home in Suresnes on June 17, 2004,
and was buried in India in the Nizamuddin Basti neighborhood
in Dehli, near the *dargah* which houses the tomb of his beloved
father. Upon hearing the news of his passing, the Dalai Lama
wrote, "I have much admiration for him. His passing is a great
loss, especially for those who follow the spiritual path, but also
believe in tolerance for other religions."[101]

> *Toward the One, the Perfection of Love, Harmony, and Beauty,*
> *the Only Being, united with all the illuminated souls who form*
> *the embodiment of the Master, the Spirit of Guidance.*

Such is the invocation of Divine Unity that was given by Pir-
o-Murshid Hazrat Inayat Khan a century ago. In a posthumous
work, *The Ecstasy Beyond Knowing: A Manual of Meditation* (2014),
Pir Vilayat included his own invocation, which can also serve as
a fitting benediction with which to conclude this section.

> *We invoke the One*
> *Whose Body is the cosmos of the galaxies and our own bodies,*
> *Whose Mind courses through our thinking,*
> *And Whose Ecstasy arouses our acts of glorification;*
> *Whose Personality is customized as our personalities,*
> *Whose Presence is always there,*
> *Whose consciousness is focalized as our consciousness,*
> *And Whose Reality is beyond our reach.*[102]

ENDNOTES

[1] Khan, Pir Vilayat, *The Call of the Dervish*, Sufi Order Publications, Sante Fe, NM, 1981; p.15. The account is also supplemented by another telling of the story by Pir Vilayat from a recorded talk in 1979.

[2] Schimmel, Annemarie, *Mystical Dimensions of Islam*, p.9; the University of North Carolina Press, Chapel Hill, NC, 1975.

[3] Qur. 41:53.

[4] Message Volume 12, *The Vision of God and Man*, pp.130-31. Barre and Jenkins, London, 1967.

[5] *The Unity of Religious Ideals*, chapter on "The Message and the Messenger: What is the Message?" 2001 Kindle edition.

[6] *Biography of Pir-o-Murshid Inayat Khan*, pp.77-78; East-West Publications, London, 1979.

[7] Khan, Pir Vilayat, *The Call of the Dervish*, p.174.

[8] *Biography of Pir-o-Murshid Inayat Khan*, p.78.

[9] *Ibid*, p.227.

[10] *Biography of Pir-o-Murshid Inayat Khan*, p.243.

[11] John 3:16.

[12] Khan, Pir Vilayat, *The Message in Our Time*, p.326; Harper & Row, San Francisco, 1978.

[13] Khan, Hazrat Inayat, *The Unity of Religious Ideals*. Chapter on "The Message and the Messenger." 2001 Kindle edition.

[14] Khan, Hazrat Inayat, *The Unity of Religious Ideals*. Chapter on *Jesus; The Spirit of Christ*. 2001 Kindle edition.

[15] *Biography of Pir-o-Murshid Inayat Khan*, p.226.

[16] *Fihi ma fihi*, quoted from Arberry, *Discourses of Rumi*, p.139, Samuel Weiser, Inc., NY, 1961.

[17] The Message Volume XII, *Confessions*. Chapter on "My Study of Religions," p.134. Servive BV, Netherlands, 1979.

[18] Khan, Hazrat Inayat, *The Unity of Religious Ideals*. Chapter on "The Religion of the Heart," p.10.

[19] Khan, Hazrat Inayat, *The Unity of Religious Ideals*. Chapter on "The Sufi's Aim in Life," 2001 Kindle edition.

[20] Message Volume VIII, Sufism, *The Sufi Message of Spiritual Liberty*. Chapter on "Peals from the Unseen," p.191.

[21] *The Unity of Religious Ideals*. Chapter on "The Purpose of the Sufi Movement," 2001 Kindle edition.

[22] *The Unity of Religious Ideals*. Chapter on "Sufism," 2001 Kindle edition.

[23] Khan, Hazrat Inayat, Social Gathekas. *Background on Sufism*, Internet at http://hazrat-inayat-khan.org.

[24] *Ibid, Sufism Beyond Religion*.

[25] *Ibid, Working for the Sufi Message*.

[26] *The Unity of Religious Ideals*. Chapter on "The Spirit of Sufism," 2001 Kindle edition.

[27] Transcribed from an audio recording of Hazrat Inayat Khan's voice.

[28] The Message Volume XII, *Confessions*. Chapter on "The Message," p.132, Servive BV, Netherlands, 1979.

[29] Khan, Hazrat Inayat, *The Complete Sayings of Hazrat Inayat Khan*, 938, p.115. Sufi Order Publications, New Lebanon, NY, 1978. Based on the original saying: "Shatter your ideals upon the rock of truth."

[30] Khan, Hazrat Inayat, Githa 3; *Concentration* (Private edition by Sufi Order, Lebanon Springs, NY).

[31] Khan, Hazrat Inayat, The *Unity of Religious Ideals,* chapter on "The Symbol of the Sufi Movement," 2012 Kindle edition.

[32] Khan, Hazrat Inayat, *The Heart of Sufism: Essential Writings of Hazrat Inayat Khan*. Chapter on "Universal Worship," 2013 Kindle edition.

[33] *Ibid.*

[34] Message Volume VIII, *Sufi Teachings*, Chapter on The Difference Between Will, Wish, and Desire, p.81. Servive BV, Netherlands, 1979.

[35] Khan, Hazrat Inayat, *The Complete Sayings of Hazrat Inayat Khan;* Vadan/Ragas, 855, p.103.

[36] *Ibid*, Gayan, Vadan/Nirtan, 471, p.48.

[37] *The Unity of Religious Ideals*, chapter on "Deity and Divinity, Part," 2001 Kindle edition.

[38] Khan, Hazrat Inayat, *Mastery through Accomplishment*, Omega Press, 1985, p. 222.

[39] Khan, Hazrat Inayat, Message Volume XIV, *The Gathas*, Morals, 1.3, "What is the Ego?" p.173. International Headquarters Sufi Movement, Geneva, 1982.

[40] Khan, Hazrat Inayat, *The Complete Sayings of Hazrat Inayat Khan*, Gayan, 7, p.6. Servive BV, Netherlands, 1979.

[41] *Ibid*, Aphorisms, 1769, p.212.

[42] Joe said this often, notably in the 1973 film, *Sunseed*.

[43] Lewis, Samuel, *In the Garden*, Lama Foundation, N.M., 1975, pp.14 &16.

[44] Faithful Doubter, *Samuel L. Lewis: Spiritual Leader of the Hippies*, 2004. Available at: http://bobby1993.livejournal.com/588012.html.

[45] I heard this attributed to Murshid Sam many years ago but do not have a written source for it.

[46] Lewis, *In the Garden*, pp.12-13.

[47] As quoted by Pir Shabda Khan in a 2018 phone conversation with the author.

[48] *The Sacred Search: World Mystical Traditions*, Pir Vilayat Inayat Khan with Thomas Atum O'Kane, 1991, C.F. Gunter and the Sufi Order Video Project. VHS videotape.

[49] *Supplimentary Papers*, Philosophy II, Section on Satan, p.11. (Private edition by Sufi Order, Lebanon Springs, NY.)

[50] Private video of a Pir Vilayat Khan talk in 1984, Unity Church, Nashville, TN.

[51] Khan, Hazrat Inayat, *The Complete Sayings of Hazrat Inayat Khan*; Gayan/Boulas, 292, p.31.

[52] St. John of the Cross, *The Ascent of Mount Carmel*.

[53] Khan, Pir Vilayat, *The Call of the Dervish*, p.149. Sufi Order Publications, 1981.

[54] *Ibid*, pp. 149,152.

[55] Friedlander, Shems, *The Whirling Dervishes*, p.23, MacMillan Publishing Company, 1975. The quote is by Jelaluddin Rumi.

[56] Khan, Hazrat Inayat, *The Complete Sayings of Hazrat Inayat Khan*; Gayan/Boulas, 275, p.29.

[57] As quoted by Pir Vilayat Khan in the context of a retreat practice.

[58] Private video of a Pir Vilayat Khan talk in 1984, Unity Church, Nashville, TN.

[59] *Ibid*.

[60] Khan, Pir Vilayat, *The Call of the Dervish*, p.154.

[61] Quoted as I heard it from Pir Vilayat.

[62] *Ibid*, p.155.

[63] Khan, Hazrat Inayat, *The Complete Sayings of Hazrat Inayat Khan*; Gayan/Suras, 554, p.64.

[64] Quoted as I heard it from Pir Vilayat on several occasions.

[65] As quoted by Pir Vilayat. It appears to be based on Yasna 30:9 of the Zend-Avesta: "And may we be such as those who bring on this great renovation, and make this world progressive till its perfection shall have been reached." Iyer, Raghavan, editor, *The Gathas of Zarathrustra*, pp.41-2; Concord Grove Press, 1983.

[66] Khan, Pir Vilayat, *Toward the One*, p.297. Harper & Row, 1974.

[67] Qur. 7:172.

[68] Private video of a Pir Vilayat Khan talk given in 1984 at Unity Church, Nashville, TN. Note: Much of the material on the alchemical retreat was based on Puran Bair's Bair's unpublished 1976 Retreat Handbook, which he had based on retreat talks by Pir Vilayat and further explanations which Pir Vilayat conveyed to him. Puran told the author in 2017 that since 1976, he has greatly revised his own approach to the retreat process in an effort to ensure that retreatants emerge from retreats as fully grounded and balanced as possible, with an emphasis on fortifying people's hearts.

[69] As quoted in *Introducing Spirituality into Counseling and Therapy*, by Pir Vilayat Khan, Omega Publications, New Lebanon, NY, 1982, p.156.

[70] Miles-Yepéz, Netanel and Nehemia Polen, *One God, Many Worlds: Teachings of a Renewed Hasidism*, 2015 Kindle edition. The quote is from a chapter entitled "Trees, Vineyards, and the Master Gardener" by Thomas Atum O'Kane.

[71] *Ibid.*

[72] The Sufi Remembrance Project 2014 is available at: http://remembrance.sufipaths.net

[73] This was a 1981 VHS interview that does not appear to have ever been commercially distributed. No further documentation is now available.

[74] On p.197 of *Science, Order and Creativity* by David Bohm and F. David Peat, Dr. Bohm states that "Current quantum field theory implies that what appears to be empty space contains an immense 'zero point energy,' coming from all the quantum fields that are contained in this space. . . . Matter is then a relatively small wave or disturbance on top of this 'ocean' of energy . . . a 'small ripple' on this ocean of energy."

[75] Quoted from a 1981 video interview of Pir Vilayat by Ellen Burstyn.

[76] Khan, Pir Vilayat, *The Call of the Dervish*, p.177.

[77] *Ibid*, p.177.

[78] *Ibid*, pp.177-78.

[79] *Ibid*, p.169.

[80] Khan, Pir Vilayat, *Introducing Spirituality into Counseling and Therapy*, p.15.

[81] Khan, Pir Vilayat, *Leader's Manual*, p.606. (Private edition by Sufi Order, Lebanon Springs, NY, 1981.)

[82] *The Sacred Search: World Mystical Traditions*, Pir Vilayat Inayat Khan with Thomas Atum O'Kane. VHS video.

[83] Khan, Pir Vilayat, *Leader's Manual*, p.636. (Private edition.)

[84] *Ibid.*

[85] *Ibid,* p.637.

[86] *Ibid.* p.629.

[87] The interview with Lex Hixon was taken from the original audio archives. An edited printed account of the interview can also be found in *Conversations in the Spirit: Lex Hixon's WBAI 'In the Spirit' Interviews: A Chronicle of the Seventies Spiritual Revolution*, edited by Sheila Hixon, 2016, Monkfish Book Publishing Company, Rhinebeck, NY.

[88] From a September 1984 audio recording of Pir Vilayat leading the Universal Worship Service at the Abode in New Lebanon, NY.

[89] Teilhard de Chardin, *Hymn of the Universe,* Mass of the World from the Offertory in Chapter 1; 1965, English translation, Harper & Row.

[90] *Sahih Al-Bukhari.*

[91] From an audio recording of Pir Vilayat Khan on June 16, 1989, during the representative's retreat on Whidby Island in Washington State.

[92] *The Sufi Message of Hazrat Inayat Khan: The Smiling Forehead,* Chapter 19, The Awakening of the Soul. 2012 Kindle Edition. Forms of this passage can be found in various editions of Hazrat Inayat Khan's works with variations, but this version appears the most succinct.

[93] Saying by Hazrat Inayat Khan as quoted by Pir Vilayat Khan in *Keeping in Touch* newsletter #91, Lahut-The Divine Inheritance. (Available at: www.centrum-universel.com)

[94] Khan, Pir Vilayat, *Awakening: A Sufi Experience,* Tarcher Perigee, 2000, pp. 29-33

[95] *Ibid,* pp.8-9.

[96] *Ibid.*

[97] *Ibid,* pp.15-16.

[98] *Ibid,* p.16

[99] From a talk by Atum O'Kane given during a training course on Spiritual Guidance in 2015.

[100] *Heart & Wings*, p. 1. Available at: www.ingrid-denegg.at.

[101] Available at: www.pirzia.org.

[102] *The Ecstasy Beyond Knowing: A Manual of Meditation*, Omega Publications, New Lebanon, NY, 2014 Kindle Edition. The quote is on an opening page following the book's Foreword.

PART II

Rabbi Zalman Schachter-Shalomi

the EARLY YEARS

Reb Zalman was born on August 17, 1924 in Zholkiev, Poland, and was raised in Vienna. His parents, Shlomo and Hayyah Gittel Schachter, were observant Jews and his father had an affiliation with the Belzer Hasidim. Reb Zalman writes:

> My father was a Hasid who developed a great interest in Western ways and ideas. He remained a devout Jew (he taught me to pray), but he also steered my education toward a pluralistic path—I went to yeshiva and at the same time attended a leftist Zionist high school where I learned Latin and modern Hebrew. I danced the hora with Marxist Zionists and also celebrated the farewell to the Sabbath with Orthodox anti-Zionists.[1]

After Austria was annexed to Nazi Germany in 1938, the Viennese synagogues were demolished and Jews were frequently killed on the streets. On one occasion, Zalman and a friend were taunted and beaten by several gentile youths, while an armed Nazi patrolman watched approvingly from a distance. They dared not fight back for fear of retaliation against their families. Shortly thereafter, Zalman's father was arrested for having an expired visa, and deported back to Poland. However, he managed to escape from the train and make his way back to

Vienna, where he clandestinely gathered his family and fled the country for Belgium. Many of Zalman's relatives would never make it out of Europe alive.

Arriving in Antwerp as an uprooted teenager, Zalman felt angry and betrayed by God that all of this should be transpiring. Needing to vent his frustrations, one afternoon he went down to the *Tz-irey Agudat Yisroel*, a local hangout for Orthodox Jewish youth in Antwerp, where he knew they would be teaching from the *Pirke Avot* (the Ethics of the Fathers) on the delights of the World to Come. Standing in the back, Zalman began to heckle the assembly, ridiculing the teachings on the next world as "pie in the sky." The students who were there to learn became very upset with his comments, but the leader, who happened to be a Habad Hasid, asked them to be patient and hear the young man out. "What else?" he gently asked Zalman. At this, Zalman poured out all his anger, telling them that there was no proof of any afterlife, that those teachings were rubbish, and quoting Karl Marx that "Religion is the opiate of the masses." The leader listened with sympathy and when Zalman had finished, he said, "Would you like to hear from someone who agrees with you?" When Zalman assented, his anger now spent, the leader sent a student out to retrieve the *Tractate Sanhedrin* commentary on the Talmud by the great Jewish theologian Maimonides.[2]

Having located the volume, the leader read a passage which explained that there is no proof of *olam ha-ba*, the world to come, and no certitude that any of the delights of heaven will be there. The passage went on to give thoughtful, reasoned answers that calmed Zalman and created an opening for him to sit down and learn with these people.

That episode was a turning point for Zalman. After that, he began to seek out other Hasidim of the Habad lineage and was able to briefly connect with Menachem Mendel Schneersohn, the son-in-law and future successor of the aged sixth Lubavitcher Rebbe, Yosef Yitzhak Schneersohn. Reb Yosef had already immigrated to America and Menachem Mendel would soon follow him there. Gradually, through his association with these Hasidim, Zalman's faith and love of the mystical Jewish traditions began to grow and this helped sustain him through the trials ahead. In this way, Zalman became an enthusiastic Hasid of the Habad lineage before leaving Europe.

The months in Antwerp provided a calm respite for Zalman as he happily continued his yeshiva studies. He reports another powerful experience, a "sacred moment" that occurred in Antwerp in 1939, when he was taking a walk outdoors in nature on the Sabbath. Suddenly the heavens opened up for him, and for a timeless moment he felt the unifying presence of God within and without. Then one of divine mysteries mentioned in the *Tanya* (the central text of Habad Hasidim) was revealed to him—the knowledge that God must necessarily remain concealed and hidden from the world. "Why?" asks Zalman.

> Because this is the only way that we can have freedom of choice. I understood why it has to be that way, and I experienced that knowledge and that freedom as God's compassionate gift. And then I prayed, asking that please, may the faith and certainty of that moment always be with me.[3]

Sadly, this formative spiritual period in his life was shortlived, as the situation soon worsened for Jews in Belgium. Zalman's family narrowly escaped to Vichy, France, where the family was interred at a refugee camp under extremely difficult conditions. After months of being forced to work to exhaustion at the camp, they were finally allowed to travel on to the port city of Marseille where they could exit Europe by boat. In early 1941, Zalman and his immediate family were able to immigrate to the United States, via the Caribbean Islands. When they reached New York, Zalman immediately connected with the Habad-Lubavitcher Hasidim* in Brooklyn, then under the leadership of Reb Yosef Yitzhak Schneersohn (1880-1950).

After years of study in the Lubavitcher yeshiva, Zalman received his rabbinic ordination in 1947. In late 1949, a year before

---

* The organizational body of this lineage uses the spelling, Chabad.

his passing, the Lubavitcher Rebbe began to encourage a new level of outreach work to American Jews, hoping to rebuild Jewish commitment and faith after the devastation of World War II. Sadly, many of the great rebbes, or Hasidic spiritual masters, of Europe had been annihilated during the Holocaust, leaving a void of knowledgeable Jewish spiritual leaders; and many survivors harbored a smoldering resentment against God for allowing this horror. These factors contributed to a widespread loss of faith in *Yiddishkeit*, the world of Judaism. Even before the Holocaust, many Jews who came to America were quickly assimilating, thinking that the old rules no longer applied in the new environment, a view not shared by the Lubavitcher Rebbe. In contrast to the secularizing tendencies and erosion of faith characteristic of many American Jews of the time, among the Lubavitchers, there was a zealous, messianic fervor to restore "righteousness" among American Jews.

Reb Zalman and his friend Rabbi Shlomo Carlebach (1925-1994), who would become famous as the "singing rabbi," were sent out to college campuses by the elderly Lubavitcher Rebbe to meet and attract wayward Jewish students back into the fold. When Reb Zalman asked his rebbe what he specifically had in mind for them to do, he replied, "If I knew, I would tell you. Go out and find out what's needed."[4] In retrospect, Reb Zalman always felt his life's work in what he later called "Jewish Renewal" was a fulfillment of that commission from his beloved rebbe.

So what did they find out? They quickly found that, in addition to their rabbinic knowledge and expertise, they needed innovative approaches to attract the young people, such as music and storytelling. Reb Zalman was able to stay within the Lubavitcher fold until the mid-1960s, but his friend, Reb Shlomo, departed sooner. In an interview with *Tikkun* magazine published just after his death in 1994, Reb Shlomo recounted how he served as the righthand of the seventh Lubavitcher Rebbe, Menachem Mendel Schneersohn (1902-1994), from 1951 to 1955 and how he used music to draw people in. However, he encountered problems due to the fact that, in those days, the

Rebbe held the position that women couldn't sing with men. Finally, Reb Shlomo went to the Rebbe and told him:

> "Last night, I had one hundred people come to learn with me and sing with me. When I told them that we had to sit separately men from women, I lost ninety people, and when I told them that women couldn't sing, I lost nine more, and the one person who remained was the biggest idiot.". . . So the Rebbe said to me, "I cannot tell you to do it your way. But I can't tell you not to do it your way. So if you want to do it on your own, God be with you." So I split.[5]

Reb Zalman parted ways with the Lubavitcher community a decade later in the mid-1960s, after having experienced LSD with Timothy Leary and writing and publicly speaking about the cosmic perspective it opened up for him. This brought Zalman a great deal of criticism from conservatives and finally led to his separation from the Lubavitcher fold. A brief quote from a 1966 interview gives the flavor of it:

> The most serious challenges to Judaism imposed by modern thought and experience are to me game theory and psychedelic experience. Once I realized the game structure of my commitments, once I see how all my theologizing is just an elaborate death struggle between my soul and the God within her, or when I undergo the deepest cosmic experience via some miniscule quantity of organic alkaloids or LSD, then the whole validity of my ontological assertions is in doubt. After seeing what really happens at the point where all is one and where God immanent surprises God transcendent and they merge in cosmic laughter, I can also see Judaism in a new and amazing light.[6]

In a 2012 interview, Reb Zalman spoke about the reasons for leaving Lubavitch:

There is a time when you have to leave the nest. Many things contributed to my departure from Lubavitch. This included my inability to maintain a certain set of Orthodox theological views and practices. There are times when you must say, "Ad kan, I can go with you this far, but from here on, I have to be my own person." But I didn't leave only because I needed more individual fulfillment, but because I wanted to be a good shepherd to the people who were coming to me for spiritual support. I simply couldn't lead most of them in the direction of a traditional Lubavitch lifestyle.[7]

During the 1950s, Reb Zalman had worked as a congregational rabbi in Massachusetts and acquired a master's degree in the pastoral psychology from Boston University in 1956. There, he studied with Rev. Howard Thurman, the great African-American mystic who was the mentor of Dr. Martin Luther King Jr., and was the person Zalman credited with opening up his interreligious sensibilities. Zalman related how he was attracted by the University brochure offering a course in "Spiritual Disciplines and Resources, with labs," but was wary of attending a class taught by a Christian minister. When he met with the professor, Rev. Thurman, he confessed his trepidation and was astonished when Thurman gave him a long, soulful look and asked him, using the Jewish term for Holy Spirit, "Don't you trust the *Ruah ha-Kodesh*?"[8] Zalman considered the implications of the question for a long moment and then affirmed that he did. Afterwards, he learned a great deal from Thurman, who went to great lengths to make Zalman feel comfortable there, even removing the cross from the altar of the chapel each morning before Reb Zalman would go there to perform his morning Jewish worship and prayers.

Zalman worked as a Hillel rabbi and as a professor of religious studies at the University of Manitoba in Canada until 1975. During this period, he began to further explore the relationship of Judaism with other religions, particularly Roman Catholicism, and developed friendships with many of the most progressive thinkers of that time, including Thomas Merton, Abraham Joshua Heschel, Gerald Heard, and Abraham Maslow.

In 1968, he earned his Doctor of Hebrew Letters at Hebrew Union College in Cincinnati, which was close enough to Our Lady of Gethsemani to allow for frequent visits with Thomas Merton during the years prior to Merton's death. In addition to Christianity, Merton was also deeply interested in Buddhism, Taoism, Judaism, and Islamic Sufism. In reference to the latter, he corresponded with the noted Islamic scholar, Louis Massignon (with whom Pir Vilayat also studied), Sidi Abdeslam (an Algerian Sufi), and Abdul Aziz (a Pakistani Sufi). Merton was especially encouraged by the reforms of Vatican II, which recognized the validity of other religions (a policy which he and Joshua Abraham Heschel together helped implement), yet his interfaith activities were only grudgingly tolerated by his superiors in the Church.

Photograph of Thomas Merton taken by Reb Zalman at the Abbey of Our Lady of Gethsemani around 1963. (Photo courtesy of the University Colorado Boulder's Zalman M. Schachter-Shalomi collection.)

His correspondence with Reb Zalman began in 1960 with an exchange of letters and books, which they sometimes annotated with comments in the margins before exchanging. They first made contact when a former student gave Merton a copy of a private edition of Reb Zalman's first book, *The First Step: A Primer of a Jew's Spiritual Life,* which is considered the first English book on Jewish meditation. Fascinated with learning more about Hasidism, he wrote to Zalman, who in turn was delighted to compare notes with a kindred soul and learn more about Christianity and its inner workings from the celebrated Trappist monk and author of *The Seven Storey Mountain.*

Merton wrote to Zalman that they were uniquely placed to understand the relationship between Church and Synagogue. Meanwhile, Zalman was reading Meister Eckhart, St. John of the Cross, and other Christian mystics and even experimenting with using plainsong to daaven the psalms in English. He wrote to Merton, "The mystic doesn't color inside the lines. He sees bigger than the people who made the lines. But this is what we need—renewal from the inside." Then he playfully added Gershom Scholem's quip, "We prefer our mystics housebroken."[9]

Both of them studied the eleventh-century classic, *Duties of the Heart* by Bahya Ibn Paquda, whom Merton described as his "favorite Jewish mystic." Ibn Paquda called the outward observance of the *mitzvot* (good deeds) "the duties of the body," but felt the inner motivations (*kavvanot*) were of equal importance, and these he called "the duties of the heart." Merton and Zalman both felt strongly that the participation of both the body and heart were necessary for true contemplative prayer. Of his understanding of Christianity, Zalman wrote, "Our problem is not so much to come to terms with the Jesus of the Gospel. That is easy. Midrash and the early Fathers of the Jewish faith parallel the Gospels so closely that we have no problem whatsoever in that. At one time, I thought that the Epistles were the furthest away from the Jewish faith, but even this is not quite so."[10]

When Reb Zalman visited Merton at the Abbey of Gethsemani, he joined in chanting the Psalms along with the monks, wrapped in his prayer tallis. He loved the Psalms, whether in Latin or in Hebrew. He was given a traditional Christian monk's habit and cowl by the abbot of the monastery, which he promised to don on Yom Kippur. All in all, it was a marvelous interspiritual friendship which ended too soon due to Merton's untimely accidental death in December 1969, in Bangkok, Thailand. He was there as a participant in a Buddhist conference, where he met and engaged in joyful dialogue with the Dalai Lama.

As postdoctoral fellow at Brandeis University, where Abraham Maslow taught, Zalman was instrumental among the group who launched the Havurah Movement of American Judaism. Following upon this, he founded B'nai Or Religious Fellowship (which later merged with ALEPH: Alliance for Jewish Renewal), as well as the Aquarian Minyan in Berkeley, California.

Years earlier, he began to study Sufism and in 1975, he was made a sheikh in the Sufi Order in the lineage of Hazrat Inayat Khan by Pir Vilayat Khan. At Pir Vilayat's request, Reb Zalman, himself a *kohein*,* also bestowed a special universal priestly blessing upon Pir Vilayat in New York soon after, connected with the tradition of the prepatriarchal high priest-king, Melchizedek, who blessed Abraham.[11] During the ceremony, Reb Zalman conferred on Pir Vilayat the title of *Kohen l'El Eliyon* (priest of God, Most High).

Reb Zalman went on to associate with many other Sufis such as Muzaffer Efendi, the Turkish Sufi master from Istanbul who initiated Zalman as a *muhib* (spiritual friend) of the Halveti-Jerrahi Order. Other Sufi friendships were made with Murshid Siddi-Hasan in Palestine; Atum O'Kane, with whom he later often co-led seminars; Pir Ibrahim Farajaje, provost at the Unitarian Starr King School for the Ministry in Berkeley; and many others.

In 1975, Reb Zalman also became a professor of Jewish mysticism and psychology of religion at Temple University in Philadelphia, a post he kept until 1987. During this period, he often joined Muzaffer Efendi and his dervishes for Sufi zikrs in New York. Following a forty-day retreat at Lama Foundation in 1984, Reb Zalman was inspired to found a movement to concentrate on spiritual eldering with the aim of bringing more joy

---

* Also spelled *kohen*. Hebrew for "priest;" typically refers to a Jewish person of the priestly lineage of Aaron.

and spiritual meaningfulness to people's retirement years. An account of that body of work is contained in his 1992 book, *From Age-ing to Sage-ing: A Revolutionary Approach to Growing Older.* In 1994, Reb Zalman was married to Eve Ilsen, a psychotherapist, singer, and storyteller, who had frequently taught in tandem with him since the late 1980s. (Reb Zalman had three previous marriages and eleven children.)

In 1990, as part of a group of rabbis involved in the "Jew in the Lotus" dialogue, Zalman traveled to Dharamsala, India, where he had the first of many encounters and interfaith exchanges with the Dalai Lama. In 1995, Reb Zalman and Eve moved to Boulder, Colorado, where he accepted the World Wisdom Chair at Naropa Institute (now Naropa University), a post he kept until 2004. After retiring from Naropa, he went on to co-found a Sufi tariqat called the Inayati-Maimuni Order with Netanel (Mu'in ad-Din) Miles-Yépez, which combines elements of the Jewish Hasidic and Islamic Sufi traditions.

CONNECTING *with the* UNIVERSALIST REBBE

I first encountered Reb Zalman at Omega Institute in Bennington, Vermont in the summer of 1981 during an Esoteric Studies week that brought together teachers from the world's major religious traditions, including Pir Vilayat Khan (Islam/Sufism), Brother David Steindl-Rast (Christianity), Swami Satchitananda (Hinduism), and Khenpo Karthar Rinpoche (Buddhism). What first got my attention was Reb Zalman's musical offering during an ecumenical service. He had everyone up out of their seats, joyously singing a robust responsorial rendition of Psalm 148 to the tune of "Michael Row the Boat Ashore," complete with for-tissimo alleluias from the congregation. ("Praise the Lord from the heavens! . . . HALLELUIA!") He certainly knew how to uplift people's hearts with song and praise!

Over the next decade, I attended a number of workshops with Reb Zalman: a seminar on Kabbalistic teachings, a week-end at the Wisdom School, a Torah and Dharma week at Elat Chayyim (co-taught by Roshi Bernie Glassman), a Shabbat

weekend in North Carolina, and so on. Years later, he gracious-
ly provided feedback and praise for my books on Sufism, *The
Garden of Mystic Love* and *Lifting the Boundaries* (the latter briefly covers Reb Zalman's relationship with Muzaffer Efendi and
other Sufis, and includes a dedication by Reb Zalman). Over
the years, I also listened to many audio tapes of Reb Zalman's
presentations and had a number of lengthy conversations with
him, which provided excellent food for the mind, heart and
soul. Close up, his gaze was very clear, warm and embracing,
and full of what he called *farginnen*, a Yiddish word he occasionally used that roughly means a deep heartfelt wishing-the-
very-best for others, rejoicing over another's good fortune—the
opposite of begrudging.

*Reb Zalman officiating a wedding in Atlanta, Georgia in 1985. (Photos by the
author).*

Here, I would like to share an experience that I had with
him which involves my wife, Sylvia. We attended a wedding
in Atlanta at which Reb Zalman officiated, and we chatted with
him before the ceremony started. After a musical interlude, but
before the bride and groom came out, Reb Zalman addressed
some words to the audience, inviting those who were married
or in relationship to use the opportunity of witnessing the marriage as an occasion for inwardly renewing their own vows of
commitment to their partners, and that all of us together, in our

own way, would send energy to the couple, praying for it to be a strong and happy union. During his remarks, Reb Zalman's glance turned toward Sylvia and there was a deep moment of connection. She recounts, "The meeting of our eyes created a feeling of floating in an ocean. The glance only lasted for a second but seemed to last longer, as though time stood still."

Three days later, she dreamed that she entered a living room and sat down on the couch next to a nice older Jewish gentleman, like a beloved uncle or grandfather, who was sitting there alone watching a mystery show on television. She felt such love radiating from him that she cuddled up next to him for a while as he continued to watch the show. When he finally turned and looked at her, she was amazed by the deep sense of love that was streaming from his eyes. Then she realized these were the eyes of God. Upon awakening, she realized that they were also the eyes of Reb Zalman. She wrote him a letter to share the dream and when we next saw him, he acknowledged the letter, chuckled, and said, "You know, that letter was such a gift, because I received it on a day when I was kind of down from a hard day and the letter brought such a ray of joy to hear what you shared about your dream. May we all experience that sense of manifesting something of the Divine in our lives."

Reb Zalman smiling (video still from the video "The Kiss of God," photo courtesy of Cathy Zheutlin and Holy Rascals Media).

Around the same year that I first encountered Reb Zalman, I also met Rabbi Shlomo Carlebach, who appeared as one of the presenters at the Light of the Mountains Sufi Healing Conference near Asheville, North Carolina. While most of the presenters gave interesting and informative talks, Reb Shlomo came in with his guitar and asked everyone to get out of their auditorium seats and gather around him for more intimacy. Then he proceeded to sing and tell stories for the next hour or two, and soon had everyone joyfully dancing, clapping, and singing along with his beautiful, stirring Jewish melodies. After that, I attended several more of Reb Shlomo's concerts and a Shabbat retreat in Alabama, where I had time to take walks with the rebbe and get to know him better.

One conversation of note occurred when Rabbi Carlebach invited me to take an afternoon walk with him in the woods on Shabbat. I had walked on the trail the previous day and it led to a beautiful overlook called the point, so I asked him, "Do you want to go down to the point?" He replied, "That is a deep question, my dearest brother." I suddenly recalled that in the morning's homily he had emphasized that there were six days of the week for work in the world, but the glorious seventh day, the Sabbath—when we cease all work and just *be* in the Divine Presence—that is *the point* of the whole week, the axis around which the other days revolve.

As we walked slowly along, I observed that, every so often, he would stop walking, glance around, and just appreciate the world around him, then continue—a practice that I picked up and now often utilize when walking in nature. We also spoke some as we walked and I confided to him that, though I was not Jewish (except for an ancestor about ten generations back), and was raised in a Christian family, I felt a strong connection with the Jewish faith—not so much with the Torah portions that dealt with the begats, and descriptions of how to build a portable sanctuary in the desert, and so on—rather, it was a general sense of reverence for the tradition.

"Perhaps Moshe Rabbeinu (Moses) isn't your man," he offered. "As a universalist Sufi, your connection may be with Abraham, the father of three religions, the one that first went beyond idol worship to the realization of the oneness of God." Then he surprised me by suggesting that perhaps I had been a Jew in a previous life, who had come back to experience other faiths. I wasn't sure if I concurred with this explanation, but I considered it an intriguing suggestion offered from the Hasidic perspective. When I later mentioned it to Reb Zalman, he noted my birthday (a few years after the end of the Second World War) and mused, "Yes, I think there could be something to that. It seems that a lot of Jews who died in the Holocaust are coming back as Sufis, Buddhists, and so forth, and working within, and even outside the traditions, to heal the divisions between the faiths."[12]

Rabbi Shlomo Carlebach in concert in Atlanta, Gerogia in 1985. (Photos by the author).

Although Rabbi Carlebach was internationally famous in Jewish circles as a performing musician and songwriter, Reb Zalman was also a gifted musician. During Reb Zalman's lifetime, he transmitted a lot of the beauty of the Hasidic tradition through melody, often setting traditional tunes, as well as newly composed melodies, to contemporary English words in order to bring them more fully into the American culture. To those who resisted changing the "traditional" Jewish liturgical melodies, Reb Zalman noted that many of the "time-honored" Jewish anthems were actually German melodies, in use for only a few centuries, and that there was no reason not to adopt American melodies as well or create new ones. As the Psalms proclaim: "I will sing unto the Lord a new song."[13] So why tightly cling to the melodies of a bygone generation to the exclusion of fresh musical possibilities?

Over the last fifty years, Reb Zalman has written many books on various aspects of Jewish Renewal and spiritual eldering, often in conjunction with co-writers, including: *Fragments of a Future Scroll* (1975); *Spiritual Intimacy: A Study of Counseling in Hasidim* (1991), *Paradigm Shift* (1993), *From Age-ing to Sage-ing* (1995), *Jewish with Feeling* (2006), *My Life in Jewish Renewal: A Memoir* (2012) and many others. The majority of these books deal with issues directly concerned with Jewish Renewal and the Hasidic masters.

However, as a longtime practitioner of Sufism with Christian roots, what has interested me the most about Reb Zalman's teachings centers around: the places where sacred traditions meet and are updated, revitalizing spiritual praxis and worship; the multilevel experience of reality and of the Divine; and the essential core and heart of what could be called the "one religion," the perennial tradition, or what Reb Zalman sometimes referred to as "the no-frills generic religion" behind the "brand-name" religious traditions. In Islam, this is recognized as the *din al-fitrah*, the natural primordial sacred stream of wisdom coming forth from the *Umm al-kitab*, the Mother of the Book, producing different spiritual traditions, each with its own sacred language and divine messenger—all of them different yet one in their essential message of unity and loving-compassion.

Therefore, the primary issues that I would like to emphasize from the prolific legacy of Reb Zalman's teaching—in addition to the connections between Hasidism and Sufism—are the following:

1. Universalism and renewal of the sacred traditions
2. The four levels of Reality and the multi-dimensionality of God
3. The ten *sephirot* and the inner council
4. Updating our God language and concepts

5. Spiritual paradigm shifts and the evolution of the God-ideal

The sources I use in presenting Reb Zalman's ideas are varied: recordings of Reb Zalman made by myself and others, articles and interviews from magazines and the internet, personal conversations, as well as books by Reb Zalman. The quotations I have chosen are mostly drawn from off-the-cuff live recordings. I quote and footnote wherever I can for accuracy, yet in many cases I have found that, instead of a directly quoting, it is more clear and concise to briefly paraphrase and synthesize recurrent ideas and concepts that Reb Zalman may have touched on in passing in various contexts. A glossary in the back of the book offers extended definitions of many of the terms used throughout the book.

UNIVERSALISM *and* RENEWAL *of the* SACRED TRADITIONS

We are now "post-Holocaust, post-Hiroshima and Nagasaki, post-Moon Walk, post-seeing the planet from outer space . . ." The renowned astronomer Fred Hoyle predicted that "when we will see what earth looks like from outer space, a revolution in our consciousness will have taken place, the likes of which have not happened before."[14] Whether or not we like it, or are ready for it, this is our current situation and, in order to continue to meaningfully engage the modern psyche, our spiritual traditions need to accommodate the new reality maps that are now operative in the world. This is the starting point from which Reb Zalman approaches the vital issues of spiritual renewal and universalism. The walls that separated and contained the sacred traditions for centuries have come down for many; the old exclusivist approach is no longer helpful or plausible for a large and growing segment of the population. Like the idea that the sun moves around the earth, the old idea that one's religious tradition is the only viable truth and all the others are all totally false and invalid no longer rings as true as it did in previous generations.

This is not to suggest that the rich and enduring sacred traditions that have nourished us for millennia should go out of existence—not at all. Rather, it is to affirm that they can incorporate modern and postmodern insights from science, physics and sociology to update their cosmologies, God-concepts, and sense of interconnectedness within the global spiritual landscape— all without giving up their important core sacred worldviews. Certainly, the egoic violence that has so often plagued historical religions when imbued with partisan or nationalistic religious claims cries out to be tempered with a truly religious compassion worthy of a universal God or Spirit which unites us all.

In regard to updating the ancient scriptures, the texts can in many cases be meaningfully reinterpreted rather than abandoned. A well-known example would be the six days of creation in Genesis 1:3-5. A common premodern interpretation is that God literally created the world a little more than 6,000 years ago in six twenty-four-hour days (even though the text stipulates that the sun—by which we measure a day—wasn't created until the fourth day), and the Deity needed to rest from His labors on the seventh day. By contrast, a common post-Darwinian interpretation, held by many believers who also value the findings of modern science, is that, if the Bible is true and it states that creation occurred in six days (or periods—*yamim* in Hebrew), a less problematic interpretation of the text would be to say that it refers to six vast eons of time; and if so, this could allow for a divinely manifested buildup of the biosphere of the earth through a natural evolutionary process. Also lending credible biblically-based support to the idea that the author did not necessarily intend six literal twenty-four-hour days is the statement in Psalms 90:4 that "a thousand years is like a day" in God's sight.

As Reb Zalman once pointed out to me, one has the legitimate right to apply a hermeneutic that reinterprets the biblical text; and according to the Jewish inner tradition, the holy scriptures have at least four levels of meaning on which they can be read (a subject to which we will return). *Exegesis* would be bringing out one of the objective, implied meanings in the text, while *eisegesis*, often employed in New Age commentaries, would be subjectively reading into the text a meaning that probably wasn't intended by the ancient author (as such, the latter wouldn't be widely accepted as a legitimate hermeneutic of the text).

During Reb Zalman's first thirty years, he embraced his Jewish faith fervently, becoming a Hasid and a rabbi, and as such, was uncomfortable with nonJewish "goyish" forms of spirituality—crosses and so forth. But with further education and experience, his outlook broadened as he began to discover commonalities between Judaism and other world religions. For instance, it came as a great surprise when he discovered that the Roman Catholic Cistercian and Jesuit orders used a form of mental prayer very similar to what he previously assumed was only known in his own tradition of Hasidism, based on the teaching of Reb Schneur Zalman of Liadi.

"I began to realize that we have gifts to give to each other," says Reb Zalman,

> and that's when I started to hang out with people in different traditions. And like Picasso, who had a "blue period," and this and that kind of period, I had a Catholic period, and I had a Protestant period, and a Hindu period, and a Buddhist period, and a Sufi period. And of course, through all this, I didn't stop being Hasid and Jew. It was just as if the flavoring and the accompanying strain— what gave harmony to my melody and gave rhythm to what I was doing—was taken from that other tradition.[15]

In the end, Zalman described himself as a "nondenominational" rabbi and "a Jewish practitioner of generic religion." Referring to his friend, Thomas Merton, another religious boundary-crosser, Zalman observed:

> When Thomas Merton, at the end of his life, was looking at Catholicism, he was no longer without a hyphen. He was a Taoist-Catholic. There is that sense of sharing— like a "Jew-fi" [Jewish Sufi]. All of us, in a way, when we

start looking at what are the other ingredients, what are the crossovers that we have, find that if we only had our tradition alone we wouldn't make it. We can only make it because we have access to more than one tradition.[16]

JEWS SEEKING FULFILLMENT
OUTSIDE *of* JUDAISM

In his early work with Jewish outreach, especially among college age students, it quickly became apparent to Zalman how many Jews had been turned off by the way Judaism was being taught at home and in the synagogue. Some had become secularized, but many other Jews, who were still experiencing an unquenched spiritual longing, were turning to Eastern religions, which seemed to offer something they were missing in their root tradition. A number of Jews had become mature students of major Eastern teachers in Zen, Vedanta and Sufism, and in time, some had gone on to become prominent roshis, swamis, and sheikhs in their own right. Reb Zalman often appeared on interfaith programs where, ironically, nearly every religious representative was Jewish by birth. When he went to purchase some incense at the Vedanta Society during the 1960s, the swami remarked, "You Jews are such a spiritual people!" The swami added that, wherever he goes in Eastern spiritual circles, he finds these organizations full of Jews. When Reb Zalman visited Joshu Sasaki Roshi, the Roshi asked him what he should tell the large numbers of Jews who were coming to the Zen Center. Zalman answered, "Tell them to do what a Jew must do, but to do it with Zen mind!"[17]

Reb Zalman pointed out that, although the exotic religions of the East appear to offer an attractive alternative for Western seekers, it is important to keep in mind that "what we get over here is Eastern religion cleaned up for export, and because of that, we don't see all the restrictive halakhic things they have in their native setting. And if you look at how Ramakrishna was chanting long hymns and so on, you'll see that there's more there than just beginning meditations like *Om Nama Shivaya*."[18]

At a "Torah and Dharma" gathering in the 1980s, Rabbi Shlomo Carlebach sent a message which offered a profound insight into the situation. He mentioned a teaching of the Izhbitzer Rebbe that anger is a defilement and a *kohein* (priest) is not to defile himself by coming in contact with the dead. The idea is that, when faced with a corpse, a certain anger against God over that death may rise up in one and subtlely contaminate one's positive feeling toward God. But alas, Shlomo continued, because of the Holocaust, every living Jew has in some way been tainted by this anger, which has adversely impacted the Jewish people's experience of the religion. The saving grace for seekers stuck in this situation has been the holy teachers from the East who are not angry with God and who have been helping Jewish seekers find another way to relate to and to get close to God again.

Besides this aspect, there are many other factors contributing to the growing modern trend of spiritually hungry people, especially in the West, turning away from the mainstream Abrahamic religions to other paths for their spiritual sustenance, or simply becoming secularized agnostics or atheists. Another fast-growing category is those who say they are "spiritual but not religious."

"What is it about religion that those who say they are 'spiritual but not religious' don't like?" asks Reb Zalman. He answers:

> The hierarchical stuff, the patriarchal stuff, the anti-feminist thing that is all the way from the Vatican through the Taliban and Mea She'arim,* and so on. The other thing is that most of the religions wanted to say something about how nature is tainted, nature is fallen. There is also the claim for "the supernatural."[19]

It is to this situation of disaffected spiritual aspirants that much of Reb Zalman's energy was focused over the years in his quest to renew and update Judaism while bringing out some of its lesser known, mystical teachings. Sadly, many nonaffiliated

---

*   The ultra-orthodox Jewish quarter in Jerusalem.

Jews have reported their experience, prior to leaving the religion, of asking their rabbis or Jewish teachers if there was any higher teaching or mystical tradition in Judaism only to receive a dismissive answer or, worse yet, a flat "no."

Reb Zalman noted that one of the reasons for the widespread estrangement from Judaism is that, since the nineteenth century, the legal, rational mode has been emphasized to the near exclusion of the experiential, loving, ecstatic side that has historically also been an important part of the Jewish tradition. When immigrants came to America, they began to do services in English and set up fixed pews—as in a church or courtroom—making it almost impossible to get up and move around or dance. In addition, the very cerebral, masculine-oriented nature of the Jewish prayer service tends to inhibit the expression of more exuberant, celebratory feelings and bodily involvement in worship in the *shul* (sanctuary). It was in an effort to redress this imbalance and bring in more of the feminine perspective that Reb Zalman began to ordain women rabbis.

THERE ARE STILL TREASURES
in the TRADITION

On the positive side, Judaism has a long, eventful history containing much of value, a rich and ecstatic Kabbalistic tradition, Dead Sea Scroll desert mystics, and a wisdom tradition that honors the divine feminine (Hokhmah/Sophia). As Reb Zalman advised a group of Sufi cherags:* When selecting Jewish scriptures, please be aware there's a lot more in the tradition than just the *Shema* ("Hear O Israel, the Lord is One") and the laws of Moses. There is that Taoist-like book of Ecclesiastes, the poetic beauty of the Psalms, the feminine wisdom from Proverbs, the deep philosophical questioning of Job, the social justice teachings from Amos, Micah, and Hosea, and even the post-Biblical tales of the Hasidim to draw on. It's not all dry prohibitions and "begats!"

---

*   Officiants in the Universal Worship Service of Hazrat Inayat Khan.

During a class on Deuteronomy, Reb Zalman contrasted the approaches of Moses and Solomon. With Moses, the tone is: "You must always obey these laws at all times and must never do these other things!" With Solomon (in Ecclesiastes), however, one gets a very different perspective: "There is a time for every season, a time to do and a time not to do." So sometimes we have to move from Moses to Solomon (like moving from Confucius to Lao Tzu). Reb Zalman observed that religious fundamentalists like the rigid fixity of books like Deuteronomy (things must never change), but do not like the mutability of Ecclesiastes (which like martial arts, teaches one how to deflect and use those energies). Clearcut teachings like the commandments of Moses work well for a guiding a child, who might be confused by Ecclesiastes; however, as one's faith matures with age, the wisdom of Solomon becomes increasingly important in navigating through the complexities of life.[20]

Rabbi Rami Shapiro, who studied with Reb Zalman and is also an ardent universalist, made the delightful discovery that the Book of Ecclesiastes' famous opening line was not necessarily the pessimistic statement that most translators of the past have assumed. Often translated as "Vanity, all is vanity" or "Futility, all is futility," the Hebrew words *Havel havalim* can alternatively be translated as referring to "breath," "vapor" or "impermanence." This discovery led Rabbi Shapiro to the realization that the text can be validly interpreted along Taoist or Buddhist lines as referring to the impermanence of things, which, in turn, inspired him to produce and publish a whole new translation of the text entitled *Ecclesiastes: Annotated & Explained*.

Similarly, Reb Zalman relates how he sat *shiva** in Boulder after his father passed on, during a time when he was teaching a course on Jewish mysticism at Naropa. He recalls,

> Allen Ginsberg, who was on the faculty there, participated in the *minyan*. Just before the Aleinu prayer, I asked him to read Psalm 49 [the one to be recited in the house

---

*   The week-long mourning period after burial for close relatives prescribed by Jewish tradition.

of the mourner] . . . and he read it beautifully, as if he
had written it himself. Then we said the *Aleinu*, including
a sentence that appears in the traditional version I grew
up with: "for they bow down to Emptiness and the Void."
The rabbis meant this as a denigration of idol worship.
But in that moment, the daavening, the shiva for my father, the teachings of Chögyam Trungpa, the reading by
Allen Ginsberg—a Jew and devoted student of Tibetan
Buddhism—all these fused together in a single instant. I
suddenly realized that "emptiness and void" (*hovel varik*)
was nothing but another perspective on what we call God,
the Holy One, the King of King of Kings, whose highest attribute the Kabbalists call *ain*, No-thing—or as the
Buddhist would say, no-thingness [*shunyata*—the void].[21]

This shows how the sacred texts and prayers, when seen with
fresh eyes that are not fixated on timeworn traditional interpretations, can open up to reveal higher levels of meaning.

In an interview with integral philosopher Ken Wilber, Reb
Zalman spoke about integrating the divine pull from the future
with the divine guidance from the past. "The traditions are our
rearview mirror. It's important to consult . . . the rearview mirror, but if we don't have it, we don't have a straight path . . . so
traditions are important to have."[22] Using the tree as a metaphor,
he likens the tradition to the roots and central wood of the tree,
which gives it strength and stability and holds it up, but adds:

Those are yesterday's rings. The new rings that are coming on every time in the present are in the growing edge
just behind the bark. I think what gives a tree the strength
that it needs to have is that it does not discard the inner
core because . . . if there was only the growing edge, the
first storm would rip it out . . . and it is powered by so
much that comes from the roots.[23]

Reb Zalman goes on to point out how the insights we
get from quantum physics and other advances must be

incorporated into our understanding of the Divine, and concludes: "If you put what works in the tradition together with the new cosmology, the new reality map, I have a sense that something remarkable is going to happen. . . . [T]his is what will be the vehicle for Teilhard de Chardin's vision of the divinization of the planet."[24]

Elsewhere, Zalman commented that his conception of God had expanded to the extent that, in his own private prayers ("daavening"), where the prayers traditionally beseech "the God of Abraham, Isaac, and Jacob," he would sometimes add "the God of Einstein, of Wilber" and so on, "because my reality map has become so much vaster and I can't talk to the little God anymore."[25] By the "little God" he means the local, anthropocentric deity who favors one nation or religion, and rules on high over a pre-Copernican universe. In his book, *Paradigm Shift*, Zalman elaborates:

> When we talked about God in the past, still we were in the Ptolomeic universe, which means that the Earth is in the center, the sun and stars and the planets all revolve around the earth, and God is the infinite, *omni*-this, *omni*-that of the universe. Most traditional theology has not been fully reformatted to the picture that emerged after Galileo, Newton, and Copernicus. Now after Einstein we surely haven't reformatted our theology."[26]

CONSIDERING CRITIQUES *of the* TRADITIONAL IMAGE *of* GOD

Reb Zalman related in an interview that once, when he was with Chögyam Trungpa Rinpoche, the rinpoche related that his son had recently asked him, "Is there a God?" Rinpoche said when he answered, "No," his son looked relieved. Then Trungpa Rinpoche looked over in a sort of challenging way at Reb Zalman, who was dressed formally for *Shabbat*, the Sabbath. Zalman told him, "Rinpoche, the God you don't believe in, I don't believe in either."[27]

On the other hand, Zalman continued, there are the "new atheists" (Richard Dawkins, Christopher Hitchens, etc.) who are arguing that we don't need such a God; but they "haven't made the paradigm shift in thinking, so they are still talking about a deistic, not even a theistic God."

> In other words, they take the Bible literally. Here's what the Zohar has to say: "Anyone who reads the Bible as if they are literal stories has never entered into the real kingdom." You know how the Sufis are always talking about the *zahir* and the *batin*, the outer and the inner. We talk about *nigleh* and *nistar* [the manifest and the hidden] . . . So the question is: "Which God are you shooting down?" If they are shooting down the God who is not the cosmic cop, who lets, for instance, Hamas do what it's doing there and people in Darfur die, then of course they have a kind of God that deserves to be smashed.[28]

Reb Zalman goes on to say that if he talks to someone who thinks God is dead or doesn't exist,

> the first thing I want to ask them is: "Tell me, what is your cosmology?" If you come up with a cosmology that is unaware—that is to say, your reality is that we are the top level of awareness, then I say, "I'm sorry, I can't go any further with you," because I believe that the sun has greater awareness than Earth and the earth has greater awareness than I. This is where *holons* come in.[*]
>
> Remember Gurdjieff was still talking about those numbers: 3, 6, 12, 24, which was his way of talking about states and levels and vibratory levels.[**] So that's why it is important to be able to ask: "What is the highest thing that you have experienced?" Then the question is: "Is it

---

[*]   A *holon* is a term coined by Arthur Koestler and championed by Ken Wilber, which describes something that is an autonomous sub-whole unit, meaning it functions as both an independent whole unit, and is also part of an even greater whole system which includes it.
[**]   See discussion on p. 200 concerning these levels.

only brain, or is there awareness beyond the brain?" If the guy says, "Everything beyond the brain is an epiphenomenon," then I say, "Goodbye, Charlie," and leave him. "Many blessings, but I can't talk to you further." . . . The question is: "What are those guys doing right now, those atheists?" And I want to say they are sending a salvo across to the fundamentalists. And if they can wake up the fundamentalists so that, in order to keep to their values, to their ideals, they would have to go inside instead of outside, I think that salvo would be helpful. So I'm looking at that as a divine appearance, as it were.[29]

Reb Zalman's own interpretation of what is happening in the brain, while significantly more nuanced, loosely resembled the view of brain scientist, Julian Jaynes, as presented in his 1982 classic, *The Origin of Consciousness in the Breakdown of the Bicameral Mind*, which viewed inspiration "from above" in terms of the right and left hemispheres of the brain. Reb Zalman occasionally referenced Jaynes' book and the case Jaynes made that the people of earlier times were getting their spirituality as if an external voice was speaking to them, when the revelation was actually an interior right hemisphere experience. Because of the partition between the two sides of the brain, the analytical left brain was hearing the intuitive voice of revelation as "other," when it actually was coming from the right brain. Only around the time of Socrates and Buddha did people gradually begin to experience the intuitive voice as coming from within. Therefore, Zalman concludes, "I believe many of the people who spoke, and the voice of God came unto them and so on and so forth, saw it more as if it were coming from the outside because that's the way our nervous system works."[30] The point is that there are more naturalistic ways to account for how humans receive divine inspiration. It isn't simply an either/or choice between the atheist's rationalist denial and the fundamentalist's interpretation that, in Biblical times, a supernatural God literally spoke to humanity with a voice coming from the clouds.

Reb Zalman also taught that each of us has hidden within ourselves an already enlightened level of our being, illumined with divine wisdom, which we can sometimes access when we meditate in silence. It sometimes communicates to us intimations of higher wisdom through "Aha!" moments, profound dreams, visions, deep intuitions, and also through the still small voice of divine guidance. We have evidence of something like this occurring not only to prophets and saints, but also to philosophers and scientists: for instance, Descartes' famous dreams of 1619, which he said revealed to him the basis of a new philosophy, and Nobel laureate James Watson's admission that the breakthrough discovery of the double helix of the DNA chain, came to him by means of a dream image of a spiral staircase.

In a class at Elat Chayyim Reb Zalman spoke about the highest level of God and explained,

> The atheist and the mystic both believe in God's nothingness. This is very important because many people are atheists because all this "somethingness" that people attribute to God tells them they are wrong. They have such a deep intuition that God couldn't possibly be that. And such an attitude, an intuition, is called negative theology. It says, "Neti, neti"—"not this, not that"—*Ain K'Elohenu*—"no, not this"—*Ain K'Adoneinu*—"nothing like that." [31]

In Islam, the same essential idea is encoded in the phrase, *Allahu Akbar*, meaning God is always greater and beyond any finite human conception.

Reb Zalman further observed:

> There is something about "the Real" that I'm not happy with, and the reason I'm not happy with it is because it has to do with *res*, the Latin word for "thing." You know? It makes a thing out of it. And part of realization is that it is "no thing." All those words which go with emptiness and *shunyata*, and so forth—they have the feeling

of "beyond thing." So when someone says, "Does God exist?" I like to say, "Deep down, there is a God, but God doesn't *exist*. What do I mean by that? I mean to say that the level of being that is the being of God does not have existence to it. Existence always means finite, something out there. *Existo* [in Latin]—to stand outside.[32]

In explaining the subtler spiritual insights to the general public, such as the nature of God, the popular tendency is to simplify and reduce the ideas to their most rudimentary, mythical level. This inevitably leads to an impoverished spiritual understanding among the people and makes religion an easy target for critics to dismiss as naive superstition. The efficacy of traditional religious interpretation is further diminished by a lack of institutional adaptivity to advances in our knowledge of the physical world. As physics and our understanding of the world continue to change, a reexamination of the old scriptural interpretations becomes necessary in order to reconcile religious precepts of the past with the new information and ramifications that were not previously available. The Dalai Lama is aware of this need and has stated in his book, *The Universe in a Single Atom: The Convergence of Science and Spirituality*, that whenever modern science establishes sound new evidence which disproves an earlier scientific theory which was endorsed in ancient Buddhist discourses, he is in favor of embracing the newer understanding and admitting that an outmoded scientific precept was referenced in the old text. He is confident that letting go of Buddhist references to antiquated scientific conceptions will not seriously undermine the essential thrust of Buddhist metaphysics or the emphasis on compassion for all sentient beings.

Where such agile and clear-thinking spiritual adaptability is tightly resisted by Jewish and Christian fundamentalists, Reb Zalman inveighs: "The template—that which Bible is about—has been frozen, has become hard. The language of Bible is being used very often, instead of to open people, to close people up." On the eve of a new age, just as another day is about to dawn, as the social institutions are breaking down and people are saying, 'What are we going to do?'" He sings the response:

> "Give me that old time religion!"—and there is that sense that I want to go and do it exactly how it was done by the people in the past in the hope that I will somehow be able to take that Humpty Dumpty that nobody can put together again and put him together again just by the fiat of using the right kind of words taken from that holy source. And what one doesn't realize is that when the words have stopped breathing, when the words have stopped living, they are just like stones—and are often being used in that way—to stone people with Bible sentences. So we find ourselves, instead of helped by that book of books, being hindered by it. It is at this point, therefore, that one of the calls we have experienced is to so clear that template which is [the] Bible—which holds these words together, which gives us a connection to the infinite—and to clean it up, to give it life again, to breathe the living air again into it. . . . In wrestling with the holy text, there something happens to us—a sort of soul stretching.[33]

Reb Zalman goes on to say that up until the mid-twentieth century, there was a commonly shared assumption that humanity, as it is now, was the center and foreordained goal of creation. Yet, when we observe the direction we are going (our denial towards addressing the looming environmental crisis, coupled with humanity's immature approach to warfare and atomic weapons, under the influence of the reptilian brain), we see that we are not likely to make it if we continue on in the same way. So it is important to go back and look at the original intention behind the creation and see where the old scriptural stories and myths took us and what evolved out of that—then see what course corrections are needed.[34]

For example, several thousand years ago, when the earth had vast uncultivated resources and the population was probably no more than 50 million people, humanity received the divine directive: "Be fruitful and multiply; replenish the earth and subdue it."[35] Today, with over seven billion humans on the planet who are facing rapidly dwindling, finite resources, and a staggering nine to 10 billion metric tons of carbon emissions currently being released into the atmosphere each year, the divine directive of Genesis has long been fulfilled and newly updated divine counsel (we could say, from the inner guidance of the Holy Spirit) is sorely needed along with a new "eco-kosher" approach to life on the planet.

DISTINGUISHING MYTH *and* ALLEGORY *from* LITERAL HISTORY

In regard to the age-old wisdom and teachings given in the form of scriptural stories of people and events in the remote past, a distinction must be made between that which in the tradition is intended as factual history and a truth which is couched in the subtle language of myth and allegory—but which is not meant to be taken literally (such as the talking serpent and the Tree of Life in the garden of Eden). Where scripture doesn't appear to be describing empirical fact, a different hermeneutic, a different level of interpretation is needed to unveil its inner meaning and intention.

In *Paradigm Shifts*, Reb Zalman asks: "What is myth?" He answers, "Generally, we perceive myths as lies. Fairy tales. But actually, myths address deep truths. A myth is a story that is true but not factual. Therefore, if I am looking for fact, the underlying meaning of a reality structure, then the myth is a great truth." He further advises that "if we are to nurture our fledgling consciousness of organic collectiveness in the newly emerging age, we will need to shelve the old myths that divide us and create new myths that unite us, which promote this new visioning."[36]

Some Bible stories may refer to historical referents while simultaneously pointing to timeless allegorical verities. For instance, in Exodus, when the enslaved ones are freed from Pharaoh's oppression to wander at length through the desert and finally enter the land of milk and honey, on a mythological level, this represents the archetypal journey of the soul, liberated from the tyranny of the ego, purified by the divine disclosure (Mount Sinai), and at last coming home to the land of one's soul, where one is nourished by the fruits of the spirit. Reb Zalman points out that in Hebrew the word for Egypt (*mitzrayim,* from the root *metzar*) means "double bind," a constricted narrowing from both sides, and adds that dependencies and addictions are the "Egypts" in which people find themselves today.

Reb Zalman goes on to say:

> I don't believe in the comic book version of the graves opening up and that all the green slimy guys are going to come out from there, so . . . I go with Teilhard de Chardin, and believe that the planet is becoming more conscious. . . . In *Paradigm Shift,* I pointed out how little we have real evidence for our religion. If we had a time machine and got to Mount Sinai—*Oy vey,* what we would see! A lot of midrash would disappear in the reality of what actually happened "factically." But this doesn't mean that mythically we [Jews] didn't build up a lot of things.[37]

So, Reb Zalman asks,

> How do we move from myth and symbol to the reality of things? That has to do with the sacred dimension. It doesn't become real unless the sacred dimension is there. I can talk about ideas but what makes an idea really present is not that it is merely there as a concept. [It is] primary experience that makes it real for us. I believe that all theology is the afterthought of a believer.[38]

First comes a very real primary experience, then one reflects on it and interprets it trying to see what it all means. "For people who read it in books, the primary does not happen first."[39] In an article entitled, "The Endgame in Job," Reb Zalman commented further on the way myth functions:

Myth is the mystic's way to stall the exoteric from calling the thought-police. Alan Watts, in his *Beyond Theology*, has demonstrated that even the most serious games of religion are nothing but games. The mystic can bear this knowledge; the exoteric mind cannot. Once the play is given away, the exoteric opts out. . . . If the exoteric were to continue, and the mystic in turn continued to expose the masks of God that the exoteric projects one by one, the exoteric would soon turn to despair. This is not a problem for the mystic (esoteric). In fact, it is precisely what the mystic hopes to have, because the mystic would want to have the exoteric embrace his own mysticism, to embrace the knowledge that this is just an "as if," which the exoteric cannot do as long as he has an optimistic view about reality being one-level.[40]

ISSUES AROUND SPIRITUAL RENEWAL

Reb Zalman observed that in order to renew and update the system, we have to understand the system files. Yet, with today's computers we know that each new update will soon be followed by still another—it's never the last word. "If we're going to say: 'Is this hubris to think we know better?' . . . I'm willing to own that," Reb Zalman affirms. "When I see the xenophobia among *frum* [strictly observant Jewish] people and misunderstanding of the value of the divine content in other religions, I feel I can't buy that. But on the other hand, I don't want to secularize." Asked, "Why be Jewish?" Zalman responds that the heart has to do heart stuff and the liver does liver stuff, but the heart can't take over the whole body or do the liver functions. It is the same with Judaism or any of the other religions, as each has its own particular note to strike in the divine symphony of life, each ideally in harmony with the others.[41]

"So if all this universal stuff is coming out, what's the good of the particular?" asks Reb Zalman. "I take an organismic point of view and I say that the organism has organs and these organs have to produce what they produce for the life of the whole planet." He says he feels it is less hubristic to think we are a cell on the global brain than to think we are the center of the universe.[42]

In *Paradigm Shift,* Reb Zalman speaks to the issue of updating, saying:

> I don't want to throw tradition away, but not everything in the Bible can be adopted whole as it is. Very often we have to ask, what was the intent then that produced such a law and how do we best fulfill the intent now? Now comes the question, what in tradition is transformative? You . . . have fundamentalists who say that every word of religion is literally true and inerrant. What they have done is created a template for Bible that has becomes so rigid that it couldn't breathe any more.[43]

Reb Zalman adds that if anyone says that renewing the tradition means diluting it, then they don't understand its purpose. Realizations aren't once and for all. There are always further ones. If renewal doesn't open the window to higher realizations, then it is just liberalization—watering down.

> The world needs for people like us to say, "Is it kosher?" looking at the ingredients. The world needs for us to ask, "Is this electricity *glatt* [*kosher*], or is it from a nuclear reactor?" These kind of halakhic questions* haven't yet come out. It's not likely that it's going to be done in Brooklyn or Mea She'arim [in Jerusalem]. But it is very important for us to ask these questions. . . ."[44]

Reb Zalman points out that Telihard de Chardin's model of the ongoing divinization of the planet points to a process of ever-expanding horizon of spiritual unfolding, where we never have the final update on our reality maps and spiritual realizations. There is also a Hasidic teaching that a seer or prophet such as Moses can only foresee events as far in advance as the

---

*   *Halakha* refers to matters of Jewish law and what is *kosher,* or lawful.

end of their own lifetime—future changes that will occur after their passing are not readily accessible to them past their allotted time.* If this be so, it means that a static model set up in the past with the spiritual realizations of that time can never serve as a complete and adequate basis for addressing the spirituality of the future. Each generation brings new relevant spiritual insights to bear as life situations continue to change and evolve.

There are two parts to the lineage: one is what Reb Zalman called the *magisterium*—a term borrowed from Catholicism which refers to the authorized accumulation of practices and spiritual wisdom of the tradition built up over the centuries— and the other is the reality map that is laminated to that magisterium. At one point, we had the Ptolemaic reality map and that was the filter, the pair of glasses, through which the spiritual insights of the tradition were viewed and understood. Since then, the Copernican revolution has taken place and today, a century after Einstein's relativity theory, we look at things very differently—we see everything as being in motion. The changeability, the impermanence of things is a core principle in Buddhism as well.

Therefore, if a religious tradition continues to ignore the changes in the reality maps that have already been collectively acknowledged by most of the society, and if it is not seen that the magisterium can be separated from the outmoded scientific worldview of the past so that its teachings are reformatted and made more relevant in the present, then inevitably obsolescence and decay will set in. The tradition will gradually find itself more and more out of step with its constituency, and sensing this irrelevancy, people will leave and look elsewhere for their spiritual needs or secularize. This is why religious renewal is so imperative.

Reb Zalman was sometimes challenged by people who said: "What right do you have to change anything in the religion?" Then they would add the "floodgate" argument—that one change will open the door to changing everything in the

---

* See "The Story of Elimelekh of Lizhensk and the Seer of Lublin," found in Reb Zalman's *A Heart Afire: Stories and Teachings of the Early Hasidic Masters.*

tradition until nothing is left. The answer, says Reb Zalman, is that you have to have knowledge of the deep structure of the tradition to see what changes can be made. Otherwise, if one has only a superficial knowledge, one will change the wrong things and do damage. The deep structure of the liturgy is what is important.[45] The Christian mass and the Jewish prayer service both have built into them an energy curve that involves the reading and contemplation of the inspired word, prayers at the foot of the altar—*Kyrie Elieson* or *Hoshiah-Na* (Lord, please save us)—hymns of thanksgiving and praise (*Gloria, Credo, Sanctus, Pesukei d'Zimra*) culminating in an ascent to the place of glorification and oneness (Eucharist or Amida and Torah portion), followed by a descent which helps one integrate that sacred, transcendent dimension or feeling of wholeness experienced on the mountain peak before going back out, renewed, into the world.

As a Hillel director, Reb Zalman noticed that when people wanted to make shifts and changes in the services, sometimes they worked and other times they didn't. When he watched people try to lead a creative service he noticed that sometimes it fell flat and sometimes it worked. Why? For one thing, the interest, concern, and involvement of the celebrant made a difference. He also learned that

> if they followed the deep structure of it, even though there would be some shifts and changes in the outer form, it didn't matter. But whenever they didn't follow the deep structure—in other words it was not developmental—one thing didn't build upon the other—then what happened was a kind of hodgepodge. Even though they used old and familiar and traditional forms, the details didn't have an inner coherence. So it's really very important that the worship that we do be something that we can live, that we can experience, and if it is only something we can put through our head or through our mouth, it wasn't enough—it had to be something we could put ourselves through."[46]

In another class, Reb Zalman explained that what Jewish Renewal—or renewal in any other tradition—is doing is deconstructing various elements used in the past, such as: What is happening when I *daaven*/pray or sing a *niggun* melody? Then the question is: How do I reconstruct it in our time to make it work with different people and different situations? How do we create that same soul response today? That is the task the Jewish Renewal Movement has undertaken.[47]

GENERIC RELIGION

The most transformative parts of the religion, says Zalman, are "the generic stuff." We are also aided by the symbols and memories triggered by music and rituals in our background religion— that's our predilection, our ancestral habits and memories.

> The understanding that we are getting now is that if you think organically, then every religion fits organically its members. Because if you see it deeper, you see that there is only one religion: generic religion, no frills religion. And if you want it with garlic and tomato sauce, you can do this way, and if you would like it to be with a Jewish taste you get this way, but the only religion that works is generic religion. Now when you begin to see this, that we on this planet can't get it together unless we talk to our counterparts in the other religions . . . [it becomes clear that] what we now need is to have believers on both sides who also see the next thing—mainly that we are all being moved forward to that place when the jigsaw puzzle will fit together.[48]

So we do not have to give up or forget our particular lineage for the sake of generic spirituality, Zalman concludes, but it is the generic part that really holds the transformational material and produces wisdom. The rest is the outer form, the window-dressing, the particular history, story, and flavor—but we do not want a flavorless generic blend either. He feels some things can be borrowed from another tradition, for instance Centering Prayer as Christian meditation. Sometimes the missing or recessive elements can be rediscovered in one's own tradition, where they have laid dormant and nearly forgotten. This was precisely the rationale medieval Jews like Abraham ben Maimonides gave for drawing on the insights, practices and piety of Sufism in order to revive that which the Jewish tradition had originally taught but from which it had later deviated during the diaspora.

Today, one doesn't normally associate Judaism with religious outreach for converts, but back during the Early Roman Empire, Jews were proselytizing and delving into universalism, so that people—known as "God Fearers" or respecters (*hanifs* in pre-Islamic Arabia)—would get to experience the universality of Judaism by accepting it at the more universal level but not at the particularist level of action (keeping the sabbath, circumcision, etc.). Isaiah points to this universalistic vision: "My house shall be a house of prayer for all people."[49] Today, this impulse is manifesting once again. As Zalman sees it: the goal is more openness between religions, but not homogenization.[50]

the FOUR LEVELS *of* REALITY *and the* MULTIDIMENSIONALITY *of* GOD

Running through the world's spiritual traditions is a fourfoldness that expresses itself in many ways: the four directions, the four elements, the four types of yoga, and the four worlds of Kabbalah and Sufism. In psychology, Carl Jung has also delineated four functions: sensation, feeling, reason, and intuition. In Kabbalistic practice, the four letters of the divine name Y-H-V-H (pronounced *Yud, Heh, Vav, Heh*—and sometimes spelled, *Yahweh*) correspond to the four levels of reality. In Arabic, the name *Allah* also fits with a four worlds schema (*Alif, Lam, Lam, Haa'*).

What are these four worlds, or modes of perception? They are the worlds of: action, feeling, knowledge and being. They correspond to the physical plane, the world of emotion, the mind world, and the transcendent world (where all is one and perfect, corresponding to the Divine Presence—that in us which

just *is*). Another way in which Reb Zalman has expressed it in
song is:

> *I am because I do.*
> *I am because I feel.*
> *I am because I know.*
> *I am because I am.*

I find the understanding of the four worlds particularly
helpful in relation to how we conceive of God and also how
we often misconceive God. The following section commences
with a brief description of how the Divine functions in each of
the worlds, followed by an overview of how these four worlds
are expressed in similar ways in the various sacred traditions
and schools of psychology. The discussion concludes with Reb
Zalman's further explications and insights into how the delineation of the four levels clarifies our understanding of God and
our own lives.

GOD *in the* PHYSICAL WORLD

In the physical world, God functions as creator and sustainer of
a material universe in which physical principles operate (such
as the laws of gravity and entropy), in which birth, death, and
natural disasters occur in accord with natural laws, and where
one karmically sows what one reaps according to the principles
of cause and effect. In this world, we wouldn't speak of supernatural, divine interventions* or qualities like divine compassion.
Rather, this level has to do with the natural material world, the
realm in which scientists, behaviorists and eighteenth century
Deists (with their mechanical clockwork conception of reality)
find at least partial affinities. Here we relate to objects, people
and bodies in terms of purely physical things, through an "I-it"
relationship, in the language of Martin Buber. In this world, if

---

* Although this is not to deny that phenomena which scientists don't
fully understand, such as spontaneous healings and stigmata, can physically
occur.

I try to say God is a thing, a substance, I go wrong and reduce God to an idol. In the physical world we are dealing only with the literal, surface, "concrete" reality of the phenomenal world, but not the interior, subjective or higher dimension of things.

Theologically, this world also corresponds to the pantheistic worldview, if we define that word in the limited sense that equates all of nature—everything which exists in the objective world of the five senses—as equivalent to the body of God, or the Goddess.* In Hebrew, the God-name most closely associated with the physical world is the plural name of God, or "the gods," *Elohim*. Reb Zalman says that "it meant at one point the whole pantheon, all the God-ing that's going on, and that God-ing shows itself most strongly in nature."[51] At this purely physical level, he says, one can't really communicate with the natural forces like gravity; instead, this aspect of the divine "face is averted from me," he says, "and only makes sure that my pulse is beating and if I take cyanide that I should die. That's part of the way that nature is set up."[52]

The physical world is where the scientist is most adept. In the physical world of the five senses, scientists can test, repeatedly verify, analyze and explain most things in a laboratory using the scientific method, yet in the other nonphysical worlds of feeling, thinking, and intuition, these methods are of little use in explaining things like love, awe, intelligence, or the intuition of a higher power.

According to the Qur'an, Allah or God cannot be seen with the physical eyes, yet God is in the seeing itself, and the Divine can be recognized in the physical *ayats* or signs which manifest in the natural world—in a glorious sunset, in rainfall and the nourishing food which sustains us, in the regularity of the seasons, and so on. Just as the footprints of a bear in the snow

---

* For example, Ramanuja, in his Gita commentary, maintains that the whole universe is the body of God. Of course, the classical theological objection to this sort of pantheism is that it leaves out the divine transcendence and identifies God with that which is changing and subject to decay. But here, we bypass that concern by delineating four dimensions of the Divine, with transcendence being the highest level, with the meaning of things in the mental world, and the personal, relational aspect of God located in the world of feeling.

point implicitly to the bear's existence, the Divine Artist is seen through His/Her art, which manifests as the physical universe. We can also recognize that we are not beating our own pulse or growing our hair; rather, it can be attributed to the Divine action. (There is a sense in which, as Alan Watts used to point out, anyone can experience this by flipping their usual perception of the body's respiration from the feeling of "I breathe it" to "It breathes me.") Again, the Qur'an supports a similar perspective in the *ayah,* in which it is revealed to Muhammad that "You did not throw when you threw [a handful of soil at the attacking army], but Allah threw."[53]

Although the story may be apocryphal, it was reported that when Russian cosmonaut Yuri Gagarin, first flew the Vostok I capsule into outer space in 1961, he peered out the window and reported, "I looked and looked and looked, but I didn't see God."[54] What was he looking for? God as a physical substance, up there and out there. It is this kind of misconception that led Buckminster Fuller and others to suggest that it is better to think of God, not as a noun, but as a verb—to see that everything that is happening in the universe is the activity of the Divine "God-ing."

The whole field of process theology, associated with Alfred North Whitehead, is predicated on the realization that people and events are not static freezeframe nouns but are everchanging verbs always in the process of moving and changing in time. Even from the standpoint of quantum physics, there are no static, "solid" atoms but only fluctuating particle-and-wave patterns of energy which, to the ordinary human eye, seem to make up discreet, solid objects which our language identifies using nouns. If we understand this about the material world, how can we continue to think of the Divine Source of Being as a noun, a thing, a discreet entity existing somewhere in time and space?

GOD *in the* FEELING WORLD

In the world of feeling, which is also the world of relationship and of dialectic, we can relate to God, not as anything that has a physical counterpart in existence (I-it), but as the beloved in an "I-thou" relationship which involves the heart. It is at this level that we can feel that God cares, and find within ourselves stirrings of the divine compassion and other qualities. In the feeling world, we liken God to a person (*persona*) in terms of function, with analogs to human relationships—as father, mother, divine child, judge, friend, sovereign, lover, avenger, comforter, and guide. All of these and more represent the masks of God, the way we idealize the Divine and make God comprehensible in the world of feeling.

In religious terms, this is the world of devotion and prayer, where one grows through a personal relationship with God, through trust, and by attuning to the spirit of the God-realized ones. Here, God is experienced as intimate and personal without being a person. It is like the difference in how we feel when we are alone as opposed to knowing that someone else is there listening and present.

The world of affect, the path of love or *bhakti* (as the Hindu tradition would name it), opens the way toward natural ego transcendence when the heart can open to fully embrace and adore another, be it God, or whoever or whatever embodies divinity for one. While our love does not naturally flow to the aspect of God who is responsible for gravity, hurricanes, and mortality, nor to the divine aspect which corresponds to the awesome infinitude of the universe, it is the aspect of God Who is the Source of love, harmony and beauty—the One with Whom we can have an intimate heart to heart talk—to Whom we can turn for refuge, forgiveness, and healing, and truly love with all our heart and soul.

It may be asked, "In the world of emotion, how does a nondualist worshiper show devotion when that divine spark is within?" The ego is also within and can easily get inflated. Devotion requires an "other" out there to adore. The quest for an outer focus of adoration and praise in religion is what gives energy to many of our rich, mythic religious rituals such as Passover and Christmas, to the contemplation of holy icons and statues, as well as Eastern traditions such as tantric Yoga, where the Divine is experienced in another human being. Likewise, an altar or a sacred shrine, such as the Ka'ba, can serve as the focus of worship, even though it is clear that God is not exclusively localized there. The nondual perspective can bring the *bhakti*- lover (the *bhakta*) to the place of union beyond subject and object when love becomes vast enough to include all of creation and beyond. This is evident in the verse from the *Gayan* of Hazrat Inayat Khan: "Before whomsoever I bow, I bend before thy throne. The heart of man is thy sacred shrine," and "Through the whole of nature I hear Thy music played, my Beloved."[55]

Each of us has an identity and an interactive role to play in the world of relationship. We also have a life script or destiny we are living out. This is what gives us individual personhood in the world. The word person is related to the Latin word *persona*, the Greek word *prosopon*, and to the goddess Persephone. The persona was the mask worn by an actor on the Greek and Roman stage as the players enacted tragic, comic, and cathartic dramas before an audience. Behind the mask remains the real being who has donned it. Just so, there is an aspect of the feeling/relational world in which "all the world's a stage" and each person wears a mask and plays a role in the divine play.

On the level where feeling is primary, the world can be experienced as a great interactive drama in which God, the one great Self of the universe, plays all the parts and experiences what it feels like to participate in the emotional ups and downs of incarnated existence, within the limitation of human form. In the Hindu spirituality of Ramakrishna, the divine play is called *lila*—the activity of the Great Mother. The word "play" here has multiple meanings: in life, we all play a role and don a temporary identity with which we identify. Play also carries the sense of something done just for the enjoyment of it—we could say God's pastime or entertainment, though not necessarily in a frivolous sense. As Reb Zalman puts it: God was in solitary confinement and bored with having nothing to experience, so God brought forth the universe as a diversion to occupy Him/Herself.[56] This is another way of expressing the idea reported in a *hadith qudsi* (holy report) of the Prophet Muhammad where

Allah reveals: "I was a hidden treasure and longed to be known, so I created the worlds." Giving the bhakti perspective, the ecstatic Egyptian Sufi, Dhul-Nun Misri, commented that it was for the sake of love that Allah was moved to bring forth the worlds.

GOD *in the* MIND WORLD

In the world of knowledge, the mind world, God is experienced as the source of consciousness, bliss, and being, the meaning behind all that exists, the One who enlightens through the true knowledge (gnosis) of reality. This is the world of intellect, of pure thought, the plane where we think philosophical ideas about God and the nature of reality. Here we meditate on what it all means and how we fit into the divine plan. This is the contemplative realm in which theologies are spun and realizations, "ahas" of consciousness, are experienced through breakthroughs in understanding. This is the way of illumination, of wisdom. The closest we can have to an analogue in the world of knowledge is something like the image of Krishna as he is unveiled to Arjuna in the Bhagavad Gita, manifesting as the Being of Splendor, donning the myriad masks of God. A space age analog might be the Hubble telescope images showing a double helix nebula which resembles a great cosmic eye, a natural symbol of consciousness, reminiscent of the Egyptian Eye of Horus. In the highest sense of knowledge or gnosis, knowledge is not just learning about external objects but participatory being/knowledge of one's true identity.

the WORLD *of* DIVINE TRANSCENDENCE

In the highest world of pure being and transcendence, all is one and God is beyond attributes and multiplicity. Here, God does not "exist" as a separate entity but just *is*, universally beyond time and space. God is Being with a capital B. We can't say anything about this level, for speech and thought are useful only in the worlds of duality, and any attempted description goes wrong, limiting the infinite aspect of God to a concept referring to the world of objects. The only way to "experience" God at this level is to become nothing, to become totally transparent so that the Divine alone is. In Sufism this is called by the Arabic word, *fana* (annihilation); in Christian tradition, *kenosis* (self-emptying), and in Hebrew, *ayin* (nothingness) and *bittul ha-yeshi* (I am nothing: God alone *is*).* Here the individual's "I am" is none other than the cosmic "I am." At this level, there is no duality and, as Reb Zalman says, "It takes One to know One."

"Today we have it easier," Reb Zalman explains,

> because we have analogs in science and we can say, "I am nothing but a chip off the old block." In other words, I'm a snippet of the Great Cosmic Hologram. . . . My deep feeling is these days that the repression of that [God] part is what is giving people great aches. And to help people to own that isn't [easy]—you can't run the ethic of "mine and yours" and capitalism and that at the same time—do know what I'm saying? This demands an organismic understanding of all life. This demands that we should see ourselves as brain cells of Mother Earth. We are the global brain. We are each a brain cell of the global brain.[57]

In Buddhism, the sense of transcendence is experienced as clear, luminous emptiness—a vast sense of joyous freedom and unconditioned awareness, beyond the limiting constraints of isolated ego consciousness. In Vedanta, transcendence is experienced in terms of liberation from the separate ego-self and union with *sat chit ananda*—the pure presence, consciousness, and bliss that underlies all manifestation. Awakening to the transcendendent dimension, then, can be experienced both in terms of merging in unity with all things, or through

---

*   Reb Zalman recommends that, rather than thinking of *bittul ha-yesh* as "becoming nothing," think in terms of "becoming transparent"—letting the light through. With a nod to Star Trek, he suggests a simple meditation in which you take a minute to experience yourself as shimmering light, as though you are being beamed onto the transporter deck of the starship, Enterprise.

discovering the freedom from self as a marvelous sense of emptiness. In the depth of the Abrahamaic spiritual traditions, the way of self-transcendence lies in experiencing unconditional love and compassion for all beings, seeing the interconnectedness of all things and entering into the spirit of "divine love" and sacred meanigfulness that has brought forth all life, and which lifts one beyond the narrow perspective of self-centeredness.

the FOUR PATHS *of* YOGA

Now that we have an idea of what distinguishes the four different levels of reality vis-à-vis God, some further background information may be useful. There are four recognized paths of yoga in Hinduism, corresponding to the four worlds: karma or hatha yoga (physical level, action), bhakti yoga (feeling), jnana yoga (knowledge), and raja yoga (being). Here, I will draw in part upon the concise descriptions of the four yogas given in the Dalai Lama's book, *Toward a True Kinship of Faiths.*

KARMA YOGA (*in the* WORLD *of* ACTION)

The path of karma yoga

> emphasizes the approach of actual work in the form of service. Here in the living out of one's everyday life and devoting oneself wholeheartedly to one's work, one cultivates the truth of God. . . . The key is to engage in one's work in a way that transcends the concerns of narrow ego-centeredness.[58]

In the *Bhagavad Gita,* Krishna advises the karma yogi to set his or her sight on the Lord, offering acts of selfless service in equanimity, without attachment to the fruits of one's action. That is, the everyday duties of the householder should be performed as conscious acts of service for their own sake, not simply for a reward nor as an action driven solely by the desire to obtain a successful end result. Yet, the Hindu sages have cautioned that one should not conclude from this that one's action is thereby rendered meaningless; rather, the emphasis is on process, the present moment of the action itself rather than the anticipated result. Lord Krishna continues: "Set thy heart upon thy work, but never on its reward. Work not for a reward, but never cease to do thy work."[59] "'I am not doing any work,' thinks the person who is in harmony, who sees the truth."[60]

In Christianity, one finds the same concept in the "holy indifference" taught by St. Ignatius. Someone once asked Ignatius how he would react if the new Pope were to disband the Jesuit Society, which Ignatius had spent so much time and energy building up. He replied: "Fifteen minutes (of prayer/meditation) in the oratory and it would all be the same to me."[61] While we have emphasized karma yoga, there are other types of yoga which operate on the physical level such as hatha yoga, with its emphasis on the health of the body.

BHAKTI YOGA (*in the* WORLD *of* FEELING)

Bhakti yoga "primarily emphasizes one-pointed devotion to the love of God." This approach

> requires attributing personal qualities to the godhead so that the devotee can experience a sense of intimacy with God, almost in the manner of a deep friendship. . . . A true practitioner of bhakti is able to totally submit the personal ego and offer his or her entire being to the love of God, such that the transcendence of ego boundaries occurs naturally in the act of deep devotion.[62]

In the eighteenth chapter of the *Bhagavad Gita,* Lord Krishna advises Arjuna on behalf of humanity:

> By love he knows Me in truth, who I am and what I am, and when he knows Me in truth he enters into My

Being.[63] . . . God dwells in the heart of all beings, Arjuna: thy God dwells in thy heart. And His power of wonder moves all things—puppets in a play of shadows—whirling them onwards on the stream of time. [64]

In Christianity, this attunement is reached through the sacred heart of Jesus. In the Sufi tradition, this is expressed in the saying of the Prophet Muhammad in which Allah reveals: "My heavens and My earth cannot contain Me, but the heart of My believing servant does contain Me." In the Jewish tradition, Jeremiah proclaims the divine word: "But this shall be the covenant that I will make with the house of Israel: After those days, says the Lord, I will put my law in their inward parts, and write it in their hearts; and I will be their God, and they shall be my people."[65] In the world of Hasidim, the Ba'al Shem Tov, is the great bhakti rebbe of love within the Jewish tradition. St. Francis and Jalaluddin Rumi hold similar ranks within the Christian and Islamic worlds.

JNANA YOGA (*in the* WORLD *of* KNOWLEDGE)

Jnana yoga, the way of gnosis,

> emphasizes the path that leads to oneness with God through knowledge. Knowledge here should not be understood in terms of intellectual discursive knowledge of facts but rather it is the knowledge of one's own nature, self-knowledge in the true sense of the word.[66]

Underlying the illusion of the ego as everyday self is a "true Self. This is called *atman,* which is the god within; and unlike our temporal, individuated self, it is eternal, unitary, and independent."[67] Jnana yoga is associated with the nondual monistic philosophy of Advaita Vedanta as expounded by sages such as Adi Shankara and Sri Ramana Maharshi. Here, there is no duality between self and the Greater Self or sole reality of Brahman; whatever seems to be separate is part of the *maya* of the false ego and the illusory world of seemingly separate objects, which the jnani sees as seamlessly interconnected. As the Gita says:

> A person is said to be established in self-realization and is called a yogi when he is fully satisfied by virtue of acquired knowledge and realization. Such a person is situated in transcendence and is self-controlled. To him, gold or stones or earth are one.[68]

The nondual perspective is found not only in Hinduism, but in the mystical side of many other paths such as Sufism, where Ibn al'Arabi is its best-known expounder, or in the Christianity of Meister Eckhart.

RAJA YOGA (*in the* WORLD *of* BEING *and* TRANSCENDENCE)

The highest path, raja yoga, which is the royal pathway to God, "involves profound contemplative exercises that integrate physical exercises with psychological approaches, such as single-pointed concentration and visualizations,"[69] which takes one beyond the duality of subject and object. It is associated with the Yoga Sutras of Patanjali as well as the older *Samkhya* philosophy in which the rishis would enter into states of *nirvikalpa samadhi* (deep concentrated meditation) for lengthy periods of time, dwelling motionlessly beyond thought, absorbed in the blissful, formless and timeless consciousness of the Eternal Oneness. The mantra corresponding with this level is *Om*. The Gita alludes to this level, saying:

> When thy mind leaves behind its dark forest of delusion, thou shalt go beyond the scriptures of time past and still to come. When thy mind, that may be wavering in the contradictions on many scriptures shall rest unshaken in divine contemplation, then the goal of Yoga is thine. [70]

The Dalai Lama concludes:

Generally the . . . way of knowledge is most suited to those with a philosophical bent of mind. . . . . The way of devotion or bhakti is suited to those with a more devotional disposition. The way of work is for those with an active personality. Finally, raja yoga is recommended for those with a more contemplative, yogic disposition.[71]

INTRODUCTION *to the* FOUR WORLDS *in* KABBALAH *and* SUFISM

In the Kabbalistic system, the four worlds are associated with the four Hebrew letters of the divine name, the *tetragrammaton, Y-H-V-H—Yud, Heh, Vav, Heh.* When written out in English, the name is Yahweh, Yahveh or Jehovah (the last variant using the Latin and Germanic J instead of a Y). Religiously observant Jews avoid writing out or pronouncing this holy name, substituting for it *Adonai,* meaning Lord, which is the word used in Christian English Bibles (*Hashem,* the Name, is also a common Jewish substitute when speaking). If the four Hebrew letters are placed in a vertical downward row, they correlate with the four worlds and their Hebrew names as follows:

Y	the world of Atzilut	(Being)	Fire element
H	the world of B'ryiah	(Knowledge)	Air element
V	the world of Yetzirah	(Feeling)	Water element
H	the world of Assiyah	(Action)	Earth element

Below are the Sufi equivalents in Arabic, using the name Allah, with their equivalent latifas or chakras:

A	Haqiqa (Hakikat)	(transcendence)	crown chakra
L	Ma'rifa (Marifat)	(mind)	throat, third eye
L	Tariqa (Tariqat)	(heart)	heart chakra
H	Shari'a (Shariat)	(physical body)	base of spine, genital area, solar plexus

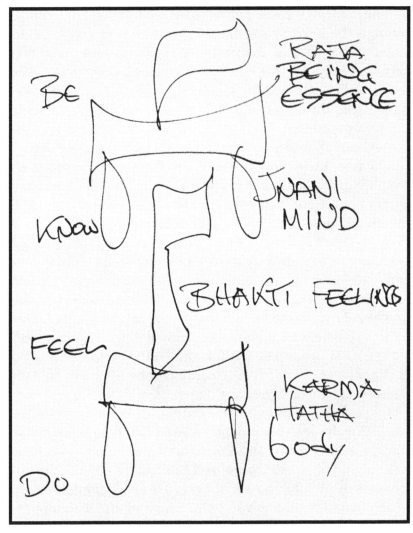

Chart of the four worlds linked with the divine name Y-H-V-H drawn by Reb Zalman and given to the author.

One caveat that must be given is that in the Sufi understanding of the four worlds (especially the Ottoman Turkish orders) the top two levels are reversed in order, so that the highest station is assigned to Ma'rifa. Why—if Haqiqa refers to the uppermost transcendent level of Truth—is Ma'rifa placed above it? Because it is understood to represent the level in which the highest Truth is realized and activated in the awakened human being.

The model is the *mi'raj* or ascent of the Prophet Muhammad through the heavens and beyond the realm of created existence to the place of Divine Unity where no separate beings exist, but only the One Absolute Source. Having transcended the created world and "disappeared" in the One, the Prophet returned to the world as a "mercy to the worlds," a vessel of the divine guidance. This state, in which one becomes the eyes through which God sees and the hands and feet through which God acts in the world, characterizes the level referred to by the Sufis as the station of Ma'rifa. To transcend the world and enter paradise consciousness (or *nirvana* in Buddhist terms) is indeed a high station, but for Sufis it is not the culmination of the path. The further stage is to become fully human, to make God a reality and embody the divine energies in one's daily life and work—opening on all four levels to the divine attributes. The Sufis use the Arabic terms *fana* and *baka* to express this mystery. First, in the words of the Prophet, one "dies before dying"—passing away from the limited self—or *fana fil'llah*, annihilation in the Divine. But the further step, the greater mystery is subsisting in Allah (*baqa* in Arabic)—or we could say "God awakening in humanity."

Of course, a similar process unfolds in the life of Buddha, who, after his enlightenment, resisted the temptation to go straight into *nirvana* instead of returning to help the world, as well as Jesus, who died to self and brought the divine compassion into the valley of human suffering, resurrecting dead hearts to abundant life. In the case of Muhammad, the literature depicts his divine encounter as resulting in intercession for the majority of his community and providing heavenly inspiration for many of the practices of Islam, such as the form and numbers of daily prayers. In Islam, the word *Haqq* (Divine Truth), which forms the root of Haqiqat, is another way of refering to God, or Allah Most High.

the FOUR WORLDS *in* PSYCHOLOGY *and* JUNG'S FOUR TYPES

Besides the Jewish and Islamic perspectives on the four levels there are also those found in modern psychology. In Carl Jung's typology, he distinguishes four types of function that closely tally with the four worlds model: sensation, feeling, thinking (reason), and intuition. Of the sensing type, Reb Zalman says that when you want to sense something (tactile, olfactory, proprioception) you experience texture, temperature, smell, hard/soft, wet/dry, and so on. Some of it is more on the animal level, especially the sense of smell. The Zen tea ceremony gives you the opportunity to take pleasure in the senses—the sheer pleasure of being there, present, slowing down and taking in every movement and sound. The bells, bread and wine, and incense in a Christian church are all ways of stimulating the senses.

Of the epistemology of feeling, Reb Zalman queries: "How does a feeling type know they are in love?" The answer is: it feels right. He says: you know you are getting rationalizations—a bunch of lame reasons—if it doesn't feel right. From a rational standpoint, it may not seem valid to say I'm doing it because it feels right, "but the knowledge of the feeler is no less knowledge."[72] The feeler goes inside and responds with how they feel—that's how they know. The sensor goes to the surface and the feeler goes deeper within, looking for centeredness and for their comfort-index.

Reb Zalman observes that most of us are unconscious about feeling. "Most feeling is binary—off/on. I love you! I hate you!" In between is bored or mildly interested. There is often an expectation that we will have great love for our spouse or family members, yet we may not always experience that intensity of feeling and that in turn can produce guilt and make us think there is something wrong in our feeling. Parents sometime undermine their children by saying, "You shouldn't feel that way about old uncle Herbie," or, "You ought to feel extremely enraptured on your wedding day." If we start believing we ought to feel something different from what we're feeling and start pretending to feel what we think others expect, that throws our calibration meter off. Then, later on, "you find that the feelings you claim to have aren't there and the feelings that are there you aren't ready to admit."

In politics, you can't legislate feeling. "You may say, 'Change your attitude, your outlook,' but you can't say 'Change your true feelings.'. . . Our language of feeling is very impoverished." Often music can be a much better conveyor of feeling than intellectual discourse, especially across cultures.

The thinker or reasoner will know something is true by operation—does it compute? In math, you add it up to check that it's true. It is coherent and reasonable. At the intuitive level, one has to go beyond the senses and beyond feeling. Sometimes it is difficult to clearly distinguish feeling from intuition. Things like faith and the desire to have children are matters of intuition beyond mere reason, mundane feeling or sensation. If you are asked, "Why have children?" you can't go to sensation for an answer because there's no sensation about that which is going on in the present to check out. You could try going to the left hemisphere and consult reasons, data and statistics for the pros and cons of whether to have children, or you could go to the right hemisphere and perhaps get a feeling of "I want" or "don't want," but none of these three options adequately addresses the question on the level of intuition. From the place of intuition, you can't really articulate an answer. You can only say, "There it is," or "I just know."[73] Thus it is fitting that even the words *knowledge* and *gnosis* (which refers to intuitive knowing beyond language) have an initial letter that usually goes unarticulated.

We can also find further corollaries to the four worlds in the various psychological schools of thought. Corresponding to the physical level is behaviorist psychology. In this system, the person is seen as part of the world of objects, conditioned by stimuli and susceptible in predictable ways to behavior modification.

The feeling level corresponds to Freudian and Depth Psychology, which points to unconscious feelings, pleasure principles and sublimated sexual urges as the underlying basis for our behavior, motivations and drives. Alfred Adler saw humans as primarily motivated by unconscious drives for personal power (inferiority/superiority issues). Freud focused mainly on pathology, on our lowest instinctual drives and desires, the behavioral level Sufis know as the *nafs al-ammara*. He reductively interpreted higher religious aspiration as a defense mechanism, a feel-good escapist fantasy of a heavenly afterlife motivated by the fear of death. The idea of God was treated as simply a projected parental superego or father complex, a product of wishful thinking as well as a means of priestly religious control. He interpreted the yogic experience of ecstatic transcendent meditation as simply a regressive flight back into the primal oceanic refuge of the mother's womb.

After working for several years with Freud, Carl Jung broke with him and forged his own system of analytical pyschology which assigned more value and weight to the collective archetypal dimensions that influence us along with the higher spiritual dimensions which can uplift our emotional lives. Jung wisely distinguished between the ego, shadow, and higher self; and although he astutely grasped the goal of psychotherapy as the wholeness of the self through integration of the opposing parts, his theories never really embraced the possibility of transcending the psyche, as emphasized in the Eastern spirituality.

Humanistic and cognitive psychology operate at the level of knowledge, epitomized by psychosynthesis, the holistic method of Roberto Assagioli, as well as Abraham Maslow's approach, which focuses not merely on pathology, but on the higher potential of the well-adjusted, high-achieving human being.

The highest level of being and intuition corresponds to Transpersonal psychology, which integrates and incorporates the higher dimension of awareness and spiritual energies beyond the limits of the skin-bound, ego-encapsulated individual self. Transpersonal psychology is widely considered to have the most potential for bridging the gap between the art of psychological and spiritual counseling.

ARCHETYPAL *and* ACCESSIBLE MODELS

Aldous Huxley, in his classic book *The Perennial Philosophy* (in the chapter on "Temperament in Religion"), matched the prophets of the various religions with various body types—mental, emotional, and physical. Huxley saw Buddha as the savior for the cerebretones in the mind world (emphasizing right knowledge, but not much devotion). He saw Jesus as the savior for the visceratones in the world of feeling, of the heart, and Moses as the savior of the somatatones in the sensate world of action (doing the commandments). In this way, we can find saints for each type.

Reb Zalman felt that a saint shouldn't be a plastic, inaccessible model, but someone like us, someone from whom we can learn lessons in dealing with life. He said sometimes the great Hasidic rebbes and saints of other traditions are thought of as having just appeared, "falling out of an eggshell, ready-made," and in this way, they become an archetype, elevated on a pedestal and unreachable. However, if we get a glimpse of the struggles they went through on their way to becoming who they became, we then encounter a more accessible model which we can truly emulate. The archetypal model is worshiped; the accessible model is followed.

Reb Zalman felt that Jesus had unfortunately become somewhat of an archetype, too high and divine to relate to in a real way—beyond the level that a person could hope to reach. Yet in the Gospels, he tells his disciples they must take up their own cross and follow his example—not that he will carry everyone's cross for them.[74] The archetypal conception has also been adopted with the pure and chaste Virgin Mary, who is the primary model available to Christian women. Like Jesus, she can become too remote if her purity is emphasized over her humanity. However, she becomes accessible when approached through her feeling heart, as the one who hears the cries of humanity and compassionately holds those who seek solace for their suffering and pain, as embodied in the image of the pieta. In the

Buddhist tradition, Kwan Yin provides this same compassionate space of refuge and consolation as the one whose heart is attuned to the suffering of the world.

The Jewish and Hindu traditions provide a somewhat wider spectrum of major feminine archetypes to choose from, as did the goddesses of Greek mythology—including some who are very down to earth: Demeter, Persephone, Artemis, Athena, Aphrodite, Hera, Hecate, and so on. These, and their male counterparts, are now utilized as constellations of inner personality types by psychologists like Jean Shinoda Bolen (author of *The Goddesses in Everywoman* and *The Gods in Everyman*). Reb Zalman concludes that if a religion doesn't have a saint for each type, it falls short of people's need.

FURTHER ELABORATIONS *on the* FOUR WORLDS *by* REB ZALMAN

Reb Zalman points out that in the nineteenth century there was tendency to deny that any levels existed other than the physical level, and so there was an effort to try to

> solve everything on the physical plane. . . . But you can never solve all the problems on one plane. There isn't enough physical stuff to go around to take care of hungers of feeling. The people who have been struggling with excess weight have found that out. The hunger that I feel, the void that I feel sometimes inside, no matter what I stuff inside of it as physical stuff, it won't handle it. The hunger happens to be on another level. It needs another level of food.[75]

In infancy, whenever hunger, loneliness, confusion or insecurity came up, we could go to the mother's breast and feel better again. As adults, if we try to go to the fridge to handle our hunger, our anxiety, our loneliness, or our spiritual needs, it doesn't work because the fridge cannot contain what is necessary for the other levels—our various needs cannot be fulfilled on the physical level alone. So, when you have a problem on one plane that can't be solved at that level, the answer is to be found on the next higher level—and that level has its own problems, to be solved at a still a higher level.

"Each world has a different operating system." In the physical world we use logic—"cause brings to effect on the level of physical action." On the level of affect, we have a dialectic, a hydraulic effect where "one pushes down, and the other raises up."[76] In the mind world, we look at how to help on this planet. We stretch to find a creative solution—looking for a synthesis of both sides. On the spiritual plane, we want to go to a level of real peace, one which has to bring together opposites, not just taking one side of a dualism.

It is customary to graphically represent the four levels stacked one above the other, with the higher levels on top. Yet the best model is not hierarchical because the four worlds are interactive. A tennis ball model is better, with the two *hehs* of the divine name joined across from each other (representing the feminine polarity), and the *yud* and *vav* likewise a connected pair (the masculine polarity), with all four interacting to make one whole sphere. In this model, neither the masculine nor the feminine side is convex only or concave only, in contrast to our usual notion that the masculine is always convex and the feminine concave.[77]

At the 1988 Wisdom School, Reb Zalman spoke about how we apprehend things in four ways:

> The I-it world is that world in which we deal with facts; the I-thou world is the world in which we deal with relationships and with feeling. . . . How would you say "gravity" in that second world, the world of I-thou? You call it love. [When] any two bodies in the universe feel attraction to each other, that's gravity . . . [and] that's love. So there are at least two levels of interpretation—one is the facticity level and the other one is the relationship level. There still is another level in which meaning is being given to something.[78]

The level on which we look at issues of why God created the universe—"that's a third level of understanding behind which there is still another level which can't even be talked about. 'The Tao that can be spoken of is not the eternal Tao; the name that can be named is not the eternal name.'"[79] That which makes crystals form and makes us as we are, is waiting as the Beloved, drawing us as theotropic beings back into itself.

The big mythological question or *koan*[*] is: Why does the infinite seek to become finite? There is a sense in which God was in solitary confinement and created the worlds as a pastime, a play, or entertainment. "As actors, we have to take the game seriously—and yet we know that the whole thing isn't finished until we become one again."[80]

In the physical world of Assiyah, things happen to us as creatures and we have karma; so at this level we have to prevent crime, law-breakers go to jail, and so on. But in the world of Yetzirah, the world of affect, the emotion is primary. The world is a stage on which dramas take place with no karma—we could say "for the entertainment of God," Who, without the creation, was in solitary confinement.

Zalman joked that in this interactive drama, in which God plays all the parts and we each experience the play from our own setting of personal consciousness, the class he is teaching brings together a group of people with whom he interacts on a weekly basis, while, for each of his students, he is but a bit player in the role of teacher who shows up in their play once a week. In this way, performing on the world stage in the realm of emotion, we interact and go through catharsis, joy, love, and fear; we get into scrapes and get out of them—even the role of villain is applauded when the curtain goes up, because he played his role in the drama well.

As Zalman explained this, a lady in the class objected that this was a very disturbing idea, to think that, for instance, with the Holocaust, God would be looking down enjoying it

---

* A koan is a paradoxical riddle or anecdote used by Zen masters in the training of students to confound logical reasoning by the intellect and lead students to a direct experience of awakening and enlightenment.

as entertainment and applauding. Zalman responded that she was confusing the level of physical reality in Assiyah, where everyone is accountable for what they do and actions have real world consequences, with how we *experience* it in the emotional world of Yetzirah. In looking at the world of feeling as an interactive drama, the idea is not that God is somewhere else, sitting back enjoying our suffering or applauding acts of villainy and heroism, rather it is God playing all the parts and experiencing it *as* us. Reb Zalman pointed out that in the *T'fillat Geshem*, the prayers for rain in the Siddur, where it speaks of Jacob, it says: "God, You have promised to be with him in the fire and in the water." It doesn't say God would deliver him from the fire and water, but that God's presence would be *with him*. From the standpoint of Yetzirah, God is experiencing it all through us from the inside, and has tremendous compassion.[81]

A deeper understanding of this perspective is afforded by the spiritual practice of "witnessing," utilized in the Vedantic and Buddhist systems, as well as the Gurdjieff tradition of self-remembering. In this practice, one enters the "witness" state, a practice usually done first in meditation, then periodically in daily life, in which one "stands back" from one's habitual absorption in one's own thoughts and actions, and begins to consciously observe the contents of consciousness, one's activities, and the automatic flow of thoughts, as though one were a silent observer, dispassionately watching a movie or someone else's consciousness, without getting caught up in it. The witness mode allows us to temporarily separate from identification with our role in the play, and opens up the perspective in which we can watch ourselves as actors and actresses in God's great interactive drama, the divine play in which ultimately God, the only Reality, is playing all the parts and is experiencing all the emotions through us.

Elsewhere, Reb Zalman indicated another facet of the world of Yetzirah: how we use what are called "sociemes" to exchange energy with others, such as wishing someone happy birthday or a good day, or various other expressions of good feeling and support. He says, imagine that you tell someone close to you that you love them, and they reply, "Yeah, I know. You told me that yesterday." The point is, when we tell someone we love them, we're not trying to give them information; rather it's a carrier wave of positive feeling.

The heart has a special capability that is not accessible through the intellect. The Zohar says of our Divine Source, "No thought can grab hold of You at all." There is no handle, no concept by which the mind can fathom or grab hold of the Source. Does this mean then that we are cut off from any connection with the Divine? The Zohar answers that there is a way through which we can connect with our Beloved Source, and that is through the medium of our feeling heart. Reb Zalman adds that "When I say, 'I love God,' I don't mean, 'I love God, the other'— [an] object. I love the center of the universe that is deeper in me than my I-ness is in me, the Source of All Identity Itself."[82]

In a 2013 interview with Zachary Amitai Malone, Reb Zalman spoke about connecting to God through prayer, as it works in the world of Yetzirah.

> I cannot contact God in [the unitive world of] Atzilut because I don't exist there. Additionally, I cannot contact God in B'riyah [the mind world] because all I can think about are God-ideas, because B'riyah is the dative of the universe, just as in the nominative of Atzilut, there is only one Being. The dative—it's all the ideas, the concepts, everything, even angels and so on and so forth; everything that has awareness is trying to focus their awareness on something particular—that's in the world of B'riyah. And in the world of B'riyah we can have good God ideas, but the heart is not able to talk to an idea. . . . The heart speaks only to another person, and this is what most philosophers and theologians do not do. They do not put themselves into the [feeling] world of Yetzirah. It's in the world of Yetzirah where Catholics find the Sacred Heart of Jesus, where Buddhists will find the Bodhisattva of Compassion, and where Jews find the Shekhinah on the Throne of God, as it were. This is

where you find the One Who Listens to Prayer, this is the Other [with whom one can have an I-Thou relationship].

I don't pray to the God of Atzilut, nor the God of B'riyah, or the God of Assiyah. If someone jumps off the Empire State Building, God forbid, and on the way down prays, "Please God, don't let me get hurt!" it won't help, because the God of Assiyah has the laws of Assiyah, the physical world. So, I have to really be in the place of Yetzirah for my prayer to grow.

Now, what does that mean? It means that the right hemisphere of the brain, where feeling and intuition reside, must be active in prayer. The left hemisphere is dominated by reason and sensation. So, when people say, "I don't know what you mean when you say 'God,'" it's because the left hemisphere doesn't have a vessel for it, . . . not that will do justice to the heart. . . . The problem is, we can't talk about [it], because we're going into the left hemisphere to find words to deal with the right hemisphere. This is why I like to sing a niggun [a Hasidic melody], because the language of the right hemisphere is closer to a niggun than it is to words.[83]

Although we have so far only spoken of four worlds, it should be noted that the Kabbalistic system also includes a higher fifth world of transcendence above Atziluth, known as the world of Adam Kadmon; however, it is not usually included when speaking of the four worlds, especially in Lurianic Kabbalah. The name Adam Kadmon refers to the primordial, unmanifest human being, the first pristine emanation of what will become personality in the lower worlds; it is the starting point where the infinite formless Godhead becomes person, so to speak. This level of divine potentiality is still united with the highest level of transcendence, known as Ain Sof. In Atziluth, the divine personality is already more present, but Adam Kadmon is like the first creative spark or impulse toward the manifestation of personality. Subsequently, in the lower worlds, personality traits appear not only in humans, but in animals and the natural world.

For those who are familiar with the teachings of G. I. Gurdjieff, he expressed the levels in terms of the number of laws per world, as reported in P. D. Ouspensky's *In Search of the Miraculous*. Reb Zalman assigned the Kabbalistic equivalents as follows: The highest world is World 1, absolute unity. Then, as the oneness descends into multiplicity, governed by more laws, it goes to World 3 (represented as the Trinity in Christianity, and *Trimurti* in Hindusim), corresponding to the world of Atzilut. World 6 corresponds to B'riyah, World 12 to Yetzirah, World 24 to spiritual Assiyah, World 48 to physical Assiyah,* and World 96 is the world in which we normally operate, a sort of *samsara* state in which there are 96 natural laws restricting what is possible for us at that level.[84] As one reaches the higher worlds, where fewer laws apply, there is more freedom, fewer delusions and obstacles to accomplishment. That is another way of speaking about these levels.

PATTERNS *of* GOOD *and* EVIL

At the 1989 Kallah gathering (a convention of Jewish Renewal teachers), someone asked Reb Zalman about good and evil in the four worlds. As part of his response, he explained that, at the physical level,

> What you have is a very neutral situation. In other words, "good" Cyclone B gas kills Jews. Do you understand? It works. Good or evil are not located in that universe of discourse. The ideas of good and evil are in the [mental] world of B'riyah. That's where we deal with the ideas of what is going to be good, how we define good, how we define evil.

---

* Reb Zalman differentiates spiritual assiyah from physical assiyah in terms of function vs. simple acting or doing. He says in physical assiyah, one has to be paid to do things, but in spiritual assiyah, one is like an artist, really enjoying the function.

He added that the world of feeling is the place where the drama, the battle takes place between good and evil. The highest level of unity is beyond the dichotomy of good and evil.

In Gainesville, Florida, Reb Zalman gave a talk on "Patterns of Good and Evil" which was based on his early paper of the same name which the participants read prior to the talk. During his presentation, Zalman offered an explanation in which he characterized the physical world as corresponding to the He of God (the power of nature, of gravity, metabolism, etc.), the feeling world as the Thou of God (the personal God with Whom we can communicate, embrace and be embraced, the only part of God we can really talk to) and the perspective of the mind world as the It of God (the cosmic aspect which is so vast and infinite that, when contemplated, it dwarfs us into insignificance). He concluded:

> So what is a miracle? A miracle is when my relationship with the Thou of God is so strong that the He of God becomes not split off from the Thou. And the It of God is merged with that. Then somehow, that has this transforming power. And there were times when we were able to call on that thing. . . . Alas, it did not happen during the Holocaust, that we got it together in a miraculous order, to be able to call upon the He and the It of God to assist all those broken Thous that were being killed. . . . Yes, God loves and, yes, God is powerful, but on the level where God loves, He has made space for us to go right and to go wrong.[85]

The final point refers to Zalman's suggestion that, in order for us to have freedom of choice and the opportunity to make mistakes and learn from our experiences (and not be like puppets), God has voluntarily made a space for our will and limited God's own divine prerogatives in order to grant us limited autonomy, just as a parent has to give a young child space to grow. But the price of our freedom is that it creates an arena where most of what we call evil occurs.

Here, what I found more interesting than the explanations above was Reb Zalman's response to a followup question, which revealed how Reb Zalman struggled like the rest of us for viable answers and how his understanding kept evolving. The questioner commented that there was something about Reb Zalman's explanation, which attempts to explain intervention in terms of I-Thouness while still trying to hold on to the concept of God, that doesn't seem to really provide a satisfying answer. Zalman responded that, to a certain extent, he agreed, but he had chosen to include some of these earlier ideas in the talk because he thought it might be helpful for some. He said that in the past he felt the explanation about the He, She, and It of God adequately answered something about how we interface with God through the Thou and through *t'shuvah* (turning to the Source) that connects us with the whole. "I'm not there today" because this whole schema is based on a reality map from the last paradigm "that is inadequate because it still speaks of God as an object, as a subject, as a noun."

> My sense of the radical immanence that has happened since, is that wherever there is a person, God has become indwelling in all the persons, in all that there is. We have moved out from the paradigm that was theistic, that saw God as the *Anima Mundi*, into a pantheistic paradigm. So all that is, is God and that which is experienced as evil is also part of that God experience in oneself. . . . My sense is that, given another one hundred years, what will emerge from our understanding of holographic notions about the universe is going to give us a whole other way of dealing with God. Already Bucky [Buckminster] Fuller has made it clear to us that God is a verb. We are dealing with God-ing; we are not dealing with the old man in the sky. The whole question is how do you revamp religion to the point that you can still address that God-ing as if that God-ing were person. What do we do with language? Language is, at this point, the pitfall for our progress—it's holding us back. We are still saying the

sun rises and sets. . . . Every time I open up the Siddur and I say, *Baruch Hu* or *Baruch shemo*—"Blessed be He" and "Blessed be His name"—I am lying to my deepest about the androgynous nature of God.[86]

Reb Zalman concluded with an analogy to updating computer software, pointing out that after you update a program you no longer want to continue running the old version which has not been updated.

FOUR LEVELS *of* MEANING *in the* SCRIPTURES

Next, we look at how scriptural interpretation works on four levels of meaning. In a mid-1980s interview with Fran Silbiger-Orrok, Reb Zalman explained that, in the world of Atzilut (at the level of *sod*, the highest level of scriptural understanding), I am God, or one with God. It is the place where the flame is one with the spark, where each person is "a chip off the old block."

> And that connection of identity that we have with God in a way is a secret. We don't like to be in a position of having to say to somebody who says, "Who are you?" to say, "I am God,". . . I'm a spark of the center of the universe, but I am God. Most of the time it would trouble us, because then people start saying, "You mean you can do anything you want?" They jump from the world of Atzilut where I am God and pull me down to the world of Assiyah, where I'm not God, where I am very much creature, finite, object, limited, and so on. Now, if somebody says, "Aha, so you can't be in two worlds at once!" the Kabbalist would say, "But that's where we are always!" We are at once in the world of Atzilut where I am God, and in the world of Assiyah where I am a thing, a creature, finite. And I'm in the world of Yetzirah where I am a person who can be an I to God's thou. . . . In the world of B'riyah, I am someone who is all amazed over what's unfolding as to how amazingly together this universe is

and each time I look I can see new aspects, new ways of knowing. . . . The secret is that I mustn't know that I am God. And I haven't got an initiation yet until I have found out that I am God.[87]

This is where the opponents of Kabbalah, the *Mitnagdim*, parted company with the Kabbalists. They totally denied that top level, the *sod*, the highest mystery of Torah, saying, "How dare you, being a creature, even talk about being God?" But I say, "I'm not talking about it, because in the world in which I talk, I'm not that." In the world of Assiyah, that's the world where I do. In the world of B'riyah, I am amazed at this universe and don't say anything because in the world in which I talk, I'm not that, but I can silently visualize with the mind and contemplate it. In Yetzirah (*remez*), the world beyond the simple meaning, I talk and have dialectical exchanges. "In the world of Atzilut, I don't even think. What happens there is that I *be*, I *be* God."

"The hermeneutic of Torah operates on these four levels: *p'shat* (the simple meaning)," *remez* (the deductive, what is hinted at in the text, what I derive from the text but is not in the text), *drash* (what I read into the text, opening up the meaning), "and *sod* (that which cannot even be said). So you have the simple meaning, the deductive, the inductive and the anagogical (not given even to words, only to intuition)."[88] These four levels of scriptural meaning are traditionally referred to as PaRDeS, an abbreviation which utilizes the first letters of each level: *p'shat*, *remez*, *drash*, and *sod*. Below, we further amplify these four levels.

Sod – the mystery or secret, esoteric level, the deepest understanding, the anagogical (an anagoge refers to the highest scriptural interpretation, which may include references to the afterlife and the eternal realms). As Zalman puts it: it is "for initiates only. Only the initiate in me can handle that interpretation." The noninitiate in me would misunderstand and make it gross.[89]

Drash – the inductive, metaphysical, allegorical, symbolical level (where one thing serves as a symbol for something else, such as a flag being a symbol of a nation, or Babylon of Rome).

Remez – the deductive, connotational, analogical level (meaning to speak using an analogy, which describes one thing by speaking of something else which is similar, such as a parable). It is the implied meaning which is alluded to or hinted at in the text. The plain meaning may also be present at the same time as that which is implied.

P'shat – the simple, denotational, literal level (the plain, basic, surface meaning of the text).

Now we can look at a few examples of scriptures at these different levels. Most scriptures can be interpreted on the level of *p'shat*, the simple, literal meaning, although some, like parables, are clearly not meant to represent factual accounts of real people. Scriptures which are to be interpreted primarily on the literal level are those such as the ten commandments, narratives, and various advice or laws such the inheritance laws recommended in Qur'an and Bible. In addition, each scripture can be interpreted on all four levels of PaRDeS.

Here is an example of a scripture as read in each of the four worlds (physical, emotional, mental, essential) which Reb Zalman gave, using Jesus' saying: "I and my father are one."[90] If I go to the bank and I am signing checks and my father is also signing checks, when the question comes up as to how many signatures are needed, I'll say,

> "one is enough because 'I and my father are one.'" On the level of business, it is very much in the world of *shari'a*. So this statement can go to the heart place, to the mind place, and to the secret place. . . . On the feeling level, if someone hurts my child, he hurts me. . .

"Then 'I and my father are one' is a meditation I do when I want to understand"[91] how to give up my otherness and discover my sameness with others. At the top, essence level, 'I and my father are one' because there is only One Being.

Reb Zalman correlates the four Christian Gospels with their levels as follows, with the caveat that a case can be made for switching the middle two:

John – Atzilut (spirit; esoteric)
Luke – B'riyah (mind)
Matthew – Yetzirah (heart)
Mark – Assiyah (body; exoteric)[92]

Below are examples of various scriptures which are most naturally read on one of the four levels of PaRDeS interpretation,* beginning with two which simply apprise the reader of the use of different levels in scripture:

It is He Who has sent down to you [Muhammad] the Book [this Qur'an]. In it are verses that are entirely clear, they are the basis of the Book; other verses are allegorical. (Qur'an 3:7)

He [Jesus] did not say anything to them without using a parable. But when he was alone with his own disciples, he explained everything. (Mark 4:34)

P'shat, the simple or literal meaning:

When you reap the harvest of your land, do not reap to the very edges of your field or gather the gleanings of your harvest. Do not go over your vineyard a second time or pick up the grapes that have fallen. Leave them for the poor and the foreigner. I am the LORD YOUR GOD. (LEVITICUS 19:9-10)

I tell you, whoever divorces his wife, except for sexual immorality, and marries another woman commits adultery. (Matthew 19:8)

If you give charity in public, it is worthwhile, but if you hide and deliver it to the poor in secret that is far better for you. (Qur'an 2:271)

---

* PaRDeS is not only used as a tool to categorize verses, but also provides the means and justification of interpreting verses in different ways.

Remez – the deductive, inferential, and analogical meaning:

Circumcise therefore the foreskin of your heart, and be no more stiffnecked. (Deuteronomy 10:16)

And if thine eye offend thee, pluck it out, and cast *it* from thee: it is better for thee to enter into life with one eye, rather than having two eyes to be cast into hell fire. (Matthew 18:9)

Verily, I say to unto you, unless you turn and become as little children, you will never enter the kingdom of heaven. (Matthew 18:3)

Let the dead bury the dead. (Luke 9:60)

The kingdom of heaven is like a mustard seed, which a man took and planted in his field. Though it is the smallest of all seeds, yet when it grows, it is the largest of garden plants and becomes a tree, so that the birds come and perch in its branches. (Matthew 13:31-32)

Compassion is a mind that savors only mercy and love for all sentient beings. (Nagarguna, *Precious Garland* 437)

Drash – the metaphysical, allegorical, and symbolical meaning:

Allah revealed to Muhammad: "I was a hidden Treasure and longed to be known, so I created the worlds."(*Hadith Qudsi*)

Matthew 2:15: "This fulfilled what the Lord had spoken through the prophet: 'Out of Egypt I called my son.'

In this New Testament quote from the Prophet Hosea, "son" is understood to refer to Jesus as he is returning as a child from Egypt to Galilee, while in the original context it refers to the nation of Israel:

"When Israel was a child, I loved him, and out of Egypt I called my son." (Hosea 11:1)

[As salt disappears in water] just so, you do not see the Real in the world. Yet it is here all the same. And this soul is the Self of all that is, this is the Real, this the Self. That thou art, O Shvetaketu. (Upanishads III)

The man who abides in the will of God wills nothing else than what God is, and what He wills. . . . The eye with which I see God is the same with which God sees me. My eye and God's eye is one eye, and one sight, and one knowledge, and one love. (Meister Eckhardt)[93]

Sod – the mysterious or secret meaning:

Before the mountains were brought forth, or ever Thou hadst formed the earth and the world, even from everlasting to everlasting, Thou art God. (Psalms 90:2)

The Tao cannot be heard; what can be heard is not It. The Tao cannot be seen: what can be seen is not It. The Tao cannot be expressed in words; what can be expressed in words is not It. Do we know the Formless which gives form to form? In the same way the Tao does not admit of being named. (Chaung Tsu)[94]

I am Alpha and Omega, the beginning and the ending, says the Lord, which is, and which was, and which is to come, the Almighty. (Revelation 1:8)

Verily, I alone am God and nothing exists (that is worthy of worship) except Me. (Sura 20:14)[*]

---

[*]   In Arabic: *Innanee ana Allahu la ilaha illa ana.*

In Appendix 2, I enlarge on the theme of higher levels of scripture discussed in this section, offering a more detailed look at how the Christian Gospels can be understood primarily along allegorical lines (*drash*), and how many of the early Fathers of the Church read them in this way.

Next, we will look at the five levels of soul in the Kabbalistic tradition, the ten *sephirot* on the Tree of Life, and the idea of an inner council representing these sephirotic qualities. By comparison, Sufism uses a system of seven levels of the soul or self, and ninety-nine divine names or qualities, ten of which we will identify as loose equivalents of the ten sephirot. While mainstream Abrahamic teachings, including Sufism, do not endorse ideas of the reincarnation of the soul, the Hasidic tradition does recognize reincarnation at the higher soul levels, using the term *gilgul.*

the LEVELS of the SOUL in KABBALAH

There are five levels of soul in the Kabbalistic system; the bottom three souls are called: *Nefesh, Ru'ah*, and *Neshamah*, and the two highest levels are called *Hayyah* and *Yehidah*. Reb Zalman explains: "Nefesh is the lowest level of soul—that which animates my body even while I'm asleep."[95] The Nefesh and the body reside in the physical world of Assiyah. Nefesh is the vital life force in the blood, the vegetative soul, which mostly dies with the body and does not reincarnate. A corpse still grows nails because it has a vegetative soul (Nefesh functions). Even a stone or plant has Nefesh (the plant breathes). Nefesh is a breath word associated with the in-breath. By contrast, the higher soul level of Neshamah is associated with the out-breath (as when God breathed into Adam's nostrils the breath of life, which was the human's in-breath). The middle level of soul, Ru'ah, corresponds to the breath when it is inside. So Nefesh is the inhalation, Ru'ah is the held breath, and Neshamah is the exhalation. The two higher souls, Hayyah and Yehidah, are not breath words.

Ru'ah is associated with the feeling world of Yetzirah. A stone does not have Ru'ah but an animal does; however, an animal doesn't have Neshamah, which is connected with the higher function of speech. The Zohar says all beings have a Nefesh, and if you polish yourself and make yourself clear you get Ru'ah; if you make that transparent, you get Neshamah. Ru'ah is where "I" and "thou" connect. Ru'ah is literally spirit; it exists in attunement, harmonizing, connecting with other people or animals (for instance, it manifests in petting a dog or cat). Ru'ah is related to emotional states and the heart, connection with others, inspiration. Sometimes the Ru'ah is very armored, sometimes open, and it can go to the place of "I-thou." When you go to a place of worship, you assess the atmosphere there—does it have energy? If not, although it may be technically perfect; it will not reach Ru'ah (a certain aliveness, excitement, willingness). If Ru'ah energy is not present, you'll probably leave.

Ru'ah helps and supports Neshamah, which has to do with the mind and a contemplative attitude. Ru'ah sometimes survives bodily death, sometimes not. Neshamah, which is associated with the world of B'riyah, does not enter the body until birth, at the first breath (while Nefesh exists there before that) and Neshamah is capable of surviving bodily death for a long time. In Judaism, if there was a birth complication, the mother's life would take precedence, up until the point that the Neshamah entered at the child's first breath, then it's a toss-up between two living souls. When two energetic people shake hands, there is Nefesh energy present in the exchange, but when two lovers touch, with their added heart energy, Ru'ah is involved. When we are consoling someone who has been through a great loss and are very present and then join hands with that person, that involves Neshamah. If your spiritual teacher gives you a blessing and it opens something within you, that touches the highest soul levels of Hayyah and Yehidah.

"Yehidah is on top of the hierarchy, meaning one-pointedness—that which is unique. As Neshamah knows by reason, by intellect and by mind, there is a knowing that Hayyah and Yehidah have—but their knowing is not conceptual, but knowing *by identity*—it takes one to know one."[96] Only the spark of the living God in you can know the living God. Hayyah knows by sinking into it, recognizing that it is that—but not by understanding or reaching for it. That knowledge is total and complete, but totally useless; it doesn't produce anything. Where would you want to go if you were about to die? That place is the only place that won't be violated by the creatureliness of death—and that's Yehidah.

"Toward the one"—that's the *uni* of the universe. The *verse* is below; the *uni* is above and beyond violation. Hayyah is a kind of higher-level Ru'ah. Ru'ah seeks raw emotion. Hayyah gets programmed with the deep will, the potential and purpose, the blueprint—the intellect that wants to unfold in a life—but Yehidah doesn't. The rebbe, the Hasidic master, wants to read the Yehidah, beyond who one is at present to who they are meant to be. Hayyah is a construer of reality; Yehidah is beyond that. The ecstasy is in Yehidah, the divine bliss. Hayyah is saying, "I want, I want it." Neshamah says, "Let me see if I can support you in that." Ru'ah says, "Let me see if I can support this with excitement." Nefesh says, "and I'll be putting in the fuel for you."[97]

In terms of brain function, Reb Zalman gave the following correspondences: Nefesh corresponds to the reptilian brain and Ru'ah to the limbic brain. Neshamah corresponds to the cortex, and Hayyah and Yehidah to the unformatted part of brain. Nefesh is stimulated through athletics, Ru'ah through the arts, and Neshamah through ideas. Hayyah is connected with our deepest aspiration and life purpose, and Yehidah's perspective lies beyond the purview of the personal self. Hayyah is the highest soul level we experience in our most uplifting altered states and corresponds to Hokhmah, the plane of wisdom, while Yehidah is even beyond that. In *Gate to the Heart*, Reb Zalman affirms that Yehidah "is essentially identical with the Divine, and as the name suggests, is the primary monad . . . a singularly unique holographic particle of God. It is clear that there is no distance, no abyss dividing Yehidah from the *yahid*, the One Infinite Being."[98]

By way of comparison, the Sufis delineate seven levels of the soul or *ruh* in Arabic. There are also seven levels of *Nafs* (ego-self development), which are based on the level of the individual's spiritual realization, from the lowest level to the most exalted God-consciousness. As I have elaborated them in detail in another book, *Garden of Mystic Love*, I will simply list the levels of Ruh here. They are: the Mineral soul, the Vegetable soul, the Animal soul, the Personal (or ego) soul, the Human soul (associated with the spiritual heart and compassion), the Secret soul (which is more God-conscious and reflective of the Divine inheritance), and the Secret of Secrets soul (the inner transcendent sphere of Divine union and identity). Roughly speaking, the bottom three levels of Ruh correspond to Nefesh, the next two to Ru'ah, the Secret soul to Neshamah and Hayyah, and the Secret of Secrets soul to Yehidah.

a CONVERSATION *on the* SOUL *with* REB ZALMAN

In September of 1987, I traveled to Philadelphia to make a weeklong Sufi retreat with a guide in the area and also arranged to stop by and see Reb Zalman at his home, part of which also served as the headquarters for P'nai Or. One of the first things I noticed was a sign on his office door that was a quote from Zorba the Greek: "A man needs a little madness or else he never dares to cut the rope and be free." After a short wait, Reb Zalman came out and we sat on the front porch and spoke at some length. During the conversation, I took the opportunity to ask Zalman if he would comment on a number of related ideas about the soul from different traditions, and how they might fit together.

I brought up the following issues: In a class on Kabbalah, Reb Zalman had previously quoted from the Zohar a statement that, "Each is given a Nefesh, and if one so merits (by refining oneself), one is granted Ru'ah." I was interested to know whether the level of Ru'ah, which one may develop, was analogous to Gurdjieff's idea of "soul-building," or as he called it, "coating the higher being bodies" through attention and inner work—which also sounds like what the Christian Church Fathers called forming "the body of the resurrection." I also mentioned Hazrat Inayat Khan's teaching on reincarnation and the Hasidic version of it, known as *gilgul*, inquiring as to how all these ideas fit together. I found his answer most interesting, as it basically uprooted the question in respect to the physical aspects of soul-building:

> You know, I really don't think that's the way this issue will be looked at in the future. We are already undergoing a revolution in the process of our thinking, and it is going to go further. Pretty soon, we simply won't be talking in these kinds of terms about the soul. These notions will be sort of beside the point, and out of date, like horse and buggy, or the old matter and spirit dichotomy they used to use, but which is no longer very useful for us.
>
> But now, let's look at what you've brought up. . . The omni-omni transcendent aspect of God [Haqiqat or Atzilut], where everything is one—that's not where the issue lies. Now, take the physical part of you [at the level of *Shariat, Assiyah*]: When we know that there is such a renewal of the body at the cellular level, that within seven years,* every cell in the body has regenerated completely, so that there is nothing at all left of the cells that formed the original body (only the pattern forms that recognizable continuity) then that gives a whole new sense of relativity to what I can point to and say, "This is my physical self." As you probably know, what is called Nefesh in Hebrew, or Nafs, the Arabic word used by the Sufis—which is associated with the breath and is the lower animal or physical level of the ego self (soul)—is intermeshed with the body, stays with it, and perishes soon after one checks out at death and the breath goes out of the body. Likewise, the Ru'ah level of the soul in Tariqat [Yetzirah] has a longer longevity as sort of a spirit independent of the body: but even that doesn't survive that long. So, your question really centers in Marifat [B'riyah]. That's where the question really lies.

---

*   During the conversation, Reb Zalman also alluded to the stages of human development in seven-year life cycles, a teaching probably drawn from Rudolph Steiner.

You know, you mentioned Gurdjieff [laughs]. I think of that story of how the Devil met Gurdjieff in Moscow. Gurdjieff said to the Devil, "Why so glum?" The Devil answered, "Nobody is coming to hell because they are not building souls!" Gurdjieff replied, "Teach me how to build souls and I'll send you some." So later some of Gurdjieff's disciples end up in hell. They ask why they are there and the Devil tells them who taught Gurdjieff the art of soul-making. Gurdjieff later sends word to the Devil, asking, "Why did have to open your mouth about it?"

Seriously, what I think Gurdjieff was getting at was how to develop the "presence"—how to *be*—to incarnate fully and fill the body with one's whole being, which is what many of the Sufi practices are all about. Soul-building—the idea that a material substance is built up—is old paradigm thinking. The new thinking will no longer speak of "resurrection bodies" or some substance or physical aspect of the soul that comes back, despite all the rinpoches and lamas. I mean, who in physics today is talking about particles and material substances? They speak in terms of waves and patterns within energy fields.

So now, let's look at this question of whether or not there is something recognizable at this level of soul [B'riyah] of which it could be said that it returns or repeats itself. I believe that there is. I have a real strong sense that it does happen; but I don't so much get the feeling that it takes place in the linear sense of one life followed by another life of that same soul in another body later on in history. Although, by and large, that's the way we talk about it in Hasidism. It comes off a little too cut and dried. So what I am saying is that I don't see it so much as a progression of lives unfolding on a horizontal time continuum, but as though many lives were simultaneously being lived transhistorically in a way that is not bound by our normal perception of the progression of time.

And then, what is it that we can say we recognize in these various incarnations as a recurring sameness? And, again, I don't believe we want to go to the physical place here and say that it is something material that comes back. I think it's more like patterns of energy—habitual wave forms and ways of experiencing that have become reinforced and congealed in your being that then "attach" to another person ["skandas" in Buddhist discourse]. So, the real question gets to be why one should have attracted that pattern-form, or karma. You know, there are all these ways of speaking about it: soul making, reincarnated souls and so forth. Everybody has their own particular slant on the subject and various cultural ways of talking about it; and they are all true at some level.

You know how even what Hazrat Inayat Khan taught about reincarnation—how the soul is a ray of the One Being, but when it descends, it sort of picks up a garment of old clothes which are the impressions that are hanging around in the higher spheres from some "other" soul's previous incarnation—it's all just another way of saying the same thing! There are just a lot of ways of talking about it. So, when it comes right down to it, you and I, none of us, are given to know all of God's secrets. So, maybe that's why the whole thing about the soul tends to want to remain somewhat of an elusive mystery. So, it will be a surprise not to have known in advance! [laughs] Maybe God would like to save back a little surprise even for Himself![99]

ACCESSING YOUR FULLY ENLIGHTENED SELF

It may be asked, does one have access to these higher levels of the soul in this life? The answer is yes. Reb Zalman advocated getting in touch from time to time, with the higher level of oneself, the fully enlightened part of one's being who understands us and knows what we need better than any guru. This wise inner-self is not always easily available when we are busy with our lives, but it is there and can be accessed by making time to tune into it and listening for its very serene voice. When one has a problem and cannot find the solution, this deeper part of our being knows what is the best course and can give us advice. Reb Zalman says there is no litmus test to see if you are hearing from the ego or a higher level, but discernment is necessary and there is a certain sense of knowing when it is the real higher level. This enlightened part is on a different timeline, and in some sense already knows what one's path in life is all about, has already done it. So, Reb Zalman said, when he was in need of the deepest guidance, he sat quietly, relaxed and opened up to consult the "already enlightened Zalman" for answers. Each of us has our own fully enlightened part who can guide us.

Although Zalman didn't specify this, I would add that even if this higher soul level at first remains difficult to access, at a minimum, one can sit quietly for a time and, when calm and collected, ask a simple unambiguous yes or no question to one's inner guide, accessing one's highest intuitive knowledge by using a method like designating one hand (or finger) for yes and the other for no. Once the question has been asked, clear the mind of any further thoughts or preconceived expectations about the issue, and after few minutes of inner silence, notice which hand or finger seems to vibrate (or feel larger, warmer, or some other discernable sensory change) indicating the inner response.

A further highly useful method, recommended by Gurdjieff, helps put one in touch with the wisdom of the deeper self particularily when facing a major choice in one's life. One is advised to take pen and paper and write down a carefully formulated question asking for inner guidance and direction. For instance: "What is the next step in my life?" or "What is my higher purpose?" or "What career should I pursue?" etc. Then, in a place where one will not be disturbed, sit quietly for twenty to thirty minutes in a comfortable, balanced position, relaxing any bodily tension, silently focusing on one's breath, and clearing the mind as completely as possible—especially avoiding any musing about the posed question. After twenty to thirty minutes, when one feels the mind has become sufficiently silent and peaceful, one ends the meditation and writes down the answer that comes at that time.

the TEN SEPHIROT *and the* INNER COUNCIL

A great deal could be said about the Kabbalistic Tree of Life and the ten sephirot and much has been written on the subject, from traditional Jewish explications to the more contemporary perspective of "Anglo-Qabbala." Our aim here is simply to provide brief descriptions of the qualities of the ten sephirot (meaning the counted divine emanations or spheres) and some of their equivalents in the Sufi tradition, as well as presenting the concept of an "inner council," of which Reb Zalman sometimes spoke.

Dating and authorship of the earliest Kabbalistic texts which enumerate the ten sephirot are difficult to determine; however, the general scholarly consensus is that most of the elucidations were worked out during the "Golden Age," a period when Jewish and Muslim mystics freely mingled in the highly tolerant Andalusian Era of Islamic rule in southern Europe and Moorish Spain (ca.711-1492). During this time, there was much cross-fertilization of mystical ideas, with Arabic texts often translated and studied by Jewish mystics. Moses Maimonides' son, Rabbi Abraham Maimuni (1186-1237) famously mingled Jewish and Sufi practices and concepts in Egypt and wrote a work disseminating these ideas. Even more widely read was Bahya ibn Pakuda's *Duties of the Heart*, which translated a significant amount of Sufi material into the context of Jewish practice. While much of the Kabbalistic system was undoubtably worked out in earlier centuries, during this period, Sufi metaphysical concepts subtly influenced the further development of the tradition, while Jewish mystical ideas no doubt reciprocally enriched the understanding of Sufis and Western occultists as well.

While God is one and encompasses all existence in an interconnected oneness, on the inner planes we humans do not usually experience ourselves as a unified whole, but rather as having many sub-personalities, as George Ivanovich Gurdjieff, Carl Gustav Jung and many other teachers and psychologists have pointed out. A number of systems of personality types have been formulated to identify the inner archetypes, including the astrological types, derived from Greco-Roman polytheism, the enneagram types, and so on. Each *sephirah* (singular of sephirot) in Kabbalah, identified from Hebrew scriptural passages, describes a quality of divine manifestation as it comes into creation from the highest unmanifest level of the Divine, which Kabbalists call *Ain Sof*. *Ain Sof* literally means "no thing," the uncreated *pleroma* ("fullness"), the eternal, transcendent divine realm above and beyond creation, where no thing exists. There are actually said to be three levels of *Ain Sof*.

While the early Kabbalistic text of *Sepher Yetzirah* and the *Zohar** provide some of the earliest identifications of the ten sephirot, the system was most clearly explicated by Isaac Luria in the sixteenth century. Luria explained the divine emanations in terms of what transpired during the creation, drawing out further ramifications beyond the somewhat brief description given in Genesis. Reb Zalman points out that Samson Raphael Hirsch translated the first verse of the Bible: "In the beginning, God *outered* Himself."[100] Luria explains that this process of "outering" came about through a process of *tzimtzum*, meaning contraction—the same word we use in birthing. So that which was first inner, then "outered" itself. The presence that is implicate, then becomes explicate; and most Kabbalists see this process of creation as ongoing, not just an event that happened once in the remote past. The Qur'an agrees that creation is not simply a one-time past fiat of creation, but sees life and renewed creation as continually generated and sustained by the Divine, proclaiming, "Every moment the Divine manifests in a new state [of glory]."[101]

Isaac Luria lays out the Kabbalistic teachings which describe how the Infinite Light (*Or Ain Sof*) at first entirely filled the worlds, leaving no room for creation; so God had to contract the divine

---

*   The *Sepher Yetzirah* dates from around the ninth century CE, possibly the sixth century or earlier. The *Zohar*, which is written in Aramaic, was first published in the thirteenth century CE by a Jewish writer named Moses de León, who ascribed the work to Shimon bar Yohai ("Rashbi"), a rabbi of the second century CE.

light in order to allow a space for the created realms. Into this dark and empty space, came a powerful laser-like discharge of light (*kav*), like a lightning bolt, into manifestation. This highly concentrated stream of divine light was channeled into manifestation, into the archetypal vessels (*kelim*) of the ten sephirot, which were formed as part of God's creation when "the *Elohim* created the primordial human in the divine image."* These ten *kelim,* or vessels were imbued with the capability of containing and rendering the light visible in the world. However, the super-charged divine beam of light was too powerful to be contained by all of the sephirot. Most of the vessels shattered and their fragments descended into creation as divine sparks. The shattering of the vessels is called *shevirat ha-kelim.* Fortunately, the higher sephirot of Keter, Binah, and Hokhmah held and didn't shatter, thus retaining their light, glory, wisdom, and redemptive power.

According to Luria, the purpose and task of manifestation lies in fixing this broken state of the cosmos by raising up and redeeming the holy sparks in creation from their fallen state, a process known as *Tikkun Olam.* Some of the sparks are redeemed by interacting with them (doing *mitzvot*—good deeds or commandments, eating kosher foods, etc.), while other lower sparks are redeemed by abstaining from giving them energy (harmful, forbidden inclinations and deeds). The divine qualities in humanity are the holy sparks within us that are there waiting to be reclaimed, activated, and exalted back toward their original heavenly condition—a kind of resurrection of the fallen world through the agency of humanity.

It is worth noting the similarity between Luria's idea of the raising of the divine sparks in the world and in ourselves, and the Orphic myth of Zagreus (Dionysus), the divine son of Zeus and Persephone, who was devoured by the Titans, who in turn were destroyed by a lightning bolt from the furious Zeus. The divine heart of Zagreus, which had not been devoured by the

---

*   Gen.1:27. *Elohim* is the plural form of "God" in Hebrew (the singlular form is *El*). Elohim is considered by Kabbalists to be endowed with the ten qualities and the primal human is identified as *Adam Kadmon.*

Titans, was recovered and Zeus proceeded to create humanity from the bodily remains of the primitive titans and the divine heart of the son of God, making humanity part brute and part divine. According to this parallel myth, humanity has to discover and manifest the divine traces within in order to rise above its lower nature.

Luria's elucidation of what went wrong in the cosmic situation furnishes another more refined explanation of why the higher divine mind, presence and wisdom is still accessible to us, yet we mostly dwell in the lower more confused world of opposites, of good and evil, of division into male and female aspects, with various opposing drives and temptations (a condition Buddhists call *samsara*). The divine sparks are covered with accretions called *K'lippot* ("shells"), thick veils of delusion and compulsion. The *K'lippot*, or shell-realm might be parallel to what Gurdjieff called the world of ninety-six constricting laws. More positively, some of the Kabbalistic teachings also focus strongly on the union of male and female polarities, which is another way of speaking about the union of God (active masculine) and the human soul (receptive feminine), or the transcendent God in Keter (the highest sephirah), with the world soul (the feminine *Shekhinah*) in Malkhut, the lowest sephirah, associated with the earth plane.*

The kabbalistic Tree of Life, which is represented as an upside down tree with its roots and highest levels in the heavens, provides a visual representation of the ten sephirot, providing a schematic diagram of the divine energies in manifestation. The tree is also divided into three columns with masculine, active qualities in the right column, the feminine, receptive qualities in the left column, as well as a middle column that integrates the left and right polarities. Reb Zalman further associates the right column with the right brain and the left column with left brain. Another way of putting it is to say that the right column represents generosity and expansion, the left severity and constraint (or contraction), while the middle column represents

---

* What this means should become clearer as we elaborate on the nature of the various sephirot below. One may also refer to Appendix I.

equilibrium between the two outer columns. Even more simply, Reb Zalman characterizes the energy of the three columns as the polar opposite energies of yes, no and their uniting conjunctive "and." (This is similar to the Sufi division of divine qualities into, respectively, *Jamal, Jalal,* and *Kamal* attributes—ie., the gentle and beautiful qualities, the severe and powerful qualities, and the perfectly balanced qualities.)

In the Jewish prayer service, it traditionally takes ten men gathered together to make a minion, the minimum for a valid congregational prayer service. Why? Because ten people ideally represent the ten sephirah types that have to come together to make *yihud,* or unified wholeness. Nine or less would be fragmented and missing some essential part of the whole. But when there are ten, it is said that the *Shekhinah,* the collective soul, is present and embodied.

With that background in mind, we can now look at the ten sephirot, starting with the highest level of manifestation, called Keter, the crown. We may note in passing that in Luria's system, Keter is linked with the transcendent aspect of God in *Ain Sof* and is not counted as part of the manifested tree, while most other Kabbalists do include Keter among the ten sephirot. Instead, Luria (along with Reb Shneur Zalman of Liadi) counts as the tenth sephirah, Da'at, a mysterious phantom sephirah of knowing (as when Adam "knew" Eve) in the middle column which unites the upper polarities of Binah and Hokhmah.

Below is a graphic representation showing the Tree of Life with its ten sephirot and lines of connection, representing the zig-zag movement of the lightning bolt of divine light as it entered and filled each sephirot on its downward trajectory into manifestation. Below the Hebrew names are their Arabic equivalents. It should be noted that the Tree of Life is in mirror image (the sephirot in the right column correspond to the right side of one's body, as if one were seeing it reflected in a mirror).

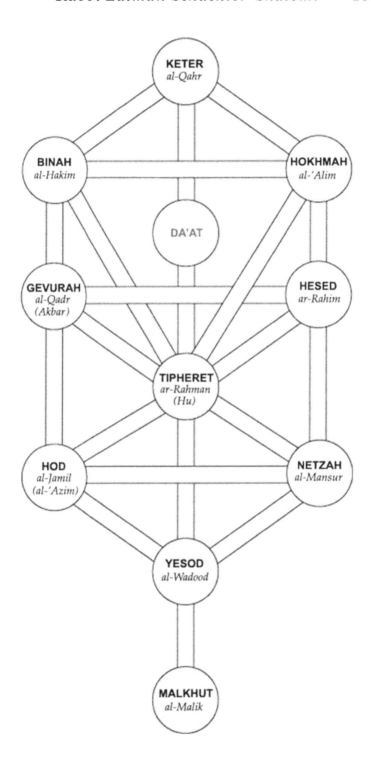

KETER represents the supreme "crown" of creation, the divine transcendence, which stretches up from the uppermost part of the tree into infinity. Located at the apex of the balanced middle column, Keter signifies the supreme Self, the cosmic "I am," a brilliant fountain of divine light—the formless Source of Being prior to the divine descent into the created realms. In relation to the human body, it is like a crown or nimbus surrounding the head. Its Arabic equivalent is *al-Qahr*, the divine over-arching sovereignty, beyond the limited human will.

HOKHMAH is the next sephirah below Keter, on the right, masculine column of the tree, associated with Adam or the father (*abba*). It represents the divine wisdom or protocritic knowledge,[*] the seat of intuitive inspiration, the active principle of knowing. It is associated with the first day of creation in Genesis, filled with the optimism of a fresh, new morning, brimming with life. Hokhmah corresponds most closely to the Arabic divine name, *al-'Alim*, meaning divine insight and clarity, omniscience, the Spirit of Guidance. Reb Zalman points out that, in the beginning, Wisdom was feminine (as in Proverbs 8:22 where Wisdom/ Hokhmah was formed first before anything else was made), but in later tradition there was a flip to the archetype of wise old man. However, one can also see Hokhmah as an intelligent young woman, as Sophia, or as Pallas Athena, who emerged directly from the head of Zeus.[102] For Kabbalists, the feminine principle normally describes a vessel that receives the outward masculine light, as the moon reflects the light of the sun, then inwardly nurtures and gives birth to the next lower sephirah. Therefore Binah, the other aspect of knowing, which is considered feminine and receptive, sequentially follows the active, masculine Hokhmah.

BINAH is located on the left column, across from Hokhmah, representing the feminine contemplative knowledge and understanding which discerns, comprehends and unfolds that which was hidden. Binah is associated with the primal mother (*imma*),

---

[*]   Protocritic knowledge refers to innate knowledge, as opposed to Knowledge which is learned or acquired through experience in the world.

Eve. In the *Tikuney Zohar*, Binah is called "the heart of under-standing." Together, Hokhmah and Binah correspond respectively to the right and left hemispheres of the brain, Hokhmah representing intuitive inner knowledge and Binah, the more experiential, analytical knowledge, which receives and clarifies the more hidden intuitions of Hokhmah. In the Zohar, it is stated that they are "two lovers that are not separate." As Reb Zalman notes, it is not possible to find Hokhmah or Binah in a pure state without the other. The two hemispheres of the brain make love together, or act in harmony with each other, sometimes one or the other being more active, but always the two work interactively. First an idea comes in Hokhmah, then it is processed in Binah, then it becomes Da'at. The hidden sephirah, Da'at (reason or vision) is their son and resides between them in the middle column, forming a unified triad of knowledge. Da'at is like the knowledge that mysteriously emerges direct from God and represents a kind of knowledge that is known not through observation and reflection, but through becoming. In terms of body location, Da'at corresponds to the cerebellum. The closest Arabic equivalent to Binah is probably *al-Hakam* (discerning wisdom, the true judge), or *al-Hakim*, the wise (which is paired frequently in the Qur'an with *al-'Alim*). Both are variations of the root word *H-K-M*, or *Hikmah* (wisdom). The Arabic divine name *ash-Shahid*, meaning eyewitness, is also related to the outer wisdom gained through observation and life experience.

HESED represents the expansive qualities of mercy, love, kindness, grace, forgiveness, attraction, and generosity, born out of wisdom and understanding. This sephirah is located on the right column and corresponds with the right shoulder and arm. It is associated with the patriarch Abraham, the generous friend of God; the feminine counterpart is Miriam,[103] for whose sake the well provided water in the desert. Hesed is associated with the water element and the word Hesed comes from the same word as Hasid—the loving, joyful followers of the Jewish mystical tradition. In Hebrew scripture, Hesed represents the first day of creation when God brought forth the light.

The perspective of Hesed is that the universe is made in order to do good, so that beneficence can come about. The shadow or extreme (or *k'lippah*) of Hesed would be over-indulgence, weakness, and uncontrolled expansion without limits or discernment. The Arabic divine names which correspond most closely to Hesed are *Rahman* and *Rahim*, meaning compassion (magnanimity) and mercy. (*Rahim* is the equivalent that Reb Zalman cited for Hesed.) There are several other divine names which reflect the qualities of Hesed: *al-Basit* (the Expander) and *al-Halim* (the Forbearing), as well as the word for love and desire, *Ishq*. Reflecting the spirit of Hesed, the Prophet Muhammad revealed in a hadith that these words of God are inscribed on the divine throne: "My mercy takes precedence over My wrath."

GEVURAH (or Din) represents the qualities of severity, judgment, power, restraint, justice, control, discipline, contraction, rigor, strength and awe. This sephirah is located across from Hesed on the left, feminine column and corresponds with the left shoulder and arm. Gevurah is also alternatively called *Din*, meaning in Hebrew to judge or govern. In Arabic, *Din* means the religion, faith, law or judgment; the word is possibly related to the Persian word, *Daena*, the eternal law, used in Zoroastrianism.

Gevurah is the constraint that balances Hesed's expansion, setting limits, bringing discipline, abstinence, tough love, and justice. Traditionally, it is associated with the left hand of God, the severe attribute of divine awe or fear of God, the hand of divine correction, which balances the right hand of Hesed with its boundless loving kindness and divine forgiveness. From Gevurah's perspective, the universe is made so that awe can come about, so God can find out what fear is and what boundaries are. In its untempered, devolved aspect (*k'lippah*), Gevurah is like a hanging judge or a religious zealot who is out to condemn and punish you without mercy or sympathy. However, a more positive expression of Gevurah would be the strong warrior or crusader who fights for justice, a parent who sets sensible disciplinary limits for a child, or a realized soul who cuts through the sham of maya and illusion. It is said that for God, rigor is not anger but Truth.

In Hebrew scripture, Din represents the second day of creation when God separated the waters with a firmament. Din is associated with the patriarch Isaac who was nearly sacrificed on the altar and experienced God's command from a place of fear and awe; and in his old age, Isaac was blind and, among his two sons, preferred Esau over Jacob. The feminine counterpart of Gevurah is Leah, the first wife of Jacob, who is characterized as *Dina Kashia*, of strong judgment. Some of the Arabic divine names that correspond to Gevurah are *al-Hasib*, the accounter and bringer of judgment, *al-Qabid*, the withholder and constrictor, and *al-Qadr*, the divine power. The word *Akbar* (meaning great, from the root word *Kabir*) points to the awesome, powerful aspect of Gevurah, and is the equivalent Reb Zalman gave for Gevurah (or alternatively, *Allahu Akbar*, meaning God is far greater than any concept of the Divine we can ever formulate.)

The dyad of Hesed and Gevurah is similar to the Arabic qualities of *jamal* and *jalal* in Islam. Whereas Hokhmah and Binah find their corresponding metaphor in the brain, Hesed-Gevurah are often compared to the right and left hands. The early Christian Church Father, Clement of Rome, spoke of the right and left hands of God, the right hand bestowing goodness and the left testing us with temptation toward evil. Somewhat more positively, Reb Zalman points out how our two hands can work together interactively in a delicate balance of push and resistance to achieve their common objective. The sephirah which balances and mediates between Hesed and Gevurah is Tipheret, located at the center of the tree.

TIPHERET represents beauty and harmony and is the center of gravity for the entire tree, mediating between Hesed and Gevurah in the two outer columns as well as occupying the transition point between the top and bottom of the tree, between heaven and earth, Keter and Malkhut (via Yesod). There are twenty-two pathways between the sephirot on the Tree of Life, and all of them connect with Tipheret in the center. If Keter represents the divine transcendence and Hokhmah-Binah the level of understanding, with Hesed-Gevurah respresenting the level of power, Tipheret is the heart of the tree and its trunk, the station of the divine immanence, the permanent presence of God. It represents the third day of creation when God formed the dry land and vegetable kingdom, beheld it and twice said that it was good.

Tipheret is also associated with the Patriarch Jacob and Jacob's ladder, positioned as the central core of the sephirotic ladder, connecting heaven and earth through the medium of the human heart, whose radiance is enhanced when connected to the upper sphere of Keter. The female counterpart is Hannah, the mother of the Prophet Samuel, whose prayer of thanksgiving exemplifies Tipheret. Tipheret represents the place of balance and equilibrium in the sacred altar of the heart, the seat of the divine presence. It is also called *rahamim*, meaning compassion, from the Hebrew root *rehem* (meaning womb). From the perspective of Tipheret, God says: "Let Me see what heavy troubles I can get people into so I can save them from it."[104] God promises to be with every victim, to console and share the suffering. Psychologically, Tipheret is the seat of the Self, or integrated individuality. The Arabic name that is closest to Tipheret is *Hu*, the divine pronoun and the word associated with the Divine Essence and Divine Presence. There is also present in Tipheret an element of *Rahman* (divine compassion—the equivalent attribute given by Reb Zalman—from the Arabic root for womb), and *al-'Adl*, the just, that which brings things into balance and harmony.

NETZAH is translated as victory or endurance; however, it might best be thought of as the practical functionality of things, the blueprints, the technical set-up or idea which is responsible for making sure a thing works efficiently. Netzah represents the fourth day of creation when the sun and moon came into being. As Reb Zalman expressed it, the perspective of Netzah is, when contemplating the evolution from chlorophyll to dodos, to humans and their inventions, to say "wow" to how it all builds up, with the rhythms and seasons working together with clockwork perfection. Netzah and Hod work together almost like twins, and in the literature, they are often defined more obscurely than the other sephirot. Together, they correspond to the two legs, Netzah on the right, as the masculine principle which gives birth to Hod on the left side. Netzah is associated with Moses (the one who gives practical rulings on how to live and manage things) and also with Rebecca, Jacob's second wife (who, Reb Zalman says, balances Isaac in Gevurah). If the upper sephirot are thought of as the domain of the higher Self, connecting to the Infinite, the lower four sephirot on the Tree of Life can be thought of as representing the lower self or personality, the more incarnate aspects. The closest Arabic equivalent for Netzah, in its Hebrew meaning of victory, is *al-Mansur,* meaning victorious with the help of God.

HOD is translated as majesty or glory; yet it may be considered the aesthetic counterpart of Netzah, that aspect which is concerned not only with Netzah's practicality and functionality, but also with how elegant, beautiful, artful, and expressive the process or design will be, reflecting something of the divine glory. Hod resides in the left feminine column of the tree, corresponds to the left leg, and represents the fifth day of creation when the birds and fish were created (with their elegant movements). Hod is associated with Aaron (the silver-tongued priest) and with Sarah, Abraham's wife (who balances Abraham in Hesed). Hod's perspective surveys all the simultaneous plays going on interactively in the universe and it thinks: "How glorious God has made it all." Reb Zalman has pointed out that in most of the books on "Anglo-Qabala," the qualities of Netzah and Hod are reversed in attribution from the more traditional Jewish identification given here. The Arabic equivalents to Hod are *al-Jamil* (divine beauty—Reb Zalman's choice) and *al-'Azim* (divine glory).

YESOD means the foundation, and corresponds to the male and female genitals and the connecting, creative function which stabilizes the opposites. The most prominent aspects of Yesod are conjugal love, justice (*tzedek*), and that which is involved with the form and foundation of things. Yesod appears in the middle column mediating between Netzah and Hod, and psychologically could be said to correspond to the ego. Yesod represents the sixth day of creation when Adam and Eve were created. Archetypally, Yesod is associated with the patriach Joseph and with Tamar, the daughter-in-law of Judah, and ancestor of King David. As the story is recounted in Genesis, Tamar, who was a widow, disguised herself with a veil as a *kedushah*, or temple maiden (prostitute), and tricked Judah into mating with her. Yet significantly, it was out of the progeny resulting from this questionable mating that King David was born, and also Jesus.

In the ancient understanding, it was felt that when a husband and wife made love on the Sabbath (or in the pre-patriarchal Canaanite world, when a temple *kedushah* mated with a man or a king in a sacred context) a mystery was enacted, a *tikkun*, or fixing of the world that brought harmony and fertility to the crops. All of this is part of the connecting energy of Yesod. The perspective of Yesod looks at how life and libido come together to produce greater life and ecstasy, and also how God is the foundation of everything that exists. The Arabic qualities which correspond with Yesod are *al-Wadud* (divine love—the equivalent Reb Zalman gave) and *al-Wahab (Wahabo)*, the provider, the generous outpouring of bounty and blessing.

MALKHUT means the Kingdom (of earth). It is where the celestial lightning bolt meets the earth and is grounded. The very ground we stand upon is Malkhut. It is the abode where the *Shekhinah*,* the feminine indwelling presence of God, dwells hidden ("in exile") in the world of matter, mirroring and drawing down that which is above. The Shekhinah is one's personal connection with divine immanence and has a connection with the larger group mind beyond the individual. As Reb Zalman puts it: "Her mystery is the silence in which she keeps her manifestation

---

*   In Arabic: *Sakina.*

hidden so that individual life forms can take shape in conscious-ness. . . . the Shekhinah does not show her face."[105]

If Keter is the divine state prior to creation, Malkhut rep-resents the world as we normally perceive it. It physically corre-sponds to the body itself, or more specifically the bottom orifice of the body. If Yesod is the sphere where forms are dreamed and conceived, it is in Malkhut that the forms actually take shape as matter. Malkhut represents the feminine, passive prin-ciple in the bottom, middle column of the sephirotic tree and its symbol is the bride, traditionally a young veiled woman seat-ed on a throne. Malkhut represents the seventh day of creation when God rested; here, God is king and doesn't have to create or do anything, but just *be*. The sephirah is associated with David (the earthy, but inspired king) and also with Rachel. The Arabic words corresponding to Malkhut are *al-Malik* (the king—the equivalent Reb Zalman gave) and *al-Mawjud* (existing or exis-tentiation, presence).

FURTHER SEPHIROTIC CONSIDERATIONS
from REB ZALMAN

The ten sephirot also correlate with the four worlds: Keter is in the very highest uncreated world, the level of Adam Kadmon (in the Lurianic system). Hokhmah is in the transcendent realm of Atzilut. Binah is in the mental realm of B'riyah. Hesed, Gevurah, and Tiferet are in the feeling world of Yetzirah. Netzah, Hod, and Yesod are in the world of spiritual Assiyah, and Malkhut is in physical Assiyah.[106] In a 1982 class on "Sephirot and the Inner Life," Reb Zalman gave the following list of equivalents for the Tree of Life:

> The place of Keter is the place of "I am that I am." The place of Hokmah and Binah is "I-me." The place of Hesed, Gevurah, Tipheret is the place of "I-Thou." The place of Netzah, Hod, Yesod is the place of "I-it." The place of Malkhut is "not I."

He went on to speak about how the two outer columns on the tree find integration in the middle column, which is the third force that reconciles the polar opposites. For instance, with the triad of Netzah, Hod, Yesod, as it shows itself in the "I-it" world of doing, it goes as follows: "Netzah says, 'Yes, that's the way we're going to do it.' Hod is saying, 'Wait a minute; that's too noisy. That's not elegant enough.' And then comes Yesod and creates that functioning combination between these two." In the "I-thou" world of Hesed, Gevurah, Tipheret, Reb Zalman says of Gevurah: the law wants to be blind and not a respecter of persons. It doesn't want to make exceptions for people to let them off the hook. Instead it has a strong, machine-like attitude that says: "The law is the law!" On the other hand is Hesed, the attitude of generosity which wants to give grace and soften the law. We find the balance in the center in Tipheret.

In the sphere of affect, of feeling, it is interpersonal. "So there is love, there is hatred, if you will, and then there is the truth about it which says: 'I know the good. I know the bad, and it's integrated; and I know that the pendulum swings.'" In relationship, one day I see a person in a good light and the next day in a bad light. "While I'm in the yes, I recognize that there will be a little bit of no, and while I'm in the no, I recognize that there will be a little bit of yes. So I've got some idea about the center in affect, in relationship."

At the higher level of 'I-me,' the issue is understanding. You give me an idea and I look at the schema and I say, "It looks great, perfect." But when I look at it the next day, I'm starting to see the flaws in it and think it's all wrong. And the third time, in a cognitive way, I look and simultaneously see each side from a more balanced place in the center. I realize it contains some good things, some not so good things, and I find the middle place of balance. This is what Gurdjieff called the third force, the reconciling force that brings the two opposing positions to integration, the gray area that is neither black nor white, neither pure good nor pure evil. It is also the reason why so often in the old spiritual literature you will see a master who tells someone to come back in three days to receive an answer—one day for yes, another for no, and finally the more integral perspective reveals itself on the third day.

Reb Zalman advises that in working with the Tree of Life, it is important to see the pathways between the sephirot and the way they interact, not just each separate sephirah, because they work and balance each other in tandem, in triads, and as ten interactive aspects of the whole. There is no pure Hesed without some Gevurah, no Netzah without Hod. So the adjustments for any imbalances are found in the pathways between the sephirot. Also, in terms of perspective, we are really on the inside of the tree, not on the outside looking in at separate fragments. If we had a rotatable three-dimensional Tree of Life that could be viewed from any angle, it would become much more clear how, for instance, Keter viewed looking down from the top middle column directly overlays Tipheret, Yesod, and Malkhut, and the kind of circular secret connection that exists between Keter at the top and Malkhut at the bottom.

In 1988, in Washington, D.C., I had a discussion with Reb Zalman over lunch about the left- and right-brain switchover as it is represented in the Tree of Life. He clarified that "the left brain has to do with the right side, and the right brain has to do with the left side." There is a switchover at Tipheret, so that the right arm goes with the left leg, the way they do when you are walking. "The switchover goes from Hokhmah to Gevurah. Hokhmah is cold and Gevurah is cold. Binah is warm and Hesed is warm, so it crosses over." Then he added, "I tell you, the whole business of crossing over and this and that doesn't make much sense to me right now." He explained that he was working with a friend on a hypercard on the Mac that he hoped could produce a three-dimensional, rotatable tree.

"Most of the time, your vantage point is from outside the tree. That itself is a sign that it's wrong," he continued. If you move from a flat surface to a three-dimensional model the whole left-right dynamic changes. "What happens now is, if you rotate it, every part can be in the middle. . . . So as you rotate it, Gevurah can be in the center and not on the left. You can have Tipheret on the right or on the left of it, depending on which way you are going to look from." Using his hands, he indicated how it could be rotated so that Gevurah could be between Hesed and Tipheret, then asked, "So which one is the middle column?" He continued: "Now, what would it be if I looked from Gevurah's point of view? If I stood in Gevurah, and one of my wings goes to Tipheret and one of my wings goes to Hesed? So it turns out that Hesed is on my left. . . . Once you see the thing three-dimensionally, you see that there has been a whole lot of conversation about this thing that doesn't make sense" because they were standing outside of the tree looking at a flat plane and dealing with the problems that caused.

Reb Zalman with the author and his family, Sylvia and daughter, Claire, in North Carolina in 1987.

He went on to mention the old children's puzzle that had sixteen squares and one missing, and you had to move the letters around to solve it. He continued, noting that in the next generation our children were doing the Rubik's cube. To solve any of these puzzles, you had to go through a stage of chaos before the solution was reached, only the Rubik's cube is far more complex. "That's where it's going—toward more complexity.... The old chess board isn't where it's at," because trying to find solutions in two dimensional space creates problems of its own which can't be solved on that level. "I think this has to do with salvation, it has to do with religion. It has to do with a lot of stuff, this insight. . . . So part of the solution is to get out of the two-dimensional universe."

In concluding this section on the sephirot, I would like to furnish a longer quote from an afternoon talk I attended at a synagogue in Charlotte, North Carolina on February 2, 1990. There, Reb Zalman spoke about the "inner council," relating it to the ten sephirot.

> Most of the time, when somebody says, "I made up my mind. I've decided I'm going to turn over a new leaf," I've found that most people are very rash in turning over new leaves with the spiritual stuff. The question was, "How come when we have an insight, we don't move right away—that there's always this lagging behind between what we know we ought to do and what we actually do?" The answer is: most of the time what we are listening to is not the council of our being but only one voice. Let's say for a moment you get inspired and it's a very strong inspiration—you had an inspiring weekend somewhere. Inside of you, a voice that hasn't had a chance to access your mouth, your awareness or your consciousness— all of the sudden this voice is beginning to talk and it is saying: "See? See? I told you! You didn't listen to me." And this voice comes out and speaks with the voice of your conscience: "Therefore you've got to make such and such a change." Then you get inspired and think:

"I really want to make this change." Then you get home and go back to your regular situation. All of the sudden that voice is no longer speaking. Why is that? Because when you made up your mind, you didn't make up your mind. You only gave voice to one part of you. What happens very often is that when you allow one voice inside of you to speak, that voice becomes a dictator.

I'll give you an example: A young person goes to Jerusalem, he/she—it doesn't matter—there gets very inspired and decides to go *frum* [orthodox], and says: "All the other voices inside of me I'm not going to listen to anymore—because they are da, da, da—and I've decided I'm going to be this." What about feelings that come up, about body and so on? "Shut up! I'm not going to listen to them anymore—they are the *Yetzer HaRa*—the inclination for evil!" Do you understand what I'm saying? They all get shut out. It's almost as if the Nouveau Frum has made a *putsch*—a revolution—and the Nouveau Frum is now in charge with a dictatorship. The radio station is blaring the whole day: "Torah, Torah, Torah!" and is not giving any voice to any other social feelings or bodily needs. You used to walk and be into health food and now you're eating greasy stuff. You buy a pair of *tzitzits*, you put on a golden *yarmulke* and start looking pasty and talking with a funny European accent and thinking, "Boy, I'm doing good— God loves me!" [audience laughter] I'm making a caricature but you've met these living caricatures. What happened was they didn't make up their mind—they suppressed. A new voice came up and this voice became the dominant voice and put down every other voice. What you often find is that the new insight did not consult the rest of the council.

I'll tell you about a very interesting person, named [Eligio] Steve Gallegos. He works with an inner totem pole. He imagines that each chakra is inhabited by a different totem animal. So he says if you want to make any important changes of life, you have to call together a council of all your totem animals and when they are willing, in the council, to have their voice and give their input and then they say 'yes,' then you have made up your mind. Most of the time when we say, "I've made up my mind" we haven't made up our mind—we have shut up nine of the ten sephirot and we are listening only to one of them. And what comes out is always something distorted, a little ugly, ungrounded. And then you begin to wonder why the backsliding comes. It comes because the other voices gang up against this one voice that took over, and then you get this pendulum where the moods swing back and forth, partly because you didn't have a consultation with the rest of your being. (We have a minion inside of us.) . . . If you talk holistically—most of the time people say, "How come I'm not listening to the voice of my conscience?" The answer is that the voice of the conscience did not consult the other voices. It's not con-science (literally, "with knowing") it's mono-science. It's not together. The only way to get it together is together. . . . Don't go for "I made up my mind," but "I consulted my council."

I have a friend whose name is Deena Metzger. She is the one to whom I am grateful for this notion: Is your inner life a democracy or is it a dictatorship? By paying attention to: What does my council have to say? By calling the parliament together: Have I heard from everyone? Sometimes you have to be a little quiet for a while because there are some voices that don't want to speak first. They are sort of timid. You have to say: Mind, from you I've heard already. Feelings, from you I've heard already. Intuition, you haven't spoken yet. Pragmatism, thank you—you have given me the spreadsheet. It's like calling in all the data, and that's what makes it possible later on to come to a decision. Not like tearing yourself from one place and going to another place, but just gradually shifting to take everything along.

In response to a questioner's request to enumerate the ten sephirot, Reb Zalman answered: In brief the ten sephirot stations you would consult, starting at the top, are:

> Will, wisdom, understanding, what attracts you, what repels you, what gives you the balance, what are the means—the tools you are going to use, how elegant is it going to be? (Will it be beautiful and effective or only one of them?) Does it have reproductive power—does it make a connection, grounding? What is its reality picture? . . . All these ten are the way we talk about integration. These are the ten voices, but only my enumeration of it. Your introspection is going to tell you what those ten voices are for you.

UPDATING OUR GOD LANGUAGE *and* CONCEPTS

Now we will look at the ways in which our old models and inherited assumptions about God may subtly distort and limit our understanding of the Divine. This condition may result in part from the limitations of our language and in part from the adult retention of simple exoteric teachings received in childhood which were never followed up by more nuanced esoteric explanations that would provide a more mature adult conception of the Divine. Children may, for instance, be told that God is a kind of great male being, separate from us and residing above us in the heavens, who listens to our prayers, loves us, watches over us, grants our wishes, protects us and our loved ones from harm and may take our souls to heaven at death if we pray to Him. (In some cases the fear of hell or divine wrath is stressed, conveying a fearful conception.)

While the more benign assurances about God may provide temporary comfort to young children, as they grow older, they will inevitably be faced with suffering and the death of loved ones, injustice in the world, and many other situations which severely challenge these simple childhood beliefs. As Reb Zalman expressed it: a child needs to hear about a good, provider God.

But when the child grows up, he (or she) will find God abandoning him more and more to his own devices and inviting a
revised theology that now can handle the good/bad Deity. Later,
there's a third stage beyond that.*

During a class on spiritual leadership at Elat Chayyim, Reb
Zalman enlarged on this theme, saying that you can't teach high
level God understandings to those who are not ready to hear
them. If you do, they may turn out to be destructive. You can't
give an advanced answer to the theodicy to a child. You can't tell
a child (the words of Job): "Yea, though He slay me, I will trust
in Him."[107] You can only stretch a person one faith level above
where they are, and no further (until that next level has been
truly assimilated).** Here, Lawrence Kohlberg's scale of moral development is helpful in mapping the stages, as well as the
work of his colleague Carol Gilligan, and James Fowler, with his
stages of faith. ***

Another important psychologist, Gordon W. Allport, spoke
of the functional autonomy of motives—how motivations
change for the same act as one grows in understanding. When
we grow older, we continue to do the same things we did when

---

* From a conversation between Reb Zalman and the author during
the 1989 Wisdom School. My notes, made at the time, indicate only that he
mentioned a third step. Presumably, that would correspond to the phase
where the Divine is discovered within and one is no longer primarily relating to God as an absolutely separate entity "out there."
** This point is also emphasized in the Spiral Dynamics system and
in Ken Wilber's teaching as well. Wilber emphasizes two essential lines of
growth: one is in terms of spiritual awakening (involving higher states of
consciousness and ego transcendence) and the other involves "growing up"
(increasing in wisdom, maturity, and ethical rectitude).
*** James Fowler has worked out six stages of faith from the primal
faith of a toddler, through the more magical, imaginative level of "intu-
itive-projective" faith (up to around age seven), extending to the "myth-
ic-literal" faith of the middle school years (involves accepting stories from
scripture literally as a matter of faith). This is usually followed by the more
critical "synthetic-conventional" faith that is common from adolescence to
young adulthood (in which one may become more skeptical of religious
claims one has previously accepted uncritically), which, for many people,
is where the levels of faith stop. However, Fowler gives two further levels:
"conjunctive" faith (around ages thirty-five to forty) where one reassesses
and clears up issues around boundaries and identity, and finally, the most
mature level of "universalizing" faith. (Modern exemplars of this level would
include Mahatma Gandhi, Thomas Merton, Martin Luther King Jr., and the
fourteenth Dalai Lama, to name but a few.)]

younger, but the rationale changes. On a low level of faith, reasons are cited to justify the commandments like: "God will be angry if you do it," or, "Jews mustn't do what the Canaanites did." But later, with more maturity and informed by higher *midrash* (interpretation) and Kabbalistic teachings, one begins to understand deeper justifications for the same acts. Then, at a much higher faith level, one may truly affirm: "Though He slay me, yet will I trust Him."

These progressive levels of faith are given in Sufism as well by teachers such as Imam al-Ghazali and, in modern times, by Hazrat Inayat Khan. Al-Ghazali speaks of three main levels of faith. At the lowest level of faith, one deals with God as with a lawyer or businessman, promising to do certain things if God will reciprocate (what Murshid Sam scorned as the lowest level of "business in love"). At a higher level, one relates to God as a loving mother or parent whom one trusts to provide for one's needs, yet one occasionally still cries out to God. At the highest level, one is as a corpse in the hands of the corpse-washer, and even surrenders to death with absolute trust in the Source. This corresponds to the high level of faith to which Reb Zalman alludes in the declaration of Job above, words affirmed by the prophet in spite of all the suffering he endured by divine permission.

Hazrat Inayat Khan enumerated four levels of belief which he said are as stepping stones to spiritual progress. The progression loosely mirrors the modalities of the four worlds. The first is an unexamined belief which conforms to what those around one believe and have told one—a mass belief which may easily change if others change their belief. This can involve inherited belief systems, prejudices and cultural assumptions.

The next level is an emotional belief in authority, in the authority of scripture, a savior, or some leader whom one trusts. It is a somewhat stronger, more idealistic belief; however, one's belief in scripture or a savior may conflict with that of another who believes in the same scripture but holds a different interpretation, and this can lead one to doubt.

The third level is a stronger belief arrived at by one's own reason. One is not simply following an authority, but can produce good, rational reasons for one's belief, and this gives it a greater power. Yet reason has its limits, and can sometimes be misguided. The highest level is an inner conviction which stands above intellectual reason, something one inwardly knows to be true to the very core of one's being, as an unshakable certainty and truth. This is the highest essence of absolute faith, called *'Ain al-Iman* in Arabic, a living torch that guides and supports one even in the most trying times.

Unfortunately, this advanced level of essential faith is not easily available to everyone. Often when people face a spiritual crisis in their lives, they may attempt to find a place of worship only to be disappointed when they discover that only the most elementary teachings are offered there. As Hazrat Inayat Khan put it (using the metaphor of music), too often a person turns toward religion, longing to hear the sublime sounds of violins, but after attending a religious service, leaves in disappointment because all they encountered was a child's rattle. When this happens on a large scale with religion, it furnishes an easy target for secularists and atheists to attack and dismiss the lowest common understanding of religion as a fairy tale for children and the sum total of what theology has to offer. Rarely are deeper spiritual insights pertaining to divine immanence, kenosis, theosis, or apophatic spirituality considered in popular writings or debates on the merits of religion. *

For those who try to approach the deeper spiritual teachings, language can still cause considerable conceptual problems, such as speaking of God as a noun or gendered pronoun, presenting enlightenment or salvation as a kind of ego achievement, or the ego as an entity that could be killed. These are the kinds of issues that are briefly touched upon in the discussion that follows.

if GOD *is* GOOD, WHENCE COMES EVIL?

Now, let's look at issues around the theodicy (If God is good and all-powerful, whence comes evil?) and how the various authors

---

*   See glossary for definitions of these terms.

of the Hebrew Bible handled the issue of evil while maintaining an emphasis on God's oneness. In speaking about the theodicy, Reb Zalman sometimes quoted the lines from Archibald MacLeish's contemporary play, *J.B.*:

> *I heard upon his dry dung heap*
> *That man cry out who cannot sleep.*
> *"If God is God He is not Good.*
> *If God is Good He is not God;*
> *Take the even, take the odd.*

There is some confusion that arises from the different ways in which scriptures depict God's relation to evil or Satan, and how God's oneness is reconciled with that. In the past, particularly in Christian culture, God has been idealized as the Good. But this has raised the issue of the origin of evil, the all-powerfulness of God, and why bad things can happen to good and righteous people (an issue addressed in the Book of Job). In the ancient world of polytheism, the gods were depicted as capricious and not bound by moral considerations. The monotheistic conception in Israel, however, idealized God as one and as requiring moral righteousness and eschewing evil.

By contrast, the Zoroastrian religion, which the Jews encountered during the Babylon captivity, spoke of twin spirits emerging from the Primal Source, a spirit of all-goodness (Ahura Mazda) and a spirit of evil and destruction (Ahriman), which gradually hardened into a doctrine of two separate Gods—thus providing one answer to the theodicy. Isaiah furnished the challenge to Zoroastrian belief from the Jewish perspective. There, God says: "I form the light, and create darkness: I make peace, and create evil: I the Lord do all these things."[108] In the Book of Job, Satan is presented as one of the sons of God. As Reb Zalman expressed it, in the old tradition, *ha-Satan* (meaning "the adversary" in Hebrew) was not an evil rebel, but was the one with whom God was able to joke and make wagers. But by the Inter-Testamental period, with the rise of Gnostic thought, Satan had become more of a bad guy.[109]

In Genesis,[110] good (*tov* in Hebrew) and evil (*raa*) enter the human condition by means of the Tree of the Knowledge of Good and Evil through the agency of the serpent (*nahash*), who is said to have legs and the power of speech, and who is described as "more subtle than any beast of the field which the Lord God had made."[111] The serpent was a widespread figure in ancient Near Eastern mythology, as was the great mother dragon, Tiamat, whom Marduk slew, fashioning the earth from her carcass, according to the old Babylonian scripture, the *Enuma Elish*. In Sumerian mythology, the human-headed serpent deity named Ningizzida (meaning "Lord of the Tree of Truth") is the son of the creator god, Enki, and is variously depicted as an underworld fertility deity with secret knowledge of creation, a god of healing, and a consort of the goddess.

These well-known motifs were likely known to the author of Genesis, yet the story has been carefully revised to reflect a more patriarchal perspective. In Genesis, the mother goddess ("the mother of all that lives," in Gen.3:20) and her wise serpent consort are negatively reframed as the culpable human progenitor, Eve, and a devious talking snake whom God curses. While St. Augustine interpreted the story as representing the fall of all humanity, tainting all humans with a sinful nature, this has never been the sense of the story's meaning in Jewish or Muslim commentary. Sufis, in fact, understand Adam and Eve's actions in eating the fruit of the tree, not as a great unintended and lamentable error, but rather, as *fulfilling* the hidden divine intention for humans to leave paradise consciousness in order to physically incarnate. For example, Hazrat Inayat Khan says in his *Gayan*: "Hail to my exile from the Garden of Eden to the earth. If I had not fallen, I should not have had the opportunity of probing the depths of life."[112] The bliss of paradise is easy, with no challenge or effort required, but the birth of consciousness is interesting—thus the motive of leaving Eden.

Yet the story of the garden is rich in meaning and carries another important theological lesson. In eating the fruit of the forbidden tree, the humans display a certain hubris, not unlike the Greek myth of Prometheus stealing fire (a symbol of consciousness) from the gods to give to humanity. The Qur'an, building on the lead of Torah, often notes that the human *nafs* or ego is unjust, because it has a Pharaoh-like tendency to arrogate to itself a presumed independence, forgetting that its very life-breath and intelligence is furnished at each moment by God, on Whom all life depends for its existence. With pride and inflation comes the risk of a fall. So humanity must constantly balance its drive for independent initiative with the humble realization that everything is done through the divine prerogative.

I once asked Reb Zalman what meaning he felt the author of Genesis had originally intended to convey with the snake in the Garden of Eden—if the snake was seen as part of God and an agent of God's will, or as a separate, more evil entity working against the divine will. He responded that, really, both are there to some degree. Primarily, the idea is a morally good God and a separate serpent, but there are other currents in it; no committee sat around and worked it out to get the theology straight. Was the revelation clear? Yes, but a number of authors had their own revelations which differed slightly. The Babylonian idea of Tiamat, Apsu and the primal world is not totally absent, nor is the God who builds up the world from the primordial chaos. He added that he did not like to refer to the traditions that preceded Judaism, such as the Canaanite, Sumerian, and Babylonian legacies as "pagan," but instead referred to them as "pre-patriarchal Judaism." For just as Buddhism emerged out of the Hindu tradition and Christianity out of Judaism, so Judaism also emerged out of the religions that came before. For instance, the Israelites adopted the Canaanite name for the High God, *El and El Shaddai,* and Abraham received bread and wine from Melchizedek, the high priest of *El Elyon.* Reb Zalman also felt that during their centuries in Egypt, the Israelites gained a lot of wisdom from the surrounding spiritual culture.[113]

Elsewhere, Reb Zalman discussed other influences of the pre-patriarchal tradition on the Bible. During a talk on Basic Training in Jewish Mysticism, he referred to the Wellhausen documentary hypothesis, which maintained that the authorship of Genesis and the rest of the Torah consisted of a weaving together of four sources (abbreviated as J, E, P, and D), authored not by Moses, but by unnamed Judean writers between the time of Hezekiah, Josiah and Ezra. Reb Zalman pointed out that, while scholars have thought for over a century that the authorship of most of the Hebrew Bible was late—even possibly as late as Maccabean times—in more recent years archeologists have found some evidence that would support earlier origins. For instance, the Ugaritic writings from 1200 BCE that were found at Rash Amra in 1928 contained mention of the righteous Akat and Dan-el, showing an earlier Canaanite version of Daniel. They also found that some of the Hebrew psalms, written down at a later date using the name of Y-H-V-H, were rewritings of hymns that were previously sung to Ba'al in Canaan.[114]

In his Wisdom school, Reb Zalman mentioned the documentary hypothesis again and said he had no trouble accepting that a seventh-century BCE priest consolidated and wove together the older material into the form we now know as the *Sefer Torah*. Yet he didn't feel that this later editing somehow diminished the Torah or made it any less divinely inspired. Rather, he felt that the anonymous redactor did a marvelous job of retro-fitting the old material together in a beautiful, organic way which would motivate both his contemporaries and future generations of Jews, and for that we owe him a tremendous debt of gratitude.

The Judean concept differed markedly from the pre-patriarchal sources of Judaism in seeing as contained in one God alone the attributes of what had been a number of deities in the polytheistic milieu—Father Sky god, Mother Earth goddess, sons and daughters of God, Underworld and Storm deities, Creator and Destroyer gods. While the realization that there is only One Being was and remains a profound spiritual insight, it created, in the exoteric religion, the conundrum of the theodicy and the necessity of attributing moral evil and destruction away from God—to Satan. Some of the members of the divine pantheon were, in the early transitional stage of Judaism, still called sons of God but were later thought of as angelic and demonic entities.

Yet a certain ambivalence in the divine character sometimes entered into God's biblical behavior. For instance, in the ancient

Babylonian version of the flood story where the Noah figure is named Utnapishtim, there were two brother gods, sons of the Most High God, Anu, and they disagreed as to whether humanity should be saved from the coming flood. Enlil, the stern first-born son, insisted that humanity was of little value and should be destroyed, but Enki, who, with the goddess Ninhursag, had created humanity, desired to save some of the human beings and came up with a secret plan to save a few people and animals in an ark and clandestinely warned Utnapishtim of the coming flood. In the later monotheistic version of the flood story, God, in assuming the role of both Enlil and Enki, appears to inwardly debate with Himself over the fate of humanity. Having first created humans and pronounced the creation good, He decides to destroy most humans and animal life with a flood, but afterwards, using the sign of the rainbow, covenants never to do it again.

One of the ways that the theme of good and evil was explored in the Torah was through a series of sibling conflicts in the Book of Genesis: Cain and Abel, Jacob and Esau, Isaac and Ishmael, Rachel and Leah. In Jungian terms, these pairs represent the twin motif, the split in the human being between the favored good self and the disowned shadow self. Another early biblical expression of how evil was managed appears in the scapegoat ceremony in Leviticus 16, where the rejected goat, Azazel, takes on the sins of the people and is exiled into the desert. In modern times, the goat (or shadow energy) has, so to speak, returned, seeking redemption, and is being handled psychologically by means of integration and reclaiming projections of our own unwanted shadows onto others.

There is another aspect of this issue which is important to consider, and that is the dark energy of the Divine that is represented in India as Shiva and as Kali. In the *trimurti* concept of Hinduism, God is idealized as Brahma, the creator, Vishnu, the sustainer, and Shiva, the destroyer. However, in the West, we don't have a theology that acknowledges the divine energies represented by Shiva or by Kali, the female destroyer, and so we find it difficult to relate to the Divine in that aspect.

Reb Zalman suggests that, in ecological terms, we could think of Shiva or Kali as the "Divine Recycler." Zalman's wife, Eve Ilsen, adds that while Lilith, the dark feminine figure in Judaism isn't too developed in Western culture, in Hindu culture she has been well-developed as Kali. The images show Kali, the dark mother, with numerous arms, one of which is held up in a "do not fear" gesture, while another hand holds a knife. She "has a necklace of skulls and a long tongue to lap up the blood of her children. . . . We tend to interpret this as evil and to be expunged in our culture," Eve continues, but in Hinduism, Kali, in the aspect of "the ferocious feminine, is the one you call on to eat the evil in you—to devour that in you which should no longer be there, which has reached the time when it is ready to decay, fall and be transformed."[115] This shows that in non-Western religious systems, God has sometimes been idealized in such a way as to recognize, even in the dark side and in the destruction of old forms and ego structures, something of the divine transformative purpose at work; in this way a redemptive value is given to the dark aspect, the so-called left hand side of God.

Why is all of this important? Because, particularly in the Common Era, Western religions have widened the gap that splits the God-ideal into a God of goodness and the devil, who by implication, is treated as a separate source of power, divorced from the Divine Oneness. While there is a limited moral payoff to this understanding with its clear separation between the polar opposites, it is at the same time problematic because any idealization of God which consigns the Divine to only the realm of "the Good" necessarily limits and fragments the Indivisible Divine Source. Human society certainly needs moral principles and guidelines to control crime and injustice, and religion plays its part by imparting moral teachings which inculcate goodness and rein in excess. Yet, this does not necessitate a theological division of God's oneness. For if God is only the author of goodness, then we must have a separate and perhaps equally powerful force, a second dark deity, to account for evil; in other words, a theology of ditheism rather than monotheism.

Here it is important to observe how the Kabbalistic Tree of Life depicts one central tree, representing the divine wholeness. Growing from this tree to the right and the left sides, are the opposing merciful and rigorous divine qualities with the middle column or trunk perfectly balancing the two sides. This clearly indicates that the divine nature is not exclusively confined to one side of the polar opposites but is a dynamic wholeness in which all things work together toward the divine purpose, a purpose which always transcends limited human assessments of what is good and evil. The Zohar states that "There is no sphere of the other side [the left side of severity] that entirely lacks some streak of light from the side of holiness."

In a 2008 article, Reb Zalman commented:

> People generally want God to be the God of the good. They don't realize that the same Source that is the Source of what we call good is the Source of evil. The Source of what we call the beautiful is the same Source of the ugly. In fact, it is the Source of Allness. When we start picking and saying we like "this" better and "that" less, we are making the division between good and evil.[116]

There is a rabbinic story (also told with variations in Sufism) which takes us to the heart of the problem of evil. It is told that, after much fasting and divine petitioning, the sages were granted to catch the *Yetzer ha-Ra*, the inclination toward evil, the one who had been causing all the mischief in the world, and put him in a lead barrel. But the *Yetzer ha-Ra* warned them that if they killed him it would be the end of the world. Within a few days, they realized what he meant. With the *Yetzer ha-Ra* removed from the scene, no one was motivated to do anything, all ambition and desire ceased, and even the chickens ceased to lay eggs; and so, reluctantly, the sages released him.[117]

There are other stories addressing this theme, such as the Hasidic tale where the Ba'al Shem Tov faced the force of darkness and was given the opportunity to seize and rid the world of the heart of evil. But when he held this blackened heart in his hand, he noticed that it was bleeding and suffering from its own alienation, so the Ba'al Shem Tov took pity on it and did not destroy it, in order that some measure of redemption might yet occur. In light of such stories, Reb Zalman concludes:

> our job is not to set up a battleground to eradicate evil, but to search out its spark of holiness. Our task is not to destroy but to build; not to hate, but to find a place of yielding; not to polarize, but to discover the points of commonality so that we can work together. Learn this lesson, dear friends, it will serve you well."[118]

If evil, then, is not to be eradicated, can we find any hidden benefit from it? In *Satan in the Old Testament*, Rivkah Scharf Klugar comments on the lesson imparted in the Book of Job, when the righteous servant, who was blessed with a fulfilled and successful life, was tested by Satan with severe trials and personal loss whose meaning Job could not comprehend. Klugar observes that, in the end, Job's experience of ultimately submitting to the divine will, and no longer insisting on his own sense of justice, represents a step beyond a submission born of blind faith in God to a realization

> born of inner insight. Satan here is truly Lucifer, the bringer of light. He brings man the knowledge of God, but through the suffering he inflicts on him. Satan is the misery of the world which alone drives man inward [from complacency] into the "other world."[119]

Similarly, in Sirach 4:17-18, it is the figure of Divine Wisdom, Hokhmah, who plagues man "with her discipline until she can trust him, testing him with her ordeals." In this way "she will lead him back to the straight road and reveal her secrets to him." This is why it is said that "the fear (or awe) of the Lord is the beginning of wisdom and knowledge of the Holy One is understanding."[120] Reb Zalman comments on this issue, stating:

One could say suffering is the school for empathy. It creates that; but that's only one element of suffering. Sometimes suffering exists in order to bring us to our senses. Sometimes suffering exists in order to show us that there are tragedies we can't overcome with our childish omnipotence in the world. We begin to see that every choice we make has its consequences. Suffering is the way in which we learn, after the fact, the consequences of our moves. Then there are some people who suffer and can't identify this reason or that reason. It's just one of those things. "Why do bad things happen to good people?" is the question behind all that, and I haven't yet found a convincing answer. Sometimes no matter what we do, we get clobbered! On a lower level of preparation and understanding we would say, "If we do only the good and the true all the time, we're going to be okay." On a higher level being good doesn't help. The biggest ethical questions are based on just that point.[121]

Zalman goes on to point out that the path of resisting evil is not a very effective response, because in doing so

we become negative ourselves. But when we come into contact with evil, there is a witnessing there. That is what Aikido and the other martial arts keep pointing out: If we get to that place, we can sidestep it and let its impetus cause it to fall. That's much better than trying to resist it with the same energy it comes at us with, because then we have to use the methods that that energy, the opposing or evil energy, uses. So, anti-terrorism is terroristic! It doesn't work either.[122]

In Islam, it is a tenant of the faith to acknowledge that everything—whether it appears to us to be good or bad—comes from the one Divine Source. That is why the ninety-nine divine names are not restricted to just the benign (or jamal) qualities. As we have seen, this idea is also important in Kabbalistic thought.

In his *Fragments of a Future Scroll*, Reb Zalman quotes two beautifully apropos sayings by the Hasidic master, Reb Moshe Lieb of Sassov:

> Realize well that you are a stranger on earth and, therefore, hold both the good and the not good as equals.

> If you truly believe and have decided in your soul that both the good and the evil come from His blessed Name, and that nothing else can be done without Him, then it is impossible that you should have pain and anxiety due to the fact that things are done against you.[123]

This is also part of the secret of Jesus' saying: "Love your enemy as yourself," and "God makes His sun rise on the evil and on the good, and sends rain on the just and on the unjust alike."[124]

Though the analytical mind likes to categorize events and people in terms of good or bad, such judgments are necessarily one-sided and subjective. For every coin has two sides; and what is good for the winning side is simultaneously bad for the losing side, while God is the One Being manifesting through both sides. And is it not a common experience that what appears at first to be a loss may turn out to be a gain, and many a gain brings with it unanticipated troubles? Here, the Ba'al Shem Tov has a most helpful suggestion. He says instead of thinking of things in terms of good and bad, think of experiences as being either bitter or sweet. The more we see the interconnectedness of life and that nothing is done outside the divine will, the more holistic our view becomes—beyond limited labels of good and bad—and the more our compassion for others can flow.

HOW OUR LANGUAGE MISLEADS US

In 1990, I traveled with my family to a synagogue in Charlotte, North Carolina, for a weekend with Reb Zalman. On Sunday afternoon he spoke for several hours and answered questions on various issues such as spiritual eldering, confusions we have about the ego, and problems with our God-language. Below is an excerpt from the talk, beginning with a response to a question about dealing with the ego:

> When anybody says, "You've got to get rid of your ego," I want to watch my pockets. The problem is not with the ego but a sick ego. . . . Sometimes it happens that the pathology of ego is due to the fact that the ego doesn't get its juice that it needs to get. Which is to say: the ego is OK as a manager but it is a lousy boss. The Self, the soul is the boss, but the ego has to be the manager—it handles a lot of stuff. And every once in a while the ego has to get a pat on the back, saying, "good, good." Every once in a while the ego needs a vacation. . . . A healthy ego is good. It's a good servant. Sometimes we talk about, "I am a child of God. I'm a servant of God." My ego is a servant of God; my soul is a child of God. Once I get the difference, I don't get lost with that one anymore.
>
> So the language of the *siddur* [the Jewish prayer book] has very often been this kind of language: "O we, who are nothing, ask You, who are everything, to do this for us." Now that is a disempowering language! So we felt it is very important to make those shifts and changes. . . . The name Y-H-V-H [contains] the word 'HoVeH' [which is associated with] breath and means "to be." And when you put the *yud* in front of it, then it means "the one who sustains and gives being." How did they translate it in the King James Version? As "Lord." The moment you get into Lord, then I'm a subject. He is the feudal boss and I'm the groveling guy below; whereas when I can say, "Y-H-V-H, the One who causes Being," then I'm not different from the One who causes my being. We are one being. He *be's* me and I'm *be-ed*. There is an "interbeing."
>
> Part of the trouble we have with language today is that we have either active or passive [tenses]. Look! I'm not sitting on the chair, and the chair isn't seating me, but the chair and I are "inter-sitting." . . . So the [Renewal

Movement] siddur is based on creating language for interbeing. . . . Example: "The sun rises. The sun sets." The fact that we say "sunrise" and "sunset" four hundred years after Copernicus keeps us from solar energy at this point. . . . "Sunrise, sunset" implies that it's out there—we are the ones who are standing still and the sun is moving. If we would have changed the language and said it the other way: "We are now turning in order to get our allotment of daily sunshine," the language would have made it click: "Ah, our allotment of sunshine is coming. Let's grab hold of it [as solar energy]!" So our old language habits can give us trouble.[125]

Since Reb Zalman mentioned the new siddur, I would like to share a few brief examples of Jewish Renewal Movement translations of the *Shema* into modern English, drawn from a late-1980s working draft edition of the Jewish prayer service.[126] The Shema is, of course, the quintessential profession of Jewish faith, which is fervently affirmed during the Jewish prayer service and repeated daily by observant Jews. The creed is attributed to Moses and is found in Deuteronomy 6:4. It was endorsed by Jesus[127] as the greatest commandment and is essentially equivalent to the Qur'anic creedal injunction: "*La ilaha ilallah,*" meaning: "Nothing exists (there are no gods) except the one Divine Reality."

The words of the *Shema* in Hebrew, as usually intoned, are: "*Shema Yisrael, Adonai Eloheinu, Adonai eḥad,*" meaning: "Hear, O Israel, the Lord our God, the Lord is one." Contained in the quote is the word *Isra-El*, the name given to Jacob after he wrestled with the Divine.[128] It means "God-wrestler," the one who struggles to serve, know and integrate the divine energies. Also, the word *Adonai* (meaning Lord) is a pious substitution for the God name Y-H-V-H in the original text, which traditionally is not to be vocalized (except it was permitted to be uttered once a year on Yom Kippur by the High Priest in the holy of holies, up until the destruction of the second Temple). Here, then, are four alternative translations of the *Shema* into modern English, from the Jewish Renewal siddur:

Listen, you who wrestle God;
The Breath of Life is our God—
The Breath of Life alone.

Hear O Israel!
The Infinite Energy
is the Infinite Oneness of all!

Hear Israel!
Being is Divine!
Being is One!

Hear O worlds;
The Self is in all,
The Self is one.

Finally, here is the version Reb Zalman used in *Gate to the Heart:*

Listen, Yisra'el,
'God-wrestler,'
Yah Who is,
Is our God;
Yah Who is,
Is one, Unique,
All there is.[129]

A further point bears mentioning regarding the God-name received by Moses in Exodus 3:4: Y-H-V-H. The King James translation, "I am that I am," is not a very accurate rendition, nor does the spelling of the name as "Jehovah" bear much resemblance to the Hebrew form. (As Rabbi Shlomo Carlebach once drolly observed: King James might have been alright as a king, but his Hebrew left something to be desired.) In the original Hebrew, the name is in the future tense and translates approximately as: "I will be what I will be," or "I am becoming what I am becoming." The name has to do with essence and therefore could even be rendered: "My essence is a continual becoming." The ramifications of this are most interesting, as it supports a view of the Divine which is dynamic and hints at the type of spiritual evolutionary vision favored by Teilhard de Chardin.

The one-hundredth Psalm provides a final example of Reb Zalman's translations, taken from his *Psalms in a Translation for Praying*. The Psalms came out of real-life experiences and were made to be sung and are often chanted. They best come alive in translation when freed of the stilted ecclesiastical phrases of past centuries. Here, in gender-inclusive language, is Reb Zalman's rendition of Psalm 100:

> *This is how you sing to God a thank-you song—*
> *you join the symphony of the whole Earth.*
>
> *In your gratefulness, you meet Him;*
> *voices echo joy in God's halls.*
>
> *In giving thanks,*
> *we engage Her blessings,*
> *We meet His goodness*
> *here and now,*
> *Her encouragement*
> *from generation to generation.*
>
> *You are filled with joy serving God's purpose;*
> *you sound your own song as you do it.*
> *Certain that God is Be-ing,*
> *we know that we are brought forth from Her—*
> *both God's companions and His flock.*
>
> *Enter into God's presence*
> *singing your own song*
> *in grateful appreciation.*
>
> *Thank you, God, You are all Blessing.*

In this world, You are Goodness,
yes Grace itself—
this is the trust we bequeath
the next generation.[130]

GOD *as* FATHER, ENTHRONED *on* HIGH

We conclude this section with a few remarks concerning God's image as cosmic parent who watches over his earthly children. Reb Zalman felt that, over the centuries, the root metaphor of God as parent had been given so much emphasis that, to a large extent, it had kept us from seeing the other relationships, the other root metaphors we have with God, particularly God as the Beloved. "Male and female they were created"—created for love. Reb Zalman pointed out that the old windows are no longer working as they once did, and the masculine/Father approach is not satisfying for everyone; some need a more feminine approach.[131] If we see this, we can participate in the task of helping to design the windows for the future. When we wear out the old root metaphors, then we need to find other metaphors that work for us. Reb Zalman often made use of computer analogies, comparing the ongoing tradition to updatable software. He also liked to say that just as plants, like the sunflower, are heliotropic—turning toward the sun—so we are theotropic beings, turning toward God as the cause and goal of everything. He advised that the crisis that all the religions are currently experiencing could best be weathered by turning to the mystical dimensions within these traditions.

In a 1998 class, Reb Zalman quoted the Ba'al Shem Tov's statement: "God's providence supervises everything." Then he added that, for the left brain, exoteric person, such a statement means: God, sitting on a throne high above the earth, "uses his omniscient spyglass and checks out if you did the right things today."

But if God is all, and everything is in God, then God knows what is going on, not by extraspection, but by introspection. *Oy!* I know what my toe is saying from

inside! How does God know? Not by object knowledge
but by subject knowledge . . . so it is a mistake to see God
up there and out there looking at the universe.[132]

Zalman added this is not to say that it is all just immanence,
as there is a complimentary transcendent view as well.

I would like to conclude this section with short teaching
parable that I heard from Reb Zalman years ago, which aptly points to the difference between the exoteric and esoteric
approaches to spirituality. Once the prophet Elijah appeared
to a holy rabbi and informed him that God was pleased with
him and would grant him one request, but he must make the
request immediately. The startled rabbi asked to be granted a
vision of paradise and his wish was instantly granted. Suddenly,
they were before the heavenly gates. But when the man looked
in, all he saw was a few rabbis seated in meditation in a lovely
landscape. "But where are all the saints who have merited paradise?" he asked. "All I see is a few rabbis sitting around." Elijah
answered: "Of all people, I thought you would know better. The
rabbis aren't in paradise; paradise is in the rabbis! They come
here, stay a while and then they go back to earth. Once they
realize that God's glory is in everyone, they want to return and
see it everywhere."

The following section concludes our survey of Reb Zalman's
teaching with a discussion of how religions, as far back as we can
trace, have been gradually undergoing changes in their basic assumptions about the nature of the Divine and our relationship
to that Ultimate Source, a phenomenon known as "paradigm
shifting." In looking at this material, I believe it is important to
bear in mind Carl Jung's cautionary advice that when we speak
about the variety of images by which humanity has idealized
the Divine, we are speaking, in epistemological terms, only of
the *God-image* (how the Ineffable Higher Power is perceived in
the human psyche through various archetypal images); for the
Absolute God to which the descriptions point is exalted far beyond any limited mental conception we could ever entertain.

SPIRITUAL PARADIGM SHIFTS *and the* EVOLUTION *of the* GOD-IDEAL

In the early part of the twentieth century, the idea of paradigm shifts in religion was not a widely known subject. The term "paradigm shift" was first popularized in the early 1960s by Thomas Kuhn in relation to revolutions in scientific thought, but soon it was also being applied to religion, since religious conceptions also undergo changes in understanding over time. Today, more and more authors and teachers are drawing on this idea as a key to understanding how religious ideas change over the centuries and how scriptures and doctrines require periodic updating and reinterpretation to maintain their spiritual vitality and relevance.

Reb Zalman was first introduced to this exciting idea as a young man in Marseille, France, when a mysterious visiting rabbi came to his yeshiva and gave a fascinating talk on the different ages of *Yiddishkeit* (Judaism*)*, based on the mystical interpretation of certain passages in the *Gemara* (Talmud). The rabbi seemed to know Arabic as well as Hebrew, and initially Zalman thought of him as "the Morrocan," until he finally learned his identity some weeks later. The enigmatic "Morrocan" turned out to be the venerable future leader of the Habad-Lubavitcher Hasidim, Rabbi Menachem Mendel Schneerson, who would become Reb Zalman's rebbe a decade later in America. When Reb Zalman came to America in 1941 and joined the Habad community in Brooklyn, the sixth Lubavitcher Rebbe, Rabbi Yosef Yitzak Schneersohn (1888-1950), who was Menachem's father-in-law, was teaching this way as well.

In brief, what the future Lubavitcher Rebbe taught was that from the time of Adam until the time of Abraham, the world was in spiritual darkness; then the revelation of God's oneness to Abraham brought light into the world. From his illumination, this light began to spread to the rest of the world. The rabbis of the Talmud spoke of a "week" of 7,000 years; the first 2,000 years were *Tohu* (chaos), followed by 2,000 years of *Torah* (divine revelation) from the time of Abraham, through Moses, David and Isaiah, up to the time when the canon of the Hebrew Bible was closed. Then came the following 2,000 years of the Messianic Era (or preparing for the Messiah—coinciding with the Christian Era), which brings us approximately to our time, an era which is expected to be 1,000 years of the Great Sabbath. (The kabbalists broke this down further into 1,000-year time periods, correlated with the sephirot, so that we are now entering into the final sabbath millennium of Malkhut.)[133]

In speaking of the various ages, Reb Zalman utilized the special Kabbalistic terminology which employs the term *deism* to indicate the early anthropomorphic concept of God, the deity who is separate from His creation, who walks in the garden, appears to people in human form, sits on a throne, likes sacrificed lambs, and gets angry and destroys cities. In deism, God is *"totaliter alitere"*—totally other than His creation—but He breaks through from time to time, making an impact on the world and then disappearing. Reb Zalman notes that when the convert, Onkelos (35-120 CE) translated the Bible into the common vernacular in the Aramaic targums, he was embarrassed over some of the more primitive anthropomorphic descriptions of God, so wherever he found a passage that said God "came down" he changed it to indicate that God "manifested." He "appeared"—as if to say, God had always been present and invisible but chose to make His presence known at that time. This also appealed more to the Greeks, many of whom had moved beyond the literal belief in Zeus and the "deistic" pantheon to a more philosophically sophisticated God who is pure spirit. The move toward a greater spiritual sophistication was also characteristic of Hellenized Jews in Alexandria, such as Philo with his *logos* doctrine.

The shift to a more spiritualized conception of God came into existence between the Axial Age (800-200 BCE) and the destruction of the second Temple in Jerusalem (70 CE), an era gradually coming to a close in modern times. Reb Zalman refers to it as the age of *theism*, with God seen as *Anima Mundi*, the world soul. In this age, words are offered up to God instead of animal sacrifices, and God is viewed as no longer moving around in space, but as existing everywhere.[134] The Theistic Era is epitomized by the saying in the Talmud:

> Just as the soul fills the body, so God fills the world. Just as the soul bears the body, so God endures the world. Just as the soul sees but is not seen, so God sees but is not seen. Just as the soul feeds the body, so God gives food to the world.[135]

The theology toward which we are now moving in the Postmodern Era is *pantheism* (or alternatively *panentheism*)— experiencing God in all things. As the Apostle Paul said: "In Him (God) we live and move and have our being."[136] Reb Zalman notes that many modern theologians add an extra "en" and use the word *panentheism* in order to be clear that it means "God is *in* all" and to avoid old associations of the word *pantheism* which equated God with only the material world. Yet Reb Zalman said he still preferred the word pantheism and felt that the distinction was not real, for if *pan-theism* means "God is everything," then that pretty much covers it. We are nothing but God taking countless forms.[137]

On the other hand, many spiritual teachers, from the early twentieth-century Zen Master Soyen Shaku to contemporary progressive theologians in all three of the Abrahamic faiths, have adopted the term *panentheism*, seeing it as the most holistic English word available for describing how the highest being, or God, "is all and one and more than the totality of existence."[138] Coined in 1828 by Karl Christian Friedrich Krause, a German idealist, using the German word *Allingottlehre*, the word *panentheism* is composed of the Greek terms "pan," meaning all, "en," meaning in, and "theism," referring to God. As a signifier of the divine oneness, the word has the advantage of "mapping" God as the inside of everything, the innermost core of things, while also acknowledging the aspect of the Divine which is transcendent of the physical world and greater than the sum of everything in the created realms.

It is worth emphasizing that, while paradigm transitions may be occurring more rapidly now than in the distant past, they have never occurred quickly but have taken centuries to change. They begin in response to changing conditions and are catalyzed by innovative spiritual visionaries and holy prophetic souls who point the way in initiating change, while the majority, led by those who are more focused on maintaining the tradition in the same form in which it has existed for generations, cling to the status quo. Each shift, as it begins, appears as heresy to the holders of the previous paradigm and is resisted with great tenacity. Only in modern times have conditions come about in most parts of the world which generally allow people freedom to voice innovative alternative ideas without fear of reprisal, or even imprisonment, torture and death. This is all part of the most recent paradigm change that has been happening over the last century or two, whose earliest stirrings can be traced back to the Renaissance.

Between the years 1346 and 1353, the Black Death ravaged Western Europe, causing the death of roughly half of Europe's population. This terrible collective trauma served as an early catalyst for the modern paradigm change from firm reliance on God's providence to humanity's secular quest for scientific knowledge in the realm of medicine and physics. Like the traumatic effect of the Holocaust on modern Jewish faith, the idea that God had allowed over a 100 million people—mostly believing Christians—to die from the plague for no discernible reason caused a great shattering of confidence in the Church, leading to a new scientific quest to gain mastery over nature and disease, with or without God.

In the Middle Ages, the Christian kabbalist and mystic theologian Joachim de Fiore (1135-1202) took the idea of the Trinity and divided time into three periods: the Age of the Father (the Old Testament period), the Age of the Son (from the time of Christ to 2,000 years later), and the final Age of the Holy Spirit (dawning about now). This final age is expected to be characterized by the indwelling divine presence, with more and more people being spirit-filled and in touch with divine guidance within, instead of relying on outer spiritual authority. Since the spirit is associated with the feminine (the Hebrew word for the Holy Spirit, *Ru'ah ha-Kodesh*, is a feminine phrase), this ties in with the astrological symbolism of Aquarius, the water-bearer,* and points to the reintegration and greatly needed balance of feminine values in the dawning era.

Others in modern times who have worked with similar ideas of progressive ages outside the Kabbalistic framework, were Reb Zalman's friend, Gerald Heard (author of *The Five Ages of Man*), Joseph Campbell (with whom Zalman's wife, Eve Ilsen, studied), John G. Bennett (Gurdjieff student and author of *The Dramatic Universe*) and most recently, Ken Wilber, who championed the related social evolutionary system of "Spiral Dynamics," developed from the ideas of Clare Graves and Jean Gebser.

TEILHARD DE CHARDIN

Another modern thinker to whom Reb Zalman often referred in this context was the distinguished Christian theologian and paleontologist, Pierre Teilhard de Chardin. Teilhard didn't speak of 2,000-year epochs, but looked at the longer range of organic life on the planet as it has evolved until now and as it continues to develop, viewing it all as progressing toward its Divine Source, just as a flower grows toward the sun. He saw life on the planet as having slowly been built up until a covering of life encompassed the planet. This he called the *biogenesis* of the planet—the elements, amoeba, minerals, plants, and animals, going up the scale in evolution to hominids. More and more, life built up on the planet, but in the earlier stages, there was not yet the development of active conscious intelligence.

Then came the next phase, the *noogenesis* of the planet—from the Greek root word *nous*, meaning mind or intelligence. By noogenesis, Teilhard indicated a buildup of gradually evolving consciousness and mental faculties, an unfurling of

---

* Water is symbolic of the feminine, the emotions, and the subconscious, although the astrological figure of the water-bearer is sometimes depicted as male.

divinely-seeded intelligence and awareness in the planet and on the planet's *biosphere*, or sphere of life, reaching its current apex of mental awareness in homo sapiens. In this way, early humans reached a level in which there occurred an awakening to the possibility of self-reflective observation of their own existence, a gift which is characteristically beyond the natural capacity of the lower animal kingdom.

This noogenesis acts to transform and, as Tielhard says, "hominize" the planet as it unfolds towards its future destiny, a process that could be likened to a feedback system whose ever-evolving innate intelligence allows it to adjust and correct imperfections in its own programming, according to a divine initiative. Through *hominization*, early hominids gradually became human and continue, as us, to become more and more truly human, a process by which humanity is destined to at last realize its inherent possibilities. As Reb Zalman put it, the divine broadcast has been going out in the universe for a long, long time, but it was not until humans began to evolve sufficiently that the antennae of our dawning consciousness began to be able to pick up the divine frequency and hear its message, at first dimly, but now with ever increasing clarity.

Today, with the dawn of scientific research into inter-species communication (for instance, with dolphins and plants) and as we begin to hear more urgently the voice of Mother Earth, Gaia, and move to live cooperatively in more harmonious response to her needs—that is all part of the noogenesis. As regards our own evolution of consciousness, we could summarize it as follows: It isn't enough to just be alive. We need to be conscious that we are alive so that we may reach towards the full potential of our awareness, and thus open the door to the next step, which is the realization of our own divine spiritual essence. Teilhard de Chardin called this stage, the divinization of the planet (or alternatively the "Christogenesis" of the planet).

There are scriptural parallels in the New Testament which provide clear theological support for Tielhard's articulated vision of divinization as the ultimate goal or "omega point" of the soul's earthly incarnation, such as Romans 8:22: "The whole creation groans and travails, waiting for the manifestation of the sons (and daughters) of God." This same teleological principle of divinization, or *theosis*, is a time-honored doctrine of the Eastern Orthodox Church, dating from at least the time of Gregory Palamos (1296-1369).

Creation, in this more dynamic evolutionary view, is not a static, one-time event in the past, but an ongoing genesis or creative process of becoming which is open-ended. As Reb Zalman pointed out, the opening word of the Book of Genesis, *Bereshit*, tends to confirm this view when it says, "*Bereshit bara Elohim et ha-shamayim ve'et ha-aretz.*" It doesn't say, as usually translated, "In *the* beginning, God created the heavens and the earth." If that is what it said, the Hebrew would have necessarily said *ba-reshit* rather than *be-reshit*. As written in Hebrew, the text translates as "*A* beginning," as if to say: "Once upon a beginning." Furthermore, when God creates Adam in Genesis 2:7, the Hebrew uses the imperfect (meaning continuous) form: "*Va'itzer Y-H-V-H Elohim et ha-Adam haphar mim ha-adamah*"—God "proceeded to create," to mold and shape man (or the earthling) from the dust (or rarification) of the ground (*adamah*).[139] This shows that the process of creating is ongoing and not over yet—it's a work in progress.

Teilhard de Chardin himself saw very clearly that humanity and all evolutionary phenomena are not static but are process, and "can never be evaluated or adequately described solely or mainly in terms of their origins: they must be defined by their direction, their inherent possibilities."[140] Therefore, he suggested, we should no longer speak of a cosmology (i.e., a static and preordained destiny, all set up in the past) but a "cosmogenesis," heading from the elementary beginning state of Alpha and moving towards a fully developed point Omega.

Tielhard de Chardin pointed out that only in this century has the germination of neo-humanity, 6,000 years after its Mediterranean unfolding, finished absorbing the last vestiges of the neolithic mosaic, thus starting the budding of the densest, most interconnected layer of the noosphere, which signals a new level of human consciousness, characterized primarily by a modern "Western-oriented" technological orientation. Certainly innovations such as the internet and cell phones point toward an acceleration in collective communication, but perhaps this global advance in interconnectivity is most iconically epitomized by the shift in mental perspective that occurred the moment we saw our round, finite and very beautiful planet Earth from the vantage point of outer space.

As psychologically powerful as the photographs were, even more so the awesome effect upon some of the astronauts who saw it directly from space. Dr. Edgar Mitchell says that he discovered his cosmic or "space identity" during his Apollo moon flights, and astronaut Rusty Schweikert attests that his extended viewing of the Earth from outside the shuttle in deep space completely transformed his outlook on life. Though Schweikert had no previous bent towards things mystical, when he contemplated the Earth from afar ("a shining gem against a totally black backdrop"), it triggered off powerful cosmic emotions in him. The planet appeared so fragile, yet supportive, loving and maternal, with no boundary lines dividing country against country; just a blue, green and brown wholeness, with clouds, uniting all the tiny beings who make their home on the planet's surface into one family—all the while silently radiating the divine splendor.

HOW *the* DIVINE IDEAL *has* CHANGED OVER TIME

For easier reference, Reb Zalman matched the various epochs with their corresponding astrological ages. In keeping with the precession of the equinox, each age is about 2,000 years, possibly 2,200 or 2,500 years, depending on the way the ages are calculated. As there is no recorded history prior to the invention of writing at Sumer in 3200 BCE, only four eons are considered here: Taurus (4000 BCE to 2000 BCE), Aries (2000 BCE to 1 CE), Pisces (1 CE to 2000 CE), and Aquarius (2000 CE to 4000 CE).

If we were to include the earlier age of Gemini, the twins (6000 BCE to 4000 BCE), during the late Neolithic period, we might be considering male and female deities who represent early versions of Shiva and Parvati, or Dionysus and Artemis, judging from the iconography at ancient sites such as Çatal Höyük in Anatolia and pre-Brahmin Mohenjo Daro in the Indus Valley.

Going back to the evidence left in prehistoric caves, the earliest deities appear to be primarily zoomorphic animal gods, associated with the old shamanic hunter-gatherer cultures, as well as the Great Mother Goddess (as evidenced by early stone statuary such as the Willendorf "Venus," which dates to around 25000 BCE.) One of the earliest animal deities who is still actively worshiped in contemporary Hinduism is Hanuman, the monkey god—emblematic of divine service—who helped Rama rescue his queen, Sita, as related in the *Ramayana*. While the prehistoric deities appear to have been animals and totemic animal spirits, over time, these deities gradually become more human, giving us such deities as Sekmet, the lion-headed goddess of Egypt, and Ganesha, the elephant-headed god of India.

the AGE *of* TAURUS, *the* BULL

Taurus was an age of polytheism and its most popular animal deity was the great bull, which in ancient times was much larger than today's bulls. In Egypt, there was Apis, the sacred bull, and Hathor, the cow goddess, and in India, Nandi, the bull mount of Shiva. In Canaan, in the subsequent Age of Aires, the high god, El, was represented in bull form, and his son, Ba'al, was represented as a calf. This (or the Egyptian Apis) is likely what the Israelites at Mount Sinai had in mind when they fashioned the idol of the golden calf. The golden idol was a throwback to the tangible form of a deistic animal god, championed by traditionalists among the Israelites who were resisting the newer theistic understanding of the transcendent God being revealed to Moses.

The bull as symbol of the Divine dates back to the earliest cave art, as seen in the great Hall of Bulls in the caves at Lascaux (ca.17000 BCE) in the Dordogne region of Southern France (which I was fortunate enough to visit as a child in 1957, before the cave was permanently closed to the public). The huge horns of bulls also adorned the sanctuary of the Goddess at Çatal Höyük in Anatolia (ca.7000 BCE), signifying the divine power. The horns are also seen in the Sumerian icons of the goddess wearing a horned tiara, as well as the Cretan "horns of consecration" during the Copper and Bronze Ages. Implicit in the symbolic connection between the bull horns and the Goddess is the ancient understanding that all life, even the phallic bull-god, comes from the cornucopia of the Great Mother, whose very body is the earth itself.

By the age of Taurus, the ascendency of the Great Mother Goddess was already wanning, as copper, then bronze armaments provided weaponry for the first armies and conquering kings, inaugurating a long period of patriarchal dominance. The oldest cuneiform tablets from Sumer already present the great goddess Inanna (called Ishtar in the subsequent Babylonian religion) from the perspective of the newly emerging patriarchal religion. In the earliest written accounts, she is the ruling queen who descends through the seven levels into the netherworld, dies, is mourned, then triumphantly resurrects, along with the rising crops, at the spring equinox, at which time she is hailed as the Queen of Heaven, an early prototype of the risen Christ at Easter. Her consort, King Dumuzi, is forced to take her place in the underworld for half the year, probably reflecting the custom of king sacrifice that was still prevalent during that era.

As Joseph Campbell pointed out, in the earliest statuary there is just the Great Mother Goddess, who alone creates the world; later the Great Mother holds a small dependent male child in her lap. Gradually her son becomes her adult consort, and finally she is replaced by the solitary male deity. The myths in the time of Taurus portray Marduk slaying the great mother sea monster, Tiamat, and Zeus defeating the titans—the offsprings of Gaia—bringing patriarchal order out of the chaos that preceded it. Even in the Psalms,[141] there is a mention of Y-H-V-H crushing the head of the sea-monster, Leviathan (whom Midrash sometimes identifies as female), and winning the victory for dry land over the primordial waters, as Reb Zalman once characterized it.

In several books of the Bible (Kings, Chronicles, Jeremiah, etc.), we are told, disapprovingly, of the continuing Israelite worship of the goddess Asherah (also known as Astarte in Canaan, and Ishtar in Mesopotamia) in the Age of Aires. Asherah was the Canaanite mother goddess and consort of El.* Her worship included lamentations for the dying and rising vegetation god Tammuz (another name for Dumuzi). The Bible also describes the sacramental eating of cakes baked in the image of the goddess and mentions her groves and tree-poles, which existed along with the altars to Ba'al on the high places. King Manasseh of Judah even installed an Asherah pole in the Temple in Jerusalem, which King Josiah removed and destroyed during his subsequent reforms.

The high mountain altars were mostly associated with the appearance of male deities. As Reb Zalman observed: "When you serve God on top of the mountain, then you are serving a male God. When you enter into the cave, into the grotto," that is the domain of the feminine, the Goddess. Thus, the priestesses of the Oracle were located in caves. Before the repression of the feminine, there were hierodules in the temple precincts, priestesses who would sexually initiate the men in a sacred context and also priests who would do the same for the women. They were transmitting the tradition of sacred union, enacted through physical love-making.[142]

Reb Zalman describes the moral and technological level of the Age of Taurus:

> The gods we knew then were totally different from what we humans were. Most of them were animal shaped to point to the essential difference between us. Such gods as we worshipped were not available to us for communication. The clergy and the gods were both male and

---

*   Asherah was also idealized as the consort of Y-H-V-H, according to several early archeological inscriptions (at Khirbet el Qom and Kuntillet Ajrud, dating from the eighth century BCE).

female. Often the hierosgamos was part of the Temple cult and celebrated by the hierodules at special calendar occasions. . . . The techology was one of clay, stone, and wood. Implements were stone axes. The hunt brought captured animals down. Life lived on other life. The steady state was war. The gods themselves warred with one another. Peace was the exception and often only a synonym for abject surrender to the stronger overlord. Cruel vengeance was the order of the day. It was both eyes for an eye. The fates acted with caprice . . . [and] human life was cheap. . . . Truth was a special privilege granted to the king by the gracious overlord god. That state of mind lasted for a long time.[143]

Perhaps as early as 2000 to 1800 BCE, on the cusp of Aires, the Israelite God of the Patriarchs first enters history in the Sumerian city of Ur, where Abraham was born. The Torah refers to Him by various names: Elohim (He-the-gods), El, "the God of Abraham," 'The God of Israel," and Y-H-V-H. In the earliest accounts in Genesis He is depicted in highly anthropomorphic imagery, but in subsequent scripture He becomes more clearly transcendent. What the biblical history records is a transition from pre-patriarchal polytheistic worship to a kind of tribal monotheism or monolatry (worshiping one God among many). This is evidenced in scriptures such as: "Thou shalt have no other gods before Me,"[144] and "Among the gods there is none like Thee."[145] The emerging God-ideal of the time is nationalistic and anthropomorphically male, with deistic relics and a portable tabernacle to house Him. By the time of Isaiah, the monotheistic understanding is becoming more and more clear—that there exists only one God, who is universal and neither male nor female, and Israel is the chosen emissary of that light to the nations ("My house shall be a house of prayer for all people."[146]). Yet the change is gradual and, centuries before Isaiah, it is possible to find among the words of Moses, declarations of pure monotheism, such as Deuteronomy 4:39: "Know therefore today, and lay it to your heart, that the Lord is God in heaven above and on the earth below; there is no other."

By Isaiah's time (ca.800-700 BCE), the God-concept in Judea is beginning to be gradually liberated from its ties to earlier settings of worship, such as the portable sanctuary in the desert and the Temple of Solomon in Jerusalem. God is presented as encompassing the heavens and earth and saying: "What kind of house could you build to contain Me?"[147] and in Isaiah 44:6: "I am the first and the last, beside Me there is no god." In time, this one universal God Who is worshiped by Jews will also be understood by Christians and Muslims to be the one and only Divine Being that exists. The Divine Source is a genus of one, conceptualized in Islam as existing uniquely without partners, and recognized in Orthodox Christianity as the three "persons" of the Trinity, Who are ultimately "one in essence."

By the Age of Pisces in the Common Era, passages begin to appear in rabbinic Midrash which move beyond the nationalistic, exclusivist concept of a God Who is only concerned with Israel. In Megilla 10, it is recounted that on the occasion when Pharaoh's men were perishing beneath the waves of the Red Sea[148] (which God had parted just long enough to allow Moses and the children of Israel to cross), the Israelites celebrated with hymns of thanks for their deliverance. The angels in heaven also wanted to join in singing songs of jubilation before God; but God stopped the angels saying, "Shhh! My other creations lie drowned in the sea and you would celebrate?"

Such is the progression of the God-ideal in Judaism from Taurus to Aries to Pisces. In the Age of Taurus, human sacrifices were offered to the gods under the impression that God literally wants the heart. In Crete, humans were sacrificed to the half-bull minotaur, Phoenician infants were sacrificed to propitiate the gods, Bronze Age kings were ritually killed for the sake of the land, and castrated priests of Attis were crucified in Phrygia.* It is on the cusp between the Age of Taurus and the Age of Aires that Abraham makes the transition to animal sacrifice, when he is given the divine command to bind and sacrifice his first born; then there is a last minute reprieve when a ram is caught in a

---

* This is probably what Deutoronomy 21:23 has in mind in cursing all those who are hung on a tree.

nearby thicket and Abraham is ordered to sacrifice the animal instead of his son.

Reb Zalman identifies the marker for the transition in Israel from Taurus to Aires as the occasion when the amazing being, Melchizedek,[*] high priest of *El Elyon* (God Most High)—the one who represents the culmination of the spiritual wisdom of the age of Pre–patriarchal Judaism—blesses Abraham with bread and wine, receives his tithe, and bequeaths to him the inheritance of the previous epoch's sacred tradition.[149] It was Abraham who broke the idols of his people and the idols within himself, and realized that, beyond all the forms and changing celestial bodies, there is just One Eternal Source behind the entire creation from which we all come and to which we return.[150]

the AGE *of* ARIES, *the* RAM

As the Age of Taurus passes, ushering in the Age of Aries, the gods more and more take on human form in a polytheistic milieu (such as the deities comprising the Greek and Canaanite pantheons). Gradually, during the period from 2000 BCE to the beginning of the Common Era, two other important developments occur. The first is the deistic beginnings of monotheism (seeded in the time of Abraham, embraced on a larger scale in the time of Akenaton and Moses, but still showing traces of a kind of nationalistic monolatry). The second development is the great collective spiritual advance that came about during the Axial Age.[**] By the end of this transitional period, the shift in Judaism to a belief that there is only one Divine Source has become strongly established. The Age of Aires corresponds to Joachim de Fiore's Age of "God the Father."

Julian Jaynes also felt that a shift or breakdown in the bicameral mind occurred sometime during the second century BCE. This produced a shift from a oral style of spirituality, in which

---

[*]   *Malki Tzedek*, "the king of righteousness" and King of Shalem (Jerusalem).
[**]   The approximate dates of the Axial Age, according to Karl Jaspers (who coined the phrase), are 800-200 BCE.

deities "out there" spoke through human oracles in visions and auditory commands (such as we see in Moses, Hammurabi, the Oracles at Delphi, and Homer in the Iliad), to a more reflective and introspective spirituality associated with the written word and the left brain.

In the Age of Aires, the early Iron Age gods on Mount Olympus, in Vedic India, Egypt and Mesopotamia are still polytheistic. There are pantheons of gods and goddesses who look like humans and require animal sacrifices. In Judaism, the ram's horn sets the tone of the era, in a nomadic, shepherd-based society. The scriptures are concerned with how to build a portable sanctuary to house the deity and there arises a priesthood of Levites, similar to the elite Brahmin priests of India. God is seen as one, but is anthropomorphically male, nationalistic, and totally other than His creation. He comes down from time to time on mountain tops and high places, delivers a message and blesses the places, which thereafter become sacred sites. He also visits the patriarchs in human form, epiphanies which are later explained as angelic appearances. He destroys cities which incur His wrath and at one point even threatens to kill Moses over the issue of circumcision.[151] In Greece, Zeus and Hermes make similar appearances among humans and also perform miraculous feats. Athena aids Perseus in defeating the dark female aspect of Medusa in Greece, Isis helps resurrect Osiris in Egypt, and so on. Babylon (*Bab-Ilu*) is named for the gate of the gods and the house of God in Israel is Beth-El. Each marked a sacred location where the deistic God had made an appearance.

Until well into the Axial Age, the conception of the afterlife is mostly limited to Sheol and Hades, a bleak cold-storage land of the shades.* The Iron Age is a time characterized by much war and conquest. The individual has few rights and is considered expendable, as conquering kings with massive armies invade and massacre whole populations, demanding to be worshiped

---

*   See King Saul's encounter with the departed spirit of Samuel, who is summoned up from underworld with the aid of the Seer of Endor in Samuel 28:7-22, and Odysseus' underworld visit with the spirit of Tiresias in Homer's *Odyssey*.

as deities. With the rise of patriarchal dominance, the older goddess worship begins to wane.

Around 600-500 BCE comes a quantum leap in the field of global human consciousness and spiritual attainment which Reb Zalman calls "a blip on the radar of the global brain." Buddha, Socrates, Plato, Aristotle, Ezekiel, Jeremiah, Pythagoras, Mahavira, Lao Tsu, Confucius, and perhaps Zarathustra, are all approximate contemporaries living on the planet at this time. A main thrust of their teaching is to proclaim the rights of the individual and the sacredness of each person, and to inaugurate the spirit of democracy in order to offset the tyrannical tendencies of the political and spiritual authorities of their day.

Buddha breaks away from the ritualistic Brahmin religion with its emphasis on priestly sacrifices and caste privilege, and instead places the emphasis on compassion, the cessation of suffering and liberation from the wheel of karma. The *Bhagavad Gita* moves toward more emphasis on conscious divine service and love, while the Upanishads begin to emphasize spiritual interiority and the discovery of one's inherent divinity. Jeremiah speaks of the Torah written on the heart, and Hosea proclaims on behalf of God, "For I desired mercy, and not sacrifice, and the knowledge of God more than burnt offerings."[152] In Babylon and Israel, there develops an expectation of a messiah, or *saoshyant* who will save the people and usher in a better world. The religions of the time begin to acknowledge the existence of hierarchies of angels, and incorporate into their teachings a nascent belief in a resurrection of souls and a heavenly afterlife.

As the cusp of Pisces draws nearer, there is also a new syncretic spirit in the air, as Alexander of Macedonia attempts to conquer and unite the known world, while knowledge is stored at the Library of Alexandria and other centers of learning. Buddhist and Pythagorean teachings are brought into contact with Egyptian Hermetic teachings, Greek mystery schools and Persian dualism. Dying and resurrecting gods and goddesses abound in the Near East, and the Greeks and Egyptians combine Osiris and Apis to create a new syncretic cult of Serapis.

Many cosmopolitan Jews begin to adopt Hellenistic ways and apply their philosophical approaches to allegorical interpretations of the Bible, while other Jews go into the desert at Qumran to avoid the degeneration they see transpiring around the second Temple in Jerusalem. Everywhere a breakdown and mixing of the old forms is occurring, ushering in a wave of Gnosticism, as gnostics seek primary experience of the Divine over ritual forms and sacrifices.

Comparing this transitional period at the dawn of the Common Era with the current breakdown of religious and social values and the New Age response, Reb Zalman proclaimed, "It's happened before!" We are currently in a chaotic transitional period very much akin to what happened at that time—a second Axial Age.

When the Second Temple in Jerusalem was finally destroyed by the Roman army in 70 CE, it marked for Israel the end of an era where observance was centered around sacred place and animal sacrifices. The subsequent buildup of Rabbinic Judaism that followed in the diaspora inaugurated a transition to worshiping the Divine in sacred time. Sabbath observance and sacred holy days, such as Passover and Yom Kipper, began to be observed in people's homes and local synagogues on specials red-letter days, effectively replacing the old Temple worship with a "temple in time." Reb Zalman adds that he is convinced that whatever divine energy was at one time present in the second Temple was no longer there by the time the physical Temple was destroyed. It had become a kind of empty shell and something new was needed. "It wasn't that sacrifices didn't work anymore because the Temple got destroyed. It was the other way around. The Temple was destroyed because it no longer was a locus where sacrifice could achieve what it has to achieve."[153] For Christians, there were holidays of Christmas, All Saints Day, Lent, and Easter, in addition to the equinox and solstice festivals as markers of sacred time. As Abraham Joshua Heschel used to say, "We Jews live more in time than we do in space. . . . The Sabbath is a palace in time."[154]

the AGE *of* PICES, *the* FISH

The Age of Pisces marks the transition from deism to theism, from the anthropomorphic God who is separate from the world to the *Logos*, the *Anima Mundi*, the Soul which fills the universe. In the Piscean Age, worship is characterized by a technology of words and incantations of powerful sacred phrases. Coming on the cusp between Aries and Pisces, Jesus is symbolized as the Lamb of God and *ichthus*, the Fish, the one who shepherds his flock and teaches his disciples to be "fishers of men." In the wake of Philo's ideas, the Christ is identified in the fourth Gospel as the eternal Word or *Logos* of God. The era corresponds to de Fiore's Age of the Son. For Jews, it is the age of the reliance on the words of the Torah and for Muslims, the Qur'an.

Reb Zalman points out that when the society shifts from a pastoral society of shepherds to a more urban society, composed primarily of city-dwellers without livestock, the effect of giving up your prized, unblemished sheep as a sacrifice in atonement for your sins is lost. There is no longer the same powerful impact and sense of contrition when you simply call up the local butcher and order some lamb meat as a sacrifice, because you didn't raise and care for the lamb yourself. And so, the era is gone and animal sacrifice, for the most part, begins to be replaced with offerings of words.

Hosea says: "Take with you words and return to the Lord. Say to Him: 'Forgive our iniquity and accept from us what is good; so we render as bullocks the offering of our lips.'"[155] The words that are offered are not "mere lip service" but are words of power, binding promises and oaths which carry real weight: "I give you my solemn word!" When the Christian priest elevates the chalice, the consecrated words of the Eucharist take on extraordinary power. Similarly, in the East, mantras, such as *Om* and *Hu* are used to attune the whole being in resonance with sacred vibrations.

In the Age of Pisces, polytheistic religion and goddess worship are slowly replaced by the worship of one universal God, until finally, in 529 CE, the Emperor Justinian closes down the "pagan" mystery schools. Christians, in a slightly different context, substitute the veneration of the Virgin Mary ("Theotokos") in place of Demeter, Isis, Artemis and the other popular goddesses of the old world. Where there was previously king and prophet, there are now senates and sanhedrins.

What takes hold is a primary myth of a binary world of good and evil, sons of light and sons of darkness, us and them, God and devil, saved and damned, and nothing in between. Truth becomes one and absolute, with no tolerance for deviating shades of gray. As Christianity gains ascendency, a believer who is one degree off from the pure truth sanctioned by orthodox dogma is now considered a schismatic heretic and is liable to ex-communication or possibly burning at the stake if intransigent. Many thousands of "heretical Christians" are killed by their co-religionists in wars over doctrinal purity and political control. Everywhere are potential anti-Christs, subtly perverting the truth with pernicious false doctrines. The war of words becomes so pronounced that in 1054, the Eastern Orthodox and Western Roman Churches split over a single word, *filioque*, in a dispute over the inclusion of the word for "and the Son" in the Nicene Creed. Later, after the Protestants split off from the Catholic Church, they too divide into further factions and engage in savage in-fighting over minute differences in belief. Only in very recent centuries are we beginning to emerge from the spell of this kind of binary dualism and triumphalism which demonizes everyone outside of one's own brand of faith.

Ken Wilber points out how both individuals and religions pass through various stages of maturity, from egocentric to ethnocentric to universalistic, as mapped by psychologist Carol Gilligan and others. As an infant, one begins at the egocentric level of self-centered concern and, as one grows up, gradually extends one's love and concern to one's family, tribe and like-minded group, evincing an ethnocentric love. For those who mature beyond this vantage point, the love and concern begins to extend universally to all sentient beings, evincing worldcentric love. This maturation process applies to religions as well as individuals.

The Crusades of the Middle Ages are emblematic of the Piscean ethnocentric religious mentality, which is triumphalist and nationalistic (or Eurocentric in the case of Christian Crusaders). The underlying assumption is that only one's group has access to Truth and divine guidance, while everyone else is dwelling in darkness and error. While there were a few saints and sages during the Age of Pisces who demonstrated some degree of universal spirituality, by and large, it is not until the transition from Pisces to Aquarius in our own time that we begin to see the dawning of a growing worldwide religious maturation that is indicative of a universalized understanding of spirituality and religion.

In *The Alphabet Versus the Goddess*, Leonard Shlain suggests that pre-literate agrarian cultures had a natural tendency toward right-brain, holistic modes, feminine values, and worship of the Goddess. But with the rise of alphabetic literacy and the strong emphasis on written scripture and the letter of the law, the brain began to undergo a subtle reconfiguration. By the Common Era, this move toward an excessive left-brain, analytical approach had thrown the genders seriously out of balance and brought with it a tendency toward dogmatic intolerance and misogyny. Over time, the Goddess and the natural world were devalued, the earthly body was denigrated in favor of spirit, and for many centuries the Great Mother Goddess of antiquity was nearly forgotten in the West. Shlain surveys the long history of religious conflicts worldwide in support of his conclusion that this imbalance, with its emphasis on the written language and abstract thinking, has inevitably led to a heightening of androcentric conflicts, with repeated wars over ideologies and the interpretation of sacred words of scripture. It is not the healthy, balanced male approach which he describes but a world dominated by immature patriarchal power, war and greedy exploitation of the land, with scant value given to egalitarian ideals or the natural world.

However, Shlain finds encouragement in the observation that the pendulum is finally swinging back toward feminine values in modern times. He believes it is linked to the emergence of widespread images (which are nonverbal or nonlanguage-reliant), starting with the invention of photography, then motion pictures, and more recently, personal computers with integrated two-handed typing. All of these factors are naturally stimulating right-brain function and laying the groundwork for a movement away from the binary conceptual world of warring opposites toward more holistic consciousness. Pisces, the age we are now completing, is represented by the perfect symbol for the era of good and evil, black and white, spirit and matter, divine and profane; for it has two separate fishes moving around each other, neither recognizing that they are really one, swimming in an ocean of unity.

Certainly, the Age of Pisces should not be characterized solely in terms of conflicting ideologies and triumphalist intolerance. One thinks of the interreligious tolerance and high level of culture achieved under Muslim rule in Andalusian Spain prior to the Spanish inquisition, the Emperor Akbar in Mughal India, Rumi and Ibn 'Arabi in the Middle East, and the example of St. Francis of Assisi, whom Joachim de Fiore considered the first fruits of the coming Age of the Holy Spirit. While Gutenberg's invention of the printing press may have intensified the war of words, it was immensely helpful in opening the road to the dissemination of knowledge which made available both ancient wisdom and the spread of modern scientific breakthroughs.

By the 1500s, new discoveries in astronomy and physics were beginning to revolutionize and secularize the way we viewed the world, and challenging some of the stagnant medieval notions of God as a monarch on high, reigning over a static earth, encompassed by a starry dome of heaven above and hell below. The American Revolution in the late eighteenth century championed a new spirit of democracy, free speech, and spiritual freedom which was gradually adopted throughout Western Europe and in numerous other countries around the world.

As humanity arrives at the cusp of the next age, it is clear that we have benefited from enormous technological advances over the past two centuries and mass communication has brought our planet closer together. Yet our technology has also heightened tensions and the dangers of planetary self-destruction, because our advances in weaponry and the ability to exploit the planet have outpaced our inner growth, maturity and wisdom. The trend toward secularization, with its exclusive focus on the material world, has inexorably led us, particularly in the West, toward a new paradigm that includes scientific materialism, existentialism and the "God is Dead" movement of the 1960s.*

The effect has been to greatly weaken and undermine our collective confidence in the religious worldviews of the past and all the associated values that our society once found so helpful. While the breakdown of outmoded forms and doctrines undoubtedly has its positive side, the downside is the desacralization and devaluation of the world in which we live. Too many people are looking toward an apocalypse as a way out. As Jung warned, it is a dangerous situation to lose the myths, beliefs and God-ideals that once sustained us and to remain this way for very long without new, more relevant myths and spiritual pathways to inspire us.

the AGE *of* AQUARIUS, *the* WATER-BEARER

We are now on the cusp of the Aquarian Age, the era which Joachim de Fiore predicted would be the Age of the Holy Spirit. Though it is still too early to tell exactly what forms the spirituality of the future will take, there are some initial indications. The symbol of Aquarius is the water bearer, suggesting an association with emotion, feeling and spirit which may lead to a quickening of our inner spiritual life springs beyond the dryness of traditional dogmas and creeds. Possibly a new *Shekhinah/Sophia* theology is indicated, a more embodied feminine approach to spirit which would water the seeds of divine immanence which esoteric spirituality has long pointed to. We might also expect science and spirituality—which are currently

---

*   Reb Zalman calls this the "death of the *name* of God"—the recognition that the old deistic and theistic conceptions are no longer tenable for a great many people in the modern world.

at odds—to discover more common ground along the lines of Fritjof Capra's classic *Tao of Physics* and the work of David Bohm, Rupert Sheldrake and Robert Lanza. The way we worship will surely change as well, for we have reached a place where the litany of words used in worship in the Age of Pisces has lost much of its potency, where increasingly people are seeking direct primary experiences rather than mere verbiage and traditional formulations based on someone else's previous experience.

In the Gospel of John, there is an instructive story which depicts Jesus traveling into Samaria and asking a woman at Jacob's well for water, at a time when Jews would normally avoid sharing things with Samaritans. After some conversation, Jesus tells the woman that he is able to give her "living water" of a kind that, after drinking it, one would never thirst again, water that would produce an inner "spring of water gushing up to eternal life."[156] She shows interest but points out that Samaritan belief differs from Jewish belief: the Jews say one must worship at the Temple in Jerusalem but the Samaritans hold that Mount Gerizim is the one true location where worship should be offered. Jesus responds with the prophetic words: "Woman, believe me, a time is coming when you will worship the Father neither on this mountain nor in Jerusalem.... A time is coming, and has already begun, when the true worshipers will worship the Father in spirit and in truth, for they are the kind of worshipers the Father seeks. God is spirit, and his worshipers must worship in spirit and in truth."[157]

This speaks to what is now emerging in the Aquarian Age, when many people are leaving the traditionally sanctioned sites of worship—churches, temples, and mosques, along with the old forms and ritual language of the past—in search of direct spiritual experience and unfiltered encounters with the Divine in the Age of the Holy Spirit. For the present, as people venture off the well-trodden roads of the spiritual map in search of new paths and tributaries, there is much uncertainty and the new directions are not always clear or assured of success. Yet the ones who persevere, who learn to read the book of themselves, and become still enough to perceive the inner voice of divine guidance, carefully distinguishing it from the voice of ego, are certainly likely to find what they are seeking. For some, the traditional roadmaps still offer the surest path; for others, what may work best is a reformatting of one of the sacred traditions, retaining some practices and principles but with new hyperlinks to other modalities which open up a deeper understanding of one's own path.

At the Wisdom School, Reb Zalman noted that Abraham Joshua Heschel had put his finger on one of the major problems with Torah study today: It is largely supplying answers for questions we are no longer asking. To a certain extent, this could be said of each of the world's ancient religious traditions as they are generally practiced today. Fortunately, these same scriptures contain a core of timeless essential truths which continue to provide humanity with guidance for today and for the future.

In the last paradigm, we were relying on one messiah or king (*mon-arch*) to fix everything for us, but now we are moving toward a spiritual democracy in which the spirit is spread out to many. As Thich Nhat Hanh has suggested, "The next Buddha may be a *Sangha* (community)."[158] A few hundred years ago, most of the monarchies of the world were overthrown because people no longer found them beneficial. After rebelling against the abuses of earthly monarchs in favor of more democratic systems, it became more difficult to relate positively to the archetype of God as king. However, there are many other less anthropomorphic divine qualities that are useful for relating to the Source: as sacred presence, as love, as truth, as wisdom, as beauty, as mercy, as power, as light, as peace, as the Ground of Being, as energy, conscious awareness, the Infinite, and so on.

In his book, *Paradigm Shift,* Reb Zalman says, "Now we are entering an age of alternative, of elasticity, in which God is being liberated from stone engravings and doctrinal codes to become organic again, in turn, freeing human consciousness to do the self-growing it was originally intended to do."[159] He feels we are now switching from a machine model to an organismic model.

What's strongly coming down now is the awareness that we are part of a larger organism. The age of the focus on the ego, on the individual self is over: that has been fulfilled, that's done. We have to start considering transpersonal psychology: who are we when we are more than one? . . . What is coming down now is the issue of ecology and awareness that this earth is not a dead hunk of matter. The Earth is alive. Our destiny is completely tied to life on this planet. We are a mirror for that awareness that is Earth. That is how a planet becomes conscious and knows itself. The planet needs people to bring about that consciousness. . . .[160]

Elsewhere, Zalman stated it this way, hyperbolically emphasizing the immanent side of the pendulum:

The help that we expect to come from the transcendent realm, from the God up there and out there, can't come that way, because the God up there and out there has gradually become one within here, to Whom it is no longer interesting to be God in the heavens, and to be sung to by the angels. But He would like to know what is it like to be a human being on a planet that almost is on a collision course with destiny and to be able to just lift that plane over the obstacles and to fly it rather than to bump into it."[161]

In the mid-twentieth century it looked as though nuclear disaster with atomic weapons was the biggest threat facing humanity. In the 1980s, Reb Zalman used to say that in his meditations he was sensing an *Oy!* of dismay from the future. During the following three decades, that threat seem to diminish in intensity. Currently, in the twenty-first century, the ecological crisis appears to be the greatest collision course that we are facing. Reb Zalman said he believes the chief commandment today, the imperative for all religions is: "Heal our Mother, the Earth." He says, "If I were to be asked what is the most important philosophical . . . and theological issue of the world today, the answer is: to come up with a cosmology that our Mother the Earth wants us to have so she can heal."[162]

Finding ways to address the looming dangers of climate change on which we can collectively agree is made difficult by the well-financed resistance of opposing corporate self-interest and a widespread strain of religious orientation that places little value on human stewardship of the Earth. If the Aquarian religion of the future is to be relevant, it will certainly need to meaningfully address humanity's relation to the environment and the worsening climate crisis. If responsible minds prevail in our planet's leadership, this may occur naturally along with the re-emergence of feminine values and a greater sensitivity to the needs of the planet. Yet we no longer have decades to procrastinate before moving in this direction.

Reb Zalman was once asked about the situation with the patriarchy and its suppression of the feminine, and he answered that just as we walk with two feet in tandem—first one foot steps forward then the other—so in the past we collectively took a step with the masculine-oriented side and we are now ready for the next step that will bring about the balance of the feminine. In a 2008 interview, he observed:

> In Kabbalah they talk about *Shekhinah*, the Divine Presence. So there is the feminine; the Divine Presence is manifesting a lot more now than it did before. Before we were closing it off saying it is evil, it is wrong. It's like the way in which people look at sexuality and so on. Now what's happening is that these two revelations are beginning to meet. Whereas before people would practice all kinds of austerity and they didn't want to have the body involved. Today with martial arts, tai-chi and with all these things we are beginning to honor the wisdom of the body and we are beginning to pay attention to the feminine because it's absolutely necessary for the survival of human beings that we should find a way to heal our planet.[163]

In 2012, Reb Zalman summarized the changes that have taken place over the last century. "No longer have we got the same division between consciousness and matter," as shown by Heisenberg and other Quantum physicists. In the field of psychology, we've moved "from behaviorism, to psychoanalysis, to humanistic psychology, to transpersonal psychology. A new paradigm is here now." Theologically, we also need to "shift the credos of the various churches from original sin to original blessing."[164]

the ASTROLOGICAL AGES *in the* CONTEXT *of the* FOUR WORLDS

Reb Zalman links each zodiacal age to one of the four worlds: Taurus is in the physical world of Assiyah, Aries is in the emotional world of Yetzirah, Pisces is in the mind world of B'riyah, and Aquarius is in the being/transcendent world of Atzilut. Elaborating on Aquarius, he says:

> In the Kabbalah this betokens an inordinate break. It points to possibilities that are altogether divine. It also is so much in harmony with what the other epoch contemplatives like [Joachim] de Fiore and [Tielhard] de Chardin have taught. We are entering the phase of the divinization of the planet. This is a mindmove of such proportions that we could say that it is totally unprecedented. All the learning accumulated in the past and stored in the collective unconscious must be sifted to be cleared of that which helped us well in the past and may in the present turn out to be a planet-killing atavism, i.e., territorial national sovereignty."[165]

Reb Zalman notes that, in the past, there was human sacrifice, then animal sacrifice and later, in the theistic Age of Pisces, words were offered up as sacrifice as well as money. Today, he says, the great sacrifice for us is not money or lives; it is time and energy—offering to give up some of our time and energy to devote to projects and to help others. He lists the shifts we've undergone, saying: In the Age of Aries, when we had powerful kings around, God was flashing transcendence to us more than immanence, and we pictured Him as king of kings and *totaliter alitere*. Later, there was a switch in Pisces, the Age of the Son, and God was pictured as *anima mundi* in Judaism. The Divine was gradually drawing closer in our collective conception. Then came the death of the name of God (boldly proclaimed on the cover of the Easter 1966 edition of *Time* magazine). The old interface wasn't working. Then *kenosis* and divine immanence began to come through. Reb Zalman says: to those who have anxiety about this and want to resist it, the question is: "Do you think that God's providence does not extend to that?"[166]

A questioner in a workshop I attended in Washington, D.C., asked Zalman whether it was wrong in Judaism to borrow from other faiths and cultures. He answered: "If you did that to Judaism in the Age of Pisces it would have killed Judaism. If you do it in the Age of Aquarius it invigorates it."[167] A decade later, when Zalman presented the main lines of paradigm shifting to a group in Jerusalem, several questioners challenged the whole premise of anything like a Hegelian model of progressive evolution toward a final truth after two World Wars and the Holocaust showed us, at some level, how little we're evolving.

Zalman agreed that "we are not there yet, but we are on the way"—not to any final truth where we will stop and say there is nothing further, but always encountering change and further horizons.[168] He said he felt the God-field is poor and empty at this point and we need to rebuild it. "Build it and they will come." When the old field collapses, then it is renewed by a new paradigm. "Feminine Shekhinah theology needs to be brought in currently." He added that every lineage has two parts to it. One is the *magisterium* and the other is the reality map that is laminated to that magisterium. At one point you had the Ptolemaic reality map and on top of that they put *Yiddishkeit*. "In Rambam's [Maimonides'] time, they were building great cathedrals to last forever, and so he figured he would formulate a great mind cathedral to last forever. Today we look at everything as being in motion, so I'm not trying here to build a mind cathedral to last forever." He pointed out that this ties in with the Buddhist view which also points to the impermanence and changeability of things. Reb Nachman of Bratzlov made the same point, saying: "The world is like a dreidel; everything keeps on turning."[169]

the SECOND AXIAL AGE

Reb Zalman's son Yotam Schachter notes that very near the end of his life, his father began to express "a preference for describing the ongoing transformation of Judaism as an Axial Age, rather than a Paradigm Shift."[170] Responding to an article by Dr. Shaul Magid in the Jewish magazine *Tikkun*, which reviewed his life's work and used the term "Paradigm Shift Judaism," Reb Zalman in his last days dictated a brief response in which he emphasized that what was involved was "a process of turning" involving a "long arc of transition from one paradigm to another," rather than "the crossing of an imaginary line."[171] It is not all a smooth, speedy transition—there are many bumps in the road.

Yotam Schachter explains that, in his father's final years, he began to see transformation to an Aquarian Judaism as a more gradual shift than he had in earlier decades. This more gradual conception better reflects the reality that "the Neo-Hasidic monotheistic paradigm coexists with the postmonotheistic paradigm" (the theological shift toward divine immanence) and suggests that we are currently living in an ongoing Axial Age of indeterminate length. Yotam adds that "the difference between an Axial Age and a Paradigm Shift is not only the pace of transformation, but how the transformation itself is understood."[172] Reb Zalman saw Judaism as a living being, a grand Jewish tree growing toward God in its own theotrophy, but within that metaphor he distinguished two ways a tree could grow. One was Judaism's growth from the outer edges of the tree, which involved Jews who incorporated elements of Buddhism and Sufism, as well as new scientific and psychotherapeutic models of reality. The second method of growth was from inside the tree, from the top and center, representing the Jewish core growth and maturation as it grows toward the sun. It is not that the sun is changing but that the tree is expanding and growing towards it.[173]

Another way in which Reb Zalman designated the new paradigm in Hasidic Judaism was in terms of a "Fourth Turning." Just as Buddhism features three turnings, with the Modern Era constituting a fourth phase,* Reb Zalman saw four turnings of Hasidism over the centuries. By the term "Hasidism," Reb Zalman indicates the universal impulse of active receptivity to the Divine, the willingness to live in the authentic Divine Presence. The first Hasidic period occurred during the time of the Essenes (*asidaioi* or *essaioi* in Greek), Dead Sea Scrollers and Theraputae in Greco-Roman Palestine, just prior to the beginning of the Common Era.

The second turning took place in the Middle Ages in two geographic areas, one among the Jewish Ashkenaz in Christian Germany (contemporaneous with the Christian "Rhineland mystics"), associated with Rabbi Yehudah He'Hasid (1150-1217)—the author of the *Sefer Hasidim*—and his family. The other wing of the second turning arose among the Sephardic Hasidim of Muslim Egypt in the family of Moses Maimonides, beginning with his son, Abraham, whose teachings and practices were strongly influenced by Sufism.

The third turning took place in Eastern Europe and Russia in the early eighteenth century, with the joyous modern Hasidic movement initiated by Rabbi Yisael ben Eliezer, the Ba'al Shem Tov, and his successor, Rabbi Dov Baer, the Maggid of Mezritch. The fourth turning of Hasidim is occurring in our time with the second Axial Age and the beginnings of the Jewish Renewal Movement, of which Reb Zalman was an important part.

the BUDDHIST CONNECTION: MEETINGS *with the* DALAI LAMA

Having reviewed many of Reb Zalman's key teachings, we can now tie together a few final threads pertaining to his

---

* The fourth turning of Buddhism is epitomized by the teachings of Chogyam Trungpa Rinpoche.

interspiritual outreach. In 1993, I attended a Torah-Dharma Week at Elat Chayyim, in Accord, New York, for a week of teachings and stories from Reb Zalman and the Jewish Zen master, Roshi Bernie Glassman. The two teachers gave complimentary teachings, compared stories, and sometimes talked shop and opened topics for discussion. One afternoon session was devoted to the question of top-down spiritual authority versus newer nonhierarchical models. Glassman relayed the experience of a modern Zen community on the West Coast where they attempted to operate communally without a designated leader, but with less than optimal results. Both teachers concurred that for learning to take place, some form of teacher-student relationship was needed, but it needn't necessarily be an authoritarian relationship. During a solo session with Reb Zalman, the class rehearsed a recitation of the *Shema Yisrael* in the style of Buddhist chanting, along with the ringing of Buddhist bells which Reb Zalman supplied. When Glassman arrived later, on signal, we launched into our Zen-Jewish (*Bu-Ju*) chanting with bells, to his great delight.

Two years later, Glassman's Zen teacher, Taizan Maezumi Roshi, died, leaving him without a living teacher. Zalman was once again teaching at Elat Chayim, so Glassman drove over to visit him and asked Reb Zalman if he would now become his teacher. Reb Zalman agreed, but with the stipulation that Glassman Roshi would also serve as his Zen teacher. Thereafter, when Glassman would visit Zalman and his wife, Eve, Zalman would greet him at the door with a grin and an invitation to "Hit me with a koan!" Zalman felt that koans would comprise an excellent study for rabbis and encouraged Glassman to develop a Jewish koan curriculum.[174]

Another milestone in Reb Zalman's interspiritual work came in the form of a dialogue with the Dalai Lama in Dharamsala in 1990. Reb Zalman and seven other rabbis representing various denominations of Judaism, were invited by the Dalai Lama to join His Holiness in India to engage in a spiritual discussion in which they would share with the exiled Buddhist leader some of the most successful ways in which Jews had kept their faith alive during their own diaspora of two thousand years. Highlights of the historic meeting were described in a book by Rodger Kamenetz entitled *The Jew in the Lotus.**

Reb Zalman began the presentation by reciting a tradition-al Jewish blessing used when encountering a king and a holy man, which was then translated for the Dalai Lama in an updat-ed form suitable for the occasion. Then each participant in the Jewish delegation gave a presentation, including both tradition-al religious and modern secularist Jewish perspectives. From all accounts, it was Reb Zalman's hour-long presentation of Kabbalah and Jewish esotericism, including an animated discus-sion of angels, mysteries, divine emanations, and levels of being which most captivated the Dalai Lama, who leaned forward on the edge of his seat, drinking in every word and occasionally commenting on points of similarity with Tibetan angelology and the like. Largely as a result of his presentation, the Dalai Lama confessed that he now could see that Judaism was much more "sophisticated" than he had previously thought.

Pir Mu'in ad-Din (Netanel) with Pir Suleyman (Zalman); photo courtesy of Netanel Miles-Yépez.

---

*   The title plays off the Buddhist mantra, *Om mani padme hum*, which translates as "Hail to the jewel in the lotus."

When queried as to the motivation behind his invitation to meet with the Jewish delegation, the Dalai Lama explained, "I think we are both chosen people! We do not have exactly the same idea, but we Tibetans believe we are chosen by Avalokiteshvara [the embodiment of Buddhist compassion and the protector deity of Tibet]. You believe you are chosen by the Creator G-d. So it is almost the same idea."[175] He added that, like the Tibetan refugees, the Jewish people had struggled for years to preserve their faith and identity outside of their homeland. The Jews perservered for centuries until, "when external conditions were ripe, they were ready to rebuild their nation. So you see, there are many things to learn from our Jewish brothers and sisters."[176]

When one member of the Jewish delegation raised the painful issue of so many modern Jews defecting to Buddhism, the Dalai Lama thoughtfully responded: "If you want to keep your people in your religion, then you must open your doors to spirituality. If you have an esoteric tradition to offer them, then they will not want to leave." He went on to say that as a result of this meeting,

> to speak quite frankly, I developed much more respect for Judaism because I found there a high level of sophistication. I think it is very important that you make these teachings available for everyone, especially intellectual people. Sometimes there is a danger in too much secrecy. Often qualified people are excluded from the practice, so I think the best thing is to be flexible. I have seen many similarities between your tradition and ours. If you make these teachings available, why would your people want Buddhist tantra? You have your own tantra! Many of your people have keen intelligence and very creative minds, and if they are not personally satisfied with what you offer them, then nobody could stop them from leaving and taking a new religion. Provide them with all the materials, all spiritual teachings. If you have these spiritual values, then there is no reason to fear; if

you have no such values, then there is no reason to hold on. If you cannot provide spiritual satisfaction to others and at the same time insist on holding on to them, then that is foolishness. This is reality.[177]

Reb Zalman would meet with the Dalai Lama on several further occasions, notably at the April 2004 Roundtable in Vancouver, Canada, which was also attended by Desmond Tutu. There, rather than attempting to affirm interspiritual unity or present "the same old cosmic truths," Reb Zalman offered a list of perplexing questions. These questions dealt with religious triumphalism and the obstacles we experience as we find our desire to grow in awareness "often blocked and opposed by forces that want to cut us off from that creative, life-affirming urge, flooding us with mind-deadening distractions and addictions to things we don't really need."[178] The four open-ended questions he raised were:

1. What cosmology does our Mother, the Earth, want us to have in order that She may be healed?
2. What is the most holistic and healthy ethos arising from that new cosmology?
3. What are the *upaya*, the 'skillful means' needed to lift our cultural trance, and to launch the awareness of the emerging cosmology?
4. What adjustments do we need to make in spiritual technologies, theology, physics, psychology, philosophy, anthropology, biology, medicine, political science, the arts, economics, communications, and most of all, ethics, in order to heal the planet?[179]

In more specific terms, he continued:

We need to ask our traditions—do our spiritual toolchests offer practices that work for urban, '9-to-5' people? If our suggestions for spiritual study and practice exceed

20 minutes in the morning, and 20 minutes in the evening, they are demanding more than most people can
afford, and will not be done. . . . When I think of the tur-
bulent mind-space we are inhabiting most of the time
today, I feel almost schizophrenic. In it, I cannot hear the
sacred, choral symphony of our common dream. Just as
we once lamented the 'twilight of the gods,' it seems that
we are now experiencing a similar 'twilight of the life-affirming archetypes!' How can we access these archetypes? How can we imbue them with power? How can
they empower us? We need to realize, once again, that we
are not on the top of the chain-of-all-being. We need to
learn once more the means of accessing the help await-
ing us on the higher planes. What do we need to do to
address the matrix of the great Life-Process on the subtle plane in order to gain an understanding of the deeper
Life-Process for ourselves? Only when we are able to do
this again will we be able to truly embark on designing
the necessary re-education of the heart and spirit.[180]

RENEWING *the* SUFI CONNECTION

Over the years, Pir Vilayat and Reb Zalman appeared together
on various interreligious panels, along with representatives of
other faith traditions. In 2000, they came together for the last
time, when both accepted invitations to speak at the State of the
World Forum in New York City. The two teachers shared a hotel
room and spent the evening together sharing conversation and
joyful song. Among the songs they sang was Pir Vilayat's favorite
Jewish melody, *Hashivenu*, a song from the Torah service recited upon the closing of the ark, whose words are drawn from
Lamentations 5:21: "Return us to You, O Lord, and we will be
restored; renew our days as of old." Although no record of their
conversation survives it is tempting to think that the founding
of a new Sufi-Hasidic tariqat may have been discussed, as it represented, at last, the fruits of their mutual spiritual initiations
nearly thirty years before.

In California and New York City in 1975, invoking the names of Melchizedek, Abraham, and Hazrat Inayat Khan, they had performed mutual initiations and bestowed on one another the titles of sheikh and *Kohein l'El Eliyon*. It was on the occasion of Reb Zalman's 1975 initiation by Pir Vilayat that he took a new Sufi name. A few years before his passing, Reb Zalman explained the way it happened to journalist Sara Davidson, who was working with Reb Zalman on a book about his final years, entitled *The December Project*. He told her that after he was introduced to Pir Vilayat Khan in the 1970s they had "become spiritual buddies, sharing their prayers and ideas."[181] Reb Zalman said he "felt a kinship with the Sufis—their ecstatic chanting, dancing, and yearning for God were similar to what he'd experienced with the Hasids in Brooklyn." Referring to Pir Vilayat, he said, "every time I found someone who'd transcended triumphalism, he was my friend."[182]

He was initiated by Pir Vilayat in Santa Cruz, California, and was surprised to be invested as a Sufi sheikh. Afterwards, Pir Vilayat told him that it was traditional to change one's name. Pir Vilayat

> thought "Zalman" was fine but "Schachter," or slaughterer, might be changed to something more uplifting. Zalman chose Shalomi, meaning "he of the peace." At that time, Egyptian President Anwar Sadat had just made his historic trip to Israel and the two countries were negotiating. Zalman said that when peace was established throughout the Middle East, he would go to court and legally change his last name to Shalomi. In the meantime, he began using Schachter-Shalomi. In 2012, when we were concluding our talks about *The December Project,* he said, raising his hands with a puckish smile, "I'm still caught in the hyphen."[183]

In 2004, Rebbe and Sheikh Zalman Suleyman* inaugurated the Inayati-Maimuni Order, designating Netanel Miles-Yépez

---

*   At some point, Reb Zalman also took the Sufi name Suleyman, which is the Arabic form of the Hebrew name Zalman.

(whose Sufi title is Pir Netanel Mu'in ad-Din) as his khalif and successor. It took many years before the right person had appeared to carry on this special work. Reb Zalman saw in Netanel the bridge that was needed between the two traditions and sent him to Pir Vilayat's senior students, Atum O'Kane and Puran Bair, for training. In the meantime, Netanel taught in the department of religious studies at Naropa University and functioned as a valuable assistant, publisher, and co-author with Reb Zalman in Boulder, Colorado. In 2004, Reb Zalman officially designated Netanel as his khalif, and turned the order over to him to develop further. Pir Zia, who was by then the acting head of the Sufi Order, was consulted and gave his wholehearted support to the new tariqat, saying: "It is my prayer that the Maimuniyya will bring healing to the tragically divided family of Abraham and guide many sincere seekers on the path that leads to the fulfillment of life's purpose. May the Message of God reach far and wide!"[184]

The official statement of the Inayati-Maimuni Order is as follows:

> The Inayati-Maimuni Order is committed to a path of spiritual development based upon both Sufi and Hasidic principles and practices. In this order, the Sufi lineage of Hazrat Inayat Khan (1882-1927), the first Sufi master to bring Sufism into the West, has been joined to the Hasidic lineage of Rabbi Israel ben Eliezer, the Ba'al Shem Tov (1698-1760), founder of the influential eighteenth-century Hasidic movement. But because it is not the first time that these two mystical paths associated with Islam and Judaism have been brought together, we endeavor to connect to and renew the spirit of the original Egyptian Sufi-Hasidism practiced by Rabbi Avraham Maimuni of Fustat (1186-1237), our forerunner, who successfully combined these paths as far back as the thirteenth century. For this reason, we are called the Inayati-Maimuniyya, honoring both Hazrat Inayat Khan's vision of Sufism as a universal approach

to spirituality and Avraham Maimuni's radical innovation which made a peaceful marriage between Jewish Hasidism and Islamic Sufism in a time of open conflict between the Abrahamic traditions. Founded in 2004 by Pir Zalman Suleyman Schachter-Shalomi and his *khalif,* Pir Netanel Mu'in ad-Din Miles-Yépez, the community is currently led by the latter.[185]

the PASSING *of* REB ZALMAN

In early 2014, I contacted Reb Zalman with a proposal for the material in this book. He liked the idea and asked me to send it to him to read when it was ready. By the end of June, I was ready to send a draft to him, but was advised to wait because Reb Zalman had fallen ill. With preparations for his ninetieth birthday celebration underway, Reb Zalman had decided to travel to Connecticut to hold his annual Shavuot retreat. By the end of the retreat, however, he had developed pneumonia and had to be hospitalized for ten days. As he was severely ill and unconscious, those close to him feared the worst. Nevertheless, he returned to consciousness and asked to be flown home to Boulder, where he died peacefully in his sleep on the morning of July 3, 2014. Sara Davidson, who had recently published a collection of interviews with Reb Zalman, described his funeral in the *Huffington Post*:

> Rabbi Zalman Schachter-Shalomi wanted no casket, no plain pine box. For his funeral, held on the Fourth of July, he wanted to be clothed in his white *kittel* (prayer robe), enfolded in his father's *tallis* (prayer shawl), sprinkled with ashes brought from Auschwitz, then shrouded in white linen and lowered directly into the earth near his home in Boulder, Colorado. He wanted the ashes buried with him in honor of his uncle, cousins, and the millions who'd died without receiving "a holy burial." . . .
>
> The funeral was held at the Green Mountain Cemetery on Independence Day, a fact that people found significant.

Three rabbis conducted the service, reflecting the many strands of faith Reb Zalman had woven together. There was a Chabad rebbe, Yossi Serebryanski, wearing a black wool coat and hat in the heat, a Conservative rabbi, Marc Soloway, and a Jewish Renewal rabbi, Tirzah Firestone.[186]

His khalif (spiritual successor) in the Sufi-Hasidic lineage he had founded, Pir Netanel Mu'in ad-Din Miles-Yépez, was one of the pallbearers. Together with Rabbi Tirzah Firestone, another senior disciple of the Rebbe, he fittingly placed Reb Zalman's body in the grave—living examples of his legacy of renewal and interspirituality.

Reb Zalman's spirit lives on, and in the end, it seems fitting to accept the Rebbe's invitation to join him in offering a blessing on the world, using the words with which he concluded one of his last books:

One of the greatest needs this planet has for healing is blessing. It is underblessed. Underblessed reality is like empty calories. A blessing enhances the possibilities for good. . . .

I want to ask the reader . . . to join with me in blessing the planet, the next generation, all species, all good intentions in people's hearts, all those who face burnout in their service to others, to the scientist and physicians who work on finding cures for cancer and AIDS, for prisoners in our penal systems who want to start a new and better life, for the prisoners of conscience to be freed, for warring nations to find the way to peace and cooperation, for those whose time has come to leave their body to be able to do so serenely and with awareness, and for the children about to be born to become agents of blessing in their turn.[187]

Amen. Amin.

ENDNOTES

[1] *The First Step: A Guide For the New Jewish Spirit*, Bantam Books, Toronto, Canada, 1983; p.1.

[2] Reb Zalman told this story many times. One version is found in an unpublished collection of Reb Zalman's writings entitled "Mareh Kohen," in a 1993 interview with Michael Paley and William Novak.

[3] Schachter-Shalomi, with Lawrence Kushner, *Davening: A Guide to Meaningful Jewish Prayer*, 2012 Kindle version, pp. xiii-xvi, Introduction.

[4] From my notes based on an audio recording of Reb Zalman from the 1980s, which I can no longer locate.

[5] *Tikkun* magazine, Fall 5758. The interview is available at: https://havurahshirhadash.org/practical-wisdom-from-shlomo-carlebach/

[6] The interview is available at: www.pardeslevavot.org./articles/haaretz-2005-10-02.html

[7] Internet article: *Sh'ma: A Journal of Jewish Ideas*, at http://shma.com/2012/03/rebbe-talk-a-conversation-with-reb-zalman-schachter-shalomi/

[8] Reb Zalman told this story many times. One place it appears is in *The First Step: A Guide For the New Jewish Spirit*, p.5.

[9] As quoted in a lecture by Professor Victoria Erhart, entitled "Unconventional Traditionalist: The Correspondence between Reb Zalman and Thomas Merton." Available at: https://www.youtube.com/watch?v=vBdwfazrBvk.

[10] *Ibid.*

[11] Gen. 14:18-20.

[12] From a 1987 conversation at Reb Zalman's home at P'Nai Or in Philadelphia, PA.

[13] Ps.96:1.

[14] From a talk by Reb Zalman at Naropa University entitled "Renewal in Traditions—Jewish as a Case in Point," Boulder, CO. 2/19/99.

[15] From a class by Reb Zalman entitled "Dialogue of the Devout," 12/1/89.

[16] From a class by Reb Zalman at the Wisdom School on "Creation: The Earth is Conscious," 11/1/88 (part 14a).

[17] From a talk by Reb Zalman on Paradigm Shift hosted by Moshe Idel, Jerusalem 5/98, Shalom Hartman Institute.

[18] *Ibid.*

[19] From a 2003 recorded talk by Reb Zalman about Rabbi Carlebach.

[20] From a talk by Reb Zalman at the Wisdom School on the subject of Deuteronomy, 4-1-17, Naropa University.

[21] Schachter-Shalomi, Reb Zalman and Joel Segel, *Jewish with Feeling; a Guide to Meaningful Jewish Practice*, Riverhead Books, New York, 2005; pp. 220-221.

[22] 7-30-07 Reb Zalman phone interview with Ken Wilber entitled "God in the Twenty-first Century."

[23] *Ibid.*

[24] *Ibid.*

[25] From a recorded talk by Reb Zalman on Paradigm Shift hosted by Moshe Idel, Jerusalem 5/98, Shalom Hartman Institute.

[26] Schachter-Shalomi, Reb Zalman, (Ellen Singer, editor), *Paradigm Shift: From the Jewish Renewal Teachings of Reb Zalman Schachter-Shalomi*; 1993 Jason Aronson, p.149.

[27] The story is also related in *Jewish with Feeling* by Reb Zalman Schachter-Shalomi with Joel Segel; p.8.

[28] 7-30-07 Reb Zalman phone interview with Ken Wilber entitled "God in the Twenty-first Century."

[29] *Ibid.*

[30] 2008 interview of Reb Zalman; 8/19/08 on "Mystic Experience and Mysticism for a New Humanity" for "Technology of the Heart" with host Sadiq Alam, Available at: http://www.techofheart.co/2008/08/interview-with-reb-zalman-on-mystic.html

[31] From a class at Elat Chayyim entitled "Entering the Gates" (part 13).

[32] From a class entitled *Renewal in Traditions: Judaism as a Case in Point*, (part 6), Aspen Community Church, Aspen, Colorado.

[33] From a class at the Wisdom School on Creation: The Earth is Conscious, 11/1/88 (part 14a).

[34] *Ibid.* (Here, the material is paraphrased.)

[35] Gen. 1:28.

[36] Schachter-Shalomi, *Paradigm Shift*, p.300.

[37] From a recorded talk by Reb Zalman on Paradigm Shift hosted by Moshe Idel, Jerusalem 5/98, Shalom Hartman Institute.

[38] *Ibid.*

[39] *Ibid.*

[40] From an article entitled, "The Endgame In Job" on the internet at http://www.jewishrenewalhasidus.org/wordpress/category/reb-zalman-articles/

[41] From a recorded talk by Reb Zalman on Paradigm Shift hosted by Moshe Idel, Jerusalem 5/98, Shalom Hartman Institute.

[42] *Ibid.*

[43] Schachter-Shalomi, *Paradigm Shift*, pp.147-148.

[44] From a 1993 video of a talk on Planetary Transformation.

[45] From a talk by Reb Zalman at Naropa entitled "Renewal in Traditions—Jewish as a Case in Point," Boulder, CO. 2/19/99.

[46] From a class by Reb Zalman entitled "Dialogue of the Devout," 12/1/89.

[47] From a series of classes by Reb Zalman on the Ba'al Shem Tov, #5.

[48] From a 1993 video of a talk by Reb Zalman on Planetary Transformation.

[49] Isa.56:7.

[50] From a workshop by Reb Zalman on Kabbalah in Washington, DC, 1988.

[51] From talk by Reb Zalman on "Patterns of Good and Evil" 2/85, Gainesville FLA.

[52] *Ibid.*

[53] Qur'an 8:17.

[54] Available at: http://www.businessinsider.com/strange-connection-between-russian-astronauts-and-god-2014-7.

[55] Khan, Hazrat Inayat, *The Complete Sayings of Hazrat Inayat Khan*; Vadan/Alankaras, 717, p.86 and Gayan/Raga, 548, p.63.

[56] Material based on a 1982 class by Reb Zalman on "Sephirot and the Inner life" (audio cassette recording).

[57] From a talk by Reb Zalman entitled "Jungian Psychology, Mysticism and Spiritual Eldering," 4a.

[58] Dalai Lama, *Toward a True Kinship of Faiths*, Doubleday, 2011 Kindle edition, chapter 3.

[59] Bhagavad Gita 2:47.

[60] Bhagavad Gita 5:8

[61] As quoted by Reb Zalman in a 1980s class on "Practical Kabbalah."

[62] Dalai Lama, *Toward a True Kinship of Faiths*, chapter 3.

[63] *The Bhagavad Gita*; translated by Juan Mascaró, Penguin Classics, 1962, verse 18:55

[64] *Ibid*, verse 18:61.

[65] Jeremiah 31:33.

[66] Dalai Lama, *Toward a True Kinship of Faiths*, chapter 3.

[67] *Ibid.*

[68] *The Bhagavad Gita* (Mascaró), verse 6:8.

[69] Dalai Lama, *Toward a True Kinship of Faiths*, chapter 3.

[70] *The Bhagavad Gita* (Mascaró), verses 2:52-53.

[71] Dalai Lama, *Toward a True Kinship of Faiths*, chapter 3.

[72] The quotes in this and the following paragraphs represent material drawn from a class discussion led by Reb Zalman on "Jung's Four Functions of the Psyche," 11-4-82.

[73] *Ibid.*

[74] Material in the above paragraphs of this section is based on a talk by Reb Zalman entitled "Jungian Psychology, Mysticism, and Spiritual Eldering," given at the Center for Jungian Studies of Southeast Florida.

[75] From a talk on Cosmology Updated, 6-10-90, San Francisco Jewish Community Center.

[76] *Ibid.*

[77] *Ibid.*

[78] From a class by Reb Zalman at the Wisdom School entitled "Creation: the Earth is Conscious," 11/1/88; part 14a.

[79] *Ibid.* Reb Zalman here quotes the famous opening line of the *Tao Te Ching* by Lao Tsu.

[80] From a 1980s class by Reb Zalman entitled "Sephirot and the Inner Life."

[81] *Ibid.*

[82] From a 1986 interview of Reb Zalman by Fran Silbiger-Orrok entitled "Kabbalah Basics."

[83] From an internet interview of Reb Zalman from 7/24/13 entitled "The Head, the Heart, and Connecting to GOD through Prayer."

[84] Talk by Reb Zalman on "Cosmology Updated," 6/10/90, San Francisco Jewish Community Center.

[85] From a talk by Reb Zalman on "Patterns of Good and Evil," February 1985, Gainesville, FL.

[86] *Ibid.*

[87] From a 1986 interview of Reb Zalman by Fran Silbiger-Orrok entitled "Kabbalah Basics."

[88] *Ibid.*

[89] From a 1981 talk in Philadelphia by Reb Zalman to Sufi cherags about the Universal Worship Service.

[90] John 10:30.

[91] From a 1981 talk in Philadelphia by Reb Zalman to Sufi cherags about the Universal Worship Service.

[92] *Ibid.*

[93] From Sermon IV of *Meister Eckhart's Sermons*, translated into English by Claud Field, 1909.

[94] The Writings of Kwang-Tze, Part II, p.69 from *The Sacred Books of the East*, Vol. XL, Adamant Media Corporation, 2000.

[95] From a 1988 Reb Zalman interview with Fran Silbiger-Orrok entitled "Teachings of the Soul." Most of the following paragraphs have been slightly paraphrased to better preserve the flow of Reb Zalman's discourse. All of the content is attributable to Reb Zalman.

[96] *Ibid.*

[97] *Ibid.*

[98] Schachter-Shalomi, Reb Zalman, *Gate to the Heart*, 2013, Albion-Andalus, Boulder, CO, p.7.

[99] From a conversation between Reb Zalman and the author at P'Nai Or in Philadelphia on 9/15/87.

[100] From a series by Reb Zalman at the Primal Myths Wisdom School Series on Torah, entitled, "The Earth is Conscious."

[101] Qur. 55:29.

[102] The discussion of the flip from the feminine to the masculine idealization of wisdom is from a 1980s class on Kabbalah at P'Nai Or.

[103] The feminine counterparts on the Tree of Life are given by Reb Zalman in an unpublished collection of his writings entitled "Mareh Kohen," (1987-88) in a section entitled "Our Need for a Theology." They are also found on pp.24-25 of *Fragments of a Future Scroll* by Reb Zalman.

[104] From a 1980s class by Reb Zalman entitled "Sephirot and the Inner Life."

[105] *Ibid.*

[106] Schachter-Shalomi, *Fragments of a Future Scroll: Hassidism for the Aquarian Age*, Leaves of Grass Press, 1975; pp.24-25.

[107] Job 3:15. From a class on Spiritual Leadership at Elat Chayyim.

[108] Isa. 45:7.

[109] From a panel discussion entitled "Journey of the Soul" at Canterbury Retreat Center in Oviedo, FL, in 1989.

[110] Gen. 2:17.

[111] Gen. 3:1.

[112] Khan, Hazrat Inayat, *The Complete Sayings of Hazrat Inayat Khan*; Gayan/Gamakas, 515, p.53.

[113] From the author's conversation with Reb Zalman at Elat Chayyim in 1993.

[114] From a talk by Reb Zalmam entitled "Basic Training in Jewish Mysticism," December 1, 1989.

[115] From a talk by Reb Zalman and Eve Ilsen entitled "Journey of the Soul" 1/12/89, Oviedo, FL.

[116] *The Spirituality of the Future* by Rabbi Zalman Schachter-Shalomi; Rabbi Arthur Waskow; 5/9/2008: Available at: www.theshalomcenter.org/node/1395.

[117] Yoma 69b from the Babylonian Talmud.

[118] From an internet article entitled "Reb Zalman: The Heart of Evil," a story retold by Rabbi David Cooper. Available at: https://www.rabbidavid-cooper.com/cooper-print-index/2010/11/8/2253-reb-zalman-the-heart-of-evil-print.html

[119] Klugar, Rivkah, *Satan in the Old Testament*, p.132, Evanston, Northwestern University Press, 1967.

[120] Prov. 9:10.

[121] "Reb Zalman: The Heart of Evil," a story retold by Rabbi David Cooper.

[122] *Ibid.*

[123] Schachter-Shalomi, *Fragments of a Future Scroll,* pp.103-04

[124] Matt. 5:44-45.

[125] From a talk by Reb Zalman in Charlotte, NC. 2/4/90.

[126] *Or Chadesh* of *P'nai Or,* late 1980s limited edition, p.236.

[127] Mark 12:29.

[128] Gen. 32:25.

[129] Schachter-Shalomi, *Gate to the Heart*, p.51.

[130] Schachter-Shalomi, Reb Zalman, *Psalms in a Translation for Praying*, ALEPH: Alliance for Jewish Renewal, 2014; p.164.

[131] From a 1980s class by Reb Zalman on Kabbalah at B'Nai Or.

[132] From a Reb Zalman class on "Core Texts of the Hasidic Masters," 1988.

[133] Schachter-Shalomi, Reb Zalman, *Paradigm Shift*, Jason Aronson, Inc., Northvale, NJ, 1993; pp.287-88.

[134] Based on a talk by Reb Zalman from a class on "Core Texts of Hassidic Masters." Reb Zalman explained the basic progression of paradigm shifts in a number of different lectures.

[135] *Talmud B. Berachoth*, 10a.

[136] Acts 17:58.

[137] Talk from "Core texts of Hassidic Masters."

[138] Shaku, Soyen, *Zen for Americans*, translated by Daisetz Teitaro Suzuki, 1906, pp. 25-26.

[139] From a talk at Naropa by Reb Zalman entitled "Hasidic Archetypes," 1/28/97.

[140] Huxley, Aldous: from the Introduction to *The Phenomenon of Man* by Teilhard de Chardin, Fontana, Fourth Edition, 1966; p.13.

[141] Ps.74:14.

[142] From a talk by Reb Zalman entitled "Jungian Psychology, Mysticism, and Spiritual Eldering," part 2b.

[143] Schachter-Shalomi, *Paradigm Shift*, p.289.

[144] Ex. 20:3.

[145] Ps. 86:8.

[146] Isa.56:7.

[147] Isa.66:1.

[148] Ex.14:27-28.

[149] Gen. 14:18-20.

[150] Qur'an 6:74-79.

[151] Ex. 4:24.

[152] Hos. 6:6.

[153] From a lecture by Reb Zalman at Vassar College entitled "Jewish Mysticism and the Paradigm Shift," Part 1 of 2.

[154] Schachter-Shalomi, *The First Step: A Guide for the New Jewish Spirit*, p.115.

[155] Hosea 14:2.

[156] Jn. 4:14.

[157] Jn. 4:21-4.

[158] *Inquiring Mind Journal*, Spring 1994.

[159] Schachter-Shalomi, *Paradigm Shift*, p.303.

[160] *Ibid*, p.145.

[161] From a 1982 talk by Reb Zalman entitled "The Descent of Divine Immanence."

[162] From a 2012 Symposium entitled "Living in the Differences," at Starr King School for the Ministry.

[163] From a 8/19/08 Reb Zalman interview with host Sadiq Alam entitled "Mystic Experience and Mysticism for a New Humanity" on "Technology of the Heart."

[164] From a 2012 Symposium entitled "Living in the Differences," at Starr King School for the Ministry.

[165] Schachter-Shalomi, *Paradigm Shift*, p.292.

[166] From a 2/1/92 Reb Zalman talk entitled "A Rainbow of Interests," Gainesville, Fla.

[167] From a Kabbalah workshop by Reb Zalman in Washington D.C., in 4/10/88.

[168] From a talk by Reb Zalman on Paradigm Shift hosted by Moshe Idel, Jerusalem 5/98, Shalom Hartman Institute.

[169] *Ibid*.

[170] From a January 20, 2015, *Tikkun*, article by Yotam Schatcher, entitled "Growing Toward God: Jewish Movement Through the Axial Age."

[171] *Ibid*.

[172] *Ibid*.

[173] *Ibid*.

[174] From an internet article by Bernie Glassman entitled, "My Rebbe is Gone!" Available at: https://zenpeacemakers.org/2014/07/my-rebbe-is-gone/

[175] Quoted from *The Jew in the Lotus*, Rodger Kamenetz in an internet article available at http://www.jcpa.org/jl/hit20.htm, entitled "A Meeting of Ancient Peoples: Western Jews and the Dalai Lama of Tibet" by Nathan Katz.

[176] *Ibid*.

[177] *Ibid*.

[178] Quoted from "The Emerging Cosmology," a transcript of Reb Zalman's presentation at HH the Dalai Lama's Roundtable, edited by Netanel Miles-Yépez, Available at: https://aleph.org/resources/the-emerging-cosmology-transcript-of-reb-zalman-at-hh-the-dalai-lamas-roundtable.

[179] *Ibid.*

[180] *Ibid.*

[181] From an internet article by Sara Davidson entitled "How the Rabbi Got His Name" available at www.saradavidson.com/blog/2014/02/how-the-rabbi-Got- his-name.html.

[182] *Ibid.*

[183] *Ibid.*

[184] Quote from internet site available at www.inayati-maimunis.org.

[185] *Ibid.*

[186] Sara Davidson, *Huffington Post*, 7-27-14.

[187] Schachter-Shalomi, *Jewish with Feeling*, 2005, pp.253-4.

APPENDIX A

Kabbalistic Meditations of Pir Vilayat Khan

Pir Vilayat occasionally led meditations utilizing the ten sephirot on the Tree of Life as a contemplative practice. Here, we introduce Pir Vilayat's approach to the sephirotic tree, based on a meditation he led in the late 1970s, enhanced by a more refined treatment in one of his last books: *The Ecstasy Beyond Knowing: A Manual of Meditation*.[1]

Pir Vilayat introduces the material by acknowledging that Kabbalah has been called the "yoga of the West." The meditation involves various principles found on the sephirotic tree, with each principle representing a certain power or attunement which, taken together, form "a map of the states of the soul, the different levels of consciousness." The sephirotic tree is pictured upside down, with the roots at the top, the place of divine transcendence. The tree is pictured with three columns: a central trunk "flanked with branches bifurcating right and left, representing a basic antinomy of bounty and restriction until we reach the culmination, which represents the existential realm,"[2] Malkhut—corresponding to divine immanence on the physical plane. In between the heavenly roots and the earthly apex at the bottom are the various archetypal qualities that are the Kabbalistic equivalent of the divine names as used in Sufism, although they are ten in number rather than ninety-nine. Above the tree is the realm of "no-thing-ness" known as Ain-Sof, "the ineffable void, the immaterial palace in which God remains eternally unattainable; albeit, it is out of this nonbeing that all being emerges."[3]

Pir Vilayat goes on to describe the qualities of the ten sephirot on the tree, offering a classical meditation on the soul's descent, eminating zigzag through the various sephirot into incarnation. He also furnishs the astrological equivalents for each sephirah. This is followed by an ascending meditation which earmarks the distinctive attunements, or approaches to reality, that characterize us as human beings, corresponding to the ten psychological types (which are represented in a Jewish minion of ten). The final version given by Pir Vilayat focuses on the divine presence in the heart of the Tree of Life and concludes with an equivalent Christian meditation on the divine presence. What follows is primarily given in Pir Vilayat's own words from a live meditation, with quotation marks indicating additional book quotations which have been interspersed.

the SEPHIROT *on the* TREE *of* LIFE

It all starts at the top of the tree with the sephirah known as Keter, a Hebrew word for "crown," which has a connection to the Arabic divine name, *Qahr* in the Islamic esoteric tradition—which indicates the highest sovereign power that prevails over all creation. On the human body, it corresponds to the crown center, the chakra located at the top of the human head. Keter represents the state of unity in which it all starts. Then we descend into a dichotomy between Hokhmah and Binah. Hokhmah represents what the Sufis mean by *Alim*—the divine wisdom or divine knowledge. Hokhmah represents "the divine intelligence, of which we become aware when we realize that if we have any understanding of the universe, it is because we think the way the universe thinks. This is . . . an inborn inherent knowledge, not based upon experience."[4]

Across from Hokhmah on the tree is Binah, representing the knowledge that has become concrete, more tangible. Then we come down to the next two principles. On the one hand, we have Hesed, which is the same word as the Hasidim, and it means exactly magnanimity. You see, the first level is understanding, realization.

The next level is power or sovereignty. So on the right side you have Hesed (or Gedula), which "represents the power of love that prevails over compulsion and manifests as grace."[5] This grace is like the magnanimity of a compassionate king. Across from Hesed on the left side is Gevurah (or Din), the sephirah of mastery and "power, the deployment of energy to ensure the actuation of the divine programming. At this stage, the contemplative discovers the role of discipline, of rigor. . . ."[6] The word Din indicates the authority, the law, and Din also refers to religious law. The word is the same in Arabic, meaning "of the religion," and in this context, the religion is experienced as restrictive, telling you what to do and what not to do. So both at the level of understanding and at the level of power, the left side is constrictive. It reduces you, confines you, while the right is expansive, cosmic, unlimited. So you could say Hesed is like the power of the king and Gevurah is the power of the policeman. The king can give grace. The policeman never gives grace, unless he is an exceptional policeman.

Next, we come to the hub of the whole tree, its center of gravity, Tipheret. In one sense, it represents the heart, the sanctuary, the holy of holies, the point of transition between what is above and what is below, between the sacred and profane, the divine and human. It is also the altar of sacrifice, and it represents the divine immanence. In Tipheret, "we encounter a further principle in the descent: affirming sacredness in the midst of the profanity that ensues from the abuse of freewill in life. . . . In the course of our ascent through the sephirotic pathways, this is where we encounter a test: only if we are willing to make some sacrifice of our personal greed or worldliness do we have access to the higher sephirot. In the course of our descent along the labyrinth of pathways, we are sworn to recollect our covenant"[7] to uphold the Divine Truth as we enter the battle of life.*

---

*   This primordial covenant (of *Alast*) in the "world of souls" is mentioned in the Qur'an (7:166) as the time when all the potential souls, while still "in the loins of Adam," pledged allegiance to their Divine Source before incarnating on earth, a material realm where one easily forgets one's true Source.

Moving further down, we have two principles; on the right side, Netzah, which represents glorification in every form—beauty, art. It "represents the splendor of the heavenly spheres reflected in our quest for beauty in form or structure, aesthetics, glorification, the triumph of excellence over mediocrity." On the other hand we have Hod, which is the intellect. So we have a pairing of emotion and intellect. Hod further "represents the cohering impact of reason and logic upon all formative processes, the mathematical laws presiding over the configuration of matter—the symphony of the spheres."[8]

Then we come down to a further point in the central trunk of the tree to Yesod, which represents the principle of vitality, regeneration, the mode of life which gives form to that which does not have a form. "Yesod is the template, the seminal etheric mold, not only determining the forms of the world, but insuring their perennity, and at the same time, uniqueness, by replication or reproduction. The quality ascribed to this sephirah is creativity."[9]

At the bottom, we have Malkhut, which represents the kingdom of earth, *Melek* (Hebrew for king; *Malik* in Arabic). So in the kingdom of earth—that is, the physical plane—all of these principles are affected and, as the soul descends, it follows these different planes with each one of these principles being complementary, one to the other. Descending through the tree, we encounter the plane of knowledge and understanding as Hokhmah-Binah, the plane of power as Hesed-Gevurah, and at Tipheret, the transition between the earth plane and the heavenly plane. This is where transmutation takes place—transfiguration, resurrection—passing from here upwards. Below, in Netzah-Hod, we have the models of physical reality, both emotional and mental, and then we come down to something more concrete in Yesod, like the molds out of which the physical world is made, and then we reach right down into the physical world with Malkhut.

For those who would like to interpret this in terms that are more familiar, especially astrological terms, you could say that Binah is Saturn, which always represents a certain limitation, and Hohkmah is Neptune. Hesed represents Jupiter—that Jupitarian quality in a person—and Din [Gevurah] represents Mars. Both are expressions of power, while Jupiter is very benevolent, although very powerful; but he can afford to be benevolent because he is so powerful. Mars is a stickler for the law—very hard, like the sacrificial priest at the altar. Tipheret is often represented by the sun, and Netzah, Venus, emotion—high emotion that manifests as art and the aesthetic expression of creativity. Hod is Mercury, Yesod, the Moon, and Malkhut, of course, the Earth.

MEDITATION *on the* DESCENT

One starts at the top in Keter by experiencing the transcendent oneness behind all things. Then we move down in Hokhmah to what the Sufis call the divine intention. At this point, it is not very concise, but still in a formative process. Then you move over to Binah, which represents the order of the universe; so the intention is becoming more actualized in the form of the order. Next, you move down from Binah into Hesed; so out of this order has developed sovereignty and an expansive sense of compassion and generosity. Then you move over to Din (Gevurah), which represents the authority, the executive, which limits the expansion and balances it with mastery. Next, you move into the heart, Tipheret, which is the point of transition, the altar where there is transmutation, transfiguration. It corresponds to the place where one affirms one's allegiance to the Divine, beyond personal considerations, in order to become the khalifa or representative of the Divine on earth. Descending further, we get into the place of glorification in Netzah, prior to the descent into a more concrete expression of the divine reality, where we find our attunement with our angelic nature, born of the worlds of light. Then we move over to the place where intellect is born, experiencing our jinn or genius nature, born of the mind world. Then one descends into the more concrete world of formation in Yesod, which is like the software behind the hardware, the programming. Here, we have the beginning of forms, the molds out of which all physical existence arises, bringing us finally to Malkhut, our existential realm on earth.

Changing directions, another classical meditation is to proceed from the bottom to the top, starting with the physical plane. There are people who say, for example, "I don't believe in anything except what I can see." Those people are right down here in Malkhut. "Anything I can see and feel, for me, that's real. But what you're talking about is really above my head."

Yesod is typified by those who appreciate the form of things; for example, the form of a ceremony. They go to church because there is beautiful music, candles, a beautiful church building, and priests in fine clothes; so they love the form. Those with an affinity for Hod may have some definite concept of God, which, in order to to be meaningful, must be clear to their minds. For example, one might hold that "God is the perfection," a kind of intellectual concept of God, Who is understandable and intelligible, in line with Plato or Plotinus—the God of the philosophers. Those attuned to Netzah value glorification and emotion—God experienced as a reality in one's emotions—and if they enjoy religious ceremonies, it is not so much the form which is appreciated, but the emotion of the service, for it communicates something of the Divine Being to them. They are generally people who have a great sensitivity to beauty and art.

The sephirah of Tipheret represents a very crucial point in one's evolution where one has to go through a kind of death, a dark night of the soul, a purification, in which one is prepared to make a sacrifice. For example, one becomes a monk, and leaves the world, giving up many things one previously enjoyed in exchange for the disciplined life of a recluse and greater intimacy with the Divine. This is the sacrificial altar.

Those with affinities in Gevurah tend to be sticklers for principles, like the principles of a monk—celibacy, obedience, and service. One may observe the dogma of the religion and attempt to understand it, not with the intellect, but with one's sense of conforming to what has been revealed without questioning it. You find that approach amongst fundamentalists. At Hesed, there is the opening of the heart, and the forms and dogmas begin to lose their importance. You find those spiritual beings who have risen above all forms and dogmas—totally unconventional—but who just have a very living heart and love all beings! Those are the Hasidim.

From the standpoint of Binah, you move back into understanding the mystery of life. Somehow things start becoming clear—what is behind it all. But even the understanding that one reaches at that moment is not enough. One has to go beyond that in Hokhmah, into what Al-Hallaj describes when he says, "If you could only have access into the divine understanding, your understanding would be shaken." So this is what the Sufis call "the consternation of intelligence," right up here in Hokhmah. And then, of course, at the top in Keter, you get into the unity. That's what one is supposed to experience in the Sufi zikr, losing oneself totally in the unity. I think, myself, that this is really the point of samadhi. Above Keter, there is still another realm of pure formlessness, Ain Sof, and below Hokhmah-Binah there is a mysterious hidden sephirah called Da'ath, but I omitted these in order not to overcomplicate things. [10]

Finally, in the more advanced contemplation of the sephirot, one goes straight down from Keter, right down through Tipheret, Yesod, and Malkhut. In this meditation, one concentrates on the top and bottom of the tree, as the two poles of transcendence and immanence, yesod being the intermediate step where the unmanifest begins to take shape in tangible forms. In between the transcendence of Keter and the immanence of Malkhut, is Tipheret in heart of the tree. Here, correlating to one's own heart, one can meditate on the eternal Divine Presence that exists beyond time and space, both within and beyond the manifest world.

the CHRISTIAN MEDITATION of
NICHOLAS OF FLÜE

Here, Pir Vilayat brings in an equivalent meditation that also has its similarities with the zikr of the Sufis and the form of a

Hindu/Buddhist mandala, a practice done by the great medieval Christian mystic, Nicholas of Flüe, also known as "Brother Klaus." Nicholas of Flüe (1417-1487), was a Swiss hermit, ascetic, and visionary, who became the patron saint of Switzerland. Before retiring from the world, Nicolas had military and political experience which put him in a position him to successfully arbitrate and resolve a civil war in Switzerland by suggesting the establishment of a federation of the various factions.

His spiritual meditation involves a circle of six symbols, surrounding an essential point at the center of the circle. In the meditation, one moves counterclockwise through the six stations of the circle, starting at the top, circling to the bottom and then back up again to where one started.

1. At the top, one concentrates on the oneness of God, a unity of being which includes the Trinity of God the Father, Son, and Holy Spirit, beyond manifestation.

2. Moving to the top left station of the circle, one envisions the descent of the Christ spirit through the angelic spheres.

3. Proceeding to the station at the bottom left of the circle, one pictures Christ being born as Jesus in the womb of the Virgin Mary, the birth of the Divine in humanity.

4. At the bottom of the circle, one concentrates on the historical Jesus, as a fully incarnated human being on earth, baptized in the Jordan and filled with the Holy Spirit, preaching the good tidings to the poor, experiencing the transfiguration, expelling the money-changers from the Temple, eating the last supper, and so on.

5. Moving upward to the bottom right of the circle, one concentrates on the crucifixion, the transition of physical death that all humans undergo.

6. Moving up to the top right station one concentrates on the resurrection and ascension of the Christ Spirit.

Then moving back to the top, one re-enters the Oneness. Nicolas found that if he concentrated in turn on all of the phases of the historical Jesus, he could simultaneously concentrate in an ever deepening way on the presence of the eternal Christ in his heart. In the language of the Sufis, the concentration is on the permanence of the eternal and formless Divine Presence in one's heart, at the center of one's being, existing timelessly beyond even the span of one's earthly incarnation—the great "I am" of the universe. The corresponding mantra or Divine name that can be intoned to evoke the Divine Essence in the heart is the Arabic sacred word, *Hu* or *Om* in Sanskrit.[11]

ENDNOTES

[1] Khan, Pir Vilayat, *The Ecstasy Beyond Knowing: A Manual of Meditation*, Part 4, chapter 6, Kabbala, Kindle edition.

[2] *Ibid.*

[3] *Ibid.*

[4] *Ibid.*

[5] *Ibid.*

[6] *Ibid.*

[7] *Ibid.*

[8] *Ibid.*

[9] *Ibid.*

[10] The above material, with the exception of the quotes from *The Ecstasy Beyond Knowing*, is taken from a 1979 talk on Kabbala by Pir Vilayat and is presented in his own words.

[11] Based on another meditation from the same 1979 talk on Kabbala by Pir Vilayat.

APPENDIX B

The Gospels as Midrash; Christ as Archetype of the Divinity in Humanity

In the second half of this book, I have referred extensively to the four worlds and the various levels of scriptural hermaneutics, furnishing various examples of scriptural interpretation that go beyond the ordinary, literal meaning of the text. Of the four levels, the two most basic are the literal, exoteric level of interpretation (*p'shat* in Hebrew) and the esoteric, parabolic, or allegorical level (including *remez* and *drash*), which implies something beyond the surface meaning of the text. In this appendix, I offer a more extended esoteric scriptural interpretation, focusing on the deeper mystical significance of the Christian Gospels as well as the archetypal implications of Christ as exemplar and revealer of the divinity in humanity. Having laid the ground with a discussion of the multidimensionality of God and of sacred scripture in the context of Sufism and Hasidism, I feel it is important to include, even if briefly, the mystical perspective of Christianity, which is the third great tradition flowing from the Abrahamic ocean of unity. At its center is the figure of the living Christ, the primary Western spiritual archetype of divinity in human form, a universal archetype to which we all inwardly have access, whether we conceptualize it as the spirit of Christ or by some other name.

In the Sufi understanding, all of the divine messengers are one in essence, inspired by one and the same source of wisdom in different times and cultures. In mystical Islam, the historical

Muhammad is considered an expression of the *Nuri Muhammad*, the first light of eternity, which is another way of describing the *Logos* or Cosmic Christ. Sufis also speak of the *Insani-Kamil*, and Jewish Kabbalists of *Adam Kadmon*, both of which represent the idealized archetype of human perfection, the primordial divine template of humanity in its glorious original state. The Eastern religions also point in various ways to the exalted nature of fully realized humanity, or one's Buddha nature; in Hinduism, a whole series of divine avatars are recognized as expressions of this ideal. Each authentic religion has its own portals to Reality, even though the pathways and messengers differ historically and culturally.

If we temporarily set aside any exclusivist claims of the Christian Church and look at the Gospel story of a man from a humble village who recognized that he was "one with the Father," and proclaimed that others were also beloved "children of the Father in heaven,"[1] we see a story that closely tallies with the Sufi message in our time, as well as the perennial philosophy. As expressed in the Sufi tradition of Hazrat Inayat Khan, the breakthrough of divine consciousness that occurred in the first century and was then associated with the singular person of Jesus is, in our time, ripe to give birth to the next step of the collective awakening of the whole humanity to its divine inheritance. This same essential idea was expressed by the early Church Father, Athanasius, who said that: "God became man so that we might become God."[2] A similar saying is attributed to the second century Church Father, Irenaeus, "Jesus Christ became what we are in order that we might become what he himself is."

"Holy, holy holy! The Lord of Hosts! The whole world is filled with God's glory!" This is the cry of the angels in Isaiah 6:3, proclaiming that everything, including humanity, is permeated with the glory and holy presence of the Omnipresent Source. Similarly, the Qur'an declares that "In whatever direction you look, there is the Divine Countenance, full of majesty and splendor,"[3] and affirms that God is nearer to us than our jugular vein.[4] The idea that humanity is created in the divine image and innately embodies divine qualities (or divine sparks) is called theomorphism—formed according to the divine pattern of the Universe. It is foundational to both Sufism and Hasidism that the universe and all beings within it exist as expressions of the Divine, although the inherent seed of divinity in humanity remains largely dormant and covered, as a hidden treasure, until its flowering. From this flowering come the fruits of spiritual awakening and unconditional love. Within the Christian tradition, Matthew Fox calls this the primal tradition of "original blessing," as opposed to the later Augustinian interpretation of "original sin."* This exalted tradition of original blessing, reflective of the divine glory, remains a scriptural heritage of the Abrahamic tradition which, over the centuries, has been largely neglected in the exoteric understanding of Judaism, Christianity, and Islam; yet it is a much needed perspective in our increasingly divisive world.

Our aim in this appendix, then, is twofold: to highlight the midrashic and allegorical dimensions of the Gospels beyond the literal reading, and in so doing, to point to the universality of the Christ archetype as an expression of the perennial theomorphic tradition which proclaims the divine potentiality—the kingdom of heaven—hidden in the human heart. This same tradition is also found in Sufism and Hasidism, but is expressed in ways that differ from the Christian presentation, as we will see.

We will begin with some introductory material, followed by a brief enumeration of the essential archetypal motifs in the Gospels, and conclude with some relevant final thoughts by Reb Zalman and Pir Vilayat.

BEHOLD, I SHOW YOU *a* MYSTERY
(*I Cor.15:51*)

If we peruse the Gospels carefully, we can observe how the evangelists repeatedly connect the events described in the Gospels with parallel events from the Jewish scriptures (TaNaKh). The context is clearly set forth that "all these things took place according to the

---

* Augustine's fourth-century doctrine of "original sin" is not accepted by Judaism, Islam, or the Eastern Orthodox Church.

scriptures," in order "that the scriptures might be fulfilled."⁵ This consistent parallelism earmarks the story as a form of Jewish midrash on the TaNaKh ("the law and the prophets") in which earlier scriptural events are implied or explicitly cited and linked with new and greater deeds of a similar character. This takes a number of forms, of which I will give three examples: Matthew's "Sermon on the Mount" cites the Mosaic commandments juxtaposed with newer, more heart-centered admonitions such as, "You have been told, 'An eye for an eye,' but I tell you," you must "turn the other cheek" to your enemies.⁶ A less explicit gospel parallelism is offered by referencing Psalm 22, where one finds in seed form much of the passion narrative including Jesus' final words on the cross.* More subtly still, John the Baptist is identified by Jesus as Elijah,⁷ the forerunner who was to come before the Messiah, and Jesus, in turn, is considered not only the secret Messiah (according to Mark) but an embodiment of the great coming prophet foretold by Moses. These two Old Testament figures then appear with Jesus during his transfiguration on the mountain, in a divine epiphany during which Jesus' garments shine with a dazzling brightness,⁸ echoing the earlier revelation on Mount Sinai and Moses' own illumination. Through such devices, the knowledgeable first-century Jewish reader would understand the underlying parallels and deeper midrashic implications which the Gospel writers intend to convey.

The New Testament was produced during an era in which parable and allegory flourished widely from Qumran to Alexandria, and techniques such as midrash, pesher, and other amplifications of the Jewish scriptures were in vogue. The author of the Fourth Gospel and Revelations, which is traditionally attributed to John, saw the spirit of Christ as the *Logos* (Word), the first light of the universe and the Alpha and Omega. Jesus is also identified as the Wisdom of God,⁹ personified in Proverbs as Lady Wisdom (Hokhmah), the artificer of the creation, who

---

* As quoted by Mark, which is generally considered to be the earliest gospel. The words of Mark 15:34, quoted in Aramaic and based on Psalm 22:2, are: "*'Eli, Eli lama sabachtani,*' which is being interpreted as, 'My God, my God, why hast thou forsaken me?'" (KJV) George Lamsa's translation based on the Aramaic Peshitta is: "My God, my God, for this I was kept!"

existed before the worlds. In the Gospel of John, Jesus states, "Before Abraham was, I am."[10] These timeless transpersonal attributes indicate that we are dealing with a mystical meta-narrative about a cosmic archetype beyond the life of an individual Galilean from Nazareth. That is the mystical, esoteric level; yet the multidimensionality of the text also allows for the story to be read on a literal level as history, albeit one filled with nonordinary miraculous elements.

We must point out the limits of historical reconstruction of the life of Jesus and why this is not our focus here. The epistles of the Paul are primarily concerned with the spiritual Christ as a path to inward transformation, and relate almost nothing about Jesus of Nazareth and his earthly life in Judea. It is the same with the other epistles in the New Testament. Furthermore, there is no contemporaneous mention of Jesus in the historical record to draw upon for further details beyond those furnished in the New Testament account. Faced with this paucity of sources outside of the Gospel narratives, scholars of recent centuries have endeavored to strip away the "supernatural" elements of the New Testament Christ of faith in order to uncover a "demythologized" historical Jesus, searching the texts to try to discern what might have actually taken place on a literal, factual level. However, after several centuries of such efforts, no widely agreed upon biography has resulted from this quest, and it is now widely conceded that such attempts inevitably reveal more about the beliefs and psychology of the scholars who produced them than about Jesus himself. Yet even if the historical documentation is slim, there is a profound significance in the way the story was presented by the authors of the New Testament.

An alternative and potentially more fruitful approach than historical analysis has been suggested by Joseph Campbell, who said that "contrary to Bultmann, this theologian who says we must demythologize religion, my vote is we should re-mythologize it."[11] This is because much of the symbolic content of the Gospels is lost when the stories are subjected to rationalist deconstruction or interpreted primarily as literal history and biography. The approach, which I believe holds more transformative potential and resonates with the insights of Sufism and the perennial philosophy, is to be found in Paul's timeless teachings concerning "the Christ spirit in you." This approach understands Jesus as the model by which human beings can discover within themselves the same Christ energies as Jesus did. This involves the unveiling of divine love and compassion within the human heart, and points to the revelation of the mystery of the divinity in humanity (or "God reconciled with humanity through Christ," in the language of the Church).

Beyond issues of Jesus' Davidic messiahship, the details of his birth, or even the manner and meaning of his death, the most essential and universal archetypal significance of the Gospels is a disclosure of how the deathless divine spirit in humanity—naturally obscured by egoic consciousness and lower impulses associated with the reptilian brain—can come to life, resurrecting the divine spirit which was buried in materialty. This resurrection and entry into the divine life comes about through the power of selfless love and reliance on our higher, transpersonal Source, when our old nature "dies." (Here, Reb Zalman frequently used the alternative metaphor that the opacity of the personal self "becomes more transparent to the Divine.") In John 12:24, Jesus states: Truly I say unto you, unless a grain of wheat dies, it remains as it is; but if it dies, it bears much fruit."

This is variously described as a "second birth" in which the seed of the divine power of love flowers in the heart (in the feeling world), or alternatively as the awakening from the sleep of spiritual slumber and forgetfulness of one's true nature (in the mind world). Spiritual transformation on the human level can also be likened to the process in which the caterpillar must shed its cocoon in order to reveal its butterfly nature. In the words of Hazrat Inayat Khan: "The first birth is the human birth, the second is the birth of God."[12] In one of his sermons, Meister Eckhart described the process in this way:

> The seed of God is in us. Given an intelligent and hard-working farmer, it will thrive and grow up to God, whose seed is in us: and accordingly its fruits will be

God-nature. Pear seeds grow into pear trees, nut seeds into nut trees, and God-seed into God.

the CHRISTIAN MYSTERY

The ancient archetypal theme of death and resurrection is embedded into the very fabric of nature with its cyclical seasons— plant life dies in the autumn, the life force goes into the roots during winter, and life returns as new growth in the spring. Likewise, the spiritual archetype of the divine exemplar who dies and is resurrected for the fecundity of the world appears in the earliest existing written records over 5,000 years ago in the scriptures of the Sumerians. The Sumerians celebrated the descent of Inanna, the goddess of love, into the underworld. There, she dies, her corpse is impaled on a stake, and the upper world goes into mourning. Thereafter, she resurrects, renews the world, and brings the crops to life during the spring equinox, around our Easter time. In the Canaanite and early Israelite tradition, the mourned, dying deity was the god Tammuz, mentioned in Ezekiel 8:14, and his consort was the great mother goddess, Ishtar (Astarte, Astoreth). With variations, this template was repeated in various cultures of the ancient world—Isis and Osiris, Demeter and Persephone, Dionysius, etc.—until the time of Jesus and Mary and Jesus' sacrificial death.

Augustine of Hippo recognized the antiquity of what later became known as Christianity: "That which is known as the Christian religion existed among the ancients, and never did not exist; from the beginning of the human race until the time when Christ came in the flesh, at which time the true religion, which already existed began to be called Christianity."[18] The Church Father and historian Eusebius also concurs, writing: "That which is called the Christian religion is neither new nor strange, but, if it be lawful to testify the truth, was known to the ancients."[14] With such statements, the Church Fathers freely acknowledge the timeless and universal aspect of the Christ story.

In the person of Jesus Christ, Paul recognized a model for individual death and transformation, saying that in Christ "I die daily"[15] and "I am crucified with Christ: nevertheless I live; yet not I, but Christ liveth in me."[16] The Prophet Muhammad famously offered similar advice, "Die before you die," as the way in which the individual "dies" to the false ego self and is resurrected by the power of the Divine within.* That is why Jesus can say, "Behold, the kingdom of God is within you,"[17] and 2 Peter 1:3-4 can state in very clear language that God has given us a gift which is "a guarantee of something very great and wonderful" and "through this gift you are sharers in the divine nature itself." Again the first letter of John proclaims: "Behold what love the Father has shown us, that we should be called children of God; and such we are."[18]

Just as Buddhism holds that every person potentially has the Buddha nature, in the mystical understanding of the Christian message, every person has the potential to discover themselves as a child of God, a bearer of the divine nature—the hidden treasure at the core of our being, the pearl beyond price. That is the good news of the Gospels. Becoming a son (or daughter) of God means that we realize ourselves as existing "in the likeness or nature of" the Divine image, that separation falls away, and we feel our connection with the All-pervading Divine presence. By contrast, just as the shadow is not the person, the false self or limited ego is clearly not God, and can never become God, although this was Pharaoh's proud boast; but when the clouds of the illusory ego-self are cleared then the sun of our True Source shines forth.

In both Biblical and Qur'anic terms, all of physical manifestation has come into being from Divine Spirit, the Source of

---

*   Dying to the false self is a metaphor that describes how one may (at least temporarily) transcend one's sense of personal ego, which is a socially agreed-upon entity that one habitually identifies as "me," yet which has no fixed intrinsic reality. The "false self" indicates a persistent self-concept, built up through identification with one's personal history, name and form, thoughts, emotions and personality. This self-image, or egoic setting of consciousness, functions usefully to provide us with a sense of identity in daily life and in society, but ultimately is an insubstantial stand-in substitute for our deeper essential being, a cover over the light of one's soul. When one's impersonal witness consciousness begins to separate from identification with the conventional ego-self, consciousness can open beyond duality and isolation to allow the divine qualities to manifest.

Being, and, metaphorically, God has breathed the divine breath*
into *ha-Adam*, the human form. The very etymology of the word
adam in Hebrew indicates an *aleph*** residing in *"dam,"* which is
the red clay of the earth out of which the human body is formed.
Thus, as manifestations of the Divine Spirit in human form, we
share a divine inheritance—something of the uncreated realm
of divine energies sustaining us—and we also have an animal
bodily nature, with all its cravings, and a "false ego" (individual
self-identity) veiling us from our deeper spiritual nature.

This understanding exists both in Christianity and Sufism,
in the Orthodox Christian teaching of Gregory Palamas and
Ibn 'Arabi respectively. Palamas explicated the teaching of divinization or *theosis*, meaning that one is able to become divine
(or discover one's divine inheritance) through sharing the nature of Christ. Ibn 'Arabi taught what is called *wahdat al-wujud*,
meaning that no reality exists except the One Divine Reality.
The profound teachings of both are in basic agreement that
the very Divine Essence (which is uncreated and transcendent)
never unites with the physical world of creation or with human
beings, but the creation is brought forth, animated and continually sustained by the divine energies or attributes (such as love,
light, truth, beauty, power, justice, etc.). All of these attributes
have negative shadow manifestations that represent distortions
of the original divine impulse or divine intention, and this accounts for the existence of imperfection, limitation, excess, and
sorrow in our "fallen" world along with its beautiful, loving, and
joyful attributes. The ten sephirot of Kabbalistic teaching furnishes yet another way of speaking of these divine attributes.

It is through a process of *kenosis*, self-emptying, or becoming transparent to the Divine, that Jesus—and potentially every
soul—has access to the divine qualities within, and is able to ex-
istentiate them, to partake of the divine action by negation of
the false self. In the Gospels, this is spoken of as losing one's self
in order to find one's Self, as seeking the pearl of great price,

---

* In Hebrew, *ruaḥ*; in Arabic, *ruh*.
** Aleph is the first Hebrew letter, corresponding to the letter a, which
in Gematria equals the number One and represents the Unmanifest Spirit.

and in praying, "Not my will but Thine be done."[19] In Islam, the divine inheritance is called "the hidden treasure" and in a hadith (saying) of the Prophet Muhammad, he conveys the divine affirmation that, in those who draw near to the Divine, God becomes the eyes through which they see, the ears through which they hear, and the hands with which they work. It is not simply that the ego has to be annihilated—for we need to have an identity and a healthy sense of self for practical reasons in everyday life—but what is needed is to see the ego as the relative and transient formation that it is: a cover over the divine spirit and the servant of the greater Reality, not its master.

The early Jewish tradition spoke extensively of the Primal Adam, the androgynous progenitor of all humanity, who was created in the divine image. The *Bereshit Rabbah*, a Jewish midrash on Genesis dating from around the fourth or fifth century CE, speaks of the original Adam as wearing garments of light, presumably before incarnating into clothes of flesh.[20] The *Bereshit Rabbah* also states that: "Rabbi Hosha'ya said, 'When the blessed Holy One created Adam, the ministering angels mistook him and sought to recite in his presence: Holy!'"[21] Psalm 8:4-5 further refers to the divine inheritance in humanity saying: "What are human beings that You spare a thought for them, or the son of man (Adam) that You care for him? Yet You have made him little less than a god, and have crowned him with glory and honor." The Qur'an carries on this tradition, characterizing the primal act of disobedience by Iblis (Satan) as his having refused Allah's command to bow before Adam—bearer of the divine breath and image—because Iblis would only bow before the divinity of Allah and couldn't perceive that Allah had animated the human form by means of Allah's own exalted Divine Spirit.[22] Iblis denied the divinity in humanity which Allah and the angels all affirmed. In a similar vein, Jesus calls the denial of the Holy Spirit in humanity an eternal sin (or state of alienation).[23]

The early Jewish Christians known as the Ebionites ("the poor") understood Jesus to be an incarnation of the "True Prophet" predicted by Moses in Deuteronomy.[24] The spirit of the True Prophet (who was thought to have appeared many times in various prophets of Israel) was associated with Adam, the primal human being, the original anointed messiah, who was created in the divine image. In the Gospel of John, Jesus had spoken of another a strikingly similar manifestation of spirit that would come after him to give the world further teachings: the *paraclete*.[25] Centuries later in Arabia, Waraqa, the Christian cousin of the wife of the Prophet Muhammad, also recognized this spirit of the True Prophet, the *namos* (law) that appeared to Moses, as having also come upon Muhammad. Closely paralleling the Christian Logos doctrine, a hadith states that the Prophet's light was the first thing created from the divine light and out of that light the rest of humanity was created. It is one and the same primordial light of conscious intelligence, whether conceptualized as *Hokhmah*, *Logos* or *Nuri Muhammad*.

These few examples point to a longstanding theomorphic tradition within the Abrahamic faiths which acknowledges the exalted essential nature of humanity, created in the divine image and endowed with the potential of realizing its own divinity. Alternatively, one could speak of the indwelling of the Holy Spirit in humanity, finding God in the heart, or the kingdom of God within. It is this awareness of the divine inheritance, and its aspect of unconditional love, which Jesus came to impart, calling sleepers to awaken from the spiritual slumber of forgetfulness.

PARABOLIC *and* SYMBOLIC CONTENT

Among the early Christians and Jews, particularly in Alexandria, allegorical writings and interpretation of the scriptures were very much in vogue. We see a clear early example of allegorical personification in Proverbs where Wisdom is personified as a woman crying out in the streets. The writers of the Dead Sea Scrolls made extensive use of the method of Hebrew *pesher*, involving innovative and symbolic interpretations of scripture as bearing allegorically on their own times, showing how, as they believed, hidden prophecies were currently being fulfilled. The Hellenistic Jewish philosopher, Philo of Alexandria (25 BCE-50 CE) interpreted the Jewish scriptures allegorically, in line with

Platonic philosophy, and appears to have influenced the Gospel of John with his doctrine of the *Logos* (first posited by Heraclitus), whom Philo identified as the first-born son of God and the Divine Wisdom. Philo also tells us that allegorical interpretation was widely practiced in the Palestinian rabbinical schools.

Among the early Church Fathers, Clement of Alexandria and his student Origen—one of the greatest minds of the early Church—stressed the allegorical and metaphorical dimensions of the scripture, beyond the literal meaning. Origen taught that within the scriptures were basic, literal teachings given for the neophytes (and also to veil certain things from hostile outsiders), higher moral teachings for the more experienced, and even deeper allegorical meanings for the spiritually mature, those whom Paul calls "the perfect."[26] Paul also refers to those things which contain an allegory in Galatians 4:24, and the author of the Epistle to the Hebrews gives a highly spiritualized account of Christ as an eternal priest after the order of Melchizedek. There, Christ is described as the true heavenly high priest in the celestial sanctuary, the great archetype which underlies all earthly temple priests, who are but poor replicas with their ineffectual animal sacrifices serving in "a sanctuary that is a copy and shadow of what is in heaven."[27] By contrast, he says, Christ, officiating in a celestial temple not made by human hands, has offered his own being as the perfect eternal sacrifice. Here the scriptures are unquestionably alluding to metaphysical realities beyond the purely literal and historical level.

In modern times, John Dominic Crossan has written about the use of parable among the first Christians and Gospel writers, saying: "When Jesus wanted to say something very important about God he went into parable; when the early church wanted to say something very important about Jesus they too went into parable."[28] In Mark's Gospel, the earliest evangelist explicitly states that Jesus taught everything in parables with the purpose of veiling the mysteries of the kingdom of God from outsiders and revealing them only to Jesus' inner circle. Jesus privately told his disciples, "The secret of the kingdom of God has been given to you. But to those on the outside everything is said in parables so that 'they may be ever seeing but never perceiving, and ever hearing but never understanding,' otherwise they might turn and be forgiven!"[29] Based on this enigmatic statement (unique to Mark's Gospel) and all that it implies, Crossan and a number of other scholars have surmised that a similar dynamic of hidden meaning is likely operating within Mark's own Gospel.

As Mark presents it, Jesus' parables function to partially veil the truth from uninitiated readers who understand the content only on a literal level, while revealing the mystery of the kingdom to those who approach with a more interiorized understanding of spiritual verities. In contrast to John's Gospel, where Jesus openly discloses his divine status, Mark portrays Jesus as veiling his messianic identity while speaking enigmatically about a "son of man" who will come on clouds of heaven in the future. Mark portrays the people and even the disciples as perplexed as to the identity of Jesus and recounts Jesus' rebuke of Peter when he openly suggests that Jesus is the Messiah of Israel. This is followed by Jesus' command to Peter and the disciples that they should not to tell this to anyone. Mark's Gospel ends without a resurrection appearance (in the earliest manuscripts); rather, the distressed women mourners are told by a young man that Jesus is risen and they hurry from the empty tomb in a state of fear, telling no one about it. Some scholars speculate that perhaps there were further verses, now lost, featuring a resurrection appearance, but there may be a very different reason for Mark's perplexing ending.

During his ministry, Jesus is shown traveling around performing many great miracles, attracting huge crowds, and entering Jerusalem in a way that points to his exalted station. Only before the High Priest Caiphas does he finally seem to indicate his messianic status, yet even here he speaks mysteriously of a "son of man" who will come on heavenly clouds;* meanwhile, there are other Gospel indications that he refused to answer his interrogators when questioned.

---

* An Aramaic metaphor meaning "with great success," according to George Lamsa.

Like Mark's presentation of the parables, all these enigmatic features in his Gospel appear to be a narrative strategy by the earliest evangelist, designed to encourage the perceptive reader to read "between the lines" about Jesus' identity and the meaning of his message. Here, it may be well to note the majority opinion of modern New Testament scholars that none of the four Gospel writers were eyewitness disciples.* Rather, the evangelists were almost certainly sophisticated Greek followers of the Way, writing in Koine Greek in the late first century, using some oral Aramaic traditions along with heavy reliance on midrashic interpretation of Old Testament "prophecies" to inform their narratives.**

Given this history of utilizing allegory and parable in the conveyance of the story of Christ, I would like to offer a brief look at some of the universal archetypal themes that find expression in the Gospels themselves. This is not meant as an invalidation of the historical, literal level, but as an unveiling and discussion of some of the deeper symbolic ramifications of the well-known story, much of which I believe the Gospel writers intentionally encoded into their texts. Some of this symbolism appears to be intended by the Gospel writers; the rest is subsequent exegesis at the metaphorical and psychological level.

ARCHETYPE *and* ALLEGORY
in the CHRIST STORY

According to the Gospel of Luke, the divine child is born into the natural world in lowly conditions, in a stable among the animals, while the angels celebrate the divine birth in the heavens. When the exalted human soul incarnates in the world, it is born into the lower realms of material bodies, with animal instincts and forgetfulness of its divine origin, as well as the joy of the heavenly hosts. As humanity thus slumbers in this state

---

*   This is based largely on the fact that Matthew and Luke appear to have relied heavily on Mark, who was not an eyewitness, and copied large portions of his text; and John's Gospel appears to have been written at least eighty years after the events described.
**   See Ps. 22, Zech. 9-14, Isa. 53, etc.

of spiritual darkness, the Christ child—representing the potential fullness of awakened human consciousness and loving compassion—is born, shining with the illumined awareness of this divine inheritance. The motif of the virgin birth shows the purity of heart necessary to bring forth the divine child and points transpersonally beyond an event that happened only in the past. As the fourteenth-century German mystic Meister Eckhart once declared in a Christmas homily:

> We are all meant to be mothers of God. What good is it to me if this eternal birth of the divine Son takes place unceasingly but does not take place within myself? And what good is it to me if Mary is full of grace if I am not also full of grace? What good is it to me for the Creator to give birth to his son if I also do not give birth to him in my time and my culture?

In Matthew, the story of the wise men indicates that the wise among us follow the star of the divine light and guidance that leads to the illumination of the soul. The motif of the tyrant (King Herod) who attempts to slay the divine child, represents the ego—who fears usurpation—and the forces of earthly opposition to the divine sovereignty. This is followed by a flight to Egypt and return, recalling Israel's captivity and exodus from Egypt in the time of Moses, and further suggesting the soul's bodily incarnation into the slavery of the lower self, followed by its liberation.

John the Baptist represents the teacher, the initiation, and the training needed for transformation; the rite of baptism symbolizes dying to the lower self in the ocean of God in anticipation of the rebirth and awakening of the greater Self, the divine inheritance within humanity. A dove descends which the evangelist identifies as the Holy Spirit descending upon Jesus.

Next, the same spirit that has descended upon Jesus at his baptism drives him into the wilderness. The temptation that follows is about battling ego inflation and the confrontation with one's own shadow energy. Jesus and Satan mythologically represent two sons, or two aspects of God the Father, and the light and dark aspects of oneself. Carl Jung understood the temptation story as the archetypal confrontation with the shadow which each of us must go through before tasting union. Jesus' refusal to grasp at divinity and personal power stands in contrast to the Biblical account of Adam and Eve yielding to this temptation when encouraged by the serpent; it also parallels Buddha's resistance to Mara's temptation under the Bodhi tree.* Significantly, the text indicates that the three temptations of Jesus are not literal, historical encounters but visionary representations, as one takes place on the pinnacle of the Temple in Jerusalem and another on a high mountain overlooking the entire world.

This episode is followed by Jesus' proclamation that the Kingdom of God is very close at hand, and the calling of the disciples, using the metaphor of becoming "fishers of men." In John's Gospel, he uses the phrase "eternal life" as a substitute term for kingdom, clarifying that "this is eternal life—to know God."[30] Then, in a series of healing stories, Mark's Gospel portrays Jesus as surpassing the similar miracles of his messianic forerunner, Elijah, by curing lepers, raising sick children from the dead, and so on, showing the immanence of the divine reign coming with power.

Viewed allegorically, the account of the feeding of the 5,000 shows how the people are spiritually fed by the Bread of Life and ΙΧΘΥΣ (Ichthus), the FISH (a well-known early Christian Greek acronym/acrostic, standing for "Jesus Christ, Son of God, Savior"), so that, in the end, the broken pieces (ie., of Israel) "with the FISH" were made into twelve overflowing baskets (ie, the restoration of the Twelve Tribes in the time of the Messiah.)

At the wedding at Cana, the "old" wine has run out and the ritual washing jars of water, symbolic of the old religious purification rites, are empty. Jesus asks for them to be refilled with water and transforms them into "new" and better wine, indicating

---

* Pir Vilayat featured the archetypal test of prophetic temptation, which is found in many sacred sacred traditions, as a key scene in "The Cosmic Celebration" pageant.

the transformative power of the divine spirit and the wine of divine love, the true fruits of religion.

When Jesus walks on the water, its shows metaphorically how the enlightened soul becomes the master of life and is able to traverse the troubled waters of life. The additional account of Peter walking on the water, which appears only in Matthew's Gospel, shows how the disciple, in the presence of his master, can also find this power within, but can easily sink when fear and the limiting egoic consciousness reassert themselves. The story symbolically demonstrates that access to the inner divine power is not exclusive to Jesus, in accord with the master's teaching that "whoever believes in me, those works which I have done he will also do, and he will do greater works than these. . . ."[31]

The narrative of Jesus raising Lazarus from the tomb illustrates the power of the Divine to bring a dead heart to life through love. Lazarus represents everyone who responds to the divine initiative and is raised from the grave of the limited self. The stone that is removed from the tomb is the blockage of the divine light by the ego self. The unwrapping of his grave-windings corresponds to his release from spiritual bondage; his calling forth from the tomb is his "yes" to the call of divine love. Christ's own intensity of love is indicated by the tears he sheds for his "dead" friend[32] and underscores God's compassion for humanity.

The account in John's Gospel of the woman charged with adultery, who is about to be stoned in the presence of Jesus, conveys the master's insight into the way we project our faults or shadow aspects onto others as scapegoats, in order to make ourselves feel better. Jesus deflates the crowd's self-righteousness and aborts the stoning with the words, "Let whoever is without sin cast the first stone." Matthew's Gospel contains many further sayings warning against hypocrisy and religious pride directed against the Pharisees, who symbolically represent the ego's tendency to experience ego inflation and to sanctimoniously look down on others. Jesus's quintessential statement on this subject is his query: "Why do you point out the speck in your brother's eye and do not notice the log in your own eye?"[33]

The episode in Matthew 18:21-22 in which Jesus advises Peter that he must forgive his brother, not merely seven times, but seven times seventy, points to the infinite forgiveness of the Father, and likewise provides a model for our own continual releasing of others from any distain or resentment we may harbor toward them. Yet, as Ghandi and Martin Luther King understood, forgiving and loving our enemies does not necessarily mean acquiescence with injustice, but always upholding the innate dignity of the other and abstaining from hatred, even when their actions must be opposed. Further light on the scriptural admonition to love others is conveyed by Reb Zalman, who clarifies that the Bible doesn't say, "Love your neighbor *as object*." The intended meaning is more like, have "love *unto* your neighbor," approaching everyone with a loving attitude, regardless of what they do with it.[34]

Another aspect of this teaching is given in the Sermon on the Mount, when Jesus extols the universal inclusiveness and unconditional love of the Divine Source, beyond limited human judgments. He says that the Father "makes his sun to rise on the evil and on the good, and sends rain on the just and on the unjust alike. . . . Be perfect, therefore, as your heavenly Father is perfect."[35] This is nondual teaching. The word "perfect" in Greek is *telios*, meaning to come to completion, to fulfill one's entire potential—to become fully human in the highest sense.

In this same discourse, Jesus also speaks of the light of God within: "You are the light of the world. A city set on a hill cannot be hidden; nor does anyone light a lamp and put it under a basket, but on the lampstand, and it gives light to all who are in the house."[36] The basket covering the light refers to the body and the physical world of the senses, which acts as a material cover over the core of divine light at the spiritual center of one's being. The basket also refers to the false sense of ego-self inasmuch as it veils the light of one's soul. The Gospel of Thomas expands the point: "Let whoever has ears listen! There is light existing within a person of light. And it enlightens the whole world: if it does not enlighten, that person is darkness."[37]

The further teaching is given that one must seek this light within oneself and bring it out, otherwise one will be overcome by the undertow of the material world: "If you bring forth what is within you, what you bring forth will save you. If you do not bring forth what is within you, what you do not bring forth will destroy you."[38] In Sufism, the seeker strives to access and increase the radiance of the divine light through concentration on the inner light and the divine attributes, such as compassion, insight, and other qualities leading to spiritual illumination.

The synoptic Gospels portray Jesus as teaching primarily through parabolic discourse. The Gospels, as usually translated, say that he taught with great authority (*mashal*) and not as the doctors of the law. Reb Zalman points out that, in Hebrew, the word *mashal* also refers to one who teaches by telling engaging stories and parables rather than by means of dry, religious legalisms.

The account of the cursing of the out-of-season fig tree in Mark's Gospel takes place just as Jesus is about to enter Jerusalem to challenge the religious authorities there. It is one of the clearest examples of what appears to be a parable about Jesus, and a kind of koan, as it makes little outward sense for the master to curse an out-of-season fig tree for not producing good fruit, and therefore likely has another intended meaning. Allegorically, it represents God decreeing that the old way of Temple worship in Jerusalem with its animal sacrifices is no longer in season and will thus be allowed to wither.

The clearing of the Temple which soon follows is symbolic of clearing away sclerosed forms of worship that have lost their living power as well as going beyond the limits of nationalism by proclaiming Isaiah's vision of God's house (meaning the entire world) as "a house of prayer for all people."[39] A further perspective on what is to supplant religious nationalism is found in John's Gospel, where he depicts Jesus informing a Samaritan woman that worship at Jerusalem and Mount Gezirim is to be replaced by "worshiping the Father in spirit and in truth."[40] Again, in the same Gospel, the reader is shown the juxtaposition of literal meaning with metaphor as the evangelist quotes Jesus' proclamation: "'Destroy this temple and in three days I will raise it up!' The Jews answered, 'It has taken forty-six years to build this temple and you will raise it up in three days?' But Jesus spoke of the temple of his body."[41]

Jesus also predicts the fall of Jerusalem, saying:

> And when you see Jerusalem surrounded by armies, then you will know that the time of its destruction has arrived. Then those who are in Judea must flee to the mountains, and those who are in the midst of the city must leave, and those who are in the country must not enter the city. For those are the days of vengeance and the fulfillment of all that is written.[42]

This passage suggests that, rather than predicting an apocalyptic end of the world, Jesus, like Jeremiah,[43] was warning that if there was no change of course among the corrupt Jewish authorities and hardline zealots, the military destruction of the earthly city of Jerusalem and its Temple by its enemies was inevitable—in this case, by the Romans. He advised the people to watch for the signs and to flee the city to safety before the time of its destruction. Here, the literal sense of the passage has too often been missed by assuming an apocalyptic, end-of-the-world symbolic interpretation which is more in keeping with the later Book of Revelation.

The Last Supper appears to have been a Jewish Passover seder in the earliest strata of tradition, with Jesus allegorically serving as the sacrificed Passover lamb. The first-century Christian document known as the *Didache* portrays the Last Supper as a Eucharistic meal of thanksgiving, and, like the Gospels of Luke and John, does not link Jesus' death to a blood atonement for the forgiveness of sins. The earliest Jewish idea of *zechuth,* or substitutionary atonement, involved forgiveness granted due to the great merit and righteousness of the one who intercedes, as seen in Abraham's prayer that Sodom and Gomorrah would be spared for the sake of ten righteous men. Isaiah 53:12 speaks of the suffering righteous servant who "bore the sin of many, and makes intercession for the transgressors." The Epistle to the Hebrews points to Jesus' death as the one ultimate sacrifice for all time which replaces the repeated animal offerings of the priests in the Temple. However, the statement, found only in Mark and Matthew's Gospel, that Jesus gave his life as "a ransom for many," has less scriptural precedent and may possibly reflect an early strand of Marcionite theology.*

The references to eating the body of Christ and drinking the wine of his blood recalls the age-old fruit and nectar of immortality that unites the seeker with the Divine, a prominent theme in

---

*   Marcion was a popular early second-century Christian leader who compiled the first New Testament cannon, consisting of one Gospel, a number of epistles by Paul, and a commentary called the *Apostolicon*. Paul's letters appear to have been largely forgotten until their Marcionite revival around 120-140 CE, and it was Marcion's publication that brought forth in response an alternative Orthodox collection comprising the full New Testament canon known today. (The Book of Revelation was canonized later.) The early Church Fathers rejected and suppressed Marcion's version, which is now lost to posterity, except where extensively quoted by its critics. Yet not all strains of Marcionite theology were successfully purged from the final canon. Marcion's proto-gnostic understanding of Paul, which was mostly rejected by the Church, involved a ditheistic conception in which the Jewish law, having been received "through angels and entrusted to a mediator"(Gal. 3:19), was no longer binding upon "saved" Christians because of a new higher revelation from a previously hidden Supreme God (the Father), Who had, in the person of Jesus, taken on the "likeness of a man" (Phil. 2:8), and, having purposely kept his true messianic identity a secret, was murdered at the hands of the lower-level "god of this world" and his *archons* (rulers over the earth), who didn't realize who they were killing. As Paul says in I Corinthians 2:8, those "who are mature in wisdom" understand this as "a mystery, a hidden wisdom which God predestined before the ages to our glory; the wisdom which none of the *archons* of this age understood; for if they had understood they would not have crucified the Lord of glory." Key to this whole interpretation of Christian salvation was the "ransom" of "saved" souls, whose release from the power of lower level principalities the High God the Father was able to secure as restitutionary compensation for the unwitting deicide that occurred when the High Father God, appearing in the "likeness" of Jesus, submitted to self-sacrifice on the cross, out of love for humans who were enslaved by the powers of sin. The atoning victory of the cross over spiritual slavery and death, as Paul says in Ephesians 6:12, was not won against enemies of flesh and blood, "but against principalities, against powers, against the *archons* of the darkness of this world, against spiritual wickedness in high places." The Church soon rejected Marcion's view because it implied an unacceptable bifurcation of God the Father into an "Old Testament" God of strict law and justice (with primarily Gevurah qualities) and a separate "New Testament" God of love and mercy (Hesed and Tipheret). This now little-known heretical view, which arose during the earliest period of the transmission of the Gospel and Paul's epistles, may offer the most cogent theological context for understanding the few references in the New Testament to Christ's death as "a ransom for many."

early mythology, from Gilgamish to Genesis. The mocking and torture of Jesus again links him to the idea of the suffering servant of Isaiah 53. Yet, this archetype this does not just describe the suffering messiah. As Reb Zalman once advised me: "We are all Isaiah 53." The ego is mortified but the greater Self is able to endure it.

The cross itself is a *conjunctio* symbol of ego and Self, or soul. The vertical human body, with arms outstretched and fastened to the cross, illustrates the way that the soul is, to a great extent, bound by limitations in this world of matter, decay and eventual death. The two thieves who are crucified on either side of Christ, one good and one bad, reflect Christ's reconciliation of light and shadow. Carl Jung saw in the cross the union of opposites and a representation of the quaternity, the four directions as emblematic of wholeness. Esoterically, the cross is an ancient pre-Christian religious symbol representing the point of intersection of the vertical line (the eternal aspect of divinity), and the horizontal line (indicative of the plane of temporal earthly life). From the human point of view, the sacred symbol of the cross carries the meaning, "I am not, Thou art (O God),"and "Not my will but Thine."[44]

Until the Middle Ages, images of Christ crucified were rare. In the earliest cross depictions, the images tended to show an empty cross and the impersonal Christ unharmed and triumphant as savior. The same idea is portrayed in some of the gnostic gospels (such as the *Acts of John*) where, during the crucifixion, the Christ spirit comes and assures his most intimate disciple that his immortal spirit is untouched by the immolation of the body of Jesus.

If we look at the meaning of the crucifixion from the level of the four worlds, the above statement reflects something of the gnostic perspective—the human side of Jesus suffers and dies on the cross, but the soul of Christ, which is divine, never dies.* The revelation, in gnostic terms, is the good news that the deepest level of the human soul, which is divine, has eternal life and cannot

---

* Qur'an 4:157 could also be understood as pointing to this mystical understanding when it says: "They slew him not nor crucified him, but it appeared so unto them."

die. When we die to the limited sense of the false self, the divinity of the soul emerges, spiritually resurrecting us from the dead and revealing us as children of God and co-heirs with Christ.

On the physical level, the human Jesus, a prophet and Messiah of Israel, dies as a martyr, is buried, and, through various vivid waking visions and revelations, his disciples experience him as resurrected, as the Living One. On the affect/relational level, Christ reveals the divine heart of compassion by laying down his life out of love for humanity, showing that God truly cares for us.

But there is an even deeper ramification than the image of a Father God sacrificing His only son out of love. Since Christ is by Christian doctrine fully human and fully divine, this points to the vital understanding that it is the very being of God Who undergoes suffering in humanity. The One Divine Being, Who, as Augustine said, "is closer to us than we are to ourselves," has entered into the drama of human life and, through each of us, is experiencing the pain and joy of life in solidarity with all humanity and all life. In God's immanent aspect as *Immanuel* ("God with us"), God is with us in our suffering and in our happiness and bliss and is never separate from us. It is only our limited ego consciousness that feels alienated from the Source, in Whom the Apostle Paul says "we live and move and have our being."[45] It is that limited sense of the false self which feels separate from God that must die to enter into Life abundant. All of this and more is symbolized in the at-one-ment of the cross. On the highest level, Christ is one with the Father, the Divine Source. This is why Jesus prays for his followers and all humanity, "that they may all be one; even as You, Father, are in me and I in You, that they also may be in Us. . ."[46]

In Mark's Gospel, the women who visit the tomb on Easter morning are told: "Do not be amazed; you are looking for Jesus the Nazarene, who has been crucified. He has risen; he is not here; behold, here is the place where they laid him."[47] Esoterically, the body refers to the outward, visible form, the exoteric Jesus, and conveys the message that the search for the body of Jesus, or any reductive fixation upon the historical person of Jesus, misses the power of the living Christ and the whole archetypal significance of what is being portrayed.

While it may be helpful to some believers to picture Jesus outwardly as a friend and counselor in their daily lives, this approach has the drawback of keeping one in the conventional mind-world of separate ego identities and does not sufficiently penetrate into the transformative depths at the core of the timeless Christian mystery. Paul teaches that Jesus Christ represents the head of the collective, corporate being of the Messiah, and all who "put on the mind of Christ" comprise his mystical body. Those who find and inwardly activate the divine Christ archetype, discover themselves as sons and daughters of God with resurrected hearts and illumined minds. This indwelling of the Divine Presence is alluded to in the words of Revelations 21:3: "And I heard a great voice out of heaven saying, 'Behold, the tabernacle of God is with humanity and God will make a dwelling place there.'"

As an archetype, Christ represents the divine Self at the core of humanity, the true Self which resurrects from the tomb of the conventional self. The crucifixion of Christ represents all the ways in which humanity is limited and suffers: addictions, political repression, slavery, injustice, natural disasters, disease, and various other personal and collective crosses that we bear. It also includes the environmental damage we inflict on the planet. Resurrection represents the release, the healing liberation that can occur, the spiritual sovereignty of the soul, the movement toward greater freedom and love in our own lives that comes with the embodiment of the Christ spirit, or true Self. The author of *The Cloud of Unknowing* says that, at the deepest level, the cross which Jesus says we must take up is really our own limited self. The willingness of Jesus to accept martyrdom represents selfless love in action, voluntarily sacrificing one's own life for the sake of others. In the meantime, the whole of humanity remains, in some sense, asleep, waiting to spiritually awaken and midwife the divinity hidden within its own nature. As Paul says: "The whole creation is eagerly waiting for God to reveal His children. . . . From the beginning till now the entire creation has been groaning in one great act of giving birth."[48]

The Gospel of Thomas contains a powerful saying of Jesus that can be taken as a meditation on the cosmic dimension of the Christ spirit.

> I am the light that is over all. I am the All. The All came forth out of me and to me All attained. Split the wood and I am there. Lift the stone, and there you will find me.[49]

Meditating on the verse with eyes closed (especially outdoors), one can allow the frontiers of one's consciousness to expand without limit, and experience one's own resonance with the all-pervading Spirit, united with the trees, stones, earth and the uncreated Source of Light that is behind the light of this world.

SOME FINAL THOUGHTS *from* REB ZALMAN

My own experience within the Christian faith has included growing up in a Protestant family, leaving the Church during my college years, and later reinvolving myself in several Christian denominations, including several years as a cantor in the Eastern Orthodox Church. Over the years, in working out my own relationship with my Christian inheritance, I occasionally consulted with Reb Zalman, whose advice was always helpful. He provided a perspective from outside the religion which was sympathetic and he was even intrigued by some aspects of Christianity and "the Nazarene Rebbe." He felt, that despite the antipathy that had historically developed between the two faiths, there was far more overlap than difference between Christianity and Judaism. He had developed friendships with many Christians over the years and was very drawn to the beauty and form of the mass. His Dominican friend Matthew Fox said he once witnessed Reb Zalman reciting the entire mass in Latin![50]

Reb Zalman was also fond of reciting the Our Father prayer in the original Aramaic language,* and he encouraged his Sufi colleague Neil Douglas-Klotz in his work of creating a Christian dance cycle (blending Jewish daavening and Sufi zikr movements) to the sung/chanted words of the Aramaic prayer of Jesus. Reb Zalman confessed that, at Christmas, he too could relish the Christian contemplation of the Divine in the form of a baby. He also related how he was once moved to tears as he stood gazing at an exquisite brown sandstone pieta in Germany, for it struck a deep Jewish chord in him reminiscent of Rachel's weeping for her children, which he further saw as the Shekhinah, the feminine Divine Presence in exile.

From the Jewish perspective, he felt that Jesus fit better the early Jewish model of the suffering Messiah who was the son of Joseph, *Mashiah ben Yosef*—the Tzadik (wise one) who is killed before the final restoration—rather than the triumphant kingly Davidic Messiah who is called the Messiah of the Penitence and is the final redeemer. "Reb Yeshu of Nazareth was a great and holy Rebbe and he, *nebah* [alas], died young . . . a martry's death; and that's what we call a Mashiah ben Yosef. In other words, . . . it is said he has to die. He is the righteous servant of Isaiah 53, who bears upon himself the sins of people."[51] But beyond that, as he explained to me, Reb Zalman saw the concept of the messiah, or *mashiah*, as something that was, in some ways fulfilled, yet not exhausted, by the coming of Jesus, since clearly the world has not yet been fully redeemed of suffering, which is part of the messianic job description. The lion has not yet metaphorically lain down with the lamb, so there is a sense in which Jews and the people of the world are still waiting for redemption; Christians too still await a second coming to finish the job.

When Jonas Salk came up with the vaccine for polio, Reb Zalman once offered, that was the coming of the messiah for polio. King Cyrus, who freed the exiled Babylonian Jews to

---

*   Some of the petitions of the Our Father prayer are reflective of the ancient Kaddish prayer ("Glorified and sanctified be God's great name. . . . May He establish His kingdom speedily in our days. . . .") which is in Aramaic and traditionally chanted as a doxology at the end of the Jewish prayer service and also prayed by mourners.

return to Israel, is also called a messiah of God in Isaiah 45:1. Seen this way, the messianic function is not just confined to one person for all time, but is more like a role one assumes for a time like a president, king, Sufi murshid or a *qutb*. Reb Zalman said he viewed Jesus as a *soter* (a savior who mediates for people) and a *Neshamah clolius*, a great soul who, from a Jewish perspective, could be seen as fulfilling the messianic role for at least three years. As for Jesus' own understanding of his messiahship and the divine intention, Zalman advised me that God moves each of us to fulfill a certain destiny but doesn't necessarily reveal more than we need to know pertaining to the future outcome of events. Yet whatever it was Jesus did and understood about his mission, he "was so perfectly guided by God in playing out his role in that situation that it has been possible for millions of people to have a window of transcendence—and that is plenty!"[52]

We conclude with Reb Zalman's further perceptions from an early work entitled, *The First Step: A Guide for the New Jewish Spirit,* which is followed by final words from Pir Vilayat Khan. Reb Zalman distinguishes between the issue of Jesus as Jewish Messiah and the experience that he models as "Son of God," which is potentially available to all who, like David, discover themselves to be a child of God, a recipient of the divine love and blessing. "Many people who are 'born again,' don't know that there is more than one brand of that experience available. Being born again is getting plugged into the universe, and no single religion has a monopoly on the universe."

Where the Christian has the experience of atonement through the power of intercession by Jesus, Reb Zalman says the Jew finds this experience through Yom Kippur, the Day of Atonement, which is not limited to only one day a year but "exists all the time." This forgiveness is associated with:

> the historical moment when our people had the first total born-again experience—the exodus from Egypt. That was when we "heard" God say in the desert, "You are forgiven." This voice comes to us from the totality of our

tradition, but also from deep within ourselves." . . . David sings in the Psalms as having heard the Voice proclaim: "You are my child. Today I have begotten you." . . . When a person "hears" this, birthing has begun. But to stop the process at this point would leave the soul in infancy. Being born again is not enough; you have to grow up too. All growth happens in stages. First you grow through the stage of "the land of milk and honey," when the world sings and supports the newly born God-spark within you. The feeling is intoxicating. Some people are so addicted to this phase that they move from one spiritual path and leader to another, hoping to avoid the next phase, when the path becomes discipline. . . . In the next phase, you are filled with excitement and enthusiasm as you tune into all the symbols of the tradition [and share with others of like mind, working] toward the establishment of a holy community. And there is more growth ahead as you move toward the maturity of the soul, the phase in which you live in intimate closeness with the Beloved.[58]

We end with the words of Pir Vilayat, who felt a deep lifelong connection with the heart of Christ. He often invoked the example of the forgiving spirit of Christ when encouraging people to let go of old resentments that weigh them down and hinder their unfoldment. The words below, garnered from a 1984 Universal Worship Service at the Abode, were extemporaneously uttered over the soft strains of Victoria's *Kyrie Eleison* and evoke the true spirit of Christ beyond considerations of theology and history:

How can we find Christ today? Not then, but today. In that man in the Washington D.C. accident, [who dived in repeatedly to save others] when so many were caught in the frozen water—in that man who gave his place to others to come first before him—that's where you find the spirit of Christ today. In the father of Iman (Ibrahim-Kiss], who was being tortured twice—by the Nazis and by the Russians—and who, in both case, was forgiving the man who was torturing him. That's where we find Christ living in our time. We find his spirit in that woman who crossed the street when that child ran across the street, and lost her life in order to save the child. We find it in the fireman who risked his life to save a child in the third floor of a burning house. That's where we see the spirit of Christ. We see it in that priest who was in a concentration camp and tried to celebrate mass, and he was beaten by the Nazis, and then he returned to where he was and celebrated the mass even more fervently than he did before! That's where we find the spirit of Christ! And we can find it in ourselves.

ENDNOTES

[1] Matt. 5:44-45

[2] Athanasius, *De Incarnatione,* 54, 3.

[3] Qur. 2:115.

[4] Qur. 50:16

[5] Jn. 19:36, etc.

[6] Matt. 5:38-9.

[7] Mk. 9:13.

[8] Mk. 9:2-13.

[9] I Cor. 1:24.

[10] Jn. 8:58

[11] New Dimensions Radio; Joseph Campbell interview with Michael Toms: "Myth, Personal Dreams, and Universal Themes," 1975.

[12] Khan, Hazrat Inayat, *The Complete Sayings of Hazrat Inayat Khan;* Gayan/Talas, 616, p.71.

[13] Retract. I, xiii, cited by Dr. Alvin Boyd Kuhn in his *Shadow of the Third Century,* Elizabeth, NJ: Academy Press, 1949, p.3.

[14] Eusebius, *Hist. Eccl.* lib. 2, ch. v.

[15] I Cor. 15:31.

[16] Gal. 2:20.

[17] Lk. 17:21.

[18] 1 Jn. 3:1.

[19] Lk. 22:42.

[20] *Bereshit Rabbah* 20:12.

[21] *Bereshit Rabbah* 8:10.

[22] Qur. 2:34.

[23] Mk. 3:29.

[24] Deut. 18:15-19.

[25] Jn. 14:25-31, 16:12-15, etc.

[26] 2 Cor. 2:6-7.

[27] Heb. 8:5.

[28] Crossan, J.D., *A Long Way from Tipperary*, Harper One; 2000, pp.167-8.

[29] Mk. 4:11-12.

[30] Jn. 17:3.

[31] Jn. 14:12.

[32] Jn. 11:35.

[33] Matt. 7:3.

[34] From a 1986 interview with Fran Silbiger-Orrok entitled "Kabbalah Basics."

[35] Matt. 5:45-46,48.

[36] Matt. 5:14-15.

[37] Thom. 24.

[38] Thom. 70.

[39] Isa. 56:7.

[40] Jn. 4:23.

[41] Jn. 2:19-21.

[42] Lk. 21-20-21.

[43] Jer. 38:17.

[44] Lk. 22:42.

[45] Acts 17:28.

[46] Jn. 17:21.

[47] Mk. 16:6.

[48] Rom. 8:14, 19, 22.

[49] Thom. 77.

[50] From an internet article entitled "Remembering Reb Zalman– Members of our Tikkun Community Share Their Memories." Available at: http://www.tikkun.org/nextgen/remembering-reb-zalman-members-of-our-tikkun-community-share-their-memories. In an unpublished collection of Reb Zalman's writings entitled "Mareh Kohen," in a 1993 interview with Michael Paley and William Novak, Reb Zalman says:

When I was at the Lama Foundation, I felt free to say mass. When I found out that they didn't have a Christian resident there, that all these people hadn't had mass in a while, I celebrated the mass without any problems. It was the first time that I was the celebrant.

[51] From the author's conversation with Reb Zalman in Washington, DC, in 1989. Some of these issues are also discussed in chapter 4 of *Paradigm Shift*, which is entitled "Jesus in Jewish-Christian-Moslem Dialogue."

[52] *Ibid.*

[53] Schachter-Shalomi, *The First Step: A Guide for the New Jewish Spirit,* pp. 117-19.

APPENDIX C

Waza'if and Sephirot by Pir Zalman Schachter-Shalomi

Waza'if to be used in conjunction with the kabbalistic *sephirot,* as discerned by Pir-o-Nagid Zalman Suleyman Schachter-Shalomi, *z'l,* and given to Pir-o-Nagid Netanel Mu'in ad-Din Miles-Yépez.*

SUNDAY (10 x) *Ya Rahim* (O Mercy) concentrating on *Hesed,* the divine quality called "loving-kindness," which gives and receives freely.

MONDAY (10 x) *Allah hu-Akbar* (God is Greater) concentrating on *Gevurah,* the divine quality called "strength," which creates boundaries.

TUESDAY (10 x) *Ya Rahman* (O Compassion) concentrating on *Tipheret,* the divine quality called "beauty," which balances the sometimes over permissive, unboundaried quality of *Hesed,* and the sometimes overly strict or severely boundaried *Gevurah.*

WEDNESDAY (10 x) *Ya Mansur* (O Victory) concentrating on *Netzah,* the divine quality called "victory," which is raw efficacy.

---

* On one occasion, these were also prescribed to be used daily, one per week over seven weeks (49 days).

THURSDAY (10 x) *Ya Jamil* (O Beauty) concentrating on *Hod*, the divine quality called "glory," which is pure elegance.

FRIDAY (10 x) *Ya Wadud* (O Lover) concentrating on *Yesod*, the divine quality called "foundation," which balances the sometimes rough and raw efficacy of *Netzah*, and the sometimes ineffectively elegance of *Hod*, in an efficient effectiveness.

SATURDAY (10 x) *Ya Malik* (O Sovereign) concentrating on *Malkhut*, the divine quality called "sovereignty," the place of the world and all action.

GLOSSARY

Apophatic theology—Negative theology; relating to the Divine through the negation of concepts, words and stories that are meant to explain the Divine. In Latin it is called the *via negativa* (negative way), and is the opposite of kataphatic theology, or *via positiva,* which attempts to understand the Divine by affirmations and positive descriptions. The fourteenth-century Christian work *The Cloud of Unknowing* is an example of the apophatic approach, as is the famous Taoist verse from the Tao Te Ching, "The Tao which can be described is not the eternal Tao."

Axial Age (800-200 BCE)—A concept coined by Karl Jaspers in his 1949 book, *The Origin and Goal of History.* The phrase refers to the pivotal era culminating around 500-600 BCE when the ritualistic theology and philosophy of the Old World began to change to become more inwardly oriented, focusing on individual liberation and salvation. Many of the world's great religious founders, philosophers, and prophets appeared during this era.

Centering Prayer—Used by many modern Christians, Centering Prayer is a method of meditation based on traditional monastic practice, which places a strong emphasis on interior silence, observing and letting go of thoughts as they arise, and using an anchoring seed-thought such as "peace," "stillness" or any sacred word as an aid to maintanining inner silence. These meditations are especially useful for lay people who can do them for 20 to 30 minutes, once or twice a day. The name was taken from

Thomas Merton's description of contemplative prayer as being "centered entirely on the presence of God," and the meditation has become popular among Christians since the early 1970s through the efforts of Trappist Abbot Father Thomas Keating and his associates. (There is a beautiful film available online of Father Thomas and Reb Zalman in conversation lovingly musing on various mystical topics. It is entitled *The Kiss of God: A Dialogue of Devoutness Between Father Thomas Keating and Rabbi Zalman Schachter-Shalomi.*)

Chishtiyya, Chishti Order—The Chishti Order is a Sufi Order with its roots in Sunni Islam and the older Adhamiyya Order. The Chishtiyya advocates love, tolerance, and openness, and utilizes Qawwali music in its practice. It arose in the town of Chisti in Afghanistan and its most famous pir is Khwaja Moinuddin Chishti (1142-1236), whose venerable tomb is in Ajmer, India. Although schooled in four branches of Sufism, Hazrat Inayat Khan traced his spiritual lineage primarily through the Chishtiyya; however, his Western-oriented Inayati Sufism is now distinct from the more traditional Chishti Order, which continues today, primarily in India.

Zikr—The word "zikr" (dhikr) means "remembrance" and is the name of an essential Sufi practice, done individually or in a group, usually involving the chanting of *Tawhid*—the phrase of unity from the Qur'an: "La ilaha ilallah," meaning: "Nothing exists but Divine Reality," or "There are no separate deities (or independent selves), but only the One Being (called Allah in Arabic)." The practice is used to go beyond one's limited sense of ego separation and lose oneself in the Divine Unity. The communal dervish zikr may be done in circles or standing in rows and may also include whirling, the chanting of various divine names and the singing of mystic hymns.

Emanationism—The idea in Neoplatonism that everything flows forth from the One, the First Principle. Plotinus (ca.204-270 CE) is the most famous exponent of emanationism. In his

Enneads, the phenomenal world is seen as emanating from the One Eternal Absolute, with the finest gradations of spirit congealing into more limited state of the material word. Emanationism stands in contrast to the creationist idea that everything was created *ex-nihilo* in the distant past by a transcendent higher power, and the scientific materialist view. Inayati Sufism takes a kind of middle ground, viewing all life and creation as constantly sustained by and flowing forth from the Source of Being, with nothing existing which is separate from the One.

Exclusivism—Religious exclusivism holds that one particular religion or sect possesses the one and only truth and way to salvation, and holds that all other faiths and philosphies are misguided, inadequate, or even demonically inspired. From this perspective, religious pluralism, interfaith sharing, and ecumenical dialogue are discouraged.

Fundamentalism—Religious fundamentalism refers to a somewhat rigid and literalistic interpretation of one's faith tradition, typically rejecting modern innovations and updated interpretations in favor of a set of beliefs and dogmas formulated during an earlier era, when the faith was supposedly "pure." Fundamentalists strive to maintain or recapture the "old-time religion" of the founder and earliest disciples and authorities of the faith, and typically emphasize one "correct" set of beliefs.

Gematria—The system used by Kabbalists to indicate the numerical value of Hebrew letters and words in order to discover added meaning, for example, in two different words of equivalent numerical value. The first Hebrew letter, *aleph* (a), has the number value of 1, *bayt* (b) is 2, and so on.

Gurdjieff's Fourth Way—George Ivanovitch Gurdjieff (ca.1872-1949) was a mystic philosopher, spiritual teacher and author of Armenian and Greek descent who transmitted from various ancient sources, including Sufism, an eclectic body of teachings designed to awaken consciousness and go beyond the traditional religious methods of the fakir, monk, and yogi to what Gurdjieff called the "Fourth Way." Reb Zalman often referred to Gurdjieff's teaching, particularily his schema of the levels of consciousness and his emphasis on the Law of Seven and the Law of Three (what Oscar Icazo would later call "Trilectics"). The latter principle, like Hegelain dialectics, and the three columns of the Sephirotic tree, emphasizes the middle way—a third reconciling or synthesizing force which is needed to go beyond the duality of opposites to a more balanced solution, or synthesis. Gurdjieff called these forces Holy affirming, Holy denying, and Holy reconciling.

Halveti-Jerrahi Order—An Ottoman Turkish Sufi Order founded by Pir Nureddin al-Jerrahi (1678-1720). The nineteenth grandsheikh of the order was Muzaffer Efendi of Istanbul, who visited America often in the early 1980s and initiated Reb Zalman as a *muhib*, or friend of the order. During that period, Reb Zalman often joined Muzaffer Efendi and the Jerrahi dervishes in their ceremonies of zikr (remembrance).

Halakha—This term refers to the precedents of Jewish law collectively drawn from the oral and written Torah, Talmudic and rabbinic law. The word literally means "the way to walk" (and how to behave) based on 613 *mitzvot* (commandments or good deeds). Halakha is the Jewish equivalent of Islamic shariah, which focuses not only on laws to keep but also on good etiquettes (*adab*), charity, and so on.

Hanifiyyah—According to Islamic tradition, there were devout monotheists known as *hanifs* in Arabia during and preceding the time of the Prophet Muhammad, who upheld the true religion of the One God taught by Abraham. They were not doctrinally Jews or Christians, but believed in the Divine Unity even in the Age of Ignorance and were held in great esteem by the Prophet.

Hasidism, Hasid—The word "Hasid" is derived from *Hesed*, or loving kindness, and is the designation given to Jewish mystics of various eras, such as the followers of the Ba'al Shem Tov (1698-1760) and Reb Shneur Zalman of Laidi (1745-1812) in Eastern Europe. The latter was the founding Rebbe of the Habad branch of Hasidism, which was Reb Zalman's lineage. A Hasid is the Jewish equivalent of a Sufi Dervish; the former follows a rebbe and the latter follows a sheikh or murshid (or the feminine equivalents). Generally, both sing mystic hymns, make prayers, practice a form of sacred dance or movement, belong to mystical orders, and revere the prophet Abraham, and the Jewish prophets.

Hermeneutics—In the religious context, hermaneutics refers to the interpretation of scripture, also called the exegesis of scripture, or the meaning that is drawn from a passage.

Hesychast—Refers to the mystical tradition of contemplative prayer in Eastern Orthodox Chrisitianity, beginning with the early Desert Fathers and Mothers and the ascetics of Cappadocia.

Immanence—In theological terms, it refers to the presence of the Divine in or encompassing the material world and dwelling within humanity, in contrast to Divine transcendence.

Inayati-Maimuni Order—A modern spiritual order (*tariqat*) combining the Sufi lineage of Hazrat Inayat Khan (1882-1927) with the Hasidic lineage of Rabbi Israel ben Eliezer, the Ba'al Shem Tov (1698-1760). The order was founded by Pir Zalman Suleyman Schachter-Shalomi and his *khalif* Netanel Miles-Yépez in 2004 in the spirit of the original Egyptian Sufi-Hasidism practiced by Rabbi Maimuni of Fustat (1186-1237), the son of Maimonides. The current head of the order is Pir Netanel Mu'in ad-Din Miles-Yépez.

Interspirituality—A term coined by Wayne Teasdale, a Christian contemplative and the author of *The Mystic Heart*, to describe the recent trend toward spiritual pluralism or "hyphenated spirituality," as Reb Zalman sometimes called it. For instance,

Brother Teasdale's spiritual teacher, Father Bede Griffiths, led a Benedictine Christian monastic community in India which incorporated elements of Hindu meditation and devotional readings from the *Upanishads* and *Bhagavad Gita* along with Biblical readings and prayer, combining the contemplative wisdom of the East with the love that is characteristic of the Abrahamic faiths in the West. Sri Ramakrishna could perhaps be regarded as the first modern exemplar of this pluralistic approach to the Divine. Hazrat Inayat Khan also taught the unity of all religions and utilized meditations, practices and scriptures from the world's major religions. Today, there is an increasing number of Jewish-Sufis, Jewish-Buddhists, Christian-Sufis, and so on, as discussed in this book. The common factor is the one essential religion or perennial wisdom that underlies the various historical faith traditions.

Jalal—An Arabic word referring to the strong, powerful qualities. For instance, a tsunami or a waterfall would be a jalal condition of water. A person with a fiery disposition has jalal qualities.

Jamal—An Arabic word referring to the beautiful, gentle qualities. For instance, a soft rain or still lake would be a jamal condition of water. A person who is mild-mannered and kind has jamal qualities. A perfect balance of jamal and jalal is called kamal.

Jewish Renewal Movement—A modern Jewish movement of which Reb Zalman Schatcher-Shalomi could be called the "father," which endeavors to reinvigorate modern Judaism with Kabbalistic and Hasidic practice. It incorporates music (traditional, new, and often English-translated), meditation, egalitarian and pacifist ideals, environmentalism, and ecumenicism in an attempt to reinvigorate traditional Judaism from what it views as a somewhat dry, rationalistic, and uninspired condition in the post-Holocaust era. The movement is transdenominational and distinct from Orthodox, Reformed, Conservative, and Reconstructionist Judaism, but its advocates may be found within diverse Jewish congregations. The earliest

Renewal organization founded by Reb Zalman was called B'nai Or, named after the "sons of light" mentioned in the Dead Sea Scrolls. The name was soon altered to P'nai Or, "Faces of Light" to reflect the egalitarian approach. In 1993, it merged with the Shalom Center, founded by Rabbi Arthur Waskow, another Jewish Renewal pioneer and activist, to become ALEPH: Alliance for Jewish Renewal.

Jinn (djinn)—According to Qur'anic teaching, among the beings of the unseen world there are, besides angels (who are made of light and unfailingly obey the divine will), beings in the mind world called jinn (known as genies in the West, from the word genius). They are said to be made of "smokeless fire" and, like humans, have free choice to do right and wrong. Thus in Islam, Iblis (Satan) is considered a jinn rather than a fallen angel. Jinns are said to possess great creativity, are able to appear in our world (often in animal form), and can make things temporarily appear out of thin air. They can assist humans or alternatively lead them astray. The Prophet Muhammad is said to have preached to the jinns, who were hungry for the knowledge of salvation.

Kabbalah—Kabbalah is the esoteric tradition of Judaism and comes from the Hebrew root *KaBeL*, meaning "to receive," or "received tradition." What is received by the mystical inner tradition is the oral teachings of the Torah which have been handed down along with the written Torah (and rabbinic writings). Two of the most important foundational Kabbalistic texts are the *Zohar* and *Sepher Yetzirah*. Kabbalistic teaching is varied and includes the understanding of the four worlds, PaRDeS (the four levels of scripture), the sephirotic Tree of Life, Gematria (the system of Hebrew letter-numbers), and Merkabah mysticism (based on Ezekiel's vision of the divine throne) among its many teachings. Other non-Jewish expressions of Kabbalah (or Qabbala) include Christian, New Age, and Occult/Esoteric Western adaptations.

Kenosis—The process of "self-emptying" of one's own will and becoming entirely receptive to the divine will. The term is found in the Greek text of Phillipians 2:7, where Jesus is described as having made himself nothing (or letting go of his personal self), rather than grasping at divinity. In the Sufi tradition, this is called *fana;* in Kabbalistic tradition, it is called *bittul ha'yeshi.*

Lubavitcher—The word "Lubavitch" means the "city of brother-ly love" in Russian and is the name of the town in White Russia where this Hasidic branch first arose under the leadership of Reb Schneur Zalman of Liadi (1745–1812). The movement is also known as Habad-Lubavitch, HaBaD being an acronym of three of the sephirot: Hesed, Binah, and Da'at (combining loving-kind-ness with wisdom and knowledge). The movement migrated to America during the early 1940s, when the sixth Lubavitcher Rebbe, Rabbi Yosef Yitzchak Schneersohn (1880–1950)—who was Reb Zalman's first rebbe—immigrated and settled in the Crown Heights section of Brooklyn, New York, and gathered many Hasidic students around him in community. After his passing in 1950, his son-in-law, Rabbi Menachem Mendel Schneerson (1902–1994), succeeded him as the guiding rebbe of the commu-nity. Today, the orginazation refers to itself as Chabad.

Mahatma—Sanskrit term for a "great soul."

Mantra—A Sanskrit word meaning a word or sound used as a meditative aid, such as OM or a phrase from the Vedas. The Sufi equivalent would be chanting or intoning one of the divine names (*esmas*) or attributes such as *Ya Rahman, Ya Rahim, Hu,* or Allah. When given as a daily practice such a word may be re-ferred to as a *wazifa.*

Mitzvah (plural: mitzvot)—Hebrew word for "commandment" which carries the sense of "a praiseworthy deed." Specifically, there are 613 mitzvot dervived from the Biblical account of the laws of Moses; 365 are prohibitions and 248 are positive commandments.

Murid (mureed)—A Sufi initiate under the guidance of a mur-shid(a), sheikh(a) or spiritual guide.

Murshid, Pir-o-Murshid—An Arabic word for "guide" or spiritual teacher. It is loosely equivalent to the title "sheikh" (shaykh), or grand-sheikh, and may indicate the head of a Sufi Order (*tariqat*). In Ottoman usage, the title "pir" indicates the founder of a tariqat. Many in the Inayati Order, including Pir Vilayat, have commonly referenced Pir-o-Murshid Hazrat Inayat Khan simply as "Murshid."

Panentheism—Literally, this word means "all-in-God," refer-ring to the idea that all that exists is in God and God is in all. The additional "en" nuances the term and subtly distinguish-es it from *pantheism* ("everything that exists *is* God"). The word panentheism retains the sense of God's transcendence *and* im-manence, acknowledging that God is simultaneously transcen-dent of the physical universe and present within it. The idea is that the Divine is all there is, the everlasting, omnipresent, infinite Source which fills and encompasses the entire universe; yet the Source of Being is not simply equivalent to the physical world, but is "greater than" and independent of the creation. The teaching of the four levels of Divine Reality in Kabbalah and Sufism makes it clear that the Divine Source is the progen-itor and sustainer of the physical world in the world of Assiyah/Shariat yet also transcends the world in Atzilut/Hakikat, all of which is implied in the term *panentheism*.

Perennial Philosophy—The term *philosophia perennis* was first used during the Renaissance, by Agostino Steuco, and later by the philosopher Liebniz. It was popularized in the twenti-eth century through Aldous Huxley's 1945 classic, *The Perennial Philosophy*. Perennialists use the word to refer to the essential universal spiritual teachings found in all the great religious tra-ditions. On the opening page of *The Perennial Philosophy*, Huxley defined the term as:

the metaphysic that recognizes a divine Reality substantial to the world of things and lives and minds; the psychology that finds in the soul something similar to, or even identical to, divine Reality; the ethic that places man's final end in the knowledge of the immanent and transcendent Ground of all being; the thing is immemorial and universal. Rudiments of the perennial philosophy may be found among the traditional lore of primitive peoples in every region of the world, and in its fully developed forms it has a place in every one of the higher religions.

Postmodern Era—An era that began in the mid-twentieth century and continues to the present (although some have spoken of a coalescing "post-postmodernism"). Postmodernism is characterized by a skepticism of all grand narratives and assertions of universal moral values, absolute truth, and objective reality. In general, postmodernism regards established modern cultural values as relative and subjective, acknowledging all points of view as equally valid (and is thus antihierarchical). In its approach to religion, postmodernism utilizes critical analysis to deconstruct and demythologize sacred scripture, relativizing claims of divine writ and triumphalist perspectives. Postmodern religion values a plurality of viewpoints and interpretations, emphasizing the individualistic, subjective nature of religious truth and experience.

Pluralism—Religious pluralism involves the understanding that there is more than one valid path to truth, often involving the perennialist view that all the world's great religious traditions are different expressions of one underlying essential core of religion or perennial philosophy. Pluralism goes beyond mere respect for other traditions to actual involvement in the training and practice of more than one religious tradition. Three clear examplars mentioned in this book are: Murshid Samuel Lewis (who was recognized as a Zen master and Sufi mystic), Reb Zalman Schachter-Shalomi (a Hassidic rebbe and Sufi sheikh), and Lex Hixon (or Sheikh Nur, who was a long-term student of Vedanta, Tibetan, and Zen Buddhism, as well as a practicing Eastern Orthodox Christian and Sufi sheikh). All three of these teachers are associated with new tariqat branches within the Sufi tradition.

Samadhi—A Sanskrit word indicating a state of meditative absorption in which the mind becomes very still. It may be defined as a state of being where "all distinctions between the person who is the subjective meditator, the act of meditation and the object of meditation merge into oneness."[1] There are several degrees of samadhi which are distinguished in Raja Yoga, the highest being *nirvikalpa samadhi*, a blissful state in which all consciousness of self and individuality temporarily dissolves.

Siddur—The Hebrew word for the Jewish prayer book.

Shunyata (Śūnyatā) —A Sanskrit word used in Buddhism and some schools of Hinduism to indicate the "emptiness, hollowness, or voidness" of the phenomenal world and of the self. The term has many meanings and may refer to the state of "nothing-ness" and freedom experienced in meditation, the idea that all things are empty of intrinsic existence, and the idea of no-self (*anatman*). The latter references Buddha's teaching that the world is empty of anything pertaining to a separate, permanent self; for what one takes to be one's self is but an elusive bundle of habits, memories, and thoughts which serve to identify oneself with a name, form, and personal history—yet this "self" is no more intrinsically real than a mirage. As used in Eastern religion, the emptiness of *shunyata* is not a depressing nihilistic void but rather a liberating sense of lightness and impermanence, a joyous freedom from the burden of having to be an illusive "somebody" with its fear of death.

Sufism, Sufi—An Arabic word which may be derived from the words *Saf* (pure), *Sophia* (wisdom), or *suf* (woollen clothes). The Sufi way is also called the *tariqat* in Arabic, meaning "the (mystical) path off the main road (*shariat*) of the religion." Sufism is often defined as Islamic mysticism or the inner teaching of Islam, but it really precedes the advent of historical Islam and its *turuq* (plural of *tariqat*), for there has always been some degree of mystical knowledge for as long as religion has existed. In the understanding of modern Sufis such as Hazrat Inayat Khan, Sufism is the mysticism of all religions and the religion of love; its expression is thus not restricted to a purely Islamic context. Other more traditional *turuq* recognize as legitimate only the form of Sufism which is practiced within the context of the religion of Islam, as revealed through the Prophet Muhammad.

Sufi Order in the West, Sufi Order International, Inayati Order—The Sufi Movement was founded by Pir-o-Murshid Hazrat Inayat Khan in 1910. In the 1950s, decades after Hazrat Inayat Khan's passing, his son Pir Vilayat Inayat Khan incorporated another branch of the Sufi Movement which he called the Sufi Order in the West. (At the time, there were almost no other Sufi orders present in the West.) Several decades later, as more Sufi *turuq* were established in the West, the name was changed to the Sufi Order International. Finally in 2015, Pir Vilayat's son and successor, Pir Zia Inayat-Khan, further revised the name of the organization in line with many of the other Sufi orders which traditionally bear the name of their founder, and thus its current name is the Inayati Order: A Sufi Path of Spiritual Liberty. Further details about the Inayati Order are set forth in this book.

Theosis—The doctrine of deification in Eastern Orthodox Christianity. The idea is not that one changes one's human nature and ontologically becomes God the Father or the Trinity, but that one selflessly participates in the divine nature and presence through alignment with the divine energies.

Theosophy—Theosophy incorporates various esoteric and occult principles in its teachings and is primarily associated with the Theosophical Society, a worldwide organization which was founded by Madame Helena Blavatsky (1831-1891), a mystic who wrote extensively on the principles and teachings of theosophy. The proponents of theosophy view it as an esoteric religious tradition which draws on the wisdom of the East as well as Western Esoterica and occultism. The Theosophical Society purports to transmit the secret hidden teaching of the ages, and sees human affairs as guided by various ascended masters and prophets of the past, seen and unseen, who have revealed this secret knowledge to worthy initiates and currently continue to guide and influence the course of human events on the higher planes.

Theotrophy—The act of metaphorically growing in and toward the light of God, as a tree grows toward the sun.

Trimurti—Refers to the Hindu trinity of Brahma (the Creator), Vishnu (the Sustainer), and Shiva (the Destroyer).

Triumphalist—A theological triumphalist sees their own religion as the one and only true way and considers all the others to be false. This can extend to military conquest in the name of one's religion and forcible conversion of people.

Universalist—A theological universalist is one who accepts the essential core of all religious traditions in an inclusive way (in contrast to a triumphalist). The universalist may be a religious pluralist or belong to one particular faith tradition yet hold that the other great religious traditions also contain inspired truth and are efficacious towards salvation. The latter view was espoused by the Roman Catholic Church in the reforms of Vatican II. The spirit of universalism in the West has been greatly influenced by Hindu universality, as introduced by Swami Vivekandana at the 1893 Parliament of World Religions. The Hindu Rig Veda succinctly states: "Truth is one; sages call it by various names." The Baha'i faith is also based on the premise that one essential truth has been taught throughout history under various names, and further teaches that in each era a more advanced teaching is revealed in a process of progressive revelation.

Universal Worship Service—The interreligious service instituted by Hazrat Inayat Khan, which features candle lighting and readings from the sacred texts of the world's great religious traditions, whose scriptures are all placed together on one altar.

Vedanta—A tradition of Hindu teaching that affirms the nondual unity of all things (*Advaita Vedanta*). Vedanta literally means "the end of the Vedas."

Wazifa—The "practice" given to Sufi mureeds for spiritual development. One's wazifa is practiced by chanting and contemplating the specific divine names or attributes (*esma* in Arabic) recommended by one's spiritual teacher.

ENDNOTES

[1] Sturgess, Stephen, *Yoga Meditation*, Watkins Publishing, London, 2014; p.27.

BIBLIOGRAPHY

Anonymous, "Practical Wisdom from Shlomo Carlebach,"
   Tikkun magazine, Fall 5758. See: https://havurahshirhadash.org/
   practical-wisdom-from-shlomo-carlebach.

Arberry, A.J. (1961), *Discourses of Rumi*, New York: Samuel Weiser, Inc.

Block, Tom (Winter, 2001), "Abraham Maimonides: A Jewish
   Sufi," *Sufi* magazine, London, England.

Bohm, David and F. David Peat (2010), *Science, Order and
   Creativity*, Routledge Classic, Abindon, Oxfordshire, England.

Cooper, Rabbi David, "Reb Zalman: The Heart of Evil." See: https://www.
   rabbidavidcooper.com/cooper-print-index/2010/11/8/2253-reb-zal-
   man-the-heart-of-evil-print.html.

Crossan, J.D. (2000), *A Long Way from Tipperary*, New York: HarperOne.

Dalai Lama (2011), *Toward a True Kinship of Faiths*, New York: Doubleday
   [Kindle edition].

Davidson, Sara (2014), "How the Rabbi Got His Name." See: www.sarada-
   vidson.com/blog/2014/02/how-the-rabbi-Got- his-name.html.

Denegg, Ingrid (2006), *Heart & Wings Memorial Issue: Pir Vilayat Inayat
   Khan*. See: https://pirdahan.blogspot.com/2017/02/chapters-twenty-
   two-through-twenty-seven.html.

Erhart, Victoria, "Unconventional Traditionalists: The Correspondence
   betweenReb Zalman and Thomas Merton." See: https://www.youtube.
   com/watch?v=vBdwfazrBvk.

Faithful Doubter (2004), "Samuel L. Lewis–Spiritual Leader of the
   Hippies." See: http://bobby1933.livejournal.com/588012.html.

Field, Claud, translator (1909), *Meister Eckhart's Sermons*. See:
   http://www.documentacatholicaomnia.
   eu/03d/1260-1328,_Eckhart,_Sermons,_EN.pdf.

Friedlander, Shems (1975), *The Whirling Dervishes*, New York: MacMillan Publishing Company.

Glassman, Roshi Bernie (2014), "My Rebbe Is Gone!" See: https://zenpeacemakers.org/2014/07/my-rebbe-is-gone.

Green, Arthur (2014), *The One Who Walked Before the Camp; a Eulogy by Rabbi Arthur Green*, ALEPH: Alliance for Jewish Renewal. See: https://aleph.org/resources/the-one-who-walked-before-the-camp-a-eulogy-by-rabbi-arthur-green+&cd=1&hl=en&ct=clnk&gl=us.

Hixon, Sheila, editor (2016), *Conversations in the Spirit: Lex Hixon's WBAI "In the Spirit" Interviews: A Chronicle of the Seventies Spiritual Revolution*, Rhinebeck, NY: Monkfish Book Publishing Company.

Iyer, Raghavan, editor (1983), *The Gathas of Zarathrustra*, Santa Barbara, CA: Concord Grove Press.

Kamenetz, Rodger (2007), *The Jew in the Lotus: A Poet›s Rediscovery of Jewish Identity in Buddhist India*, New York: HarperCollins Publishers.

Khan, Hazrat Inayat (1979), *Biography of Pir-o-MurshidInayat Khan*, London: East-West Publications.

Khan, Hazrat Inayat, Githa 3 (1923), *Concentration*, New Lebanon, NY: Sufi Order Publications [private edition].

Khan, Hazrat Inayat (1985), *Mastery Through Accomplishment*, New Lebanon, NY: Omega Press.

Khan, Hazrat Inayat (1979), Message Volume VIII, *Sufi Teachings, The Sufi Message of Spiritual Liberty*, Farnham, Surrey, England: Servire Publishing.

Khan, Hazrat Inayat (1979), Message Volume XII: *Confessions*, Farnham, Surrey, England: Servire Publishing.

Khan, Hazrat Inayat (1967), Message Volume XII: *The Vision of God and Man*), London: Barrie & Jenkins.

Khan, Hazrat Inayat (1982), Message Volume XIV, *The Gathas*, International Headquarters Sufi Movement, Geneva, Switzerland.

Khan, Hazrat Inayat (1923), *Social Gathekas: Background on Sufism*. See: http://hazrat-inayat-khan.org.

Khan, Hazrat Inayat (1978), *The Complete Sayings of Hazrat Inayat Khan*, Lebanon Springs, NY: Sufi Order Publications.

Khan, Hazrat Inayat (2013), *The Heart of Sufism: Essential Writings of Hazrat Inayat Khan*, Boston, MA: Shambala Publications [Kindle edition].

Khan, Hazrat Inayat (2012), *The Sufi Message of Hazrat Inayat Khan: The Smiling Forehead*, Charlotte, NC: Library of Alexandria, Baker & Taylor [Kindle edition].

Khan, Hazrat Inayat (2012). *The Unity of Religious Ideals*, Commodius Vicus e-Publisher [Kindle edition].

Khan, Hazrat Inayat (1979), *The Unity of Religious Ideals*, New Lebanon, NY: Sufi Order Publications.

Khan, Pir Vilayat (2000), *Awakening: A Sufi Experience*, Los Angeles, CA: TarcherPerigee.

Khan, Pir Vilayat (1982), *Introducing Spirituality into Counseling and Therapy*, New Lebanon, NY: Omega Publications.

Khan, Pir Vilayat, *Keeping in Touch* newsletter #91, *Lahut—The Divine Inheritance*. See: www.centrum-universel.com.

Khan, Pir Vilayat (1981), *Leader's Manual*, Lebanon Springs, NY: Sufi Order Publications [private edition].

Khan, Hazrat Inayat (1923), *Supplementary Papers*, Lebanon Springs, NY: Sufi Order Publications [private edition].

Khan, Pir Vilayat (1981), *The Call of the Dervish*, Sante Fe, NM: Sufi Order Publications.

Khan, Pir Vilayat(2014), *The Ecstasy Beyond Knowing: A Manual of Meditation*, New Lebanon, NY: Omega Publications, [Kindle edition].

Khan, Pir Vilayat (1978), *The Message in Our Time*, San Francisco: Harper & Row.

Khan, Pir Vilayat (1974), *Toward the One*, New York: Harper & Row.

Khan, Pir Vilayat with Thomas AtumO'Kane (1991), *The Sacred Search: World Mystical Traditions*, New Lebanon, NY: C.F. Gunter and the Sufi Order Video Project [VHS videotape].

Klugar, Rivkah (1967), *Satan in the Old Testament*, Evanston, IL: Northwestern University Press.

Kuhn, Alvin Boyd (1949), *Shadow of The Third Century*, Elizabeth, NJ: Academy Press.

Lewis, Samuel (1975), *In the Garden*, San Cristobal, NM: Lama Foundation.

Mascaró, Juan, translator (1962), *The Bhagavad Gita*; London: Penguin Classics.

Miles-Yepez, Netanel, editor (2015), *One God, Many Worlds: Teachings of a Renewed Hasidism*, Boulder, CO: Albion-Andalus Books [Kindle edition].

Or Chadesh of P'nai Or, late 1980s, preliminary draft edition, Philadelphia, PA: P'Nai Or Fellowship.

Schachter-Shalomi, Reb Zalman and Joel Segel (2005), *Jewish with Feeling: A Guide to Meaningful Jewish Practice*, New York: Riverhead Books.

Schachter-Shalomi, Reb Zalman and Ellen Singer, editor (1993), *Paradigm Shift: From the Jewish Renewal Teachings of Reb Zalman Schachter-Shalomi*, Northvale, NJ: Jason Aronson Inc.

Schachter-Shalomi, Reb Zalman (1975), *Fragments of a Future Scroll: Hassidism for the Aquarian Age*, Germantown, PA: Leaves of Grass Press.

Schachter-Shalomi, Reb Zalman (2013), *Gate to the Heart*, Boulder, CO: Albion-Andalus.

Schatcher-Shalomi, Reb Zalman, *Mareh Kohen*; undated, unpublished collection from late 1980s.

Schachter-Shalomi, Reb Zalman (2014), *Psalms in a Translation for Praying*, Philadelphia, PA: ALEPH: Alliance for Jewish Renewal.

Schatcher-Shalomi, Reb Zalman, *Reb Zalman, Among the Sufis*, excerpt of a 3/19/94 audio recording at the Hillel Foundation in Berkeley, CA. Co-sponsored by the Aquarian Minyon, transcribed by Reuven Goldfarb with the assistance of Eliyahu Khaled McLean). See: http://sufi-tariqah.de/tarchiv/rebzalman.html.

Schachter-Shalomi, Reb Zalman, "The Emerging Cosmology," edited by Netanel Miles-Yépez. See: https://aleph.org/resources/the-emerging-cosmology-transcript-of-reb-zalman-at-hh-the-dalai-lamas-roundtable.

Schachter-Shalomi, Reb Zalman, "The Endgame in Job." See: http://www.jewishrenewalhasidus.org/wordpress/category/reb-zalman-articles.

Schatcher-Shalomi, Reb Zalman (1983), *The First Step: A Guide For the New Jewish Spirit*, Toronto, Canada: Bantam Books.

Schachter-Shalomi, Reb Zalman, with Lawrence Kushner (2012) *Davening: A Guide to Meaningful Jewish Prayer* Woodstock, VT: Jewish Lights [Kindle edition].

Schachter-Shalomi, Reb Zalman, with SadiqAlam, "Mystic Experience and Mysticism for a New Humanity" interviewed on Technology of the Heart (2008). See: http://www.techofheart.co/2008/08/interview-with-reb-zalman-on-mystic.html.

Schimmel, Annemarie (1975), *Mystical Dimensions of Islam*, Chapel Hill, NC: The University of North Carolina Press.

Shaku, Soyen (1906), *Zen for Americans*, translated by DaisetzTeitaro Suzuki, Whitefish, MT: Kessinger Publishing.

Sh'ma: A Journal of Jewish Ideas, 2012, "Rebbe Talk: A
Conversation with Reb Zalman Schachter-Shalomi
(with Rabbi Or Rose)." See: http://shma.com/2012/03/
rebbe-talk-a-conversation-with-reb-zalman-schachter-shalomi.

Sturgess, Stephen (2014), *Yoga Meditation*, London: Watkins Publishing.

Teilhard de Chardin (1965), *Hymn of the Universe,* English translation, New
York: Harper & Row.

Teilhard de Chardin (1966), *The Phenomenon of Man*, New York:
HarperCollins Publishers.

Muller, Friedrich Max, *The Sacred Books of the East*, Volume XL
(2000), Adamant Media Corporation; Oxford, England: Claredon Press
(Elibron Classic Replica Edition of 1891 edition).

Khan, Pir Zia Inayat, "Reb Zalman Schachter-Shalomi,"

The Sufi Remembrance Project (2014). See: http://remembrance.sufipaths.
net.

Waskow, Rabbi Arthur (2008), "The Spirituality of the Future by Rabbi
ZalmanSchachter-Shalomi."See: www.theshalomcenter.org/node/1395.

ABOUT THE AUTHOR

Gregory Blann has been an active student of Sufism and the world's religions for forty years. He received initiation from Pir Vilayat Khan in the Inayati Order in 1980 and served as a representative in that order for a number of years. He met Reb Zalman Schachter-Shalomi and began Kabbalistic studies with him in 1981. In 1990, he received initiation in the Turkish Halveti-Jerrahi Order from Sheikh Nur al-Jerrahi (Lex Hixon), and also studied with Safer Efendi. He was given the Sufi name Muhammad Jamal, and became a Jerrahi sheikh in 1994.

He received a degree in music and art from Vanderbilt University in 1974 and continued his studies at Massachusetts College of Art in Boston, also training for ten years in Carnatic South Indian music during the 1980s. Over the years, he has worked in the graphic arts industry, taught and performed international folk dance, led local Sufi groups in Nashville, Tennessee, and taught Sufism in various cities throughout the United States. He has also been a frequent participant in ecumenical dialogues and panels, serving on the board of the Interfaith Alliance of Middle Tennessee.

Gregory's previous books include *Garden of Mystic Love* (on the history and teachings of Sufism) and *Lifting the Boundaries* (an account of the life and contemporary Sufi teachings of Muzaffer Efendi). He is an advocate of universal spirituality, affirming the essential core of unity, love, and compassion in all the world's great spiritual traditions, beyond narrow sectarian divisions and the distortions which manifest as religious violence.

CPSIA information can be obtained
at www.ICGtesting.com
Printed in the USA
JSHW081953130223
37654JS00001B/25